Chinese Dialectology:

A Selected and Classified Bibliography

中國方言學分類參考書目

Paul Fu-mien Yang, S.J.

楊福綿編著

The Chinese University Press

Hong Kong

International Standard Book Number: 962–201–211–6

The Chinese University Press
The Chinese University of Hong Kong
SHATIN, N.T., HONG KONG

Typesetting and printing by Union Printing Company

In Fond Memory of My Parents
Paul Yang Ch'ang-hsi (1897–1972)
Mary Yang Ts'ui Ching-ch'ing (1893–1975)

CONTENTS

FOREWORD xvii

PREFACE xix

EXPLANATORY NOTES xxiii

LIST OF PERIODICALS xxv

LIST OF ABBREVIATIONS xxxix

1. BIBLIOGRAPHIES AND COLLECTED ESSAYS (0001–0113)

   1.1. Bibliographies (0001–0061) 1
      1.1.1. General and Mandarin Dialects (0001–0044) 1
      1.1.2. Wu Dialects (0045–0047) 4
      1.1.3. Hakka Dialects (0048–0050) 4
      1.1.4. Yüeh Dialects (0051–0052) 4
      1.1.5. Min Dialects (0053–0061) 4
   1.2. Biographies and Bibliographies of Individual Scholars (0062–0092) 5
      1.2.1. Biographies (0062–0084) 5
      1.2.2. Bibliographies (0085–0092) 6
   1.3. Collected Essays (0093–0113) 7
      1.3.1. Encyclopedias (0093–0096) 7
      1.3.2. Collected Essays (0097–0113) 7

2. HISTORY OF CHINESE DIALECTOLOGY (0114–0172)
   2.1. General Studies (0114–0146) 9
   2.2. Institutional Activities (0147–0150) 11
   2.3. Dialect Surveys (0151–0162) 11
   2.4. Studies on Individual Dialects (0163–0172) 12

3. METHODOLOGY OF CHINESE DIALECTOLOGY (0173–0337)
   3.1. General Methods (0173–0190) 14
   3.2. Dialect Surveys (0191–0222) 15
      3.2.1. General (0191–0208) 15
      3.2.2. Linguistic Geography (0209–0213) 16
      3.2.3. Questionnaires (0214–0222) 16
   3.3. Descriptive Methods (0223–0278) 17
      3.3.1. General (0223–0231) 17
      3.3.2. Phonetic Descriptions (0232–0257) 18

            3.3.2.1. General (0232–0248)   18
            3.3.2.2. Phonetic Correspondences (0249–0257)   19
        3.3.3. Lexical Descriptions (0258–0272)   19
        3.3.4. Grammatical Descriptions (0273–0278)   20
    3.4. Romanizations and Dialect Characters (0279–0337)   21
        3.4.1. General and Mandarin Dialects (0279–0294)   21
        3.4.2. Wu Dialects (0295–0301)   22
        3.4.3. Yüeh Dialects (0302–0308) '..   22
        3.4.4. Min Dialects (0309–0319)   23
        3.4.5. Interdialectal Romanization (0320–0331)   23
        3.4.6. Dialect Characters (0332–0337)   24

4. ARCHAIC AND OLD DIALECTS (0338–0462)
    4.1. Archaic and Old Dialects in General (0338–0349)   25
    4.2. Chou and Ch'in Period (0350–0369)   25
        4.2.1. General Studies (0350–0358)   25
        4.2.2. Ch'u Dialects (0359–0369)   26
    4.3. Han Period (0370–0401)   27
        4.3.1. General Studies (0370–0372)   27
        4.3.2. Fang-yen (0373–0397)   27
        4.3.3. Shuo-wen chieh-tzu (0398–0401)   29
    4.4. Wei, Chin, and Six Dynasties Period (0402–0412)   29
    4.5. Sui and T'ang Period (0413–0432)   30
    4.6. Sung Period (0433–0439)   31
    4.7. Yüan, Ming, and Ch'ing Period (0440–0450)   32
    4.8. Dialects in Local Gazetteers and Literary Works (0451–0456) 33
    4.9. Hsin fang-yen (0457–0462)   33

5. MODERN DIALECTS IN GENERAL (0463–0554)
    5.1. Languages and Dialects of China (0463–0481)   35
    5.2. Classification of Chinese Dialects (0482–0486)   36
    5.3. History of Chinese Dialects (0487–0493)   36
    5.4. Sociocultural Aspects of Chinese Dialects (0494–0506)   37
    5.5. General Studies on Chinese Dialects (0507–0554)   38
        5.5.1. General (0507–0513)   38
        5.5.2. Multidialectal Dictionaries (0514–0525)   38
        5.5.3. Phonetics and Phonology (0526–0543)   40
        5.5.4. Vocabulary and Grammar (0544–0554)   41

6. NORTHERN MANDARIN DIALECTS (0555–0886)

    6.1. Northern Mandarin Dialects in General (0555–0574) 42

        6.1.1. General Studies (0555–0560) 42

        6.1.2. Phonetics and Phonology (0561–0569) 42

        6.1.3. Vocabulary (0570–0574) 43

    6.2. Peking Dialect (0575–0744) 43

        6.2.1. General Studies (0575–0604) 43

            6.2.1.1. Peking Dialect and Common Language (0575–0583) 43

            6.2.1.2. Historical Development (0584–0593) 44

            6.2.1.3. Sociocultural Aspects (0594–0604) 44

        6.2.2. Phonetics and Phonology (0605–0668) 45

            6.2.2.1. General (0605–0635) 45

            6.2.2.2. Initials (0636–0641) 47

            6.2.2.3. Finals (0642–0645) 47

            6.2.2.4 Tones (0646–0668) 47

        6.2.3. Vocabulary and Grammar (0669–0711) 49

            6.2.3.1. Vocabulary (0669–0685) 49

            6.2.3.2. Morphology (0686–0696) 50

            6.2.3.3. Syntax (0697–0711) 51

        6.2.4. Contrastive Studies (0712–0720) 52

        6.2.5. Textbooks (0721–0734) 52

        6.2.6. Dictionaries (0735–0744) 53

    6.3. Hopei (0745–0776) 54

        6.3.1. General Studies (0745–0750) 54

        6.3.2. Northern Peking (Jehol) (0751–0755) 54

        6.3.3. Paoting (0756–0757) 55

        6.3.4. Tientsin (0758–0760) 55

        6.3.5. Hochien (0761–0765) 55

        6.3.6. Other Localities (0766–0769) 56

        6.3.7. Contrastive Studies (0770–0776) 56

    6.4. Northeastern Provinces (0777–0794) 56

        6.4.1. General Studies (0777–0782) 56

        6.4.2. Various Localities (0783–0787) 57

        6.4.3. Contrastive Studies (0788–0794) 57

    6.5. Shantung, Northern Kiangsu and Honan (0795–0886) 58

        6.5.1. Shantung (0795–0855) 58

            6.5.1.1. General Studies (0795–0802) 58

6.5.1.2. Phonetics and Phonology (0803–0810) 58
6.5.1.3. Vocabulary and Grammar (0811–0814) 59
6.5.1.4. Anch'iu (0815–0817) 59
6.5.1.5. Chiaohsien (0818–0823) 59
6.5.1.6. Various Localities (0824–0839) 60
6.5.1.7. Dictionaries (0840–0844) 61
6.5.1.8. Contrastive Studies (0845–0855) 61
6.5.2. Northern Kiangsu (0856–0859) 62
6.5.3. Honan (0860–0886) 62
6.5.3.1. General Studies (0860–0864) 62
6.5.3.2. Chungho (0865–0866) 63
6.5.3.3. Huochia (0867–0868) 63
6.5.3.4. K'aifeng (0869–0870) 63
6.5.3.5. Loyang (0871–0874) 63
6.5.3.6. Other Localities (0875–0880) 63
6.5.3.7. Contrastive Studies (0881–0886) 64

7. NORTHWESTERN MANDARIN DIALECTS (0887–0959)
7.1. Northwestern Mandarin in General (0887–0891) 65
7.2. Hopei (formerly Chahar) (0892–0898) 65
7.3. Shansi (0899–0925) 66
7.3.1. General Studies (0899–0904) 66
7.3.2. Phonology (0905–0913) 66
7.3.3. Vocabulary and Grammar (0914–0920) 67
7.3.4. Contrastive Studies (0921–0925) 67
7.4. Shensi, Kansu, Mongolia and Sinkiang (0926–0959) 68
7.4.1. Shensi and Kansu (0926–0948) 68
7.4.1.1. General Studies (0926–0931) 68
7.4.1.2. Lanchow (0932–0934) 68
7.4.1.3. Shanghsien (0935–0937) 68
7.4.1.4. Sian (0938–0940) 69
7.4.1.5. Other Localities (0941–0943) 69
7.4.1.6. Contrastive Studies (0944–0948) 69
7.4.2. Mongolia and Sinkiang (0949–0959) 69
7.4.2.1. General Studies (0949–0954) 69
7.4.2.2. Contrastive Studies (0955–0959) 70

8. EASTERN MANDARIN DIALECTS (0960–1009)
8.1. Kiangsu (0960–0993) 71

8.1.1. General Studies (0960–0961) 71

8.1.2. Nanking (0962–0972) 71

8.1.3. Yangchow (0973–0978) 71

8.1.4. Nant'ung (0979–0981) 72

8.1.5. T'aihsing (0982–0983) 72

8.1.6. Tanyang (0984–0985) 72

8.1.7. Other Localities (0986–0990) 72

8.1.8. Contrastive Studies (0991–0993) 73

8.2. Anhwei (0994–1009) 73

8.2.1. General (0994–0995) 73

8.2.2. Hofei (0996–0997) 73

8.2.3. Other Localities (0998–1002) 73

8.2.4. Hweichow Dialects (1003–1009) 74

8.2.4.1. General Studies (1003–1007) 74

8.2.4.2. Contrastive Studies (1008–1009) 74

9. SOUTHWESTERN MANDARIN DIALECTS (1010–1120)

9.1. Hupei (1010–1035) 75

9.1.1. General Studies (1010–1014) 75

9.1.2. Hankow (1015–1022) 75

9.1.3. Hsishui (1023–1024) 75

9.1.4. Kuangchi (1025–1027) 76

9.1.5. Other Localities (1028–1029) 76

9.1.6. Contrastive Studies (1030–1035) 76

9.2. Szechwan (1036–1094) 76

9.2.1. General Studies (1036–1047) 76

9.2.2. Phonetics and Phonology (1048–1056) 77

9.2.3. Vocabulary (1057–1063) 78

9.2.4. Grammar (1064–1065) 78

9.2.5. Ch'engtu (1066–1072) 78

9.2.6. Chungking (1073–1076) 78

9.2.7. Omei (1077–1079) 79

9.2.8. Other Localities (1080–1084) 79

9.2.9. Dictionaries (1085–1088) 79

9.2.10. Contrastive Studies (1088–1094) 79

9.3. Yunnan, Kweichow and Kwangsi (1095–1120) 80

9.3.1. Yunnan (1095–1107) 80

9.3.1.1. General Studies (1095–1100) 80

9.3.1.2. Phonetics and Phonology (1101–1103)   80

9.3.1.3. Vocabulary and Grammar (1104–1107)   81

9.3.2. Kweichow (1108–1110)   81

9.3.3. Kweilin, Kwangsi (1111–1113)   81

9.3.4. Contrastive Studies (1114–1120)   81

10. ISOLATED MANDARIN DIALECTS (1121–1168)

10.1. Dungan (1121–1164)   83

10.1.1. General Studies (1121–1128)   83

10.1.2. Orthography (1129–1136)   83

10.1.3. Phonetics and Phonology (1137–1144)   84

10.1.4. Vocabulary and Dictionaries (1145–1146)   84

10.1.5. Grammar and Textbooks (1147–1164)   84

10.2. Nanp'ing (1165–1166)   85

10.3. Hainan (1167–1168)   86

11. WU DIALECTS (1169–1359)

11.1. Wu Dialects in General (1169–1195)   87

11.1.1. Historical Studies (1169–1175)   87

11.1.2. General Studies (1176–1184)   87

11.1.3. Phonetics and Phonology (1185–1189)   88

11.1.4. Vocabulary and Grammar (1190–1195)   88

11.2. Kiangsu (1196–1315)   88

11.2.1. Shanghai (1196–1272)   88

11.2.1.1. General Studies (1196–1198)   88

11.2.1.2. Phonetics and Phonology (1199–1213)   89

11.2.1.3. Vocabulary (1214–1224)   89

11.2.1.4. Grammar (1225–1229)   90

11.2.1.5. Textbooks (1230–1262)   90

11.2.1.6. Dictionaries (1263–1272)   92

11.2.2. Changchow (1273–1276)   93

11.2.3. Soochow (1277–1294)   93

11.2.3.1. Phonetics and Phonology (1277–1285)   93

11.2.3.2. Vocabulary (1286–1291)   94

11.2.3.3. Grammar (1292–1294)   94

11.2.4. Wuchiang (1295–1296)   95

11.2.5. Wuhsi (1297–1298)   95

11.2.6. Other Localities (1299–1303)   95

11.2.7. Contrastive Studies (1304–1315)   95

11.3. Chekiang (1316–1359) 96
    11.3.1. Ningpo (1316–1323) 96
    11.3.2. T'anghsi (1324–1326) 97
    11.3.3. Wenchow (1327–1334) 97
    11.3.4. Wenling (1335–1340) 97
    11.3.5. Hangchow (1341–1343) 98
    11.3.6. Other Localities (1344–1355) 98
    11.3.7. Contrastive Studies (1356–1359) 99

12. HSIANG DIALECTS (1360–1384)
12.1. Hsiang Dialects in General (1360–1365) 100
12.2. Ch'angsha (1366–1370) 100
12.3. Shuangfeng (1371–1373) 101
12.4. Yüehyang (1374–1375) 101
12.5. Other Localities (1376–1380) 101
12.6. Contrastive Studies (1381–1384) 101

13. KAN AND HAKKA DIALECTS (1385–1520)
13.1. Kan Dialects (1385–1400) 102
    13.1.1. General Studies (1385–1386) 102
    13.1.2. Nanch'ang (1387–1390) 102
    13.1.3. Other Localities (1391–1398) 102
    13.1.4. Contrastive Studies (1399–1400) 103
13.2. Hakka Dialects (1401–1520) 103
    13.2.1. History of the Hakkas (1401–1414) 103
    13.2.2. Sociocultural Aspects (1415–1424) 104
    13.2.3. Historical Studies (1425–1427) 104
    13.2.4. General Studies (1428–1440) 105
    13.2.5. Szuhsien (1441–1461) 105
        13.2.5.1. Phonetics and Phonology (1441–1452) 105
        13.2.5.2. Vocabulary (1453–1457) 106
        13.2.5.3. Grammar (1458–1461) 106
    13.2.6. P'ingyüan (1462–1463) 107
    13.2.7. Tap'u (1464–1465) 107
    13.2.8. Haifeng and Lufeng (1466–1468) 107
    13.2.9. Sathewkok (1469–1471) 107
    13.2.10. Taiwan (1472–1475) 107
    13.2.11. Other Localities (1476–1482) 108
    13.2.12. Contrastive Studies (1483–1488) 108

13.2.13. Textbooks (1489–1509) 109

13.2.14. Dictionaries (1510–1520) 110

14. YÜEH DIALECTS (1521–1860)

14.1. Yüeh Dialects in General (1521–1818) 111

    14.1.1. Historical Studies (1521–1530) 111

    14.1.2. General Studies (1531–1542) 111

    14.1.3. Sociocultural Aspects (1543–1559) 112

    14.1.4. Phonetics and Phonology (1560–1610) 113

        14.1.4.1. General (1560–1582) 113

        14.1.4.2. Initials (1583–1586) 114

        14.1.4.3. Finals (1587–1592) 115

        14.1.4.4. Tones (1593–1610) 115

    14.1.5. Vocabulary (1611–1622) 116

    14.1.6. Grammar (1623–1644) 117

    14.1.7. Contrastive Studies (1645–1671) 118

    14.1.8. Textbooks (1672–1778) 120

    14.1.9. Dictionaries (1779–1818) 126

14.2. Kwangtung (1819–1849) 129

    14.2.1. Hong Kong (1819–1821) 129

    14.2.2. Tungkuan (1822–1825) 129

    14.2.3. Szeyap (1826–1840) 129

        14.2.3.1. General (1826–1828) 129

        14.2.3.2. Hsinhui (1829–1831) 130

        14.2.3.3. T'aishan (1832–1840) 130

    14.2.4. Yangchiang (1841–1844) 130

    14.2.5. Other Localities in Kwangtung (1845–1849) 131

14.3. Kwangsi (1850–1860) 131

15. SOUTH MIN DIALECTS (1861–2220)

15.1. South Min Dialects in General (1861–1981) 132

    15.1.1. Historical Studies (1861–1904) 132

        15.1.1.1. General (1861–1864) 132

        15.1.1.2. Phonetics and Phonology (1865–1882) 132

        15.1.1.3. Vocabulary and Grammar (1883–1904) 133

    15.1.2. General Studies (1905–1923) 134

    15.1.3. Sociocultural Aspects (1924–1930) 136

    15.1.4. Phonetics and Phonology (1931–1946) 136

    15.1.5. Vocabulary (1947–1952) 137

15.1.6. Grammar (1953–1968)   137

15.1.7. Contrastive Studies (1969–1974)   138

15.1.8. Textbooks (1975–1977)   139

15.1.9. Dictionaries (1978–1981)   139

15.2. Amoy (1982–2023)   139

  15.2.1. Phonetics and Phonology (1982–1999)   139

  15.2.2. Grammar (2000–2005)   140

  15.2.3. Textbooks (2006–2012)   141

  15.2.4. Dictionaries (2013–2023)   141

15.3. Ch'aochou and Swatow (2024–2064)   142

  15.3.1. Ch'aochou (2024–2051)   142

    15.3.1.1. General Studies (2024–2028)   142

    15.3.1.2. Phonetics and Phonology (2029–2038)   142

    15.3.1.3. Grammar (2039–2042)   143

    15.3.1.4. Contrastive Studies (2043–2045)   143

    15.3.1.5. Textbooks and Dictionaries (2046–2051)   143

  15.3.2. Swatow (2052–2064)   144

    15.3.2.1. Phonetics and Phonology (2052–2053)   144

    15.3.2.2. Vocabulary and Grammar (2054–2056)   144

    15.3.2.3. Textbooks (2057–2061)   144

    15.3.2.4. Dictionaries (2062–2064)   144

15.4. Other Localities in Fukien and Kwangtung (2065–2075)   145

15.5. Taiwan (2076–2196)   145

  15.5.1. Historical Studies (2076–2083)   145

  15.5.2. General Studies (2084–2097)   146

  15.5.3. Sociocultural Aspects (2098–2105)   147

  15.5.4. Phonetics and Phonology (2106–2126)   147

  15.5.5. Vocabulary (2127–2129)   149

  15.5.6. Grammar (2130–2141)   149

  15.5.7. Contrastive Studies (2142–2147)   150

  15.5.8. Textbooks (2148–2181)   150

  15.5.9. Dictionaries (2182–2196)   152

15.6. Hainan Island (2197–2220)   153

  15.6.1. General Studies (2197–2200)   153

  15.6.2. Haik'ou and Wanning (2201–2203)   153

  15.6.3. Wench'ang (2204–2220)   153

15.6.3.1. Phonetics and Phonology (2204–2214) .. 153

15.6.3.2. Grammar and Textbooks (2215–2220) 154

16. NORTH MIN DIALECTS (2221–2275)

16.1. North Min Dialects in General (2221–2226) 155

16.2. Foochow (2227–2259) 155

16.2.1. Phonetics and Phonology (2227–2238) 155

16.2.2. Vocabulary (2239–2243) 156

16.2.3. Grammar (2244–2245) 156

16.2.4. Contrastive Studies (2246–2248) 156

16.2.5. Textbooks (2249–2255) 156

16.2.6. Dictionaries (2256–2259) 157

16.3. Kienow, Kienyang, and Shaowu (2260–2266) 157

16.3.1. Kienow (2260–2261) 157

16.3.2. Kienyang (2262–2263) 157

16.3.3. Shaowu (2264–2266) 157

16.4. P'ut'ien and Hsienyu (2267–2275) 157

16.4.1. P'ut'ien (2267–2271) 157

16.4.2. Hsienyu (2272–2275) 158

LIST OF CHINESE AND JAPANESE PUBLISHERS 159

ROMANIZED INDEX OF AUTHORS 167

FOREWORD

In January 1980 my friend Paul Yang came back from a trip to Peking and gave me a letter from my former student Wang Fu-shih 王輔世 with whom I had done dialect surveys in 1947 and 1948. Wang is now at the Institute of Minorities Studies 民族研究所. The letter bridged a gap of thirty years of silence concomitant with the political situation of those years.

The next month I made a trip to Europe and there I was asked to speak on March 12 to the students of the Chinese Language Department at Leiden University (Netherlands); they wished to hear about my dialect research done in China between 1941 and 1948. It was a nostalgic experience to re-read articles published between 1943 and 1958 on that subject. It was also at Leiden University that I for the first time saw the new journal *Fang-yen* 方言 that has been published in Peking for a year or two.

Now, after these experiences, I have before me the bibliography of Chinese dialects authored by my friend Paul Yang. This book could not have come at a better time. The field of Chinese dialectology is now again being opened up; I do not mean to say that there has not been any work done between 1949 and the present; this book in itself shows that this is not the case. On the contrary, a free flow of information and an exchange of scholars between China and the other countries of the world has again begun. Now, with this bibliography, one can assess how far research has progressed and what problems should be tackled by new generations. I am very thankful for the author's zeal and scholarship.

WILLEM A. GROOTAERS
Graduate School of Linguistics
Sophia University
Tokyo, Japan

PREFACE

In 1974, my *Chinese Linguistics: A Selected and Classified Bibliography* was published. In the Introduction of that book, I stated that a separate bibliography on Chinese dialectology would be published at a later date. During the past six years, I have been collecting and editing bibliographical entries; now the new bibliography is ready to be received by the public. This bibliography may serve as a companion or second volume to the first bibliography. Its scope and format is the same as the first.

The purpose of this bibliography is to provide scholars and students of Chinese language and linguistics with comprehensive bibliographical information concerning various aspects of Chinese dialectology: bibliographical, historical, methodological, ancient and modern dialects. Included are historical, sociocultural and descriptive studies on a dialect group in general, or on a given specific dialect in particular. Historical studies include historical development of phonology, vocabulary and grammar. Sociocultural studies include sociolinguistic studies, popular sayings and proverbs, and dialect literature in general. Descriptive studies of individual dialects include phonetics and phonology, vocabulary, grammar, contrastive analysis, textbooks and dictionaries for learning the respective dialects. Contrastive studies include methods for learning dialects, phonetic, lexical and grammatical correspondences.

In scope, the work includes all important published studies—both books and articles that have appeared in periodicals, excluding daily newspapers—in the principal languages of the world: Chinese, Japanese, English, French, German, Dutch, Russian, etc. Entries in Oriental languages are given in their respective native writing systems with romanizations and English translations in order that this bibliography can be used by those who are less familiar with Oriental languages and writing systems.

The priority for selection and inclusion of linguistic contributions to Chinese dialectology, is given to modern and contemporary works, chiefly covering those works published between the middle of the nineteenth century and the present time (1979). The criteria for inclusion of an item are the scientific and linguistic value of a work or an article as determined by a careful examination of its contents and its relative importance to the total available information on a particular topic. Availability is another criterion for inclusion. This means that the book or article is either easily accessible through libraries or can easily be purchased commercially. Some rare items, however, although at present still not available for personal inspection, are included (marked with [not seen]) because they have been either cited by authorities or listed in reputable bibliographies. Often, complete bibliographical information, such as pagination, for these items was not provided. Unpublished Ph.D. dissertations and M.A. theses, now easily obtainable through university libraries or through University Microfilms International, Inc., are also included. Literary works written in dialect styles and translations of the *Bible* are excluded from this bibliography because they are not strictly linguistic studies and are not easily accessible to the public. For those who wish to find references on dialect literatures, the following works can be conveniently consulted: For Wu dialect literature, Osada's bibliography (#0045); for Yüeh dialect literature, Tenri Daigaku's bibliography (#0051); for Min dialect literature, Murakami's bibliography (#0054); for translations of the *Bible,* Shiga's book (#0031).

For the classification of modern Chinese dialects, I have adapted Yüan Chia-hua's system (see #0146) with some minor modifications. The complete system is as follows:

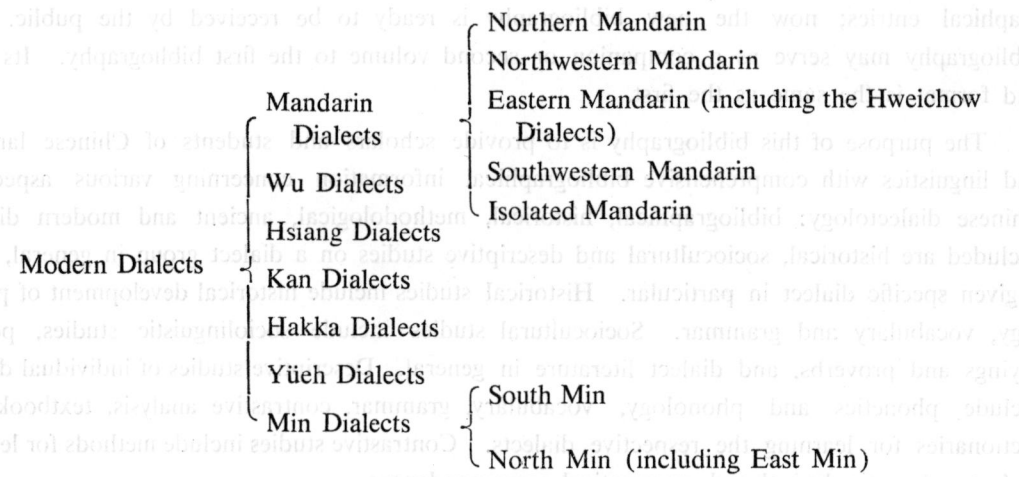

Modern Dialects
- Mandarin Dialects
  - Northern Mandarin
  - Northwestern Mandarin
  - Eastern Mandarin (including the Hweichow Dialects)
  - Southwestern Mandarin
  - Isolated Mandarin
- Wu Dialects
- Hsiang Dialects
- Kan Dialects
- Hakka Dialects
- Yüeh Dialects
- Min Dialects
  - South Min
  - North Min (including East Min)

However, for the convenience of bibliographical arrangement and balance of sub-classification, I have listed the Mandarin sub-dialect groups under separate numerical headings, and have put Kan and Hakka under one general heading, as Li Fang-kuei and many others have done. At present, there is not a definitive sub-classification of dialect varieties within a major dialect group, and very often, it is difficult to make such a sub-classification due to the dirth of linguistic data, and/or ambiguous dialectal features. Furthermore, there is divergence between geographical distributions and politico-administrative divisions; namely, one dialect can be found in more than one district (*hsien*) or province (*sheng*). In this bibliography, although great efforts have been made to pay close attention to linguistic features, geographical distributions, and politico-administrative divisions, the sub-classifications of dialects, however, are by no means definitive, but rather are plausible and in certain cases merely convenient.

There is another matter that needs some clarification, namely, the difference between the Peking dialect and the Standard Language (called Kuo-yü or P'u-t'ung-hua). The phonology of these two is identical since the Standard pronunciation is based on Peking dialect phonology. The vocabulary is somewhat different since the Standard Language excludes certain words considered to be Peking patois. The grammar, both morphology and syntax, is the same. In this bibliography, I have included mainly works that specifically refer to the Peking dialect. Works that can be regarded as dealing with both forms are excluded here. These works can be found in my *Chinese Linguistics: A Selected and Classified Bibliography* (#0042), Section 10: Modern Chinese. The reader is invited to consult it when necessary.

During the stages of gathering materials and preparing entry cards, I was aided by my teaching assistants Miss Christine M. Casati and Mr. James R. Jennings. Miss Casati has typed and proofread many entry cards. Mr. Jennings was very helpful in proofreading and in compiling indexes. Fr. Ignatius Chin-chang Ch'en, S. J. has copied many Chinese and Japanese titles. Their assistance has speeded up the completion of the manuscript. To them I would like to express my deep appreciation and gratitude. I am also indebted to Mr. Richard Lai, Director of the Chinese University Press, and to Mr. Ho Chun-chung, Production Assistant of the Press, for their arrangements and assistance in publishing this work. Last but not least, I would like to express my thanks and appreciation to Fr. Willem A. Grootaers, C.I.C.M. who, during the past twenty-five years, has inspired and encouraged my study of Chinese dialectology and who is kind enough to write a foreword for this work.

Despite the numerous proofreadings to which this bibliography was subjected, errors and omissions may still be present. Criticisms and suggestions will be gratefully accepted and appreciated.

In memory of their encouragement and assistance in my academic labors, this book is gratefully dedicated to my parents.

PAUL FU-MIEN YANG, S.J.
Georgetown University
Washington, D.C.
June 14, 1980

EXPLANATORY NOTES

I. AUTHORS AND TRANSLATORS

1. The order followed is surname first, then given name. In case of pseudonyms, the real name, if known, follows in square brackets [ ].
2. Unknown authors are indicated by the term *Anonymous.*
3. Proper names following the term *Transl. by* indicate the translator.
4. Names of book revisors and reviewers follow usual signature order for Western names, but surname first, then given name, for East Asian names.

II. TITLES OF BOOKS AND ARTICLES

1. A colon separates the author's name from the title of his work.
2. Book titles are in italics, but article titles in Roman type.

III. PLACE OF PUBLICATION AND NAME OF PUBLISHERS

1. A period and a dash (. —) separate book titles from place of publication.
2. Place of publication is given in English spelling or in romanization for East Asian place names, followed by a colon.
3. The name of the publisher and the year of publication, separated by a comma, follow the place of publication.
4. For the name of publishers and place of publication in respective East Asian languages, see List of Chinese and Japanese Publishers (pp. 159–165).

IV. PAGINATION OF BOOKS

1. Pagination of books follows the year of publication, separated by a comma.
2. The combination of small Roman numerals (for preface, table of contents, etc.) and of Arabic numerals (for the main text) is indicated if found in the work itself. Otherwise, Arabic numerals alone, separated by commas, are used. If relevant for a book, starting and ending pagination is linked by a hyphen (–).
3. In multi-volume works, pagination for each volume is given in succession, separated by a semi-colon.
4. Books of note found cited in works examined but which gave no pagination and as yet not themselves seen by this bibliographer are indicated by the term [not seen].

V. TITLE, VOLUME, NUMBER, YEAR, AND PAGINATION OF PERIODICALS

1. Periodical titles follow article titles, separated by a period and a dash (. —). Periodical titles in italics are usually abbreviated. See List of Periodicals (pp. xxv-xxxvii).
2. Volume of a periodical is given immediately after its title, without any mark of separation, next its issue number follows, separated by a colon, then the year, separated by a comma. But issue numbers, either published within a given year or coinciding with the twelve months of the calendar year, follow the year.
3. Pagination of an article is given after the year or the issue number, whatever be the case, separated by a comma. Starting and ending pagination is linked by a hyphen. In some Chinese periodicals (for example, the *CKYW*), the concluding part of an article may be found either on a preceding page or on a succeeding page, and thus be

separated from the main body of the article. In such cases, the main successive pagination is given first, then the concluding pagination.

4. Articles of note found cited in works examined but which gave no pagination and as yet themselves not seen by this bibliographer are indicated by the term [not seen].

VI. ADDITIONAL REMARKS AND REVIEWS

1. Additional remarks as well as reviews of book or article follow the main entry, separated by a diagonal (/). Among the additional remarks is information concerning bibliography and contents, series and collection titles, etc.

2. Reviews of the book or article follow the same format of an article entry except that the names of reviewers follow the order stated in I.4, and occur as final information given for reviews.

VII. TRANSLATION OF TITLES

1. Chinese, Japanese, Korean, and Russian titles are translated into English and are given in square brackets.

2. A book or article that is a translation follows the format already outlined. The original title of the translated work is likewise given in square brackets.

VIII. USE OF CHINESE, JAPANESE, AND KOREAN CHARACTERS

1. At the end of those entries indicating books or articles written by Chinese, Japanese, or Korean scholars, the respective characters follow: proper name first, then the title of the book or article. Characters for reviewers' names follow the title, separated by a diagonal.

2. Double quotation marks (『 』) in the title of an article indicate either titles of books or specific terms. Single quotation marks (「 」) indicate titles of a series or a collection. Book titles within a book are unmarked.

IX. ROMANIZATION, TRANSCRIPTION, AND ENTRY ORDER

1. Chinese, Japanese, Korean, and Russian titles are romanized according the following systems: Wade-Giles for Chinese; Hepburn for Japanese; McCune-Reischauer for Korean; and Library of Congress for Russian, with omission of diacritical mark (˘).

2. International Phonetic Alphabet symbols are kept if they occur in original titles, and are used for transcription of certain dialect sounds.

3. The order of entries in the main body of the text, List of Periodicals, List of Chinese and Japanese Publishers, and Romanized Index of Authors is according to standard alphabetical order. For the convenience of arrangement, the order of spelling for Wade-Giles romanization is also adapted to the standard alphabetical order.

X. ROMANIZATION OF PLACE NAMES

1. European, American, and Asian place names are found in standard English forms.

2. Well known Chinese place names are transcribed according to accepted English forms. Other Chinese place names are transcribed according to Wade-Giles spelling without hyphens.

XI. CROSS REFERENCES

1. Cross references to a book or an article appearing in this bibliography are indicated by their entry numbers in parentheses.

2. Reference to an original title of a translated work is indicated the same way.

LIST OF PERIODICALS

AAGB Ajia-Afurika Gengo Bunka Kenkyū. Tokyo. 1968–
Journal of Asian and African Studies.
アジア・アフリカ言語文化研究

AAs Acta Asiatica. Tokyo. 1960–

AATS Ajia-Afurika Gengo Bunka Kenkyūjo Tsūshin. Tokyo. 1966–
アジア・アフリカ言語文化研究所通信

AcOr Acta Orientalia. Copenhagen. 1922–

Afrika und Übersee. Berlin. 1910–

AGDR Aichi Gakuin Daigaku Ronsō (Ippan Kyōiku Kenkyū). Nagoya. 1965–
愛知學院大學論叢（一般教育研究）

AGK Ajia Gengo Kenkyū. Tenri. 1951–1955.
アジア言語研究

AL Anthropological Linguistics. Bloomington. 1958–

ALH Acta Linguistica Hafniensia (continued Acta Linguistica). Copenhagen. 1939–

AM Asia Major, new series. London. 1949–

An-hui ta-hsüeh yüeh-k'an. Anch'ing (Anking). 1960–1962.
安徽大學月刊

Anthropologie. Paris. 1890–
Anthropos International Review of Ethnology and Linguistics. Freiburg. 1906–

AO Archiv Orientální. Prague. 1933–

AOH Acta Orientalia Academiae Scientiarum Hungaricae. Budapest. 1950–

Archives Néerlandaises de Phonétique Expérimentale. The Hague. 1927–

BEFEO Bulletin de l'École Française d'Extrême-Orient. Hanoi, Saigon, Paris. 1901–

BGRS Bungaku Ronshū. Fukuoka. 1953–
文學論輯

BIE Bulletin of the Institute of Ethnology, Academia Sinica. Taipei. 1956–
中央研究院民族學研究所集刊

BIHP Bulletin of the Institute of History and Philology, Academia Sinica. Canton, Peking, Shanghai, Kunming, Chungking, Taipei. 1928–
中央研究院歷史語言研究所集刊

BIHPEV Bulletin of the Institute of History and Philology, Extra Volume, Academia Sinica. Taipei. 1960–
中央研究院歷史語言研究所集刊外編

BMFEA Bulletin of the Museum of Far Eastern Antiquities. Stockholm. 1929–

Books Abroad. Norman, Okla.

BPTJ Biuletyn Polskiego Towarzystwa Językoznawczego. Wroclaw & Krakow. 1927–
Bulletin de la Société Polonaise de Linguistique.

BSL Bulletin de la Société de Linguistique de Paris. Paris. 1869–

BSOAS Bulletin of the School of Oriental and African Studies. London. Formerly *BSOS.*

BSOS Bulletin of the School of Oriental Studies. London. 1917–

BUA Bulletin de l'Université l'Aurore. 3rd series. Shanghai. 1940–1949.

Bulletin Catholique de Pékin. Peking. 1905–1945.

Bulletin de la Maison Franco-Japonaise. Tokyo. 1927–

CAAAL Computational Analysis of Asian and African Languages. Tokyo. 1975–
アジア・アフリカ語の計數研究

CBKK Chūbun Kenkyū. Tenri. 1961–
中文研究

CCHP Ch'ung-chi hsüeh-pao. Hong Kong.
1962–
Chung Chi Journal.
崇基學報

CCS Collectanea Commissionis Synodalis.
Peking. 1929–
公教教育叢刊

CGGG Chūgoku Gogaku. Tokyo. 1947–
Bulletin of the Chinese Language Society
of Japan.
中國語學

CGKK Chūgoku Gogaku Kenkyūkai Kaihō.
Tokyo. 1951–1954.
中國語學研究會會報

CGKR Chūgoku Gogaku Kenkyūkai Ronshū.
Nara.
中國語學研究會論集

Ch'ao-chou liu Ching hsüeh-hui nien-k'an.
Peking. 1923–1926.
潮州留京學會年刊

CHCK Ch'ing-hua chou-k'an. Peking. 1921–
1937.
清華週刊

CHHP Ch'ing-hua hsüeh-pao. Peking.
1924–; Taipei: New series, 1956–
Tsing Hua Journal of Chinese Studies.
清華學報

Chi-Lin. Princeton. 1968–
Unicorn.
麒麟

Chiang-hai hsüeh-k'an. Nanking. 1958–1963.
江海學刊（月刊）

Chiang-hsi chiao-yü yüeh-k'an. Nanch'ang.
1934–1937.
江西教育月刊

Chiang-nan shih ti ts'ung-kao. 1942.
江南史地叢考

Chiang-su chiao-yü. Nanking. 1955–1963.
江蘇教育（半月刊）

Chiao-yü kung-tso. Nanch'ang. 1955–1958.
教育工作（半月刊）

Chiao-yü yü wen-hua. Taipei. 1950–
教育與文化

Chien-kuo yü-wen yüeh-k'an. Ch'engku
(Shensi). 1942.
建國語文月刊

Chih-chiang hsüeh-pao. Hangchow. 1935–
1936.
之江學報

Chih-hsüeh yüeh-k'an. Ch'engtu. 1942–1945.
志學月刊

Chih-yen Chih-yen pan-yüeh-k'an. Soochow.
1935–1940.
制言半月刊

Chine. Peking. 1921–1925.

Chinese Repository. Canton. 1832–1951.

Chinese Social and Political Science Review.
Peking. 1916–1941.
中國社會及政治學報

Ching-kang-shan ta-hsüeh hsüeh-pao. Ching-
kangshan. 1960.
井岡山大學學報（綜合版）

Ch'ing-nien chieh. Shanghai. 1931–1947.
青年界

ChinRec Chinese Recorder. Shanghai, Foochow. 1868–

Ch'u-pan chou-k'an. Shanghai. 1934–1937.
出版週刊

Chūbun Gakkaihō. Tokyo.
中文學會報

Chūgoku Bungaku Ronsō. Tokyo. 1968–
中國文學論叢

Chūgoku Sōgō Kenkyū. Tokyo. 1975–
中國綜合研究

Ch'un sun. Peking. 1929–1930.
春笋（季刊）

Chung-hua chiao-yü chieh. Shanghai. 1913–
1937; 1947–1949.
中華教育界（月刊）

Chung-hua tsa-chih. Taipei. 1963–
中華雜誌

Chung-kuo yü-wen. Shanghai. 1939–1940.
中國語文

Chung-shan hsüeh-pao. Canton. 1941–1944.
中山學報

Chung-shan ta-hsüeh shih-fan hsüeh-yüan chi-k'an. P'ingshih.
中山大學師範學院季刊

Chung-shan ta-hsüeh yen-chiu-yüan wen-k'o yen-chiu-so chi-k'an. Canton. 1943.
中山大學研究院文科研究所集刊

Chung-yang ta-hsüeh pan-yüeh-k'an. Nanking. 1929–1930.
中央大學半月刊

Chung-yang ta-hsüeh wen-i ts'ung-k'an. Nanking. 1933–1936.
中央大學文藝叢刊（半年刊）

Chungkuk hakpo. Seoul. 1963–
Journal of Chinese Studies.
中國學報

CKYW Chung-kuo yü-wen. Peking. 1952–1966; 1978–
中國語文

CKYWT Chung-kuo yü-wen. Taipei. 1952–
中國語文（臺北）

CLAO Cahiers de Linguistique Asie Orientale. Paris. 1977–

CLTH Chi-lin ta-hsüeh hsüeh-pao. Ch'angch'un. 1959–1963.
吉林大學學報（語言，文學）

Concentric, The. Taipei. 1966.

CR China Review. Hong Kong. 1872–1901.

CSTHW Chung-shan ta-hsüeh wen-shih-hsüeh yen-chiu-so yüeh-k'an. Canton. 1933–1935.
中山大學文史學研究所月刊

CSTY Chung-shan ta-hsüeh yü-yen li-shih yen-chiu-so chou-k'an. Canton. 1927–1930.
中山大學語言歷史研究所週刊

CTCK Ch'i-ta chi-k'an. Chinan (Tsinan). 1932–1935.
齊大季刊

CTHP Cheng-chih ta-hsüeh hsüeh-pao. Taipei. 1960–
The National Chengchi University Journal.
政治大學學報

CTWC Chung-shan ta-hsüeh wen-hsüehyüan chuan-k'an. Canton. 1943.
中山大學文學院專刊

CWYH Chung-kuo wen-hua yen-chiu hui-k'an. Ch'engtu. 1940–1948.
Bulletin of Chinese Studies.
中國文化研究彙刊（年刊）

CYYK Kuo-li Chung-yang yen-chiu-yüan yüan-k'an. Taipei. 1954–
Annals of Academia Sinica.
國立中央研究院院刊

DA Dissertation Abstracts. Ann Arbor.

DAI Dissertation Abstracts International. Ann Arbor.

DBDK Daitō Bunka Daigaku Kiyō Bungakuhen. Tokyo. 1964–
大東文化大學紀要文學編

Developing Economics. Tokyo. 1962–

Dōshisha Gaikoku Bungaku Kenkyū. Kyoto. 1971–
同志社外國文學研究

Ethnohistory. Window Rock, Ariz. 1954–

Fang-chih yüeh-k'an. Nanking. 1934–1935.
方志月刊

FCWH Fu-chien wen-hsien. Taipei. 1968–
福建文獻

FDKR Fukushima Daigaku Kyōikugakubu Ronshū. Fukushima.
福島大學教育學部論集

FJHC Fu-jen hsüeh-chih. Peking. 1928–1947.
輔仁學誌

Folklore Studies. Peking. 1942–

FPC Fang-yen yü P'u-tung-hua chi-k'an. Peking. 1958–1961.
方言與普通話集刊

FPT Fang-yen ho P'u-t'ung-hua ts'ung-k'an. Peking. 1958–1959.
方言和普通話叢刊

Free China Review. Taipei. 1951–

FSNC Fu So-chang chi-nien t'e-k'an. Taipei. 1951.
Special Publication of the Institute of History and Philology, Academia Sinica, in Memorial of Director Fu Ssu-nien.
傅所長紀念特刊

FTTH Fu-tan ta-hsüeh hsüeh-pao. Shanghai. 1962–1963.
復旦大學學報（哲學社會科學）

Fu-chien shih-fan hsüeh-yüan hsüeh-pao. Foochow. 1956–1963.
福建師範學院學報（社會科學）

Fu-chien wen-hua. Foochow. 1932–1936.
福建文化

FY Fang-yen. Peking. 1979–
方言（季刊）

Gakusō. Tokyo. 1964–
學叢

General Linguistics. University Park, PA. 1955–

Gengo. Tokyo. 1972–
言語（月刊）

Gengo Seikatsu. Tokyo. 1959–
言語生活

Geographical Journal. London. 1893–

GK Gengo Kenkyū. Tokyo. 1939–
Journal of the Linguistic Society of Japan.
言語研究

GnK Gengo no Kagaku. Tokyo. 1970–
言語の科學

Hai-wang. T'angku. 1934–1935.
海王（旬刊）

Hang-chou ta-hsüeh hsüeh-pao. Hangchow. 1959–1963.
杭州大學學報（人文科學）

HDBK Hokkaidō Daigaku Bungakubu Kiyō. Sapporo. 1952–
北海道大學文學部紀要

Hei-lung-chiang chiao-yü. Harbin. 1956–1961.
黑龍江教育（月刊）

HJAS Harvard Journal of Asiatic Studies. Cambridge, Mass. 1936–

HKCW Hsiang-kang Chung-wen ta-hsüeh Chung-kuo wen-hua yen-chiu-so hsüeh-pao. Hong Kong. 1968–
The Journal of the Institute of Chinese Studies of The Chinese University of Hong Kong.
香港中文大學中國文化研究所學報

HKHP Hua-kang hsüeh-pao. Taipei. 1965–
華岡學報

HKR Hikone Ronsō. Hikone. 1949–
彥根論叢

HMTH Hsia-men ta-hsüeh hsüeh-pao. Amoy. 1954–1963.
廈門大學學報（社會科學）

HNPK Ho-nan po-wu-kuan kuan-k'an. K'aifeng. 1936–1937.
河南博物館館刊

HNTH Ho-nan ta-hsüeh hsüeh-pao. K'aifeng. 1934.
河南大學學報

Ho-fei shih-fan hsüeh-yüan hsüeh-pao. Hofei. 1959–1963.
合肥師範學院學報

Ho-nan chiao-yü yüeh-k'an. K'aifeng. 1934–1935.
河南教育月刊

Ho-pei ta-hsüeh hsüeh-pao. Tientsin. 1961–
1963.
河北大學學報（社會科學）

Hōgen. Tokyo. 1931–1938.
方言

Hōgen Kenkyū Nenpō. Tokyo. 1964.
方言研究年報

HSCK Hsüeh-shu chi-k'an. Taipei. 1952–
1958.
學術季刊

Hsi-fang yü-wen. Peking. 1957–1958.
西方語文（季刊）

Hsi-nan yen-chiu. Kunming. 1940.
西南研究

Hsia-men t'u-shu-kuan sheng. Amoy. 1932–
1937.
廈門圖書館聲（月刊）

*Hsiang-ch'in ta-hsüeh shih-fan hsüeh-yüan chi-
k'an.* Canton. 1934.
勤勤大學師範學院季刊

Hsiao-hsüeh yen-chiu. Nanking. 1936.
小學研究

Hsin-chiang ta-hsüeh lun-wen chi. Urumchi.
1963.
新疆大學論文集（人文科學）

Hsin Chung-hua. Shanghai. 1933–1937, 1949.
新中華（半月刊）

Hsin hsi-pei. Lanchow. 1942–1943.
新西北（半月刊）

Hsin p'ing-lun. Chungking. 1940–1944.
新評論（半月刊）

Hsin-she hsüeh-pao. Singapore. 1967–
新社學報

Hsin-sheng-pao: Yü-yen yü wen-hsüeh.
Peking. 1946–1948.
新生報：語言與文學

Hsin wen-tzu chou-k'an. Shanghai. 1950–
1952.
新文字週刊

Hsin wen-tzu pan-yüeh-k'an. Nanning. 1936.
新文字半月刊

Hsin Ya-hsi-ya. Nanking. 1942–1943.
新亞細亞（月刊）

Hsin yü-wen. Shanghai. 1947.
（上海時代日報）新語文

Hsin yüeh. Shanghai. 1928–1933.
新月（月刊）

Hsüeh-feng. Anch'ing (Anking). 1930–1937.
學風（月刊）

Hsüeh-szu. Ch'engtu. 1942–1943.
學思（半月刊）

Hsüeh-ts'ui. Taipei. 1948–
學粹

HTCK Hsia-men ta-hsüeh chi-k'an. Amoy.
1927.
廈門大學季刊

Hu-pei wen-hsien. Taipei. 1966–
湖北文獻

Hua-chung shih-fan hsüeh-yüan hsüeh-pao.
Wuhan. 1955–1960.
華中師範學院學報（語言文學）

Hua-hsüeh yüeh-k'an. Taipei. 1972–
Sinological Monthly.
華學月刊

Hua-nan shih-yüan hsüeh-pao. Canton. 1960.
華南師院學報（中國語言文學專號）

Hua-nien chou-k'an. Shanghai. 1932–1937.
華年週刊

Hua-tung shih-ta hsüeh-pao. Shanghai. 1956–
1961.
華東師大學報（人文科學）

HYSY Hsin-ya shu-yüan hsüeh-shu nien-k'an.
Hong Kong. 1959–
新亞書院學術年刊

IAN Izvestiia Akademiia Nauk SSSR,
Otdelenie Gumanitarnykh Nauk.
Leningrad.

IANK Izvestiia Akademiia Nauk Kazakhskoi
SSSR. Moscow.

Iazyki Narodov SSSR. Leningrad. 1968.

JAOS Journal of American Oriental Society. New Haven. 1851–

JAS Journal of Asian Studies. Ann Arbor. 1957–

JBGH Jinbun Gakuhō. Tokyo. 1952–
人文學報

JBK Jinbun Kenkyū. Osaka. 1949–
Studies in the Humanities, Journal of the Literary Association of Osaka City University.
人文研究

JCL Journal of Chinese Linguistics. Berkeley. 1973–

JCLTA Journal of the Chinese Language Teachers Association. South Orange. 1966–

Jen-wen hsüeh-pao. Hsinchuang (Taipei-hsien). 1970–
人文學報

Jen-wen k'o-hsüeh lun-ts'ung. Taipei. 1948.
人文科學論叢

Jen-wen yüeh-k'an. Shanghai. 1930–1937.
人文月刊

Jinbungaku. Kyoto. 1948–
人文學

Jinsei. Tokyo. 1967–
人生

JL Journal of Linguistics. Cambridge. 1965–

Journal of American Folklore. Boston. 1888-

Journal of Child Language. London. 1974–

Journal of Speech and Hearing Research. Washington. 1958–

Journal of The Chinese University of Hong Kong. Hong Kong. 1973–1979.
香港中文大學學報

JRAS Journal of the Royal Asiatic Society of Great Britain and Ireland. London. 1826–

JRASHK Journal of the Royal Asiatic Society of Great Britain and Ireland. Hong Kong Branch. Hong Kong. 1959–

JRASNC Journal of the Royal Asiatic Society of Great Britain and Ireland. North China Branch. Shanghai. 1858–

Kago Gekkan. Shanghai. 1939–1944.
華語月刊

K'ai-feng nü-shih hsiao-k'an. K'aifeng. 1937.
開封女師校刊

K'ai-feng shih-fan hsüeh-yüan hsüeh-sheng k'o-hsüeh hsi-tso. K'aifeng. 1957.
開封師範學院學生科學習作

K'ai-feng shih-yüan hsüeh-pao. K'aifeng. 1956–1963.
開封師院學報

Kai-tsao tsa-chih. Shanghai. 1946–1947.
改造雜誌（半月刊）

Kakyō Seikatsu. Tokyo. 1962–
華僑生活

Kan-su shih-fan ta-hsüeh hsüeh-pao. Lanchow. 1959–1963.
甘肅師範大學學報（人文科學）

Kao-hsiung shih-yüan hsüeh-pao. Kaohsiung. 1972–
Kaohsiung Teachers College Journal.
高雄師院學報

KGK Kangaku Kenkyū. Tokyo. 1963–
漢學研究

KGR Kōbe Gaidai Ronsō. Kobe. 1949–
Kobe City University Journal.
神戶外大論叢

KHCK Kuo-hsüeh chi-k'an. Peking. 1923–1946; 1950–1952.
Journal of Sinological Studies.
國學季刊

KHHP K'o-hsüeh hui-pao. Taipei. 1953–
科學彙報

KHLT Kuo-hsüeh lun-ts'ung. Peking. 1927–1930.
國學論叢

KHMC Kuo-hsüeh-men chou-k'an. Peking. 1925–1926.
（北京大學研究所）國學門週刊

KHMY Kuo-hsüeh-men yüeh-k'an. Peking. 1926–1927.
（北京大學研究所）國學門月刊

KHTK Kuo-hsüeh ts'ung-k'an. Peking. 1941–1945.
國學叢刊

KHYK Kuo-hsüeh yüeh-k'an. Peking. 1945.
國學月刊

Kita Kyūshū Daigaku Gaikokugo Gakubu Kiyō. Kita Kyush. 1958–
北九州大學外國語學部紀要

Kita Kyūshū Daigaku Ronbunshū. Kita Kiyō. Kita Kyushu. 1958–
北九州大學論文集

K'o-hsüeh. Shanghai. 1915–1929.
科學（月刊）

Ko-yao tseng-k'an. Peking. 1923.
歌謠增刊

KSBR Kansai Daigaku Bungaku Ronshū. Osaka. 1951–
關西大學文學論集

KSCB Kansai Daigaku Chūgoku Bungakkai Kiyō. Osaka.
關西大學中國文學會紀要

KSIV Kratie Soobshcheniia Instituta Vosto-kovedeniia. Moscow. 1951–
Short Report of the Institute of Oriental Studies.

KTJDK Kyōto Joshi Daigaku Kiyō. Kyoto. 1949–
京都女子大學紀要

Kuan-ch'a. Shanghai. 1946–1949.
觀察（週刊）

Kuang-hsi shih-yüan hsüeh-pao. Kweilin. 1959.
廣西師院學報（人文科學版）

Kuang-tung chiao-yü. Canton. 1956–1962.
廣東教育（月刊）

Kuang-tung chiao-yü yü wen-hua. Canton. 1950–
廣東教育與文化

Kuang-tung chien-she yen-chiu. Canton. 1946–1947.
廣東建設研究

Kuei-chou chiao-yü. Kweiyang. 1955–1958.
貴州教育（月刊）

Kung-hsien. Shanghai. 1927–1928.
貢獻（旬刊）

Kuo feng. Nanking. 1932–1936.
國風（半月刊）

Kuo-hsüeh chuan-k'an. Shanghai. 1926–1927.
國學專刊（雙月刊）

Kuo-hsüeh hui-pien. Shanghai. 1924–1925.
國學彙編

Kuo-hsüeh lun-heng. Soochow. 1933–1937.
國學論衡（半年刊）

Kuo-yü t'ung-hsün. Taipei. 1946–1948.
國語通訊

KWYK Kuo-wen yüeh-k'an. Kunming. 1940–1949.
國文月刊

KYAO Ko-yao chou-k'an. Peking. 1922–1937.
歌謠週刊

KYCK Kuo-yü chou-k'an. Peking. 1931–1937.
（北平世界日報）國語週刊

KYCK (Pei-hsin) Kuo-yü chou-k'an. Peking. 1925.
國語週刊（北新書局）

KYHK Kuo-yü hsün-k'an. Peking. 1929.
國語旬刊

Lan-chou ta-hsüeh hsüeh-pao. Lanchow. 1957–1958.
蘭州大學學報（人文科學）

Languages and Linguistics. Washington, D.C. 1966–

Languages and Linguistics: Working Papers. Washington, D.C. 1970–

Leuvense Bijdragen. Tijdschrift voor Moderne Philologie. Louvain. 1897–

Lg Language. Journal of the Linguistic Society of America. Baltimore. 1925–

Li-shih yü k'ao-ku. Chinan (Tsinan). 1937. 歷史與考古（月刊）

Lien-ho shu-yüan hsüeh-pao. Hong Kong. 1962–
United College Journal.
聯合書院學報

Lingua. International Review of General Linguistics. Amsterdam. 1947–

Linguistics. An International Review. The Hague. 1963–

LNHP Ling-nan hsüeh-pao. Canton. 1929–1949.
嶺南學報（季刊）

Maître Phonétique, Le. London. 1889–

Meiji Daigaku Jinbun Kagaku Kenkyūjo Kiyō. Tokyo. 1962–
明治大學人文科學研究所紀要

Min-chu p'ing-lun. Hong Kong. 1949–1966.
民主論評

Min-sheng chou-k'an. Nanking. 1936.
民生週刊

Min-su. Canton. 1928–1933.
民俗（週刊）

Min-ta Chung-kuo wen-hsüeh-hsi ts'ung-k'an. Peking. 1934.
民大中國文學系叢刊（半年刊）

Min-to tsa-chih. Shanghai. 1916–1929.
民鐸雜誌（月刊）

Minzokugaku Kenkyū. Tokyo. 1935–
民族學研究

Missiewerk, Het. Nijmegen. 1919–

MS Monumenta Serica. Peking, Nagoya, Los Angeles, St. Augustin. 1938–
華裔學志

MSBGK Min Shin Bungaku Gengo Kenkyūkai Kaihō. Osaka. 1962–
明清文學言語研究會會報

MSBGKT Min Shin Bungaku Gengo Kenkyūkai Kaihō Tankan. Osaka.
明清文學言語研究會會報單刊

Muséon. Revue d'Études Orientale. Louvain. 1915–

Nagasaki Kenritsu Kokusai Keizai Daigaku Ronshū. Nagasaki. 1967–
長崎縣立國際經濟大學論集

Nan-ch'iang yüeh-k'an. Nanking. 1936–1937.
南強月刊

Narody Azii i Afriki. Moscow. 1961–

NCGH Nippon Chūgoku Gakkaihō. Tokyo. 1950–
Bulletin of the Sinological Society of Japan.
日本中國學會報

Nei Meng-ku ta-hsüeh hsüeh-pao. Huhehot. 1959–1962.
內蒙古大學學報（社會科學）

Newsletter of the American Oriental Society. New Haven. 1979.

NGBK Nagoya Daigaku Bungakubu Kenkyū Ronshū (Bungaku). Nagoya. 1951–
名古屋大學文學部研究論集（文學）

Norsk Tidsskrift for Sprogvidenskap. Oslo. 1928–

NSTH Nü-shih-ta hsüeh-shu chi-k'an. Peking. 1930–1931.
女師大學術季刊

NYHP Nan-yang hsüeh-pao. Singapore. 1940–
南洋學報

NYTH Nan-yang ta-hsüeh hsüeh-pao. Singapore. 1967–
南洋大學學報

NYWH Nan-ying wen-hsien. Tainan. 1954–
南瀛文獻

OGDG Ōsaka Gaikokugo Daigaku Gakuhō. Osaka. 1952–
大阪外國語大學學報

OJKK Ochanomizu Joshi Daigaku Jinbun Kagaku Kiyō. Tokyo. 1952–
お茶の水女子大學人文科學紀要

OLZ Orientalische Literaturzeitung. Berlin. 1898–

ONK Onsei no Kenkyū. Tokyo. 1928–
音聲の研究

Onoma Bibliographical and Information Bulletin. Louvain. 1950–

Orbis Bulletin International de Documentation Linguistique. Louvain. 1952–

Oriens. Journal of the International Society for Oriental Research. Leiden. 1948–

OSGK Onseigakkaihō. Tokyo. 1926–
Bulletin of the Phonetic Society of Japan.
音聲學會報

Panse. Kyoto.
ぱんせ

Papers from the Sixth Regional Meeting of the Chicago Linguistics Society. Chicago. 1970.

Phonetica. International Journal of Phonetics. Basel. 1957–

Phonetica Pragensia. Prague. 1967–

PICO Proceedings of the International Congress of Orientalists. 1873–

P'in-yin. Peking. 1956–1957.
拼音

P'ing-nü hsüeh-pao. P'ingtung (Taiwan). 1975–
屛女學報（屛東女子中學　年刊）

PJL Philippine Journal of Linguistics. Manila. 1970–

POLA Project on Linguistic Analysis. Columbus, Berkeley. 1962–

Problemy Vostokovedeniia. Moscow. 1959–
Problems of Oriental Studies.

RBS Revue Bibliographique de Sinologie. The Hague-Paris. 1955–

RO Rocznik Orientalistyczny. Warsaw. 1920–

Romance Philology. Berkeley & Los Angeles. 1947–

SBGK Shinmatsu Bungaku Gengo Kenkyūkai Kaihō. Osaka. 1961–
清末文學言語研究會會報

SCPL Shih cheng p'ing-lun. Hangchow. 1936.
市政評論（月刊）

SCTH Szu-ch'uan ta-hsüeh hsüeh-pao. Ch'engtu. 1955–1963.
四川大學學報（社會科學）

SCWH Szu-ch'uan wen-hsien. Taipei. 1962–
四川文獻

Seinan Gakuin Daigaku Bunri Ronshū. Fukuoka. 1960–
西南學院大學文理論集

Shan-tung sheng-li t'u-shu-kuan chi-k'an. Chinan (Tsinan). 1931–1936.
山東省立圖書館季刊

Shan-tung ta-hsüeh hsüeh-sheng k'o-hsüeh lun-wen chi-k'an. Chinan. 1956.
山東大學學生科學論文集刊（人文科學）

Shan-tung ta-hsüeh wen-shih ts'ung-k'an. Tsingtao. 1934.
山東大學文史叢刊

Shan-tung wen-hsien. Taipei. 1974–
山東文獻

Shih-tai ch'ing-nien. Chinan (Tsinan). 1936.
時代青年（月刊）

Shina oyobi Shinago. Osaka.
支那及支那語

Shinagaku. Kyoto. 1920–
支那學

Shinago. Tokyo. 1932–1940.
支那語（月刊）

Shinago Kenkyū. Tenri. 1938.
支那語研究

Shinago Zasshi. Tokyo. 1941–
支那語雜誌

Shinagogakuhō. Tokyo. 1935–
支那語學報

Shizen to bunka. Kyoto. 1952.
自然と文化

Shu ho jen. Taipei. 1969–
書和人

Shu-mu chi-k'an. Taipei. 1966–
書目季刊

Shūkan Tōyōgaku. Sendai. 1959–
集刊東洋學

Sinica. Frankfurt. 1926–1939.

Sitzungsberichte der Kaiserliche Akademie der Wissenschaften. Vienna. 1848–

SK Shina Kenkyū. Shanghai. 1918–
支那研究

Sovetskaia Etnografiia. Moscow. 1951–

Sovetskoe Vostokovedenie. Moscow. 1940–

SPhon Studia Phonologica. Kyoto. 1961–

Språkliga Bidrag. Lund.

STHP Shih-ta hsüeh-pao. Taipei. 1956–
師大學報

STKT Shih-ta kuo-hsüeh ts'ung-k'an. Peking. 1930–1932.
師大國學叢刊

STTH Shan-tung ta-hsüeh hsüeh-pao. Chinan (Tsinan). 1951–1963.
山東大學學報（人文科學）

Studia Serica. Ch'engtu. 1940–1950.
華西協合大學中國文化研究所集刊
（年刊）

Studies in English Literature and Linguistics. Taipei. 1979–

STYK Shih-ta yüeh-k'an. Peking. 1932–1934.
師大月刊

Sui-yüan lü P'ing hsüeh-hui hsüeh-k'an. Peking. 1934–1935.
綏遠旅平學會學刊

Sung Kyun Kwan University Journal. Seoul. 1954–
成均館大學校論文集

SWYK Shuo-wen yüeh-k'an. Shanghai, Chungking. 1939–1947.
說文月刊

Szu-ch'uan chiao-yü t'ung-hsün. Ch'engtu. 1948–1949.
四川教育通訊（月刊）

Szu-wen. Nanking. 1940–1943.
斯文（半月刊）

Ta-hsüeh. Ch'engtu. 1942–1947.
大學（月刊）

T'ai-pai pan-yüeh k'an. Shanghai. 1934–1935.
太白半月刊

T'ai-p'ing-yang. Shanghai. 1917–1925.
太平洋（月刊）

Tai-tan. Chiuchiang. 1935.
待旦（季刊）

TCLP Traveaux de Cercle Linguistique de Prague. Prague. 1929–1939.

Teikoku Gakushiin Kiji. Tokyo. 1942–1947.
帝國學士院紀事

TFHP Tung-fang hsüeh-pao. Singapore. 1957–
東方學報

TFTC Tung-fang tsa-chih. Shanghai. 1904–1948; Taipei. 1967–
The Eastern Miscellany
東方雜誌

TFWH Tung-fang wen-hua. Shanghai. 1942–1943.
東方文化（月刊）

THG Tōhōgaku. Tokyo. 1951–
Eastern Studies
東方學

THGHK Tōhō Gakuhō, Kyōtō. Kyoto.
1931–
Journal of Oriental Studies.
東方學報（京都）

THHP Tung-hai hsüeh-pao. Taichung.
1959–
Tunghai Journal.
東海學報

TICOJ Transactions of the International
Conference of Orientalists in Japan.
Tokyo.
國際東方學者會議紀要

*T'ien-chin shih-fan-hsüeh-yüan k'o-hsüeh lun-
wen chi-k'an.* Tientsin. 1957.
天津師範學院科學論文集刊（人文科學）

T'ien-chin wen-hua. Tientsin. 1948.
天津文化（半月刊）

TLTC Ta-lu tsa-chih. Taipei. 1950–
The Continent Magazine.
大陸雜誌

Tōhōgaku Ronshū. Tokyo. 1954–1955.
東方學論集

Tokushima Daigaku Gakugeibu Kiyō. Tokushima. 1953–
德島大學學藝部紀要（人文科學）

Tongyanghak. Seoul.
東洋學

Tou-sou. Hong Kong. 1976–
抖擻

Tōyō Kenkyū. Tokyo. 1961–
東洋研究

TP T'oung Pao. Leiden. 1890–
通報

TPS Transactions of the Philological Society.
Oxford. 1854–

TPWH T'ai-pei wen-hsien. Taipei. 1949–
臺北文獻

TPWW T'ai-pei wen-wu. Taipei. 1952–
臺北文物

TRGH Tenri Daigaku Gakuhō. Tenri.
1949–
天理大學學報

*Trudy Instituta Iazyka i Literatury, Akademiia
Nauk, Kirgizskoi, SSR.* Frunze. 1956–

*Trudy Instituta Iazykoznaiia Akademiia Nauk
Kazakhskoi SSR.* Alma-Ata. 1944–

TSCK T'u-shu chi-k'an. Peking. 1934–1947.
圖書季刊

Tse-shan pan-yüeh-k'an. Ch'engtu. 1940–
1941.
責善半月刊

TSGH Tōkyō Shina Gakkaihō. Tokyo.
1955–
東京支那學會報

TSKC T'u-shu-kuan-hsüeh chi-k'an. Peking.
1926–1937.
圖書館學季刊

TSST Tai-wan sheng-li shih-fan ta-hsüeh
kuo-wen yen-chiu-so chi-k'an. Taipei.
1957–
Journal of Research Institute of Chinese
Literature of Taiwan Normal University.
臺灣省立師範大學國文研究所集刊

TSTH Tu-shu t'ung-hsün. Chungking,
Shanghai. 1940–1948.
讀書通訊（半月刊）

TSYK T'u-shu yüeh-k'an. Chungking.
1941–1945.
圖書月刊

T'ung-sheng yüeh-k'an. Nanking. 1940–
1943.
同聲月刊

TWFW T'ai-wan feng-wu. Taipei. 1951–
臺灣風物

TWSN Taiwan seinen. Tokyo. 1960–
臺灣青年

TWWH T'ai-wan wen-hsien. Taipei. 1949–
臺灣文獻

TYGH   Tōyō Gakuhō.   Tokyo.   1911–
Reports of the Oriental Society.
東洋學報

Tz'u-shu yen-chiu.   Shanghai.   1979–
辭書研究

UZIV   Uchenye Zapiski Instituta Vostokove-
deniia.   Moscow-Leningrad.   1950–
Transactions of the Institute of Oriental
Studies.

VANK   Vestnik Akademiia Nauk Kazakhskoi
SSR.   Alma-Ata.   1944–

VLU   Vestnik Leningradskogo Universiteta.
Istoriia, Iazyka, Literatura.   Leningrad.
1946–

Vox.   Hamburg.   1925–1936.

Wen-chou shih-fan hsüeh-yüan hsüeh-pao.
Wenchow.   1963.
溫州師範學院學報（人文科學）

Wen-feng hsüeh-pao.   Canton.   1947–1948.
文風學報

Wen-hsüeh (Canton).   Canton.   1947–1948.
文學（月刊）

Wen-hsüeh ch'uang-tso.   Kweilin.   1942–1944.
文學創作（月刊）

Wen-hsüeh tsa-chih.   Canton.   1933–1934.
文學雜誌

Wen-hua tsa-chih.   Kweilin.   1941–1943.
文化雜誌（月刊）

Wen shih.   Peking.   1934.
文史

Wen-shih hsüeh-pao.   Kowloon.   1964–
文史學報

Wen-shih hui-k'an.   Tainan.   1959–
文史薈刊（年刊）

Wen-shih tsa-chih.   Chungking.   1941–1948.
文史雜誌（半月刊）

Wennti.   Wennti Papers.   New Haven.   1952–
問題

WHTH   Wu-han ta-hsüeh jen-wen k'o-hsüeh
hsüeh-pao.   Wuhan.   1956–1963.
武漢大學人文科學學報

WHWC   Wu-han ta-hsüeh wen-che chi-k'an.
Wuhan.   1930–1942.
武漢大學文哲季刊

WLHP   Wen-lan hsüeh-pao.   Hangchow.
1936–1937.
文瀾學報（季刊）

Word.   Journal of the Linguistic Circle of New
York.   New York.   1945–

WSC   Wen shih che.   Chinan.   1951–1958;
1961–1963.
文史哲（月刊）

WSCH   Wen shih che hsüeh-pao.   Taipei.
1950–
Bulletin of the College of Arts, National
Taiwan University.
文史哲學報

WSTC   Wen-shih tsa-chih.   Chungking.
1941–1948.
文史雜志（半月刊）

WTKK   Wen-tzu kai-ko.   Peking.   1957–
1963.
文字改革

*Wu-han ta-hsüeh Szu-ch'uan t'ung-hsüeh-hui
hui-k'an.*   Wuchang.   1934.
武漢大學四川同學會會刊

WZKM   Wiener Zeitschrift für de Kunde des
Morgenlandes.   Vienna.   1887–

Yamato Bunka.   Tenri.   1934–
日本文化

YCHP   Yen-ching hsüeh-pao.   Peking.   1927–
1949.
Yenching Journal of Chinese Studies.
燕京學報

YLT   Yü-yen-hsüeh lun-ts'ung.   Shanghai-
Peking.   1957–
語言學論叢

YSDR Yokohama Shiritsu Daigaku Ronsō. Yokohama. 1958–
橫濱市立大學論叢（人文學科系列）

YSYK Yu-shih yüeh-k'an. Taipei. 1953–
幼獅月刊

Yü szu. Peking. 1925.
語絲（周刊）

Yü-wen. Shanghai. 1937; Chungking. 1959–1960.
語文（月刊）

Yü-wen i-k'an. Taipei.
（國語日報）語文乙刊

Yü-yen yü wen-hsüeh. Peking. 1937.
語言與文學

Yüeh-pao. Shanghai. 1937.
月報

YWC Yü-yen wen-hsüeh chuan-k'an. Canton. 1936–1937.
語言文學專刊

YWCH Yü-wen chiao-hsüeh. Shanghai. 1956–1960.
語文教學

YWCS Yü-wen chih-shih. Peking. 1952–1960.
語文知識

YWHH Yü-wen hsüeh-hsi. Peking. 1951–1960.
語文學習（月刊）

YWTC Yü-wen tsa-chih. Hong Kong. 1979–Language Forum.
語文雜誌

YYWH Yü-yen wen-hsüeh. Hohehot. 1958–1960.
語言文學（雙月刊）

ZDMG Zeitschrift der Deutschen Morgenländischen Gesellschaft. Leipzig. 1847–

Zphon Zeitschrift für Phonetik, Sprachwissenschaft und Kommunikationsforschung. Berlin. 1947–

LIST OF ABBREVIATIONS

C. S.	Chinese summary	pl.	plate(s)
Chap.	Chapter	portr.	portrait
col.	column(s)	print.	printed, printing
comp.	compiler, compiled (by)	pt.	part
d. p.	double pages	publ.	published (by)
E. S.	English summary	repr.	reprint, reprinted
ed.	editor, edited (by), edition	rev.	revised (by)
enl.	enlarged	s. p.	separate pagination
ERIC	Educational Resources Information Center Clearinghouse on Languages and Linguistics	tab.	table(s)
		transl.	translated (by)
		U.	University
F. S.	French summary	UM	University Microfilms International order number
illus.	illustrated		
mimeogr.	mimeographed	unpubl. doc. diss.	unpublished doctoral dissertation
n. d.	no date		
n. p.	no pagination	v. p.	various pagination
p.	page(s)	vol./vols.	volume/volumes

1. BIBLIOGRAPHIES AND COLLECTED ESSAYS (0001–0113)
1.1. Bibliographies (0001–0061)
1.1.1. General and Mandarin Dialects (0001–0044)

0001   Chang, Ch'ün: *Min-kuo hsüeh-shu lun-wen so-yin.*—Taipei: Chung-hua wen-hua, 1954, xii, v, 238 p./   140-143: Dialects. [Index to Chinese periodicals since the founding of the Republic.]
章羣：民國學術論文索引

0002   Ch'en, Tun: Chiu-chi chung kuan-yü fang-yen chih chu-tso.—*CSTY* 8:85–87, 1929, 112–114.   [Dialect works found in ancient texts.]
陳鈍：舊籍中關於方言之著作

0003   Ch'en, Tun: Kuan-yü fang-yen lun-wen te mu-lu.—*CSTY* 8:85–87, 1929, 115–117. [A list of articles on dialects.]
陳鈍：關於方言論文的目錄

0004   Chiu, Rosaline Kwan-wai: *Language contact and language planning in China (1900–1967): A selected bibliography.*—Québec: Les Presses de l'Université Laval, published for the International Center for Research on Bilingualism, 1970, xviii, 273 p./ *JCLTA* 6:3, 1971, 113-114, Winston L.Y. Yang.

0005   Chūgoku Gogaku Kenkyūkai: *Chūgoku gogaku bunken mokuroku 1945.8–1957.7.*—Tokyo: Kōnan shoin, 1957, iii, 61 p./ 32–34: Dialects. [Bibliography on Chinese linguistics—August 1945–July 1957.]/ Restricted to Japanese sources.
中國語學研究會：中國語學文獻目錄 1945.8–1957.7

0006   Chūgoku Gogaku Kenkyūkai: *Chūgoku gogaku bunken mokuroku II. 1957.8–1961.12.*—Tokyo: Kōseikan, 1963, iii, 61 p./ 30–32: Dialects. [Bibliography on Chinese linguistics II.—August 1957–December 1961.]/   Restricted to Japanese sources.
中國語學研究會：中國語文獻目錄 II. 1957.8–1961.12.

0007   Chung-kuo k'o-hsüeh-yüan Li-shih yen-chiu-so Ti-i erh so & Pei-ching ta-hsüeh Li-shih-hsi: *Chung-kuo shih-hsüeh lun-wen so-yin.*—Peking: K'o-hsüeh, 2 vols., 1957, iv, 421; viii, 676, 116 p./ Vol. II, 367–372: Dialects. [Index to articles in periodicals on Chinese history.]
中國科學院歷史研究所第一、二所，北京大學歷史系：中國史學論文索引

0008   Chung-kuo k'o-hsüeh-yüan Yü-yen yen-chiu-so (comp.): *Chung-kuo yü-yen-hsüeh lun-wen so-yin. Chia pien.*—Peking: Shang-wu, 1978, viii, 210 p./ Covers pre-1949 publications. [Index to articles in periodicals on Chinese linguistics. Volume I.]
中國科學院語言研究所編：中國語言學論文索引　甲編

0009   Chung-kuo k'o-hsüeh-yüan Yü-yen yen-chiu-so (comp.): *Chung-kuo yü-yen-hsüeh lun-wen so-yin. I pien* (Tseng-ting pen).—Peking: Shang-wu, 1978, vi, 326 p./ Covers 1950–1963. [Index to articles in periodicals on Chinese linguistics. Volume II. (Enl. ed.).]
中國科學院語言研究所編：中國語言學論文索引　乙編（增訂本）

0010   Cordier, Henri: *Bibliotheca Sinica: Dictionnaire bibliographique des ouvrages relatifs à l'Empire chinois.*—Paris: Librairie Orientale & Américaine, 5 vols., 1922–1924, 4439 col.; Taipei: Ch'eng-wen, 1966, repr./ XIII. Language and literature.

0011   Dunn, Robert (comp.): *Chinese-English and English-Chinese dictionaries in the Library of Congress.*—Washington, D.C.: Library of Congress, 1977, vii, 140 p./   Including dialect dictionaries.

0012   Gordon, Leonard H.D. & Shulman, Frank J.: *Doctoral dissertations on China: A bibliography of studies in Western languages, 1945–1970.*—Seattle & London: U. of Washington Press, 1972, xviii, 317 p./ *JAOS* 95, 1975, 128, David R. Knectges./   See below (0032).

0013   Gotō, Kimpei: Postwar Japanese studies on the Chinese language.—*MS* 20, 1961, 368–393./ An annotated bibliography; 382–387: Dialects.

0014   Hsia, T'ing-yü: Pen so so ts'ang ti-fang-chih chung kuan-yü fang-yen chih chi-tsai.—*CSTY* 8:85–87, 1929, 118–120. [Dialect records found in the collection of local gazetteers at the Institute of Language and History, Sun Yat-sen University.]
夏廷棫： 本所所藏地方志中關於方言之記載

0015   Kawauchi, Katsuaki: Chūgokugo (Kango) hōgen kenkyū bunken mokuroku. — *Hōgen kenkyū nenpō* 7, 1964, 69–93. [Bibliography of Chinese dialect studies.]
川內且昭： 中國語（漢語）方言研究文獻目錄

0016   Kuo-li   Chung-yang   t'u-shu-kuan (comp.): *Chung-kuo chin erh-shih-nien wen shih che lun-wen fen-lei so-yin.*— Taipei: Kuo-li Chung-yang t'u-shu-kuan & Cheng-chung shu-chü, 1970, xl, 852 p./   Covers   1948–1968;   121–126: Chinese dialects. [Subject index to articles in the last 20 years on Chinese literature, history and philosophy.]
國立中央圖書館： 中國近二十年文史哲論文分類索引

0017   Kuo-li T'ai-wan ta-hsüeh t'u-shu-kuan: *Chung-wen ch'i-k'an lun-wen fen-lei so-yin.*—Taipei: National Taiwan U. Library, 1960–. [A classified index to Chinese periodicals.]
國立臺灣大學圖書館： 中文期刊論文分類索引

0018   Kyōto Daigaku Jinbun Kagaku Kenkyūjo: *Tōyōshi kenkyū bunken ruimoku.* —Kyoto: Kyōto Daigaku Jinbun Kagaku Kenkyūjo, 1934– (publ. in 1935–)./ From 1963 publ. under the title *Tōyōgaku bunken ruimoku.*/   Section XV.   Philology. [Annual bibliography of Oriental studies, 1934–.]
京都大學人文科學研究所： 東洋史研究文獻類目（自1963年改爲：）東洋學文獻類目

0019   Lin,   Yü-t'ang: Kuan-yü Chung-kuo fang-yen te yang-wen lun chu mu-lu.— *KYAO* 89, 1925, 6–8; *Yü-yen-hsüeh lun-ts'ung* (0105), 213–217. [A list of Western language publications on Chinese dialects.]
林語堂： 關於中國方言的洋文論著目錄

0020   Loon, Piet van der (ed.): *Revue bibliographique de Sinologie* (Année 1955). —The Hague and Paris: Mouton, 1957./ Annual. Section XV. Language; *TP* 45, 1957, 219–220, P. Demiéville; *JAOS* 61, 1961, 446–448, C.S. Goodrich.

0021   Lust, John: *Index Sinicus: A catalogue of articles relating to China in periodicals and other collective publications 1920–1955.*—Cambridge: W. Heffer & Sons, 1962, xxx, 663 p./   332–334: Dialects.

0022   Möllendorff, P.G. & O.F. von: *Manual of Chinese bibliography, being a list of works and essays relating to China.*— Shanghai: Kelly & Walsh, 1876, viii, 378 p./   2–15: Grammars, dictionaries, handbooks.

0023   Nihon   Gakujutsu   Kaigi   (ed.): *Bungaku, tetsugaku, shigaku bunken mokuroku, III. Tōyō bungaku gogakuhen.* —Tokyo: Nihon Gakujutsu Kaigi, 1954, 8, 138 p.; *Hoi* [Supplement] 1958, 2, 127 p. [Bibliography of materials on literature, philosophy and history, III. Oriental literatures and languages.]
日本學術會議：文學、哲學、史學文獻目錄，Ⅲ.東洋文學語學篇；補遺

0024   Ōta, Tatsuo: Chūgoku gogaku annai.— *KGR* 18:3, 1967, 67–83./ 79–80: Dialects. [A bibliographical guide to Chinese linguistics.]
太田辰夫：中國語學案內

0025   Permanent International Committee of Linguists: *Linguistic Bibliography for the Year 1939–.* —Utrecht and Antwerp: Spectrum, 1949–./   Section on languages of Southeast Asia: Sino-Tibetan languages.

0026 Rai, Tsutomu: *Chūgoku on'in kenkyū bunken ryakumoku.*—Tokyo: The Author, 1956, 50 p./ Mimeogr. [A bibliography of studies on Chinese phonology.]

賴惟勤：中國音韻研究文獻略目

0027 Rai, Tsutomu: Chūgokugo on'in kenkyū bunken mokuroku kō.—*Chūgoku bungaku ronsō* 1, 1968, 126–156; 2, 1970, 1–35; 3, 1972, 1–22; 4, 1973, 1–22./ Pt. II. Dialects. [A bibliography of studies on Chinese phonology.]

賴惟勤：中國語音韻研究文獻目錄稿

0028 Rokkaku, Tsunehiro: *Kindai Nihon no Chūgokugo kyōiku.*—Tokyo: Harima Shobō, 1961, 277 p., illus./ 225–247: List of textbooks for teaching Mandarin and other dialects published during the Meiji period. [The teaching of Chinese in modern Japan.]

六角恒廣：近代日本の中國語教育

0029 Rokkaku, Tsunehiro: *Chūgokugo kankeisho shomoku (1867–1945).*—Tokyo: Waseda Daigaku Gogaku Kyōiku Kenkyūjō, 1968, 104 p. [A bibliography related to the Chinese language (1867–1945).]/ Published in Japan. Including dialect studies, arranged chronologically by date of publication.

六角恒廣：中國語關係書書目 （1867—1945)

0030 Shafer, Robert (ed.): *Bibliography of Sino-Tibetan languages.* — Wiesbaden: Harrassowitz, 2 vols.: Vol. I, 1957, xi, 211 p.; Vol. II, 1963, ix, 141 p./ I, 38–59: Dialects; II, 67–83: Dialects; *BSL* 60, 1965, fasc. 2, 248, A.G. Haudricourt.

0031 Shiga, Masatoshi: *Chūbunyaku Seisho (Bible) no kisoteki kenkyū.*—Tenri: The Author, 1973, 204 p./ 3–31: Lists Bibles translated into various dialects. [A basic study on Chinese translations of the Holy Bible.]

志賀正年：中文譯聖書 （ Bible ）の基礎的研究

0032 Shulman, Frank Joseph: *Doctoral dissertations on China, 1971–1975: A bibliography of studies in Western languages.*—Seattle & London: U. of Washington Press, 1978, xx, 329 p./ See (0012).

0033 Skachkov, P.E.: *Bibliografiia Kitaiia.*—Moscow: Izdatel'stvo Vostochnoi Literatury, 1960, 691 p./ 476–491: XVIII. Language and writing; *RBS* 6, 1960, 3, M. Doleželova-Velingerová. [Chinese bibliography.]

0034 Ting, Chieh-min: Fang-yen k'ao.—*TSST* 10, 1966, 789–812; Hong Kong: Lung-men shu-tien, 1967, repr., 74 p. [An annotated bibliography of researches on Chinese dialects.]

丁介民：方言考

0035 Ting, Stella: American doctoral dissertations in Chinese linguistics: A bibliography.—*JCL* 1:1, 1973, 170–182.

0036 Torii, Hisayasu: *Chūgoku gengo kenkyū shomoku (kō).*—Tenri: The Author, 1961, 33 p. [A catalogue of researches on Chinese proverbs (draft).]/ Including dialect proverbs classified under respective provinces.

鳥居久靖：中國諺語研究書目（ 稿)

0037 Ts'ui, Chi: *Fang-yen* k'ao.—*TSKC* 6:2, 1932, 143–210. [*Fang-yen* studies.] /A bibliography on the *Fang-yen* and other related works.

崔驥：『方言』考

0038 Wang, Chung-min et al.: *Kuo-hsüeh lun-wen so-yin.*—Peking: Chung-hua t'u-shu-kuan hsieh-hui, 1st issue comp. by Wang, Chung-min, 1929, 19, 230 p.; 2nd issue comp. by Hsü, Hsü-ch'ang, 1931, 16, 196 p.; 3rd issue comp. by Liu, Hsiu-yeh, 1934, 36, 386, 13 p.; 4th issue comp. by Liu, Hsiu-yeh, 1936, 35, 481, 4 p.; 5th issue comp. by Hou, Chih-chung, 1955, 2 vols., 533 p.; Taipei: Chung-ting wen-hua, 1967, repr., 4 issues, 3 vols., 5th issue excluded. [Index to articles in periodicals on Chinese humanities.]

王重民、徐緒昌、劉修業、 侯直忠編：國學論文索引

0039   Wang, William S-Y.: Bibliography of Chinese linguistics.—*Current trends in linguistics,* II. (0109), 188–499./ An earlier version of (0040).

0040   Wang, William S-Y. & Lyovin, Anatole: *CLIBOC: Chinese linguistics bibliography on computer.*—Cambridge: Cambridge U. Press, 1970, 513 p., 3 maps in pocket./ 332–489: Abstracts.

0041   Yang, Paul Fu-mien: Chinese dialectology 1955–1965.—*Orbis* 15, 1966, 90–159./ A bibliographical survey.

0042   Yang, Paul Fu-mien: *Chinese linguistics: A selected and classified bibliography.*—Hong Kong: The Chinese U. of Hong Kong, 1974, xxvi, 292 p./ *JCL* 3:2–3, 1975, 259–265, Timothy Light; *JAOS* 96, 1976, 479–480, Teng Shou-hsin; *JCLTA* 11:3, 1976, 216–217, G.W. Roy; *JAS* 36:2, 1977, 349–350, Jerry Norman.
〔 楊福綿： 中國語言學分類參考書目 〕

0043   Yang, Winston L.Y. & Yang, Teresa S.: *A bibliography of the Chinese language.*—New York: Paragon Book Gallery (distributor), 1966, xiv, 171 p./ XI. Dialects; *JAS* 26, 1967, 488–489, Henry H. Tai; Restricted to Western-language sources.

0044   Yuan, Tung-li: *China in Western literature.* A continuation of Cordier's *Bibliotheca Sinica* (0010).—New Haven: Far Eastern Publications, Yale U., 1958, xix, 802 p./   394–397: Dialects.
〔 袁同禮 〕

1.1.2.   Wu Dialects (0045–0047)

0045   Osada, Natsuki; Ogawa, Tamaki; Ōta, Tatsuo; Kurata, Junnosuke & Sakamoto, Ichirō: Gogo kenkyū shomoku kaisetsu.—*KGR* 3–4, 1953, 56–103. [A bibliographical study of the Wu dialects.]
長田夏樹，小川環樹，太田辰夫，倉田淳之助，坂本一郎： 吳語研究書目解說

0046   Sherard, Michael: Wu dialect studies in Western literature.—*FY* 3, 1979, 183–195; C.S./ 193–195: Bibliography.
〔 司馬侃：歐美之吳語研究 〕

0047   Yang, Paul Fu-mien: Chinese dialectology 1955–1965 (0041), 132–134: Wu dialects.

1.1.3.   Hakka Dialects (0048–0050)

0048   Hashimoto, Mantarō: Baazeru hōshoshi.—*CGGG* 1971:12, 8–14. [A visit to the Basel Missionary Library.] / About publications on the Hakka dialect.
橋本萬太郎：バアゼル訪書誌

0049   Ishida, Takeo: Taiwan ni okeru Hakkago no kankei shomoku kaidai.—*HKR* 4, 1954, 56–67. [An annotated bibliography concerning the Hakka dialect of Taiwan.]
石田武夫： 台灣における客家語の關係書目解題

0050   Yang, Paul Fu-mien: Chinese dialectology 1955–1965 (0041), 136–138: Hakka dialects.

1.1.4.   Yüeh Dialects (0051–0052)

0051   Tenri Daigaku Chūgokugo Gakka Kenkyūshitsu: *Nihon genson Etsugo kenkyū shomoku (kō).*—Tenri: Tenri U., 1952, 44 p. [Bibliography of books and articles on Cantonese now extant in Japan (draft).]
天理大學中國語學科研究室： 日本現存粵語研究書目（ 稿 ）

0052   Yang, Paul Fu-mien: Chinese dialectology 1955–1965 (0041), 138–140: Yüeh dialects.

1.1.5.   Min Dialects (0053–0061)

0053   Liu, Chien-jen: Kuang-fu hou te T'aiyü yün-shu.—*TWFW* 17:6, 1968, 73–88. [Taiwanese rhyme books published after 1945.]
劉健仁：光復後的臺語韻書

0054   Murakami, Yoshihide: *Binnan hōgen bunken mokuroku (kō).*—Tenri: Oyasato Kenkyūjo, 1969, 46 p. [A classified bibliography on the South Min dialects (draft).]/ Including bibliography on popular and religious literature.
村上嘉英：閩南方言文獻目錄（ 稿 ）

0055 Ting, Pang-hsin et al.: Min-yü fang-yen yen-chiu hsüan mu.—*Shu-mu chi-k'an* 11:2, 1977, B1–B41. [A selected bibliography of studies on the Min dialects.]
丁邦新等：閩語方言研究選目

0056 Wu, Chao-wan (ed.): *Min-nan-yü shih yen-chiu wen-hsien mu-lu.*—Taipei: Wu Shou-li & family, 1969, 41 p., 1 portr. [A list of works on the study of the history of the South Min dialect.]/For Prof. Wu Shou-li on the occasion of his 60th birthday.
吳昭婉：閩南語史研究文獻目錄

0057 Wu, Shou-li: *Chin wu-shih-nien lai T'ai-yü yen-chiu chih tsung ch'eng-chi.*—Taipei: The Author, 1955, 129 p. [General results of Taiwan dialect studies in the last fifty years.]
吳守禮：近五十年來臺語研究之總成績

0058 Wu, Shou-li: T'ai-wan fang-yen yen-chiu wen-hsien mu-lu.—*TPWH* 6, 1963, 67–89. [A bibliography of studies on the dialects of Taiwan.]
吳守禮：臺灣方言研究文獻目錄

0059 Wu, Shou-li: T'ai-wan fang-yen yen-chiu wen-hsien mu-lu hsü pien.—*Min-nan-yü shih yen-chiu wen-hsien mu-lu* (0056), 12–40./ From 1947 to 1966. [A bibliography of studies on the dialects of Taiwan, continued.]
吳守禮：臺灣方言研究文獻目錄續編

0060 Wu, Shou-li: Fu-chien-yü te wen-hsien chien chieh.—*Jinsei* 2, 1968, 4–19. [A short introduction to a bibliography on the Fukien dialect.]
吳守禮：福建語的文獻簡介

0061 Yang, Paul Fu-mien: Chinese dialectology 1955–1965 (0041), 140–147: Min dialects.

1.2. Biographies and Bibliographies of Individual Scholars (0062–0092)

1.2.1. Biographies (0062–0084)

0062 Bielenstein, Hans: Bernhard Karlgren (1889–1978).—*Newsletter of the Ameri-*can *Oriental Society,* February–March, 1979, 2.

0063 Chao, Yüan-jen: Wo-te yü-yen tzu-chuan.—*BIHP* 43, 1971, 303–317; *Aspects of Chinese sociolingustics* (0098), 1–20 (revised and condensed English version). [My linguistic autobiography.]
趙元任：我的語言自傳

0064 Chao, Yuen Ren: Bernhard Karlgren as 高本漢.—*JCL* 7, 1979, 144.

0065 Chou, Yin-meng: Yang Hsiung ho t'a-te *Fang-yen.*—*CKYW* 1956:5, 37–40. [Yang Hsiung and his *Fang-yen.*]
周因夢：揚雄和他的『方言』

0066 Chou, Yin-meng: Po-wen ch'iang-chi te Kuo P'u.—*CKYW* 1956:7, 39–43. [Kuo P'u: A learned scholar and a man of good recollection.]
周因夢：博聞強記的郭璞

0067 Cordier, Henri: Sir Thomas Francis Wade.—*JRAS* 1895, 911–916; *TP* 6, 1895, 407–412.

0068 Cordier, H.: Nécrologie: Dr. Gustave Schlegel.—*TP* 4, 1903, 407–415.

0069 Cordier, H.: Nécrologie: Ernest Johann Eitel.—*TP* 10, 1909, 92–94.

0070 Draye, H.: The 65th birthday of Willem A. Grootaers.—*Onoma* 21:3, 1977, 577–580.

0071 Fu, Mao-chi: Shen-ch'ieh huai-nien Lo Ch'ang-p'ei hsien-sheng.—*CKYW* 1979:1, 16–17. [In esteemed memory of Prof. Lo Ch'ang-p'ei.]
傅懋勣：深切懷念羅常培先生

0072 Grootaers, Willem A.: Chao Yüan-jen (Yuen Ren Chao), China's leading dialectologist.—*Orbis* 3, 1954, 328–335./ Biography and bibliography.

0073 Hsü, Kao-juan: Tung T'ung-ho hsien-sheng hsiao-chuan.—*BIHP* 36, 1965, pt. 1, i-ii. [A short biography of Prof. Tung T'ung-ho.]

徐高阮：董同龢先生小傳

0074 Iakhontov, S.E.: A. A. Dragunov.—*KSIV* 18, 1956, 89–95./ 94–95: List of publications (1928–1955).

0075 Leslie, Ronald & Davidson, Jeremy: *Author catalogues of Western Sinologists.* —Canberra: Australian National U., 1968, lvii, 257 p./ *TP* 54, 1968, 125–126, D. Holzman.

0076 Lo, Ch'ang-p'ei: Pai Ti-chou hsiao-chuan chi chu-shu t'i-yao.—*BIHP* 4:4, 1934, 491–494. [A short biography of Pai Ti-chou and a list of his major works.]

羅常培：白滌洲小傳及著述提要

0077 Malmqvist, N.G.D.: Bernhard Karlgren in memoriam.—*JCL* 7, 1979, 142–143.

0078 Pop, Sever: *Willem A. Grootaers, notice biographique et bibliographique.*— Louvain: Centre Internationale de Dialectologie Générale, 1960, 16 p., portr.

0079 Ting, Pang-hsin: Chin chi yü-yen-hsüeh-chia Tung T'ung-ho hsien-sheng.— *YSYK* 40:6, 1974, 56–59; *Chung-kuo yü-yen-hsüeh lun chi* (0113), 415–425. [Life and work of Tung T'ung-ho: A linguist.]/ Biography and bibliography.

丁邦新：謹記語言學家董同龢先生

0080 Ting, Pang-hsin: Kao Pen-han hsien-sheng tsai Han-hsüeh shang te kung-hsien. —*Hua-hsüeh yüeh-k'an* 87, 1979, 47–52. [B. Karlgren's contributions to Sinology.]

丁邦新：高本漢先生在漢學上的貢獻

0081 Tung, Tso-pin: Fang-yen-hsüeh-chia Yang Hsiung nien-p'u.—*CSTY* 8:85–87, 1929, 82–88. [A chronological biography of a dialectologist: Yang Hsiung.]

董作賓：方言學家揚雄年譜

0082 Wei, Chien-kung: Pai Ti-chou chuan. —*KHCK* 4:4, 1935, 121–123. [A short biography of Pai Ti-chou.]

魏建功：白滌洲傳

0083 Yang, Paul Fu-mien: Lo Ch'ang-p'ei (9 August 1899–12 September 1958). —*Orbis* 8, 1959, 594–598./ Biography and bibliography.

0084 Yang, Paul Fu-mien: Tung T'ung-ho (September 12, 1911–June 18, 1963). —*Orbis* 16, 1967, 306–309./Biography and bibliography.

1.2.2. Bibliographies (0085–0092)

0085 Anonymous: Chao Yüan-jen hsien-sheng chu-tso mu-lu.—*BIHP* 29, 1958, 923–930. [Selected bibliography of Dr. Yuen Ren Chao.]

無名氏：趙元任先生著作目錄

0086 Anonymous: *Liste chronologique des ouvrages et opuscules publiés par le Dr. G. Schlegel, 1862–1901.*—Leiden: E. J. Brill, 1902, 24 p.

0087 Chou, Yin-meng & Liao, Hsün-ying: Lo Ch'ang-p'ei hsien-sheng chu-tso mu-lu.—*CKYM* 1959:2, 97–98. [Bibliography of Lo Ch'ang-p'ei.]

周因夢，廖珣英：羅常培先生著作目錄

0088 Dil, Anwar S.: Bibliography of Yuen Ren Chao's works.—*Aspects of Chinese sociolinguistics* (0098), 402–415./ From 1915 to 1976.

0089 Glahn, Else: A list of works by B. Karlgren.—*BMFEA* 28, 1956, 45–54./ 1908–1954.

0090 Misawa, Reiji & Suenobu, Yasuo: Sakamoto Ichirō sensei chosaku mokuroku sōkō.—*KGR* 18:3, 1967, 103–106. [A list of publications by Prof. Sakamoto Ichirō (draft).]

三澤玲爾，末延保雄：坂本一郎先生著作目錄草稿

0091 Ting, Pang-hsin: Tung T'ung-ho hsien-sheng (1911–1963) chu-tso mu-lu.— *YSYK* 40:6, 1974, 80. [A list of the publications of Prof. Tung T'ung-ho (1911–1963).]

丁邦新：董同龢先生（一九一一——一九六三）著作目錄

0092 Wu, Chao-wan: Ts'ung-i [=Wu, Shou-li] hsien-sheng pien chu nien-piao.—*Min-nan-yü shih yen-chiu wen-hsien mu-lu* (0056), 2–11. [A chronological list of works by Prof. Wu Shou-li.]
吳昭婉：從宜〔吳守禮〕先生編著年表

1.3. Collected Essays (0093–0113)

1.3.1. Encyclopedias (0093–0096)

0093 Chūgoku Gogaku Kenkyūkai (ed.): *Chūgoku gogaku jiten.*—Tokyo: Kōnan shoin, 1958, xxiii, 1129 p./ *RBS* 4, 1958, 531, W. Simon; *Orbis* 15, 1966, 95–96, Paul Fu-mien Yang. [Encyclopedia of Chinese linguistics.]
中國語學研究會：中國語學事典

0094 Chūgoku Gogaku Kenkyūkai (ed.): *Chūgoku gogaku shinjiten.*—Tokyo: Kōseikan, 1969, 12, 339 p.; 1970, 2nd ed., with minor corrections. [New encyclopedia of Chinese linguistics.]
中國語學研究會：中國語學新事典

0095 Heibonsha (ed.): *Ajia rekishi jiten.*—Tokyo: Heibonsha, 10 vols., 1959–1962. [Encyclopedia of Asian history.]
平凡社：アジア歴史事典

0096 Heibonsha (ed.): *Seikai meicho daijiten.*—Tokyo: Heibonsha, 8 vols., 1960–1962. [Encyclopedia of world famous books.]
平凡社：世界名著大事典

1.3.2. Collected Essays (0097–0113)

0097 Arisaka, Hideyo: *Kokugo on'inshi no kenkyū.*—Tokyo: Sanseidō, 1957, rev. & enl. by Kindaichi Kyōsuke, viii, 694 p. [Studies on Japanese historical phonology.]
有坂秀世著，金田一京助刊行：國語音韻の研究（增補新版）

0098 Chao, Yuen Ren. Ed. by Dil, Anwar S.: *Aspects of Chinese sociolinguistics.*—Stanford: Stanford U. Press, 1976, xiv, 415 p., maps; 402–415: Bibliography of Yuen Ren Chao's works./*JAOS* 97, 1977, 410, Alvin P. Cohen; *JCLTA* 12:1, 1978, 88–91, Chauncey C. Chu.

0099 Chou, Fa-kao: *Chung-kuo yü-wen yen-chiu.*—Taipei: Chung-hua wen-hua, 1955, ii, 168 p., maps./*RBS* 2, 1957, 544, C.Y. Wu; *KHHP* 5:3, 1956, 6–8, Chang Hsi-chen. [Studies on Chinese language and literature.]
周法高：中國語文研究 / 張席珍評

0100 Chou, Tsu-mo: *Han-yü yin-yün lun-wen chi.*—Shanghai: Shang-wu, 1957, 283 p./ *RBS* 3, 1957, 550, C. Y. Wu. [Collected essays on Chinese phonology.]
周祖謨：漢語音韻論文集

0101 Chou, Tsu-mo: *Wen-hsüeh chi.*—Peking: Chung-hua, 1966, 2 vols., iv, 930 p. [Essays on Chinese language and writing.]
周祖謨：問學集

0102 Egerod, Søren & Glahn, Else (eds.): *Studia Serica Bernhard Karlgren dedicata.*—Copenhagen: Ejnar Munksgaard, 1959, ix, 282 p., 13 pl./ *Lg* 37, 1961, 180–186, H. M. Stimson.

0103 Hsien-tai Han-yü kuei-fan wen-t'i hsüeh-shu hui-i mi-shu ch'u (ed.): *Hsien-tai Han-yü kuei-fan wen-t'i hsüeh-shu hui-i wen-chien hui-pien,*—Peking: K'o-hsüeh, 1956, 334 p., 5 pl./ *RBS* 2, 1956, 405, M.A.K. Halliday. [Proceedings of the Academic Committee for the Standardization of Modern Chinese.]
現代漢語規範問題學術會議秘書處編：現代漢語規範問題學術會議文件滙編

0104 Joos, Martin (ed.): *Readings in linguistics.*—Washington, D.C.: American Council of Learned Societies, 1957, viii, 421 p./ Including several articles on Peking phonetics and phonemics.

0105 Lin, Yü-t'ang: *Yü-yen-hsüeh lun-ts'ung.*—Shanghai: K'ai-ming, 1933, iii, 376 p.; Taipei: Wen-hsing, 1967, repr./ *WHWC* 6:3, 1937, 671–684, Li Hsiao-t'ung. [Collected essays on linguistics.]
林語堂：語言學論叢 / 厲嘯桐評

0106 Lo, Ch'ang-p'ei. Ed. by Chung-kuo k'o-hsüeh-yüan Yü-yen yen-chiu-so: *Lo Ch'ang-p'ei yü-yen-hsüeh lun-wen hsüan-chi.*—Peking: Chung-hua, 1963, iii, 238 p., tables. [Selected linguistic works of Lo Ch'ang-p'ei.]

羅常培著，中國科學院語言研究所編：羅常培語言學論文選集

0107 Ni, Hai-shu (ed.): *Chung-kuo yü-wen te hsin-sheng. La-ting-hua Chung-kuo wen-tzu yün-tung 20 nien lun-wen chi.*—Shanghai: Shih-tai, 1949, 581 p. [New life in the Chinese language and writing. Collected essays on the Latinization movement during the past 20 years.]

倪海曙編：中國語文的新生，拉丁化中國文字運動二十年論文集

0108 Ogawa, Tamaki: *Chūgokugogaku kenkyū.*—Tokyo: Sōbunsha, 1977, 361, 13 p./ With English table of contents. [Studies in Chinese linguistics.]

小川環樹：中國語學研究

0109 Sebeok, Thomas A. (ed.): *Current trends in linguistics, II. Linguistics in East Asia and South East Asia.*—The Hague & Paris: Mouton, 1967, xix, 979 p.

0110 Tung, T'ung-ho. Ed. by Ting, Pang-hsin: *Tung T'ung-ho hsien-sheng yü-yen-hsüeh lun-wen hsüan chi.*—Taipei: Shih-huo, 1974, i, 434 p. [Selected articles on linguistics by Prof. Tung T'ung-ho.]

董同龢著，丁邦新編：董同龢先生語言學論文選集

0111 Ushijima, Tokuji; Kōsaka, Jun'ichi & Tōdō, Akiyasu (eds.): *Gengo.*—Tokyo: Taishūkan, 1967, 472 p., maps./ *Chūgoku bunka sōsho* 1. CGGG 1968:4, 9-17, Suzuki Naoji; *Gengo seikatsu* 198, 1968, 70–71, Matsumoto Akira. [Chinese language.]

牛島德次，香坂順一，藤堂明保編集：言語／中國文化叢書1／鈴木眞治評，松本昭評

0112 Wen-tzu kai-ko ch'u-pan-she (comp.): *P'u-t'ung-hua lun-chi.*—Peking: Wen-tzu kai-ko, 1956, 3, 191 p. [Collected essays on the Common Language.]

文字改革出版社：普通話論集

0113 Ya, Hsüan (ed.): *Chung-kuo yü-yen-hsüeh lun chi.*—Taipei: Yu-shih wen-hua shih-yeh kung-szu, 1977, iii, 470 p. [Collected essays on Chinese linguistics.]

瘂弦：中國語言學集論

2. HISTORY OF CHINESE DIALECTO-LOGY (0114–0172)

2.1. General (0114–0146)

0114 Chang, Shih-lu: *Chung-kuo yin-yün-hsüeh shih.*—Shanghai: Shang-wu, 1938, 2 vols., vi, 222; ii, 363 p.; Hong Kong: T'ai-hsing, 1963, repr. one vol./ Vol. 2, 345–358: Dialect studies. [History of Chinese phonology.]
張世祿：中國音韻學史

0115 Chao, Yuen Ren: My field work on Chinese dialects.—*CAAL* 1, 1975, 3–7; *Aspects of Chinese sociolinguistics* (0098), 26–33 (revised and condensed version).

0116 Chou, Fa-kao: Chung-kuo fang-yen-hsüeh fa-fan.—*Chung-kuo yü-wen yen-chiu* (0099), 82–97, 5 maps. [Introduction to Chinese dialectology.]
周法高：中國方言學發凡

0117 Chou, Fa-kao: *Chung-kuo yü-yen-hsüeh te kuo-ch'ü hsien-tsai ho wei-lai.*—Hong Kong: Hsiang-kang Chung-wen ta-hsüeh, 1966, 21 p., E.S. [The past, present and future of Chinese linguistics.]/ Including dialectology.
周法高：中國語言學的過去現在和未來

0118 Chou, Fa-kao. Transl. by Liu, San-fu: Chūgoku gengogaku no kakyo genzai to mirai.—*Seinan Gakuin Daigaku Bunri Ronshū* 17:1, 1976, 33–51. [The past, present and future of Chinese linguistics.] (0117)
周法高著，劉三富譯：中國言語學の過去，現在と未來

0119 Chou, Fa-kao: Erh-shih shih-chi te Chung-kuo yü-yen-hsüeh.—*Journal of The Chinese University of Hong Kong* 1, 1973, 297–322; *YSYK* 40:6, 1974, 9–21; *Chung-kuo yü-yen-hsüeh lun chi* (0113), 1–35; also repr. in Paul Fu-mien Yang's *Chinese linguistics: . . . bibliography* (0043), 268–292./ V. Dialectology. [Chinese linguistics in the 20th century.]
周法高：二十世紀的中國語言學

0120 Chung-kuo yü-wen pien-chi-pu: Shih-nien-lai wo-kuo yü-yen-hsüeh-chieh chi-shih.—*CKYW* 1959: 10, 501–506; (Addenda:) 11, 556–557. [A chronological record of linguistic studies in the past ten years.]/ 1949–1959.
中國語文編輯部：十年來我國語言學界記事

0121 Egerd, Søren: Dialectology.—*Current trends in linguistics* (0109), 91–129.

0122 Franke, Herbert: *Sinologie.*—Bern: A. Franke Ag. Verlag, 1953, 216 p./ 47–50: Dialect studies.

0123 Grootaers, Willem A.: Twintig jaar Chinese linguistiek.—*Handelingen van het achttiende vlaamse filologencongres* (Louvain, 1950), 67–72.

0124 Grootaers, Willem A.: Chinese dialectology (1948–1951).—*Orbis* 1, 1952, 210–218.

0125 Grootaers, Willem A.: Language study in China (1951–1952).—*Orbis* 2, 1953, 165–175./ 169–174: Dialect studies.

0126 Hatano, Tarō: O Rei-ki kyōju no Min-dai hōgen no kenkyū ni tsuite.—*YSDR* 14:2–3, 1962, 50–59. [Studies done by Prof. Wang Li-ch'i on the dialects of the Ming dynasty.]
波多野太郎：王利器教授の明代方言の研究について

0127 Ho, Chung-ying: Chung-kuo fang-yen-hsüeh kai-lun.—*TFTC* 21:2, 1924, 31–63. [Introduction to Chinese dialectology.]
何仲英：中國方言學概論

0128 Hu, P'u-an: *Chung-kuo hsün-ku-hsüeh-shih.*—Shanghai: Shang-wu, 1939, v, xviii, 359 p./ Chap. IV. The *Fang-yen* school. [History of Chinese traditional semantics.]
胡樸安：中國訓詁學史

0129   Lehmann, Winfred (ed.): *Language and linguistics in the People's Republic of China.*—Austin & London: University of Texas Press, 1975, ix, 168 p./ 10–40: The Common Language and the language of everyday life; *JCL* 5, 1977, 134–144, Liao Chiu-chung; *JAOS* 98, 1978, 294, Teng Shou-hsin.

0130   Li, Fang-kuei: Linguistics in Taiwan.— *Current trends in linguistics* (0109), 177–187./ 178–182: Chinese language and dialects.

0131   Lo, Ch'ang-p'ei: Hsi-yang-jen yen-chiu Chung-kuo fang-yin te ch'eng-chi chi ch'i ch'üeh-tien.—*KYCK* 72, 1932, Feb. 11. [Achievements and deficiencies of studies on Chinese dialect pronunciations by Westerners.]
羅常培：西洋人研究中國方言的成績及其缺點

0132   Lo, Ch'ang-p'ei: Ming Ch'ing hsüeh-che tui-yü fang-yin yen-chiu te kung-hsien.—*KYCK* 69, 1933, Jan. 21; 70, 1933, Jan. 28; 71, 1933, Feb. 4. [Contributions to the study of dialect pronunciations by scholars of the Ming and Ch'ing dynasties.]
羅常培：明清學者對於方音研究的貢獻

0133   Lo, Ch'ang-p'ei: Fang-yin yen-chiu chih tsui-chin-te chin-chan.—*KYCK* 73, 1933, Feb. 18. [Recent advances in the study of dialect pronunciations.]
羅常培：方音研究之最近的進展

0134   Lo, Ch'ang-p'ei: Chung-kuo fang-yin yen-chiu hsiao shih.—*TFTC* 31:7, 1934, 141-153; *Lo Ch'ang-p'ei . . . hsüan-chi* (0106), 142–156. [A short history of studies on Chinese dialects.]
羅常培：中國方言研究小史

0135   Pop, Sever: *La dialectologie.*—Louvain: The Author, 1950, 2 vols., 1v, 1334 p./ Vol. II, 1101–1119: Chinese dialectology; *Word* 8, 1952, 260–262, A. Martinet.

0136   Solntseva, N.V.: Chinese language study.—*Fifty years of Soviet Oriental studies* (Moscow: Nauka, 1967), 28 p.

0137   Ting, Pang-hsin: Chung-yang yen-chiu yüan chin shih nien lai chih yü-yen-hsüeh yen-chiu.—*Chung-kuo yü-yen-hsüeh lun chi* (0113), 36–45. [Linguistic researches at the Academia Sinica during the past ten years.]
丁邦新：中央研究院近十年來之語言學研究

0138   Tōdō, Akiyasu: Postwar studies of the Chinese language [in Japan].—*Current trends in linguistics* (0109) 633–644./ 638–641: Studies on Chinese dialects.

0139   Ts'en, Ch'i-hsiang: *Yü-yen-hsüeh shih kai-yao.*—Peking: K'o-hsüeh, 1958, xvi, 332 p./ 23–26: *Fang-yen*; 153–159: Sinitic. [An outline of the history of linguistics.]
岑麒祥：語言學史概要

0140   Tung, T'ung-ho: Chin san-shih nien te Chung-kuo yü-yen-hsüeh.—*HSCK* 1:4, 1953, 17–26./ 23–24: Chinese dialects; *Tung T'ung-ho . . . hsüan chi* (0110), 371–382. [Chinese linguistics during the past three decades.]
董同龢：近三十年的中國語言學

0141   Tung, T'ung-ho: Recent studies on phonetics and phonology in China.— *Phonetica* 6, 1961, 216–228./ 218–221: Survey of modern Chinese dialects; *Tung T'ung-ho . . . hsüan chi* (0110), 383–395.

0142   Wang, Li: Chung-kuo yü-yen-hsüeh shih.—*CKYW* 1963: 3, 232–245, 265; 4, 309–326, 347; 5, 411–427, 431; 6, 496–510, 474; 1964: 1, 62–75; 2, 103–105; Hong Kong: Lung Men, 1967, repr., 99 p./ 10–15 (241–245, 265): The rise of dialectology. [History of Chinese linguistics.]
王力：中國語言學史

0143 Wang, Li-ta: *Han-yü yen-chiu hsiao-shih.*—Peking: Shang-wu, 1959, viii, 162 p./ An adapted translation of Chapter V. of *Chūgoku gogaku jiten* (0093). [A short history of Chinese linguistics.]/ Including Chinese dialectology.

王立達：漢語研究小史

0144 Yang, Paul Fu-mien: The Catholic missionary contribution to the study of Chinese dialects.—*Orbis* 9, 1960, 158–185.

0145 Yang, Fu-mien: Taiwan ni okeru gengogaku.—*CGGG* 1961:3, 18–20. [Linguistics in Taiwan.]

楊福綿：臺灣における言語學

0146 Yüan, Chia-hua et al.: *Han-yü fang-yen kai-yao.*—Peking: Wen-tzu kai-ko, 1960, x, 330 p./ Chap. II. Chinese dialectology; *CKYW* 1960:4, 190–192, Fang Ch'ing; *RBS* 6, 1960, 382, Li Fang-kuei; *Orbis* 15, 1966, 109, Paul Yang. [Outline of Chinese dialects.]

袁家驊等：漢語方言概要 / 方青評

2.2. Institutional Activities (0147–0150)

0147 Chung-yang yen-chiu-yüan: *Chung-yang yen-chiu yüan Li-shih yü-yen yen-chiu-so szu-shih chou-nien chi-nien t'e-k'an.*—Taipei: Academia Sinica, 1968, 213 p., portr., pl. [In commemoration of the fortieth anniversary of the Institute of History and Philology.]/ History of the Institute and biography and bibliography of all its members.

中央研究院：中央研究院歷史語言研究所四十周年紀念特刊

0148 Grootaers, Willem A.: Report on linguistic institutes of China (till Dec. 1957). —*Orbis* 7, 1958, 205–211.

0149 Tung, T'ung-ho: Linguistic activities of Academia Sinica.—*Communications et rapports du Premier Congrès International de Dialectologie Générale* (Louvain, du 21 au 25 Août 1960), IV, Louvain, 1965, 264–271; *Tung T'ung-ho . . . hsüan chi* (0110), 397–404.

0150 Yang, Paul Fu-mien: Academic institutions.—Chinese dialectology 1955–1965 (0042), 91–93.

2.3. Dialect Surveys (0151–0162)

0151 Anonymous: Kao-teng chiao-yü-pu ho Chiao-yü-pu fa-ch'u kuan-yü Han-yü fang-yen p'u-ch'a te lien-ho chih-shih.— *CKYM* 1956:5, 48. [A joint directive of the Ministry of Higher Education and the Ministry of Education concerning a general survey of Chinese dialects.]

無名氏：高等教育部和教育部發出關於漢語方言普查的聯合指示

0152 Chang, Kung-kuei: Chiang-su-sheng fang-yen tiao-ch'a chih-tao-tsu ch'eng-li. —*CKYW* 1956:12, 45. [The coordination group for the dialect survey of Kiangsu province is established.]

張拱貴：江蘇省方言調查指導組成立

0153 Chao, Yuen Ren: My fieldwork on the Chinese dialects.—*CAAAL* 2, 1975, 3–7; *Aspects of Chinese sociolinguistics* (0098), 26–33 (a revised version).

0154 Cheng, Chien-pai: Szu-ch'uan-sheng shang pan-nien chiang wan-ch'eng 32 tien fang-yen tiao-ch'a.—*CKYW* 1957:5, 39. [Szechwan province to complete dialect surveys of 32 localities during the first half of the year 1957.]

鄭堅白：四川省上半年將完成32點方言調查

0155 Fang, Tsu-kao: Ch'üan-kuo Han-yü fang-yen ch'u-pu p'u-ch'a chi-pen wan-ch'eng.—*CKYM* 1959:10, 507. [Basic accomplishments of the preliminary general survey of Chinese dialects.]

方祖高：全國漢語方言初步普查基本完成

0156 Shang, Yün-ch'uan: Liao-ning-sheng p'u-ch'a tsu pu-chih chü-t'i kung-tso.— *CKYM* 1957:5, 32. [The Liaoning Province Dialect Survey Team plans substantial work.]

尚允川：遼寧省普查組佈置具體工作

0157   Tung, T'ung-ho. Transl. by Ogawa, Tamaki: *Chūgoku ni okeru gengo chōsa.* —Kyoto: Harvard-Yenching Institute, 1957, 31, 5 p.; E.S. Also repr. in *Chūgokugogaku kenkyū* (0108), 296–324. [Linguistic survey of the Institute of History and Philology.]

董同龢著，小川環樹譯： 中國における言語調査

0158   Wu, T'ien-shih: Chiang-su-sheng te fang-yen tiao-ch'a kung-tso shih tsen-yang wan-ch'eng te.—*CKYW* 1958:12, 594–595. [An account of the completion of the work on dialect surveys of Kiangsu province.]

吳天石： 江蘇省的方言調查工作是怎樣完成的

0159   Wu, Tsung-chi: Hua-pei Hua-tung Hua-chung shih sheng fang-yen p'u-ch'a kung-tso hsien-k'uang.—*CKYW* 1957:7, 30–34. [The present status of the work on general dialect surveys in ten provinces of north, east, and central China.]

吳宗濟： 華北華東華中十省方言普查工作現況

0160   Yang, Ch'ang-li: An-hui-sheng chao-k'ai fang-yen p'u-ch'a kung-tso hui-i.—*CKYW* 1957:6, 24. [Anhwei province convenes for general survey of dialects.]

楊長禮： 安徽省召開方言普查工作會議

0161   Yang, Paul Fu-mien: Chinese dialectology 1955–1965 (0042), 99–109: General survey of Chinese dialects.

0162   Yang, Shih-feng: Yü-yen tiao-ch'a yü yü-yin shih-yen.—*FSNC* 1951, 27–31. [Linguistic surveys and phonetic experiments.]

楊時逢： 語言調查與語音實驗

2.4.   Studies on Individual Dialects (0163–0172)

0163   Hashimoto, Mantarō: Jun'yango no kenkyū.—*Chūgoku gogaku jiten* (0093), 353–356. [The study of the Dungan language.]

橋本萬太郎：ジュニヤン語の研究

0164   Hashimoto, Mantarō: Jun'yango (Sobieto-Dongāngo) kenkyū shomoku kaidai. —*GK* 41, 1962, 66–81. [Annotated bibliography of works dealing with the Dungan (Soviet-Dungan) language.]

橋本萬太郎：ジュニヤン語（リビュト・ドウンガーン語）研究書目解題

0165   Hashimoto, Mantarō J.: Current developments in Zhunyanese (Soviet Dunganese) studies.—*JCL* 6:2, 1978, 243–267; References, C.S.

〔橋本萬太郎：東干語言學的現況〕

0166   Hashimoto, Mantarō: Bingo kenkyū no kinkō.—*AATS* 12, 1971, 1–3, 10. [Recent studies on the Min (Fukien) dialects.]

橋本萬太郎：閩語研究の近況

0167   Murakami, Yoshihide: Protestanto senkyōshi no Binnango kenkyū—Iminzoku tendō to gengo no mondai.—*Yamato Bunka* 44, 1966, 52–72; 154–155: E.S. [On the study of the South Min dialect by Protestant missionaries—Problems of language in the missionary work among foreign peoples.]

村上嘉英： プロテスタント宣教師の閩南語研究 ──異民族傳道と言語の問題

0168   Murakami, Yoshihide: Nihonjin no Taiwan ni okeru Binnango kenkyū.— *Yamato Bunka* 45, 1966, 62–108; 149: E.S. [On studies of the South Min dialect by Japanese in Taiwan.]

村上嘉英： 日本人の臺灣における閩南語研究

0169   Murakami, Yoshihide: Tsūzoku insho ni mirareru Chūgokujin no Binnango kenkyū.—*Yamato Bunka* 46, 1967, 18–36; 172: E.S. [On studies of the South Min dialect by Chinese as seen in popular rhyming dictionaries.]

村上嘉英： 通俗韻書に見られる中國人の閩南語研究

0170 Sherard, Michael: Wu dialect studies in Western literature (0046).

0171 Wu, Shou-li: Min-nan-yü yen-chiu chin-k'uang.—*Shu ho jen* 55, 1967, 1–8. [Recent studies on the South Min dialect.] 吳守禮：閩南語研究近況

0172 Wu, Shou-li: Min-nan-yü yen-chiu te chin k'uang.—*Jinsei* 1, 1967, 14–20. [Recent studies on the South Min dialect.] 吳守禮：閩南語研究的近況

3. METHODOLOGY OF CHINESE DIALECTOLOGY (0173–0337)

3.1. General Methods (0173–0190)

0173 Ballard, William L.: Dialectology.—*Chi-Lin* 3, 1968, 74–88.

0174 Chao, Yüan-jen: *Yü-yen wen-t'i.*—Taipei: T'ai-wan ta-hsüeh Wen-hsüeh-yüan, 1959, 220 p.; Taipei: Shang-wu, 1968, 2nd rev. ed., 223 p./ Lecture 7. Dialects and the standard language; Lecture 8. What is standard pronunciation. [Linguistic problems.]
趙元任：語言問題

0175 Chao, Yuen Ren: *Language and symbolic systems.*—Cambridge: Cambridge U. Press, 1968, xv, 240 p./ 130–133: Dialects and the standard language.

0176 Chu, Hsing: *Yü-yen-hsüeh kai-lun.*—Tientsin: T'ien-chin jen-min, 1957, iii, 200 p./ 48–52: Dialects; *CKYW* 1958:11, 543–545, Chao Chen-to. [Introduction to general linguistics.]
朱星：語言學概論／趙振鐸評

0177 Ho, Chung-ying: *Chung-kuo fang-yen-hsüeh kai-lun* (0127). [Introduction to Chinese dialectology.]
何仲英：中國方言學概論

0178 Kao, Ming-k'ai: *P'u-t'ung yü-yen-hsüeh.*—Shanghai: Tung-fang, 1954, 2 vols., ii, 305; ii, 274 p./ Pt. 1, Chap. IV. Local dialects; Chap. V. Social dialects. [General linguistics.]
高名凱：普通語言學

0179 Kao, Ming-k'ai: *P'u-t'ung yü-yen-hsüeh* (Tseng ting pen).—Shanghai: Hsin chih-shih, 1957, rev. and enl. ed., vii, 503 p./ Pt. 1, Chap. IV. Local dialects; Chap. V. Social dialects. [General linguistics.]
高名凱：普通語言學（增訂本）

0180 Kao, Ming-k'ai: *Yü-yen lun.*—Peking: K'o-hsüeh, 1965, vii, 525 p./ Pt. 3, Chap. III. Local and social dialects. [Language.]
高名凱：語言論

0181 Lin, Yü-t'ang: Yen-chiu fang-yen ying yu te chi-ko yü-yen-hsüeh kuan-ch'a-tien.—*Ko-yao tseng-k'an* 1923, 7–11; *Yü-yen-hsüeh lun-ts'ung* (0105), 239–248. [Several linguistic viewpoints needed for dialect studies.]
林語堂（玉堂）：研究方言應有的幾個語言學觀察點

0182 Mao, Ch'iu-pai: Lun fang-yen.—*Ch'ing-nien chieh* 2:5, 1932, 47–55. [On dialects.]
毛秋白：論方言

0183 Po, Han: Fang-yen te shih-yung ho yen-chiu.—*Wen-hua tsa-chih* 2:3, 1942, 18–29. [The use and study of dialects.]
伯韓：方言的使用和研究

0184 Shang-hai Wai-kuo-yü hsüeh-yüan & Ha-erh-pin Wai-kuo-yü hsüeh-yüan (eds.): *Yü-yen-hsüeh yin-lun.*—Peking: Shih-tai, 1958, 318 p./ 60–77: Dialects and the standard language. [Introduction to linguistics.]
上海外國語學院，哈爾濱外國語學院：語言學引論

0185 Shen, Chien-shih: Chin hou yen-chiu fang-yen chih hsin ch'ü-shih.—*Ko-yao tseng-k'an* 1923, 16–19. [New trends in the study of dialects from the present on.]
沈兼士：今後研究方言之新趨勢

0186 Sung, Chen-hua & Wang, Chin-cheng: *Yü-yen-hsüeh kai-lun.*—Ch'angchun: Chi-lin jen-min, 1957, v, 306 p./ 218–224: Dialects, dialectology and Chinese dialects. [Introduction to linguistics.]
宋振華，王今錚：語言學概論

0187 Tung, T'ung-ho: *Yü-yen-hsüeh ta-kang.*—Taipei: Chung-hua ts'ung-shu, 1964, ii, iv, 180 p./ Publ. posthumously; 16–17: Chinese dialects; 149–153: Dialectology. [Outline of linguistics.]
董同龢：語言學大綱

0188 Yüan, Chia-hua: Lüeh t'an Han-yü fang-yen yen-chiu.—*YLT* 2, 1958, 133–144. [Briefly discussing Chinese dialect studies.]
袁家驊：略談漢語方言研究

0189 Yüan, Chia-hua: Fang-yen.—*Han-yü fang-yen kai-yao* (0146), Chap. I. [Dialects.]

袁家驊：方言

0190 Yüan, Chia-hua: Han-yü fang-yen-hsüeh.—*Han-yü fang-yen kai-yao* (0146), Chap. II. [Chinese dialectology.]

袁家驊：漢語方言學

3.2. Dialect Surveys (0191–0222)
3.2.1. General (0191–0208)

0191 Anonymous: Pei-ta yen-chiu-so Kuo-hsüeh-men fang-yen tiao-ch'a-hui hsüan-yen shu.—*KYAO* 47, 1924, 1–3; *TFTC* 21:7,1924,144–147. [A declaration of the Dialect Survey Society of the Chinese Department, Peking University.]

無名氏：北大研究所國學門方言調查會宣言書

0192 Chou, Tso-jen: Ko-yao yü fang-yen tiao-ch'a.—*KYAO* 31, 1923, 1–3. [Investigation of folk songs and dialects.]

周作人：歌謠與方言調查

0193 Ch'uan, Fu: Tiao-ch'a fang-yin te ching-yen.—*KYCK* 126, 1934, Feb. 24. [My experience from surveys of dialect pronunciations.]

船夫：調查方音的經驗

0194 Chung-kuo yü-wen tsa-chih she (ed.): *Yü-yen tiao-ch'a ch'ang-shih.*—Peking: Chung-hua, 1956, 175 p./ *CKYW* 1957: 1, 48, Yin Meng. [General knowledge of linguistic surveys.]

中國語文雜誌社：語言調查常識／因夢評

0195 Li, Chin-hsi: Lun ch'üan-kuo fang-yen yen-chiu tiao-ch'a chih chung-yao chi ch'i kung-tso chi-hua.—*Chien-kuo yü-wen yüeh-k'an* 1:1, 1942, 1–7. [On the importance and working plans of the nation-wide studies and surveys of dialects.]

黎錦熙：論全國方言研究調查之重要及其工作計劃

0196 Li, Jung: Tsen-yang pien-hsieh pen-ti-jen hsüeh-hsi P'u-t'ung-hua te shou-ts'e ho fang-yen tiao-ch'a pao-kao.—*CKYW* 1956:11, 3–9. [How to compile a handbook for learning the Common Language for dialect speakers and to write a report on dialect surveys.]

李榮：怎樣編寫本地人學習普通話的手冊和方言調查報告

0197 Li, Sen: Kuan-yü chih-ting 'Fang-yen tiao-ch'a yen-chiu ta-kang' te i-hsieh wen-t'i.—*Yü-yen tiao-ch'a ch'ang-shih* (0194), 165–175. [Some problems concerning the drawing up of an outline for dialect surveys and researches.]

李森：關於制訂『方言調查研究大綱』的一些問題

0198 Lin, Yün-lai: Kuang-tung-sheng fang-yen shih tien tiao-ch'a ching-yen tien-ti.—*CKYW* 1957:8, 49. [Selected points from past experience for the tentative dialect survey of Kwangtung province.]

林運來：廣東省方言試點調查經驗點滴

0199 Liu, Yu-hsin: Tsen-yang hsün-lien hsüeh-sheng ts'ung-shih fang-yen tiao-ch'a kung-tso.—*CKYW* 1956:12, 34–36. [How to train a student to engage in the work of dialect surveys.]

劉又辛：怎樣訓練學生從事方言調查工作

0200 Pei-ching ta-hsüeh yü-yen-hsüeh chiao-yen-shih Han-yü fang-yen-hsüeh chi fang-yen tiao-ch'a chiao-hsüeh hsiao-tsu: Fang-yen tiao-ch'a shih-hsi kung-tso te t'i-hui.—*CKYW* 1960:1, 35–36. [An appreciation of the practicality of dialect surveys.]

北京大學語言學教研室漢語方言學及方言調查教學小組：方言調查實習工作的體會

0201 Ting, Sheng-shu & Li, Jung: Han-yü fang-yen tiao-ch'a.—*Hsien-tai Han-yü kuei-fan wen-t'i . . . . hui-pien* (0103), 80–88. [The survey of Chinese dialects.]

丁聲樹、李榮：漢語方言調查

0202 Ting, Sheng-shu: Kuan-yü chin i-pu k'ai-chan Han-yü fang-yen tiao-ch'a yen-chiu te i-hsieh i-chien.—*CKYW* 1961:3, 4–6. [Some opinions concerning a further step in the survey and study of Chinese dialects.]

丁聲樹：關於進一步開展漢語方言調查研究的一些意見

0203 Ts'en, Ch'i-hsiang: Fang-yen tiao-ch'a fang-fa kai-lun.—*YWC* 1:1, 1936, 23–73. [Methods of dialect surveys.]

岑麒祥：方言調查方法概論

0204 Ts'en, Ch'i-hsiang: *Fang-yen tiao-ch'a fang-fa.*—Peking: Wen-tzu kai-ko, 1956, ii, 82 p./ *CKYW* 1957:2, 44–45, Ho Yü, Wen Tuan-cheng; *Orbis* 15, 1966, 104, Paul Yang. [Methods of dialect surveys.]

岑麒祥：方言調查方法 / 何育、溫端政評

0205 Wei, Chien-kung: "Tao-ti tsen-ma-yang?" (fang-yen tiao-ch'a).—*KHMC* 1:3, 1925, 19–24. [How to make a dialect survey?]

魏建功：『到底怎麼樣？』（方言調查）

0206 Yang, Hsiao-min: Chia-ch'iang shao-shu min-tsu ti-ch'ü te Han-yü fang-yen tiao-ch'a yen-chiu kung-tso.—*CKYW* 1960:12, 431–432. [Increase the surveys and studies of Chinese dialects spoken in the districts of national minorities.]

楊筱敏：加強少數民族地區的漢語方言調查研究工作

0207 Yin, Huan-hsien: T'an fang-yen tiao-ch'a.—*Hsin wen-tzu chou-k'an* 35, 1950, 2–3. [A discussion of dialect surveys.]

殷煥先：談方言調查

0208 Yin, Huan-hsien: T'ui-kuang P'u-t'ung-hua yün-tung chung te fang-yen tiao-ch'a kung-tso.—*WSC* 1956:1, 16–22; *P'u-t'ung-hua lun-chi* (0112), 176–191. [The work of dialect surveys during the movement for propagation of the Common Language.]

殷煥先：推廣普通話運動中的方言調查工作

3.2.2. Linguistic Geography (0209–0213)

0209 Grootaers, Willem A.: La géographie linguistique en Chine. Nécessité d'une nouvelle méthode pour l'étude linguistique du chinois.—*MS* 8, 1943, 103–166; 10, 1945, 389–436, 4 maps, 6 pl./ *Lg* 25, 1949, 80–83, James R. Ware.

0210 Grootaers, Willem A.: La méthode géographique en linguistique et en folklore. —*BUA* 9:35, 1948, 221–233, 4 maps.

0211 Grootaers, Willem A.: Problems of a linguistic atlas of China, presented by the Bureau of Linguistic Geography Catholic University, Peiping.—*Leuvense Bijdragen* 38, 1948, 57–72, 1 map. / *BSL* 45, 1949, 273–277, Paul Demiéville.

0212 Grootaers, Willem A.: Shina nōson ni okeru bunka shoyōso aida no kankei no ichirei.—*Shizen to Bunka* 3, 1952, 59–69; 59–60: E.S. [Inter-relationship of cultural factors in the rural communities of China.]
Grootaers, W.A.：支那の農村に於ける文化諸要素間の關係の一例

0213 Ho, Teng-sung [Willem A. Grootaers]: Chung-kuo yü-yen-hsüeh chi min-su-hsüeh chih ti-li-te yen-chiu.—*YCHP* 35, 1948, 1–27. [A study of Chinese linguistic geography and folklore.]
賀登崧：中國語言學及民俗學之地理的研究

3.2.3. Questionnaires (0214–0222)

0214 Chao, Yüan-jen: *Fang-yen tiao-ch'a piao-ko.*—Peiping: Academia Sinica, Vol. I, 1930, 82 p.; Vol. II, 1934, 9 p. [A questionnaire for dialect surveys.]
趙元任：方言調查表格

0215 Chinese Linguistics Project (ed.): *Fang-yen tz'u-hui tiao-ch'a shou-ts'e.*—Princeton: Chinese Linguistics Project, 1972, [vi], 285 p., with romanized Mandarin index. [Handbook of words for dialect surveys.]
方言詞彙調查手冊

0216 Chin, Yu-ching: Tsen-yang shih-yung *Han-yü fang-yen tiao-ch'a tzu-yin cheng-li k'a-p'ien.*—*CKYM* 1957:3 40–43. [How to use the *Han-yü fang-yen tiao-ch'a tzu-yin cheng-li k'a-pien* (0221).]

金有景：怎樣使用『漢語方言調查字音整理卡片』

0217 Chung-kuo K'o-hsüeh-yüan Yü-yen yen-chiu-so: *Fang-yen tiao-ch'a tz'u-hui shou-ts'e.*—Peking: K'o-hsüeh, 1955, iii, 34 p. [Handbook of words for dialect surveys.]

中國科學院語言研究所：方言調查詞彙手冊

0218 Chung-kuo K'o-hsüeh-yüan Yü-yen yen-chiu-so: *Fang-yen tiao-ch'a tzu-piao.*—Peking: K'o-hsüeh, 1955; 1964, rev. ed., xii, 82 p./ *Orbis* 15, 1966, 103, Paul Yang. [Questionnaire of characters for dialect surveys.]

中國科學院語言研究所：方言調查字表

0219 Li, Jung: *Han-yü fang-yen tiao-ch'a shou-ts'e.*—Peking: K'o-hsüeh, 1957, xii, 157 p./ *Orbis* 15, 1966, 103–104, Paul Yang. [A handbook for the surveys of Chinese dialects.]

李榮：漢語方言調查手冊

0220 Ting, Sheng-shu & Li, Jung: *Han-yü fang-yen tiao-ch'a chien-piao.*—Peking: K'o-hsüeh, 1956, vi, 59 p./ *Orbis* 15 1966, 102, Paul Yang. [Simplified list of characters for the Chinese dialect surveys.]

丁聲樹，李榮：漢語方言調查簡表

0221 Ting, Sheng-shu & Li, Jung: *Han-yü fang-yen tiao-ch'a tzu-yin cheng-li k'a-p'ien.*—Peking: K'o-hsüeh, 1956. / *CKYW* 1957:2, 45, Chiao Ping; *Orbis* 15, 1966, 102–103, Paul Yang. [Phonetically arranged card index for the Chinese dialect surveys.]

丁聲樹，李榮：漢語方言調查字音整理卡片／趙秉評

0222 Ting, Sheng-shu & Li, Jung: *Ku chin tzu-yin tui-chao shou-ts'e.*—Peking: K'o-

hsüeh, 1958, xii, 214 p./ *RBS* 4, 1958, 547, A. Rygaloff; *Orbis* 15, 1966, 103, Paul Yang. [A handbook of the Ancient and Modern pronunciation of characters.]

丁聲樹，李榮：古今字音對照手冊

3.3. Descriptive Methods (0223–0278)
3.3.1. General (0223–0231)

0223 Chao, Yüan-jen: Fang-yen chi-lu chung Han-tzu te kung-yung.—*CYYK* 1, 1954, 117–128. [The function of Chinese characters in the recording of dialects.]

趙元任：方言記錄中漢字的功用

0224 Ch'en, Han-ch'ing & Chu, Chien-sung: Yung shu-hsüeh fang-fa miao-shu fang-yen te ch'a-pieh.—*FY* 1979:1, 75–80. [Towards using mathematical methods in the description of differences in dialects.]

陳漢清，朱建頌：用數學方法描述方言的差別

0225 Ch'en, Wang-tao: Fang-yen te chi-lu.—*T'ai-pai pan-yüeh-k'an* 1:1, 1934, 50–52. [Recording of dialects.]

陳望道：方言的記錄

0226 Cheng, Robert L.: Second-language learner's classification of Chinese dialects and related languages.—*GK* 63, 1973, 27–43.

〔鄭良偉〕

0227 Ho, Shu-yung: T'an-t'an tsen-yang chieh-shao fang-yen.—*YWCS* 1956:7, 50–51. [Discussion on how to introduce dialects.]

何叔永：談談怎樣介紹方言

0228 Hsieh, Hsin-i: A new method of dialect subgrouping.—*JCL* 1:1, 1973, 64–92./ *JCL* 2:1, 1974, 88–104, Steven P. Baron.

0229 Huang, Chao-p'ing: Kuan-yü pien-tsuan *Fang-yen ku lin* te hua.—*SWYK* 1, 1939–1940, 107–108; 1:9, 1939, 7–8. [A few words about a project for compilation of *Fang-yen ku lin.*]

黃肇平：關於編纂『方言詁林』的話

0230 Jung, Chao-tsu: Cheng-chi fang-yen te wo chien.—*KYAO* 35, 1923, 1–4. [My opinion on the collection of dialect materials.]

容肇祖：徵集方言的我見

0231 Ya, Yüan: Tui chieh-shao fang-yen te i-hsieh hsiao i-chien.—*YWCS* 1956:1, 44–45. [Some opinions for the introduction of dialects.]

亞元：對介紹方言的一些小意見

3.3.2. Phonetic Descriptions (0232–0257)
3.3.2.1. General (0232–0248)

0232 Chang, Che-sheng; Shih, Wen-t'ao & Yeh, Hsiang-ling: Chi-t'i pi-chiao yü-yin tsai fang-yen tiao-ch'a kung-tso chung te chung-yao-hsing.—*CKYW* 1960:10, 327–330. [The importance of collective work in comparing phonetic data during the work of dialect surveys.]

張嚞生，施文濤，葉祥苓：集體比較語音在方言調查工作中的重要性

0233 Fu Mao-chi: Yin-wei te chi-pen li-lun ho shih-chi wen-t'i.—*Yü-yen tiao-ch'a ch'ang-shih* (0194), 46–69. [Fundamental theories and practical problems in phonemics.]

傅懋勣：音位的基本理論和實際問題

0234 Hsü, Shih-jung: *P'u-t'ung-hua yü-yin chiang-hua.*—Peking: Wen-tzu kai-ko, 1958, 4, 1, 128 p./ Including phonetics of Pekinese and other dialects. [Lectures on the phonetics of the Common Language.]

徐世榮：普通話語音講話

0235 Hsü, Wei-han: *Han-yü yü-yin chiang-hua.*—Tientsin: T'ien-chin jen-min, 1959, v, 109 p./ Chap. IX. Dialect sounds. [Lectures on Chinese phonetics.]

許威漢：漢語語音講話

0236 Li, Jung: Tsen-yang ch'iu-ch'u Han-yü fang-yen yin-hsi te lun-k'uo.—*CKYW* 1956:12, 27–33. [How to draw an outline of the phonetic system of a Chinese dialect.]

李榮：怎樣求出漢語方言音系的輪廓

0237 Li, Jung: Fang-yen li te wen pai i-tu.—*CKYW* 1957:4, 22–23. [The differences between the literary and colloquial readings in Chinese dialects.]

李榮：方言裏的文白異讀

0238 Li, Jung: Han-yü fang-yen p'u-ch'a te kung-tso fang-shih ho chi-yin fang-fa.—*CKYW* 1957:5, 10–15. [Working plans and methods of phonetic transcription for a general survey of Chinese dialects.]

李榮：漢語方言普查的工作方式和記音方法

0239 Lin, Yü-t'ang: Fang-yen tiao-ch'a-hui fang-yin tzu-mu ts'ao-an.—*KYAO* 55, 1924, 1–6; 85, 1925, 1; *Yü-yen-hsüeh lun-ts'ung* (0105), 239–248. [A draft of a dialect alphabet by the Dialect Survey Society.]

林語堂：方言調查會方音字母草案

0240 Lin, Yü-t'ang et al.: Fang-yen piao-yin shih-li.—*KYAO* 55, 1924, 7–15; 66, 1924, 1–3. [Examples of phonetic transcriptions from the dialects (15 dialects).]

林語堂：方言標音實例

0241 Lo, Chi-kuang: Tsen-yang fen-hsi yü-yin ho miao-hsieh yü-yin.—*Yü-yen tiao-ch'a ch'ang-shih* (0194), 32–45. [How to analyze and describe speech sounds.]

羅季光：怎樣分析語音和描寫語音

0242 Ts'en, Ch'i-hsiang: *Kuo-chi yin-piao yung-fa shuo-ming.*—Shanghai: Shang-wu, 1957, 62 p./ 36–39: Peking and Canton dialects. [A guide to the use of the International Phonetic Alphabet.]

岑麒祥：國際音標用法說明

0243 Tsu-mo [Chou, Tsu-mo]: Shuo fang-yin yen-chiu.—*KYCK* 194, 1935, June 15. [On the study of dialect sounds.]

〔周〕祖謨：說方音研究

0244 Tung, Shao-wen: *Yü-yin ch'ang-shih (Kai-ting pan).*—Peking: Wen-hua chiao-yü, 1959, rev. & enl. ed., vi, 186 p./ Chap. XII–XVI. Phonetics of Chinese dialects. [Essentials of phonetics.]

董少文：語音常識（改訂版）

0245 Wang, Fu-shih: Tsen-yang fen-hsi ho chi-lu Han-Tsang-yü-hsi yü-yen te sheng-tiao.—*Yü-yen tiao-ch'a ch'ang-shih* (0194), 83–105. [How to analyze and record the tones of the Sino-Tibetan languages.]

王輔世：怎樣分析和記錄漢藏語系語言的聲調

0246 Yang, Nai-szu: *Ch'ieh-yün* yin-hsi yü fang-yen tiao-ch'a.—*CKYW* 1957:7, 35–36. [The phonetic system of the *Ch'ieh-yün* and dialect surveys.]

楊耐思：『切韻』音系與方言調查

0247 Yü, Shih-ch'ang: Yin-wei hsi-t'ung te fen-hsi ho miao-hsieh.—*Yü-yen tiao-ch'a ch'ang-shih* (0194), 70–82. [The analysis and description of phonemic systems.]

喻世長：音位系統的分析和描寫

0248 Yüan, Chia-hua: Fang-yen yen-chiu.—*Han-yü fang-yen kai-yao* (0146), Chap. XII:1. [The study of dialects.]

袁家驊：方言研究

3.3.2.2. Phonetic Correspondences (0249–0257)

0249 Chang, Kung-kuei: T'an yü-yin tui-ying kuan-hsi.—*CKYW* 1957:1, 12–16. [A discussion on phonetic correspondences.]

張拱貴：談語音對應關係

0250 Chang, Kung-kuei: T'ung-kuo fang-yin lai chang-wo Pei-ching yü-yin.—*YWCH* 1957:3, 33–34. [Mastering Peking pronunciation through the pronunciation of the dialects.]

張拱貴：通過方音來掌握北京語音

0251 Chao, Yüan-jen: Kuo-yü t'ung-i chung fang-yen tui-pi te ko fang-mien.—*BIE* 29, 1970, 37–42. [Various aspects of the dialect contrasts in the standardization of the National Language.]

趙元任：國語統一中方言對比的各方面

0252 Chen, Matthew Y.: Cross dialectal comparison: A case study and some

theoretical considerations.—*JCL* 1:1, 1973, 38–63.

0253 Li, Jung: Tsen-yang ch'iu-ch'u fang-yin ho Pei-ching-yin te yü-yin tui-ying kuei-lü.—*CKYW* 1956:6, 7–14; 7, 37. [How to find out the rules of phonetic correspondences between the dialects and Pekinese.]

李榮：怎樣求出方音和北京音的語音對應規律

0254 Ma, Ying-po: Fang-yin ho Pei-ching-yin tui-ying kuei-lü te chiao-hsüeh.—*FPT* 1, 1958, 175–181. [The teaching of rules of phonetic correspondences between the dialects and Pekinese.]

馬鏊伯：方音和北京音對應規律的教學

0255 Shih, Wen-t'ao: Tsen-yang yün-yung yü-yin tui-ying kuei-lü.—*CKYW* 1961:5, 30–32. [How to use the rules of phonetic correspondences.]

施文濤：怎樣運用語音對應規律

0256 Wang, Tsung-yao: Wo shih che-yang lai ch'iu fang-yin ho Pei-ching-yin te yü-yin tui-ying kuei-lü te.—*Kuei-chou chiao-yü* 1957:6, 30–34. [My approach to finding the rules of phonetic correspondences between the dialects and Pekinese.]

王宗瑤：我是這樣來求方音和北京音的語音對應規律的

0257 Yang, Ch'ang-li: Chiao-hsüeh fang-yin ken Pei-ching yü-yin chu-yao tui-ying kuan-hsi te i-tien t'i-hui.—*YWCH* 1959: 12, 37–38. [Some personal experiences in teaching the rules of phonetic correspondences between the dialects and Pekinese.]

楊長禮：教學方音跟北京語音主要對應關係的一點體會

3.3.3. Lexical Descriptions (0258–0272)

0258 Chan, Po-hui: Shou-chi ho cheng-li Han-yü fang-yen tz'u-hui.—*CKYW* 1958: 11, 526–530. [The gathering and arrangement of a Chinese dialect vocabulary.]

詹伯慧：收集和整理漢語方言詞彙

0259   Chan, Po-hui & Huang, Chia-chiao: Kuan-yü Han-yü fang-yen tz'u-hui tiao-ch'a yen-chiu te wen-ti.—*WHTH* 1963:1, 121–136. [Problems concerning surveys and studies of the vocabulary of Chinese dialects.]
詹伯慧，黃家教：關於漢語方言詞滙調查研究的問題

0260   Chang, Che-sheng: Kuan-yü pien-chih fang-yen tz'u-hui tiao-ch'a piao-ko te jo-kan wen-t'i.—*CKYW* 1961:2, 23–25. [Problems concerning the compilation of questionnaires for surveys of dialect vocabulary.]
張喆生：關於編制方言詞滙調查表格的若干問題

0261   Ch'eng, K'ang: Man-t'an Pei-p'ing yü-hui te sou-chi ho cheng-li.—*KWYK* 69, 1948, 11–15. [Casual remarks on the collection and arrangement of Peiping dialect vocabulary.]
程亢：漫談北平語彙的蒐集和整理

0262   Chou, Ch'ang-chi: *P'u-t'ung-hua Min-nan fang-yen tz'u-tien* te pien-hsieh wen-t'i.—*Tz'u-shu yen-chiu* 2, 1979, 172–187. [Problems in compiling the *Common Language-South Min dialect dictionary*.]
周長楫：『普通話閩南方言詞典』的編寫問題

0263   Ho, Wei: *Kuan-yü pien-tsuan Han-yü fang-yen tz'u-tien* te chi-ko wen-t'i.—*CKYW* 1960: 10, 331–333. [Some problems concerning the compilation of a Chinese dialect dictionary.]
賀巍：關於編纂漢語方言詞典的幾個問題

0264   Jao, Ping-ts'ai & Li, Hsin-k'uei: Pien-hsieh Kuang-tung fang-yen tz'u-tien te chi-ko wen-t'i.—*CKYW* 1965:1, 51–58./ *RBS* 11, 1965, 441, F. K. Li. [Several problems in compiling a Cantonese dialect dictionary.]
饒秉才，李新魁：編寫廣東方言詞典的幾個問題

0265   Jao, Ping-ts'ai; Ou-yang, Chüeh-ya & Chou, Wu-chi: Kuan-yü *Kuang-chou-hua fang-yen tz'u-tien.*—*Tz'u-shu yen-chiu* 2, 1979, 163–171. [Concerning the *Kuang-chou-hua fang-yen tz'u-tien.*]
饒秉才，歐陽覺亞，周無忌：關於『廣州話方言詞典』

0266   Lyovin, Anatole: A Chinese dialect dictionary on computer: Progress report.—*POLA*, 2:7, 1968, C1–C43.

0267   Ma, Hsüeh-liang: Sou-chi tz'u-hui ho pien-p'ai tz'u-hui te fang-fa.—*Yü-yen tiao-ch'a ch'ang-shih* (0194), 106–125. [The method of gathering and arranging vocabulary.]
馬學良：蒐集詞彙和編排詞彙的方法

0268   Streeter, Mary: Dictionary on computer: 1971.—*POLA* 15, 1971, 63–138; map, illus.

0269   T'ien, Shui: Tui chieh-shao fang-yen tz'u-hui te chi-tien i-chien.—*YWCS* 1956: 8, 52–54. [Some opinions concerning the introduction of dialect vocabulary.]
天水：對介紹方言詞滙的幾點意見

0270   T'ien, Shui: Kuan-yü fang-yen tz'u te wen-ti.—*YWCS* 1958:5, 33–36. [Problems concerning dialect vocabulary.]
天水：關於方言詞的問題

0271   Wang, William S. Y.: Project *DOC*: Its methodological basis.—*JAOS* 90, 1970, 57–66./ DOC=Dictionary on computer./ The immediate object is to reconstruct the phonological histories of the main Chinese dialects.

0272   Yüan, Chia-hua: Fang-yen tz'u-hui.—*Han-yü fang-yen kai-yao* (0146), Chap. XII:2. [Dialect vocabulary.]
袁家驊：方言詞滙

3.3.4.   Grammatical Descriptions (0273–0278)

0273   Chan, Po-hui & Huang, Chia-chiao: T'an Han-yü fang-yen yü-fa ts'ai-liao te shou-chi ho cheng-li.—*CKYW* 1965:3, 211–223. [On the collection and arrangement of grammatical materials of Chinese dialects.]
詹伯慧，黃家教：談漢語方言語法材料的收集和整理

0274 Chin, P'eng: Chi-lu yü-fa ts'ai-liao ying chu-i te wen-t'i.—*Yü-yen tiao-ch'a ch'ang-shih* (0194), 126–134. [Problems to be considered in recording grammatical materials.]
金鵬：記錄語法材料應注意的問題

0275 Hsia, Hsi-chün: Fang-yen tiao-ch'a pu ying hu-shih tz'u-hui yü-fa.—*CKYW* 1960:1, 36–37. [Vocabulary and grammar ought not to be overlooked in dialect surveys.]
夏錫駿：方言調查不應忽視詞滙語法

0276 Li, Jung: Tsen-yang chi tz'u-hui ho yü-fa li-chü.—*CKYW* 1957:1, 17–23. [How to record vocabulary and grammatical structures.]
李榮：怎樣記詞滙和語法例句

0277 Yü, Shih-ch'ang: Tsen-yang sou-chi yü-fa ts'ai-liao chin-hsing yü-fa yen-chiu. —*Yü-yen tiao-ch'a ch'ang-shih* (0194), 135–148. [How to gather grammatical materials and carry out grammatical study.]
喩世長：怎樣蒐集語法材料進行語法研究

0278 Yüan, Chia-hua: Fang-yen yü-fa.— *Han-yü fang-yen kai-yao* (0146), Chap. XII:3. [Dialect grammar.]
袁家驊：方言語法

3.4. Romanizations and Dialect Characters (0279–0337)

3.4.1. General and Mandarin Dialects (0279–0294)

0279 Anonymous: A uniform system of romanization for Mandarin.—*ChinRec* 33, 1902, 138–139.

0280 Anonymous: Mandarin romanization. —*ChinRec* 34, 1903, 347–349.

0281 Anderson, Olov Bertil: *A concordance to five systems of transcription for Standard Chinese.*—Lund: Studentlitteratur, 1970, 228 p./ *AM* 17:1, 1971, 90, G. Weys.

0282 Chang, Chao: *Han-yü yin-chieh p'in-fa hui-pien.*—Peking: Wen-tzu kai-ko, 1963, ix, 140 p. [Systems of phonetic transcription of Chinese syllables.] / 21 systems.
張照：漢語音節拼法滙編

0283 Chiang, Ching-fu: *Kuo-yü Lo-ma-tzu.* —Shanghai: Chung-hua, 1936, 52 p. [National Romanization (Gwoyeu Romatzyh).]
蔣鏡夫：國語羅馬字

0284 Chu, Hsing: Fang-yin fu-hao te pi-chiao yen-chiu.—*Ho-pei Shih-fan hsüeh-yüan yüan-pao* 1956:1, 70–88. [A comparative study of phonetic symbols for dialects.]
朱星：方音符號的比較研究

0285 Crawford, T.P.: A system of phonetic symbols for writing the dialects of China. —*ChinRec* 19, 1888, 101–110.

0286 Darroch, John: Phonetic representation of Mandarin.—*ChinRec* 33, 1902, 521–523.

0287 Gardner, C. S.: The Western transcription of Chinese.—*JRASNC* 62, 1931, 137–147.

0288 Hu, Ying: San-pai-wu-shih-nien lai tsai Chung-kuo te Lo-ma-tzu P'in-yin chi-lüeh. —*KYCK* 1933, 105–106. [A brief note on romanizations in China in the past 350 years.]
胡英：三百五十年來在中國的羅馬字拼音紀略

0289 Legeza, Ireneus László: *Guide to transliterated Chinese in the modern Peking dialect.*—Leiden: E.J. Brill, 3 vols., Vol. I. Conversion tables of the currently used international and European systems with comparative tables of initials and finals, 1968, viii, 176 p.; Vol. II. Conversion tables of the outdated international and European individual systems with comparative tables of initials and finals, 1969, 262 p.; Vol. III. (in preparation)./ *AM* 15:1, 1969, 128; 15:2, 1970, 257, Hugh D.R. Baker.

0290   Lo, Ch'ang-p'ei: *Kuo-yin tzu-mu yen-chin shih.*—Shanghai: Shang-wu, 1934, v, 80 p., tab./ 4–9: Bibliography. [A history of the Chinese phonetic alphabet and transcriptions.]

羅常培：國音字母演進史

0291   Lo, Ch'ang-p'ei: *Han-yü p'in-yin tzu-mu yen-chin-shih.*—Peking: Wen-tzu kai-ko, 1959, 59 p., tab./ A reprint of (0290). [A history of the Chinese phonetic alphabet and transcriptions.]

羅常培：漢語拼音字母演進史

0292   Mullie, Joseph: La romanisation du chinois.—*Bulletin Catholique de Pékin* 6:70, 1919, 230–235; 71, 263–267.

0293   Pai, Ti-chou: Han-tzu piao-yin fang-fa chih yen-chin.—*KHCK* 4:4, 1935, 87–119. [Evolution of the methods of transcription of Chinese characters.]

白滌洲：漢字標音方法之演進

0294   Simon, Walter: *The new official Chinese Latin script, Gwoyeu Romatzyh.*—London: A. Prosthain, 1942, 63 p./ With tables, rules, illustrative examples.

3.4.2.   Wu Dialects (0295–0301)

0295   Anonymous: Shanghai romanization.—*ChinRec* 34, 1903, 401–404.

0296   Anonymous: Ningpo romanization.—*ChinRec* 34, 1903, 457–460.

0297   Chao, Yüan-jen: Su-chou fang-yin chu-yin fu-hao yü k'uan-shih kuo-chi yin-piao tui-chao piao.—*KYAO* 2:15, 1936, 8. [A comparative table of phonetic symbols and broad IPA for the Soochow dialect.]

趙元任：蘇州方音注音符號與寬式國際音標對照表

0298   Ch'ien, Hsüan-t'ung: Su-chou chu-yin tzu-mu ts'ao-an.—*KYCK* (Pei-hsin) 28, 1925, 1–7. [A draft of an alphabet for the Soochow dialect.]

錢玄同：蘇州注音字母草案

0299   Lu, Chi: *Su-chou chu-yin ts'ung-shu.*—Soochow: Su-chou chu-yin fu-hsing hui, n.d., 136 p. [Collected work on phonetic transcriptions of the Soochow dialect.]

陸基：蘇州注音叢書

0300   Lu, Chi & Fang, Pin-kuan: *Su-chou chu-yin fu-hao.*—Shanghai: Shang-wu, 1931, 32 p. [A phonetic alphabet for the Soochow dialect.]/ With short phrases and sentences.

陸基，方賓觀：蘇州注音符號

0301   Ni, Hai-shu: Shang-hai-yin te p'in-yin k'o-pen.—*YWCS* 1952:1, 7–9; 2, 25–27; 3, 16–18; 4, 23–25. [A Pinyin textbook of Shanghai dialect pronunciation.]

倪海曙：上海音的拼音課本

3.4.3.   Yüeh Dialects (0302–0308)

0302   Anderson, O.B.: Om transkriptionen av kantonesiskan.—*Språkliga bidrag* 5, 1955, 75–103.

0303   Barnett, K.M.A.: A transcription for Cantonese: Notes on Yuen Ren Chao's *Cantonese primer* (1691).—*BSOAS* 13: 3, 1950, 725–745.

0304   Bridie, William: Cantonese romanization.—*ChinRec* 35, 1904, 309–311.

0305   Egerod, Søren: The tonal spelling of Cantonese.—*TP* 46, 1959, 369–375./ *RBS* 4, 1958, 555, Li Fang-kuei; A critical review of Ulring's article (0307).

0306   Tam, Wing-kwong: *A new phonetic alphabet for the Cantonese dialect of the Chinese language.*—Hong Kong: Yau Sang Printing Press, 1953, 28 p./ A kana-type phonetic alphabet.

〔譚榮光〕

0307   Ulring, Tor: The transcription of Cantonese: A critical review of some current systems of "tonal spelling" and a presentation of a new rational transcription.—*TP* 46, 1958, 81–110./ *RBS* 4, 1958, 554, Li Fang-kuei.

0308 Wen-tzu kai-ko ch'u-pan-she (ed.): Kuang-tung-sheng szu-chung fang-yen p'in-yin fang-an.—*WTKK* 15, 1960, 21–25. [Romanization of four dialects in Kwangtung.]
文字改革出版社：廣東省四種方言拼音方案

3.4.4. Min Dialects (0309–0319)

0309 Cole, W.B.: Romanized script in Fukien.—*CR* 1920, 856–858.

0310 Feng, Mao-sung: Hai-nan-hua p'in-yin tzu-mu.—*CSTY* 85–87, 1929, 57–63. [A phonetic alphabet for the dialect of Hainan.]
馮茂松：海南話拼音字母

0311 Huang, Tien-ch'eng: Ts'ung Min-nan te pai-hua tzu k'an-ch'u p'in-yin wen-tzu te yu-tien.—*CKYW* 1953:7, 16–19. [The advantages of the Pinyin system as seen from the *péh-oē-jī* romanization of the South Min dialect.]
黃典誠：從閩南的『白話字』看出拼音文字的優點

0312 Li, Mao-hsiang: Min-nan yü-yin Lo-ma-tzu p'in-yin hsüeh-hsi fa.—*TWFW* 21:3, 1971, 44–54. [Method of learning the romanization system of the South Min dialect.]
李茂詳：閩南語音羅馬字拼音學習法

0313 Lin, Pen-yüan: T'ai-wan pai-hua tzu te shang-ch'üeh.—*TPWW* 6:4, 1958, 17–28. [A discussion on the *péh-oē-jī* romanization of Taiwanese.]
林本元：臺灣白話字的商榷

0314 Lin, Pen-yüan: Min-nan pai-hua tzu te fen-hsi.—*TPWH* 1968:1–4, 269–284. [An analysis of *péh-oē-jī* romanization of the South Min dialect.]
林本元：閩南白話字的分析

0315 Murakami, Yoshihide: Hakuwaji no hensen to Binnangoyaku seisho.—*Yamato Bunka* 49, 1968, 96–118. [The development of *péh-oē-jī* romanization and the translations of the Holy Bible into the South Min dialect.]
村上嘉英：白話字の變遷と閩南語譯聖書

0316 Phillips, Hugh Stowell: The Kien-Ning romanised dialects.—*ChinRec* 35, 1904, 517–519.

0317 Pitcher, P.W.: Amoy romanization, its history, purpose and results.—*ChinRec* 35, 1904, 567–573.

0318 Wang, Yü-te: Fukkengo no kyōkai Rōmaji ni tsuite.—*CGGG* 1957:3, 3–10. [Church romanizations of the Fukien dialect.]
王育德：福建語の教會ローマ字について

0319 Wang, Yü-te: Kyōkai Rōmaji no hanashi.—*TWSN* 5, 1960, 31–34; 6, 43–46. [On Church romanization.]
王育德：教會ローマ字の話

3.4.5. Interdialectal Romanization (0320–0331)

0320 Gaultier, A.: Une écriture alphabétique du chinois est-elle possible?.—*BUA* 3:7, 1946, 139–155.

0321 Grooaters, Willem A.: Dialectes chinois et alphabétisation, à propos de la Romanisation Interdialectique.—*BUA* 7:2, 1946, 207–232.

0322 Jasmin, Ernest: L'origine, les progrès et la nature de la R.I. [Romanisation Interdialectique].—*CCS* 14, 1941, 360–402.

0323 Jasmin, Ernest: *Romanisationis Interdialecticae Abecedarium in usum discipulorum.*—Szepingkai: Catholic Mission, n.d., 57 p./ *CCS* 6:12, 1933, 1083, Anonymous.
〔羅馬字母綴法ＡＢＣ教科書〕

0324 Jasmin, Ernest: *Romanisation Interdialectiques: Léxique des caractères les plus usuels orthographies en R.I. et classés selon l'ordre de Debesse.*—Hong Kong: Nazareth, 1933, 48 p./ *CCS* 6:12, 1933, 1083–1084, E.J.

0325 Jasmin, Ernest & Rutten, J.: *Dictionarium Romanisationis Interdialecticae.*—Peiping: Lazariste Pétang, 1935, 5, 96 p./ *CCS* 8:2, 1935, 210, Anonymous.

〔羅馬字母綴法字典〕

0326 Lamasse, Henri: *Nouveau répertoire de la Romanisation Interdialectique, ou léxique alphabétique de 4,300 caractères couramment usités en langue chinoise écrits en "Phonétique Nationale" traduite en français et en anglais chaque graphie de la R.I. a un seul caractère.*—Hong Kong: Nazareth, 1951, 126 p.

〔拉體文字新體字典〕

0327 Lamasse, Henri & Jasmin, Ernest: L'écriture alphabétique du chinois en fonction de la langue ancienne et avec la possibilité de passer d'un dialecte actuel à l'autre.—*CCS* 4, 1931, 639–657, 775–793, 935–947, 1061–1073; 5, 1932, 85–93, 381–393. A simplified version by Jasmin: *CCS* 5, 1932, 732–735; 6, 1933, 818–820, 881–887, 28–31.

0328 Lamasse, Henri & Jasmin, Ernest: La Romanisation Interdialectique.—*Bulletin Catholique de Pékin* 1934, 43–50, 92–99.

0329 Lamasse, Henri & Jasmin, Ernest: *L'écriture alphabétique du chinois.*—Hong Kong: Nazareth, 1934, 76 p./ Subtitle: Rendue littéraire, pratique et intelligible sous une forme unique dans tous les styles modernes et dans tous les dialectes actuellement en usage, par Romanisation Interdialectique, c'est-à-dire, orthographie, fonction de la langue ancienne.

0330 Luc, Khynh [Rutten, J.]: *Chinese-English-French dictionary, featuring a modern practical Chinese script.*—Shanghai: T'ou-sè-wè, 1945, xxii, 702 p./ With an introduction to the R.I. system.

〔盧謹：中英法綜合辭典〕

0331 Luc, Kynh [Rutten, J.]: *An easy modern script for Chinese of all dialects taught in forty-five lessons. The teacher's book.*—Hong Kong: Nazareth, 1946, xii, 36 p.

3.4.6. Dialect Characters (0332–0337)

0332 Chang, Wei-kang: Fang-yen tzu.—*YWCS* 1954:2, 11–12. [Dialect characters.]

張爲綱：方言字

0333 Chou, Yu-kuang: Fang-yen yü fang-yen wen-tzu.—*Hsin wen-tzu pan-yüeh-k'an* 82, 1952, 1–9. [Dialects and dialect characters.]

周有光：方言與方言文字

0334 Hsieh, Hsüan: *Fang-yen tzu k'ao.*—Shanghai: Hui-wen-t'ang, 1923, 2, 122 p. [Etymological study of dialect characters.]

謝璿：方言字考

0335 Li, Ts'ung-yün: Fang-yin fu-hao yü hsin fang tzu.—*CTWC* 4, 1943, 48–55. [Phonetic symbols for the dialects and new dialect characters.]

李叢雲：方音符號與新方字

0336 Parker, Edward Harper: Characterless Chinese words.—*CR* 9, 1879, 85–88./ List of colloquial words in five dialects, including Cantonese.

0337 Shen, Ch'un: Fang-yen yü hsin tzu.—*KWYK* 20, 1943, 10–11./ *KWYK* 26, 1944, 34–35, Liu Nai-lung. [Dialects and new characters.]

沈純：方言與新字／劉迺隆評

4. ARCHAIC AND OLD DIALECTS (0338–0462)

4.1. Archaic and Old Dialects in General (0338–0349)

0338 Chang, Kun: Dialect variations in Chinese historical phonology.—*BIHP* 46, 1975, 613–635.

0339 Demiéville, Paul: Archaïsmes de prononciation en chinois vulgaire.—*TP* 40, 1950, 1–59.

0340 Kriukov, M.V.: Drevnekitaiskie dialekty i problema datirovki pis'mennykh pamiatnikov.—*NAA* 6, 1967, 69–82; E.S. [The ancient Chinese dialects and the problem of dating written documents.]

0341 Li, Jung: Ts'ung hsien-tai fang-yen lun ku ch'ün-mu yu i, erh, szu teng.—*CKYW* 1965:5, 337–342, 355, 5 tabl./ *RBS* 11, 1965, 230–231, S.N. Cartier. [A theory on the existence of the 1, 2, and 4 Divisions in the ancient Chinese *g'*-initial based on evidence from modern dialects.]
李榮：從現代方言論古『羣』母有一、二、四等

0342 Lo, Hsin-t'ien [Lo, Ch'ang-p'ei]: Hsien-tai fang-yen chung te ku-yin i-chi.—*WSTC* 1:2, 1941, 7–13. [The phonological traces of Ancient Chinese in modern dialects.]
羅莘田：現代方言中的古音遺迹

0343 Mullie, Joseph L.M.: La survivance de la voyelle *a* de l'ancien chinois dans le dialecte pékinois du nord.—*MS* 6, 1941, 73–112.

0344 Noguchi, Masayuki: Kango hōgen-on ni zansonsuru chūkoon no kenkyu (1).—*DBDK* 9, 1971, 71–106. [A study on Ancient Chinese as preserved in the pronunciations of modern Chinese dialects (1).]
野口正之：漢語方言音に殘存する中古音の研究㈠

0345 Serruys, Paul L.-M.: Note on archaic Chinese dialectology.—*Orbis* 9, 1960, 42–57.

0346 Serruys, Paul L.-M.: Chinese dialectology based on written documents.—*MS* 21, 1962, 320–344./ *RBS* 8, 1962, 436, Li Fang-kuei.

0347 Yang, Paul Fu-mien: *Modern dialects and the reconstruction of Archaic Chinese —Initial consonant clusters.*—Washington, D.C.: Georgetown University, 1968, 27 p.

0348 Yang, Paul Fu-mien: *On the reconstruction of Old Chinese based on modern dialect data.*—Paper delivered at the 4th Meeting of the Conference on Sino-Tibetan Linguistics, Indiana U., October 8–9, 1971, 13 p.

0349 Yang, Paul Fu-mien: Prefix kə- in modern Chinese dialects and Proto-Chinese. —*MS* 33, 1977–1978, 286–299.

4.2. Chou and Ch'in Period (0350–0369)
4.2.1. General Studies (0350–0358)

0350 Hsü, Jen-fu: *Meng-tzu* fang-yen k'ao. —*Chih-hsüeh yüeh-k'an* 1942:5, 14–18; 6, 9–11. [A study of dialect words found in *Mencius*.]
徐仁甫：『孟子』方言考

0351 Li, Hsing-chih: *Meng-tzu* shu chung chih fang-yen su-yü.—*Tse-shan pan-yüeh k'an* 1:11, 1940, 4–5. [Dialect words and popular sayings found in *Mencius*.]
李行之：『孟子』書中之方言俗語

0352 Lin, Yü-t'ang: Yen Ch'i Lu Wei yang-sheng chuan-pien k'ao.—*Yü-yen-hsüeh lun-ts'ung* (0105), 82–87. [A study of denasalization in the ancient states of Yen, Ch'i, Lu, and Wei.]
林語堂：燕齊魯衞陽聲轉變考

0353 Lin, Yü-t'ang: *Chou-li* fang-yin k'ao. —*Yü-yen-hsüeh lun-ts'ung* (0105), 88–91. [A study on the dialect pronunciations in *Chou-li*.]
林語堂：『周禮』方音考

0354 Lin, Yü-t'ang: *Tso-chuan* chen wei yü shang-ku fang-yin.—*Yü-yen-hsüeh lun-ts'ung* (0105), 92–132./ *Hsin yüeh* 1, 1928, 1–2, Wei Chü-hsien. [Archaic dialect sounds and the authenticity of *Tso-chuan.*]

林語堂：『左傳』眞僞與上古方音／衞聚賢評

0355 Lin, Yü-t'ang: Ch'en Sung Huai Ch'u ko han tui-chuan k'ao.—*Ch'ing-chu Ts'ai Yüan-p'ei hsien-sheng 65 sui lun-wen chi* (Peiping: Academia Sinica, 1933–1935), 425–428. [A study of the alternation of the *ko* and *han* rhymes in the ancient states of Ch'en, Sung, Huai, and Ch'u.]

林語堂：陳宋淮楚『歌』『寒』對轉考──『慶祝蔡元培先生六十五歲論文集』

0356 Ting, Hsing-wang: Wen-tzu-hsüeh shang Chung-kuo ku-tai fang-yen kou-ch'en.—*Hsüeh-feng* 5:3, 1935, 1–16; 5:4, 17–45. [A research in the logography of old Chinese dialects.]

丁興潫：文字學上中國古代方言勾沉

0357 Tōdō, Akiyasu: Jōko Kango no hōgen—Tokuni Shū Shin hōgen no tokushoku ni tsuite.—*Tōhōgaku ronshū* 1, 1954, 85–104; 04: E.S. [Archaic Chinese dialects—with reference to the special features of dialects of the Chou and Ch'in dynasties.]

藤堂明保：上古漢語の方言──特に周秦方言の特色について

0358 Yoshida, Megumu: Shunju Sengoku jidai no tetsugaku sho ni okeru hōgen—*Rongo* to *Bokushi* no baai.—*Jinbungaku* 38, 1958, 118–135. [Dialects from philosophical writings of the Spring-Autumn and Warring States periods—*Confucian Analects* and *Motzu.*]

吉田惠：春秋戰國時代の哲學書における方言──『論語』と『墨子』の場合

4.2.2. Ch'u Dialects (0359–0369)

0359 Chou, Tsu-mo: Ch'ien-kung *Ch'u-tz'u yin* chih hsieh-yün shuo yü Ch'u yin.—*FJHC* 9:2, 1940, 117–124; *Wen-hsüeh chi* (0101), 168–176, 6 pl. (fragments of the *Ch'u-tz'u yin* from Tun-huang). [Rhyming pronunciations and sounds of the Ch'u dialect in Ch'ien's *Ch'u-tz'u yin.*]

周祖謨：龔公『楚辭音』之協韻說與楚音

0360 Forkes, Eduard: Die sprache des alten Ch'u.—*TP* 27, 1930, 1–11.

0361 Hsiang, Hsia: *Li-sao* p'ien Ch'u-yü fang-yen-tz'u yin-cheng.—*TLTC* 34:3, 1967, 5–8. [Phonetico-semantic study of Ch'u dialect words found in the *Li-sao* chapter of *Ch'u-tz'u.*]

向夏：『離騷』篇楚語方言詞音證

0362 Hsiang, Hsia: Ch'ü Yüan fu *Chiu-ko T'ien-wen Chiu-chang* Ch'u-yü fang-yen-tz'u yin-cheng.—*TLTC* 35:11, 1967, 7–11. [Phonetico-semantic study of Ch'u dialect words found in the *Chiu-ko, T'ien-wen* and *Chiu-chang* chapters of *Ch'u-tz'u.*]

向夏：屈原賦『九歌』『天問』『九章』楚語方言詞音證

0363 Lin, Lien-hsien: *Ch'u-tz'u* yin-shuo shu-p'ing chü-yao.—*CCHP* 5:2, 1966, 126-149. [A critical account of phonetic interpretations of *Ch'u-tz'u* rhymes.]

林蓮仙：『楚辭』音說述評舉要

0364 Lin, Lien-hsien: *Ch'u-tz'u* yün yü hsien-tai Han-yü fang-yen tsai ku tiao yen-chiu chung te chiao-hu tso-yung.—*CCHP* 7:2, 1968, 177–186. [An approach to Ancient Chinese rhymes through the comparative study of the rhymes of *Ch'u-tz'u* with contemporary Chinese dialects.]

林蓮仙：『楚辭』韻與現代漢語方言在古調研究中的交互作用

0365 Liu, Tse: Ch'u-yü shih-i.—*WCCK* 1:1, 1930, 141–172. [Ch'u dialect words.]

劉賾：楚語拾遺

0366 Lo, Hung-k'ai: *Ch'u-tz'u* chang-chü cheng-yin Ch'u-yü k'ao.—*STKT* 1:2, 1931, 17–20. [A study of the Ch'u dialect words found in the text of *Ch'u-tz'u*.]

駱鴻凱：『楚辭』章句徵引楚語考

0367 Matake, Naoshi: Ryō-Shū Shin Kan inbun no yōin kara mita Kaon to Soon.—*Mekata hakase kanrei kinen Chūgokugaku ronshū* (Tokyo, 1964), 375–401. [The dialect pronunciations of Hsia and Ch'u as seen from the rhymes used during the Chou, Ch'in and Han dynasties.]

眞武直：兩周秦漢韻文の用韻から見た夏音と楚音 ——『目加田博士還曆記念中國學論集』

0368 Takeji, Sadao: *Soji no hōgensei.*—*Tokushima Daigaku Gakugeibu Kiyō* 14, 1965, 1–10. [On the dialect character of *Ch'u-tz'u*.]

竹治貞夫：『楚辭』の方言性

0369 Tung, T'ung-ho: Yü Kao Pen-han hsien-sheng shang-ch'üeh tzu-yu ya-yün-shuo chien lun shang-ku Ch'u fang-yin t'e-se.—*BIHP* 7, 1938, 533–543; *Tung T'ung-ho . . . . hsüan chi* (0110), 1–11. [Notes on Karlgren's 'Free rime system' and the phonological characteristics of the archaic Ch'u dialect.]

董同龢：與高本漢先生商榷『自由押韵』說兼論上古楚方音特色

4.3. Han Period (0370–0401)

4.3.1. General Studies (0370–0372)

0370 Lin, Yü-t'ang: Han-tai fang-yin k'ao. —*Yü-szu* 31, 1925, 84–87. [A study of the dialects of Han times.]

林語堂：漢代方音考

0371 Lin, Yü-t'ang: Hsi Han fang-yin ch'ü-yü k'ao.—*Kung-hsien* 2, 1927, 1–8; 3, 15–30; *Yü-yen-hsüeh lun-ts'ung* (0105), 16–44; 2 maps. [A study of the geographical distribution of dialects during the Former Han dynasty.]

林語堂：西漢方音區域考

0372 Lin, Yü-t'ang: *Han-tai fang-yin k'ao* hsü.—*HTCK* 1:3, 1927, 1–7. [A preface to *Han-tai fang-yin k'ao*.]

林語堂：『漢代方音考』序

4.3.2. Fang-yen (0373–0397)

0373 Chmielewski, Janusz: Sur la dissyllabisation des mots en chinois ancien d'après les glosses de Kouo P'o dans le *Eul-ya* et le *Fang-yen*.—*PICO* 21, 1948 (publ. in 1949), 270–271 (summary).

0374 Chou, Tsu-mo & Wu, Hsiao-ling: *Fang-yen chiao-chien chi t'ung-chien.*—Peking: K'o-hsüeh, 1956, xxii, 95, 1 map; 1x, 249 p./ *CKYW* 1957:3, 47, Chang Ch'i-hua; *CKYW* 1963:5, 428–431, Hu Chih-fan; *Orbis* 15, 1966, 97–98, Paul Yang. [The *Fang-yen*—A critical edition and index.]

周祖謨，吳曉鈴：方言校箋及通檢 / 張其華評，胡芷藩評

0375 Fukuda, Jōnosuke: Yōyū *Hōgen* no seiritsu ni tsuite.—*Tōhōgakkai sōritsu nijūgoshunen kinen Tōhōgaku ronshū* (Tokyo: Tōhōgakkai, 1972), 739–753. [The formulation of Yang Hsiung's *Fang-yen*.]

福田襄之助：揚雄『方言』の成立について ——『東方學會創立二十五周年記念東方學論集』

0376 Kong, Jae-sŏk: Handae *Bangŏn* chung Chosŏn bangŭm e kwanhayŏ.—*Tongyanghak* 5, 1975, 335–347. [Korean dialect pronunciations found in *Fang-yen* of the Han dynasty.]

孔在錫：漢代「方言」중朝鮮方音에관하여

0377 Lo, Ch'ang-p'ei: Yang Hsiung *Fang-yen* tsai Chung-kuo yü-yen-hsüeh shih shang te ti-wei.—*Lo Ch'ang-p'ei . . . . hsüan-chi* (0106), 177–179. [The place of Yang Hsiung's *Fang-yen* in the history of the Chinese language.]

羅常培：揚雄『方言』在中國語言學史上的地位

0378 Ma, Kuang-yü: *Fang-yen chiao shih.*—Taipei: Shang-wu, 1970, ii, 92 p. [A commentary on the *Fang-yen.*]

馬光宇：方言校釋

0379 P'u, Chih-chen: *Fang-yen* mu-t'i ch'ung-chien yen-chiu.—*CKYW* 1966:1, 30–33. [A study on the recurrence of semantic groups in *Fang-yen.*]

濮之珍：『方言』母題重見研究

0380 Serruys, Paul L.-M.: The names of the 'lizard' in the old Chinese dialects.—*Orbis* 1, 1952, 489–499, 1 map.

0381 Serruys, Paul L.-M.: The study of the old Chinese dialects, the name for the 'wildcat' in *Fang-yen,* VIII, 2.—*Oriens* 6, 1953, 354–371, 1 map.

0382 Serruys, Paul L.-M.: *Prolegomena to the study of Chinese dialects of Han times according to Fang-yen.*—Berkeley: U. of California, 1956, xi, 605 p./ Unpubl. doc. diss.

0383 Serruys, Paul L.-M.: The word for 'salt' in *Shuo Wen.*—*Oriens* 11, 1958:1–2, 203–223./ *RBS* 4, 1958, 560, M.J. Künstler.

0384 Serruys, Paul L.-M.: *The Chinese dialects of Han time according to Fang Yen.*—Berkeley and Los Angeles: U. of California Press, 1959, xix, 350 p., maps./ *JAOS* 79, 1959, 309–310, Li Fang-kuei; *RBS* 5, 1959, 483, N.C. Bodman; *TP* 47, 1959, 435–441, M.J. Künstler; *BSOAS* 23, 1960, 165–167, G.B. Downer; *Lingua* 9, 1960, 306–309, A.F.P. Hulsewé; *MS* 19, 1960, 518–523, *Chūgokugogaku ken-kyū* (0108), 339–351, Ogawa Tamaki; *TYGH* 43:3, 1960, 86–91, Kōno Rokurō; *AOH* 13, 1961, 333–335, B. Csongor; *Orbis* 15, 1966, 98, Paul Yang.

0385 Serruys, Paul L.-M.: Five word studies on *Fang Yen,* Pt. I.—*MS* 19, 1960, 114–209; Pt. II, *MS* 21, 1962, 223–319./ *RBS* 6, 1960, 411, W. Simon; 8, 1962, 450, H. M. Stimson.

0386 Serruys, Paul L.-M.: The dialect words for 'tiger' in Middle Han times.—*MS* 26, 1967, 225–285.

0387 Serruys, Paul L.-M.: *Fang Yen* IV, 5 and 31: 'Knee covers' and 'apron.'—*BIHP* 39, 1969, 245–267.

0388 Tagawa, Kazumi: Yō Yū to sono cho *Hōgen* ni tsuite.—*DBDK* 14, 1976, 141–147. [Yang Hsiung and his work *Fang-yen.*]

田川一己：揚雄とその著『方言』について

0389 Tateishi, Hiroo: Kaku Hoku no onchū ni tsuite (jō)—*Hōgen* ni okeru hansetsu jōji.—*KGK* 13:8, 1971, 65–80. [Kuo P'u's phonetic annotations (A)—The first fan-ch'ieh characters in *Fang-yen.*]

立石廣男：郭璞の音注について（上）——『方言』における反切上字

0390 Tateishi, Hiroo: Kaku Hoku no onchū ni tsuite (ge)—*Hōgen* ni okeru chokuon-chū o chūshin ni.—*KGK* 13:14, 1975, 185–198. [Kuo P'u's phonetic annotations (B)—Focusing on the chih-yin annotations in *Fang-yen.*]

立石廣男：郭璞の音注について（下）——『方言』における直音注を中心

0391 Ting, Wei-fen: *Fang-yen* i.—Ku-ya-t'ang ts'ung-shu ed., 14 chüan. [Phonetico-semantic annotations to *Fang-yen.*]

丁惟汾：方言譯——「詁雅堂叢書」本

0392 Ts'ai, Feng-ch'i: *Fang-yen* sheng-chuan shuo.—*SWYK* 2:8, 1940, 17–23. [Sound alternations in *Fang-yen.*]

蔡鳳圻：『方言』聲轉說

0393 Tung, Chün-yen: *Fang-yen yin cheng.*—Taipei: Wen-chin, 1975, ii, ii, ii, 130 p. [A phonological study of *Fang-yen.*]

董俊彥：方言音證

0394 Wang, Pu-chou: *Fang-yen* sheng-lei k'ao hsü li.—*HNTH* 1:2, 1934, 1–22. [Examples of the initial groups in *Fang-yen.*]

王步洲：『方言』聲類考叙例

0395 Yang, Hsiung (53 *B.C.–A.D.* 18): *Yu-hsüan shih-che chüeh-tai yü shih pieh-kuo fang-yen.*—Shanghai: Shang-wu, 1937, 13 chüan, 2 vols., ix, ii, 326, 4, 2 p., with commentaries by Kuo, P'u and Tai, Chen./ *Ajia rekishi jiten* (0095) 8, 261, Nishida Taiichirō; *Seikai meicho daijiten* (0096) 5, 479–480, Tōdō Akiyasu. [Dialects words and phrases used in different parts of the empire.]/ For a critical ed. and index to *Fang-yen*, see Chou & Wu (0374).

揚雄撰，郭璞注，戴震疏證：輶軒使者絕代語釋別國方言／ 西田太一郎評介；藤堂明保評介

0396 Yang, Shu-ta: Tu *Fang-yen* shu-hou.—*Chi-wei-chü hsiao-hsüeh shu-lin* (Peking: Chung-kuo k'o-hsüeh-yüan, 1954), 271–272. [A postscript to *Fang-yen*.]

楊樹達：讀『方言』書後 ——『積微居小學述林』

0397 Yen, Keng-wang: Yang Hsiung so chi hsien-Ch'in fang-yen ti-li ch'ü.—*HYSY* 17, 1975, 37–56. [The geographical areas for the pre-Ch'in dialects recorded by Yang Hsiung.]

嚴耕望：揚雄所記先秦方言地理區

4.3.3. Shuo-wen chieh-tzu (0398–0401)

0398 Ho, Ko-en: *Shuo-wen* li so chien te fang-yen.—*LNHP* 3:2, 1943, 110–136. [The dialects as found in *Shuo-wen*.]

何格恩：『說文』裏所見的方言

0399 Kuo, Yü-ts'ai: *Shuo-wen* fang-yen i-lu hou-chi.—*HNPK* 4, 1936, 1–10; 5, 1936, 1–7; 7–8, 1937, 1–8. [An afterword on the collation of dialect words found in *Shuo-wen*.]

郭豫才：『說文』方言逸錄後記

0400 Li, Tao-chung: Hsü shih *Shuo-wen* so ch'eng pieh-kuo shu-yü yü Yang shih *Fang-yen* i t'ung t'iao cheng.—*WLHP* 2:2, 1936, 1–32. [Notes on similarities and dissimilarities of dialect words in Hsü's *Shuo-wen* and Yang's *Fang-yen*.]

李道中：許氏『說文』所稱別國殊語與揚氏『方言』異同條證

0401 Ma, Tsung-huo: *Shuo-wen chieh-tzu yin Fang-yen k'ao.*—Peking: K'o-hsüeh, 1959, 2, 2, 45 d. p. [A research on the citing of dialect words in *Shuo-wen chieh-tzu.*]

馬宗霍：說文解字引方言考

4.4. Wei, Chin, and Six Dynasties Period (0402–0412)

0402 Ch'en, Yin-k'o: Tung Chin nan-ch'ao chih Wu-yü.—*BIHP* 7:1, 1936, 1–4. [The Wu dialect during the Southern dynasty of the Eastern Chin (ca. A.D. 317–589).]

陳寅恪：東晉南朝之吳語

0403 Chou, Tsu-mo: Lun *Wen-hsüan yin* ts'an-chüan chih tso-che chi ch'i fang-yin.—*FJHC* 8:1, 1939, 113–126; E.S.; *Wen-hsüeh chi* (0101), 177–191; 6 pl. [The authorship of the *Wen-hsüan yin* and his dialect pronunciations.]

周祖謨：論『文選音』殘卷之作者及其方音

0404 Chu, Fang-p'u: Chin-tai fang-yen k'ao.—*TFTC* 28:3, 1931, 63–74. [A study on the dialects of the Chin dynasty.]

朱芳圃：晉代方言考

0405 Juhl, Robert A.: *A survey of the rhyming of poets from the Wei dynasty into the early T'ang.*—Madison: U. of Wisconsin, 1972, v, 139 p.; appendices, var. pag./ Unpubl. doc. diss., *DAI* 33:7, 1973, 3619A; UM 72–23,745. Chap. VI. Rhyming and dialects in Liu Ch'ao times; maps.

0406 Juhl, Robert A.: Phonological evolution of the Chinese rhymes: Wei to Liang.—*JAOS* 94, 1974, 408–430.

0407 Juhl, Robert A.: The literary dialect of Xie Zhuang.—*JCL* 3:2–3, 1975, 129–153.

〔謝莊〕

0408 Juhl, Robert A.: The literary dialect of Tao Qian.—*JCL* 4:1, 1976, 83–107.

〔陶潛〕

0409   Juhl, Robert A.: The literary dialect of Liang Yuan Di.—*JCL* 5:1, 1977, 26–58.
〔 梁元帝 〕

0410   Lo, Ch'ang-p'ei & Chou, Tsu-mo: *Han Wei Chin Nan-Pei-ch'ao yün-pu yen-pien yen-chiu.* (Ti-i fen-ts'e).—Peking: K'o-hsüeh, 1958, iv, 322 p./ Chap. VI & VII. Dialects of the Han dynasty; *RBS* 4, 1958, 542, N.G.D. Malmqvist; *MS* 22, 1961, 394–412, Paul L.-M. Serruys. [An investigation of the rhyme categories in the poetry and rhyme prose of the Han, Wei, Chin and the Northern and Southern dynasties. Pt. I.]
羅常培，周祖謨： 漢魏晉南北朝韻部演變研究（第一分冊）

0411   Mather, Richard B.: A note on the dialects of Lo-yang and Nanking during the Six Dynasties.—*Wen-lin: Studies in the Chinese humanities* (Ed. by Chow, Tse-tsung, Madison: U. of Wisconsin Press, 1968), 247–256.

0412   Ting, Pang-hsin: *Chinese phonology of the Wei-Chin period: Reconstruction of the finals as reflected in poetry.*—Taipei: Academia Sinica, 1975, iii, 296 p./ 261–268: The Wei-Chin dialects.
〔 丁邦新：魏晉音韻研究 〕

4.5.   Sui and T'ang Period (0413–0432)

0413   Arisaka, Hideyo: Zuidai Shina hōgen. —*Hōgen* 6:1, 1936, 29–45.; *Kokugo on'inshi no kenkyū* (0097), 285–302. [Chinese dialects during the Sui dynasty.]
有坂秀世：隋代の支那方言

0414   Arlotto, Anthony: Velars in T'ang standard.—*MS* 26, 1967, 224–236.

0415   Chang, Lu: Chung-ku fang-yin ch'a-pieh wen-t'i.—*CKYW* 1957:10, Back cover. [The problem of phonetic differences in the dialects of Ancient Chinese.]
章璐：中古方音差別問題

0416   Chou, Fa-kao: *Yen-shih chia-hsün hui chu.*—Taipei: Academia Sinica, 1960, 4 ts'e; Supplementary notes.—*BIHPEV* 4,

1961, 857–897. [Collected commentaries on *Yen-shih chia-hsün.*]
周法高：顏氏家訓彙注

0417   Chou, Tsu-mo: *Yen-shih chia-hsün* yin-tz'u p'ien chu-pu.—*FJHC* 12:1–2, 1943, 201–220; *Wen-hsüeh chi* (0101), 2, 405–433. [Addenda to the commentaries on Chap. XVIII (On phonology) of *Yen-shih chia-hsün.*]
周祖謨：『 顏氏家訓 』音辭篇注補

0418   Chou, Tsu-mo: Kuan-yü T'ang-tai fang-yen chung szu-sheng tu-fa te i-hsieh tzu-liao.—*YLT* 2, 1958, 11–16. [Some linguistic materials concerning the reading of four tones during the Tang dynasty.]
周祖謨： 關於唐代方言中四聲讀法的一些資料

0419   Csongor, B.: A note on T'ang dialects. —*MS* 26, 1967, 286–294.

0420   Fukunaga, Seiya: Tōdai Chōan'on saikōsei no kiso.—*KTJDK* 9, 1954, 1–32. [The basis for the reconstruction of the phonological system of the Ch'angan dialect during the T'ang dynasty.]
福永靜哉：唐代長安音再構成の基礎

0421   Kōno, Rokurō: Tōdai Chōan'on ni okeru bi-bo ni tsuite.—*CBKK* 4:1, 1954, 29–39. [The initial *wei* in the pronunciation of the Ch'angan dialect in T'ang times.]
河野六郎： 唐代長安音における『 微 』母について

0422   Kōsaka, Jun'ichi: Tō Sō zokugo to Kanan hōgen.—*CGKK* 1951:5, 3–5. [The colloquial of the T'ang and Sung periods and the dialects of Southern China.]
香坂順一：唐宋俗語と華南方言

0423   Liang, Chen-shih: Ch'ieh-yün hsi-t'ung yü hsien-tai Han-yü fang-yen.—*Kuang-hsi shih-yüan hsüeh-pao* 1959:3, 89–115. [The phonetic system of Ch'ieh-yün and modern Chinese dialects.]
梁振仕：『 切韵 』系統與現代漢語方言

0424 Lo, Ch'ang-p'ei: *Ch'ieh-yün* yü yü chih yin-chih chi ch'i so-chü fang-yin k'ao.—*BIHP* 2, 1931, 258–385. [The value of the *Ch'ieh-yün* rhymes *yü* and *yü* and the ancient dialects in which their distinction was based.]

羅常培：『切韻』『魚』『虞』之音值及其所據方音考

0425 Lo, Ch'ang-p'ei: *T'ang Wu-tai hsi-pei fang-yin.*—Shanghai: Academia Sinica, 1933, xxiii, 8, 223 p.; *Seikai meicho daijiten* (0096) 4, 426–427, Matsumoto Akira. [The Northwestern dialects of the T'ang and Five Dynasties.]

羅常培：唐五代西北方音／松本昭評介

0426 Maspero, Henri: Sur quelques textes anciens de chinois parlé.—*BEFEO* 14:4, 1914, 1–36.

0427 Maspero, Henri: Le dialecte de Tch'ang-ngan sous les T'ang.—*BEFEO* 20:2, 1920, 1–124./ *Seikai meicho daijiten* (0096) 4, 439–440, Hashimoto Mantarō.

橋本萬太郎評介

0428 Ōshima, Shōji: Tōdai nanpō hōon no ichi yōsō—Ri Zen *Monsen* onchū ni han'eiseru Kōto jion ni tsuite.—*HDBK* 26:1, 1977, 29–185. [An aspect of southern pronunciation during the T'ang dynasty—On the Chiangtu pronunciation reflected in Li Shan's phonetic annotation on *Wen Hsüan*.]

大島正二：唐代南方方音の一様相——李善『文選』音注に反映せる江都字音について

0429 Pulleyblank, E.G.: The rhyming categories of Li Ho.—*CHHP* 7:1, 1968, 1–25.

0430 Rai, Tsutomu: Chūko Kango to gendai hōgen.—*Chūgoku gogaku jiten* (0093), 149–161. [Ancient Chinese and modern dialects.]／ Modern dialect phonology compared with Sino-Xenic transcriptions.

賴惟勤：中古漢語と現代方言

0431 Shao, Jung-fen: Tun-huang su wen-hsüeh chung te pieh-tzu i-wen ho T'ang Wu-tai hsi-pei fang-yin.—*CKYW* 1963:3, 193–217./ *RBS* 9, 1963, 490, S.N. Cartier. [The variant and different characters found in the popular literature of Tun-huang and their relationship to the northwestern dialects of the T'ang dynasty.]

邵榮芬：敦煌俗文學中的別字異文和唐五代西北方音

0432 Yen, Chih-t'ui (A.D. 531–591). Transl. by Teng, Ssu-yü *Family instructions for the Yen clan: Yen-shih chia-hsün.*—Leiden: E.J. Brill, 1968, xxxiv, 245 p./ An annotated translation with introduction; Chap. XVIII. On phonology.

〔顏之推著，鄧嗣禹譯：顏氏家訓〕

4.6. Sung Period (0433–0439)

0433 Chang, Yung-mien: Kuan-yü Sung Yüan hua-pen su-yü fang-yen te cheng-li.—*CKYW* 1957:12, back cover. [Concerning the collection and compilation of popular and dialect words found in the Hua-pen of the Sung and Yüan dynasties.]

張永綿：關於宋元話本俗語方言的整理

0434 Chou, Tsu-mo: Sung-tai Pien Lo yü-yin k'ao.—*FJHC* 12:1–2, 1943, 221–285; E.S.; *Han-yü yin-yün lun-wen chi* (0100), 189–235; *Wen-hsüeh chi* (0101), 581–655. [The dialect of K'aifeng and Loyang during the Sung dynasty.]

周祖謨：宋代汴洛語音考

0435 Chou, Tsu-mo: Sung-tai fang-yin.—*Wen-hsüeh chi* (0101), 656–662; *Wen shih* 4, 1965. 107–110./ *RBS* 11, 1965, 400, K. Kaden. [Dialect sounds during the Sung dynasty.]

周祖謨：宋代方音

0436 Hung, Hui-ch'ou: Ming-tai i-ch'ien chih Chung-kuo fang-yen k'ao-lüeh.—*Hsüeh-feng* 6:2, 1936, 1–10. [A study on the pre-Ming dynasty dialects of China.]

洪惠疇：明代以前之中國方言考略

0437 Kallgren, Gerty: Study in Sung time colloquial as revealed in Chu Hi's *Ts'üan-shu.*—*BMFEA* 30, 1958, 1–167./ *RBS* 4, 1958, 577, W. Simon.

0438 Maspero, Henri: Le dialecte de Tch'ang-ngan sous les T'ang (0427)./ Includes studies on the phonology of 9th-century Chinese.

0439 Sakai, Ken'ichi: Sōdai on'in kenkyū josetsu.—*CBKK* 4:2, 1955, 36–51./ *RBS* 1, 1955, 272, C. Y. Wu. [An introductory study of Chinese phonology during the Sung dynasty.]

坂井健一：宋代音韻研究序說

4.7. Yüan, Ming, and Ch'ing Period (0440–0450)

0440 Ai, Ch'iang: *Shui-hu* tso-che tui-yü fang-yen t'u-yü te yün-yung.—*Wen-hsüeh ch'uang-tso* 1:1, 1942, 62. [The utilization of dialect and patois by the author of *Shui-hu chuan.*]

艾羌：『水滸』作者對於方言土語的運用

0441 Chang, Wei-ching: *Shui-hu* li chi-ko fang-yen-tz'u te i-i.—*CKYW* 1958:10, 500. [The meaning of several dialect words found in *Shui-hu chuan.*]

張衛經：『水滸』裏幾個方言詞的意義

0442 Chu, Chü-i: *Yüan-chü su-yü fang-yen li-shih.*—Shanghai: Shang-wu, 1956, 368 p./ *RBS* 2, 1956, 380, M.A.K. Halliday; *Orbis* 15, 1966, 98, Paul Yang. [Common phrases and dialect words from Yüan dramas annotated.]

朱居易：元劇俗語方言例釋

0443 Hattori, Shirō: The Chinese dialect on which the transcription of the *Yüan-ch'ao mi-shih* was based.—*AAs* 24, 1973, 35–44.

0444 Hsü, Chia-jui: *Chin Yüan hsi-ch'ü fang-yen k'ao.*—Peking: Shang-wu, 1956, xvii, 53, 34 p./ *RBS* 2, 1956, 379, M.A.K. Halliday; *CKYW* 1960:5, 244–247, P'an Keng. [A study of dialects in Chin and Yüan dramas.]

徐嘉瑞：金元戲曲方言考／潘庚評

0445 Huang, Li-chen: *Chin Yüan pei-ch'ü yü-hui chih yen-chiu.*—Taipei: Shang-wu, 1968, 2, 1, 1, 2, 200, 17 p. [A study of the vocabulary of the northern dramas during the Chin and Yüan dynasties.]/ Chap. I. Dialects and popular words.

黃麗貞：金元北曲語彙之研究

0446 Iriya, Yoshitaka: *T'ung-su p'ien, Chih-yü pu-cheng, Heng-yen lu, Fang-yen tsao, Erh-yen sōgō sakuin.*—Kyoto: Kyōto Daigaku Chūgoku Gobungaku Kenkyūshitsu, 1950, 91 p./ Mimeogr. [Combined index to *T'ung-su p'ien, Chih-yü pu-cheng, Heng-yen lu, Fang-yen tsao* and *Erh-yen.*]

入矢義高：通俗篇，直語補正，恒言錄，方言藻，邇言綜合索引

0447 Ōta, Tatsuo: *Jijo eiyū ten no gengo.*—*NCGH* 26, 1974, 141–156. [Language of *Erh-nü ying-hsiung chuan.*]/ 2. Dialect; 3. Peking dialect.

太田辰夫：『兒女英雄傳』の言語

0448 Sakai, Ken'ichi: *Monkishū* kakuchi kyōon ni tsuite—Gendai hōon kenkyū shiryō to-shite.—*KGK* 10, 1973, 33–60. [On the provincial pronunciations of various regions of *Wen-ch'i chi*—as materials for the study of modern dialects.]

坂井健一：『問奇集』各地鄉音について――現代方音研究資料として

0449 Stimson, Hugh M.: Old Mandarin dialects, Old Pekingese, and the rhymes of the *Zhōngyuán Yīnyùn.*—*Proceedings of Symposium on Chinese Linguistics* (Ed. by Robert L. Cheng et al., Taipei: Student Book Co., 1978), 221–232.

0450 Ting, Pang-hsin: *Wen-ch'i chi so-chi chih Ming-tai fang-yin.*—*Chung-yang yen-chiu yüan ch'eng-li wu-shih chou-nien chi-nien lun-wen chi* (Taipei: Academia Sinica, 1978), 577–592. [Dialect pronunciations during the Ming dynasty as recorded in *Wen-ch'i chi.*]

丁邦新：『問奇集』所記之明代方音――『中央研究院成立五十周年紀念論文集』

4.8. Dialects in Local Gazetteers and Literary Works (0451–0456)

0451 Fu, Ch'ao-yang: Fang-yen tz'u li shih. —*YWHH* 1954:7, 50–57; 8, 67–71; 9, 70–75; 11, 43–48; 1955:1, 40–47; 4, 41–46. [Dialect words explained.]/ Taken from modern literary works.

傅朝陽：方言詞例釋

0452 Fu, Ch'ao-yang: *Fang-yen-tz'u li-shih.* —Peking: T'ung-su tu-wu, 1957, 348 p./ *CKYW* 1957:11, 47–48, Hui; Mao Hsi-p'ang; I Ting; *RBS* 3, 1957, 597, M. Prjadochin. [Dialect words explained.]

傅朝陽：方言詞例釋 / 灰，毛西旁，一丁評

0453 Hatano, Tarō: *Chūgoku shōsetsu gikyoku shii kenkyū jiten, Sōgō sakuin hen.* —Yokohama: Yokohama Shiritsu Daigaku, 1956–1963, 7 vols.; I. *Hatsuon sakuin* [phonetic index], 1956, 8, 80 p.; *Hitsuga sakuin* [stroke index], 1956, 8, 91 p.; II. *Hatsuon sakuin*, 1957, 3, 107 p.; *Hitsuga sakuin*, 1958, 3, 151 p.; III. *Hatsuon hitsuga sakuin*, 1958, 3, 121 p.; IV. *Hatsuon hitsuga sakuin*, 1959, 7, 129 p.; V. *Hatsuon hitsuga sakuin*, 1960, 3, 160 p.; VI. *Hatsuon sakuin*, 1961, 15, 145 p.; VII. *Hatsuon sakuin*, 1963, 11, 100 p./ *Yokohama Shiritsu Daigaku Kiyō*, Series A. 9, 10, 14, 16, 20, 23, 25, 27. / *RBS* 2, 1956, 378, G. Weys; 6, 1960, 406, A. Lévy. [A combined index to seven lexical works on Chinese fiction and drama composed during the Tokugawa period (1603–1867).] / Phonetic and stroke indexes.

波多野太郎：中國小說戲曲詞彙研究辭典，綜合索引篇，發音索引，筆劃索引 ——『橫濱市大學紀要』

0454 Hatano, Tarō (comp.): *Chung-kuo fang-chih so-lu fang-yen hui-pien* (Jap. *Chūgoku hōshi shoroku hōgen kaihen*). —Yokohama: Yokohama Shiritsu Daigaku, 1963–1972, 9 vols.; 1, 1963, 218, 140 p.; 2, 1964, viii, 353, 89 p.; 3, 1965, xvi, 405, 39 p.; 4, 1966, xix, 500, 74 p.; 5, 1967, xix, 569, 77 p.; 6, 1968, xxviii,

390, 98 p.; 7, 1969, xv, 429, 90 p.; 8, 1970, xvii, 4, 404, 103 p.; 9, 1972, xv, 7, 264, 75, 14, 31 p./ *RBS* 11, 1965, 437, M. Cartier; *Orbis* 15, 1966, 97, Paul Yang. [Collection of dialects as recorded in some Chinese local gazetteers.]

波多野太郎：中國方志所錄方言滙編

0455 Lu, Tan-an: *Hsiao-shuo tz'u-yü hui shih.*—Peking: Chung-hua, 1964, clxxii, 916 p./ *Orbis* 15, 1966, 98–99, Paul Yang. [Vocabulary of Chinese novels, collected and annotated.] / Including dialect words.

陸澹安：小說詞語滙釋

0456 Shih, Wen-t'ao: Lüeh-lun ti-fang chih li fang-yen tzu-liao te tso-yung wen-t'i.—*Chiang-hai hsüeh-k'an* 1963:4, 43–49. [A short discussion on the problems concerning the functions of dialects recorded in local gazetteers.]

施文濤： 略論地方志裏方言資料的作用問題

4.9. Hsin fang-yen (0457–0462)

0457 Chang, Ping-lin: *Hsin fang-yen.* (Fu *Ling wai san-chou yü*).—Ed. by the Che-chiang t'u-shu-kuan (Chekiang Library), 11 chüan./ Chang-shih ts'ung shu. [New dialects. With appendix: *Ling-wai san-chou yü.*]

章炳麟：新方言（附嶺外三州語）——「章氏叢書之一」

0458 Ch'en, Ch'i-t'ung: *Kuang Hsin fang-yen.*—Peiping, 1928, 2 chüan; Nagoya: Tenzan shuppansha, 1976, repr., 110 p. [Expanded additions to the *Hsin fang-yen* (0457).]

陳啓彤：廣新方言

0459 Fang, Yung: Hsü *Hsin fang-yen.*—*An-hui ta-hsüeh yüeh-k'an.*—1:3, 1933, 1–10; 1:4, 1933, 1–12. [Addenda to the *Hsin fang-yen* (0457).]

方勇：續『新方言』

0460 Kao, Ching-ch'eng: *Hsin fang-yen* pu (chiu tse).—*KHYK* (Peking) 1:2, 1945, 7–9. [Addenda (9 items) to the *Hsin fang-yen.*]

高景成：『新方言』補（九則）

0461 T'ung, Chen-hua: Tu *Hsin fang-yen* cha-chi (Chang T'ai-yen).—*Yü-wen* 1:2, 1937, 8–9. [Notes on reading Chang's *Hsin fang-yen.*]

童振華：讀『新方言』箚記（章太炎）

0462 Wang, Lun: Hsin fang-yen tsa-chi.—*Kuo-feng* 3:5, 1933, 5–14; *Chih-yen* 3, 1935, 1–16; 4, 1935, 1–22; *Kuo-hsüeh lun-heng* 5–A, 1935, 12–24. [Miscellanea on new dialects.]

王綸：新方言雜記

5. MODERN DIALECTS IN GENERAL (0463–0554)

5.1. Languages and Dialects of China (0463–0481)

0463 Chao, Yuen Ren: Languages and dialects in China.—*Geographical Journal* 102, 1943, 63–66; *Aspects of Chinese sociolinguistics* (0098), 21–25; 1 map.

0464 Chou, Fa-kao: Chung-kuo ching-nei te yü-yen.—*Min-chu p'ing-lun* 6:15, 1955, 2–6; *Chung-kuo yü-wen yen-chiu* (0099), 13–27. [Languages within the borders of China.]
周法高：中國境內的語言

0465 Chou, Yu-kuang: Chung-kuo Han-yü fang-yen te fen-pu.—*Hsin wen-tzu pan-yüeh-k'an* 71, 1951, 3–4. [The geographical distribution of Chinese dialects in China.]
周有光：中國漢語方言的分布

0466 Gotō, Asatarō: *Butsu-In Tai Shina gengo no kōryū.*—Tokyo: Daitō Shuppansha, 1942, 3, 4, 330 p./ Chap. II. Chinese language and dialects. [The linguistic interchange between Indo-China, Thai, and China.]
後藤朝太郎：佛印・泰・支那言語の交流

0467 Grootaers, W.A. & Ogawa, Tamaki: Chūgokugo no hōgen.—*Chūgoku gogaku jiten* (0093), 64–73. [Chinese dialects.]
Grootaers, 小川環樹：中國語の方言

0468 Iachontov, S.E.: Geograficheskoe rasprostranenie dialektov kitaiskogo iazyka.—*VLU* 1967:1, 76–83. [The geographical extension of Chinese dialects.]

0469 Kratochvíl, Paul: *The Chinese language today.*—London: Hutchinson U. Library, 1968, 199 p., map./ 13–19: Affiliation and dialects of Chinese; *Lg* 45, 1969, 423–439, Sandra A. Thompson.

0470 Li, Fang-kuei: Languages and dialects of China.—*The Chinese yearbook* (Shanghai: Commercial Press) 1937, 59–65; 1938–1939, 43–51; 1944–1945 (Shanghai: The China Daily Tribune Publishing Co., 1946), 129–137; also Seattle: U. of Washington, mimeogr. of a rev. version of 1941; *Free China Review* 22:5, 1972, 26–31; *JCL* 1:1, 1973, 1–13, a rev. version./ *JCL* 1, 1973, 471–474, James A. Matisoff.

0471 Li, Fang-kuei. Transl. by Ogawa, Tamaki: Chūgoku ni okeru shominzoku no gengo to hōgen.—*Shinagaku* 11:4, 1946, 48–66; *Chūgokugogaku kenkyū* (0108), 275–295 (a new translation). [Languages and dialects of China.] (0470)
李方桂著，小川環樹譯：中國に於ける諸民族の言語と方言

0472 Ogaeri, Yoshio: *Tairiku no gengo to bungaku.*—Tokyo: Sanseidō, 1940, 2, 9, 260 p.; photos, portr. [The language and literature of the China mainland.]/ Translations and essays.
魚返善雄：大陸の言語と文學

0473 Ogaeri, Yoshio: Shinago.—*Seikai gengo gaisetsu* (Ed. by Ichikawa, Sanki, et al.—Tokyo: Kenkyūsha, 1952–1955), Vol. II, 778–832./ 819–824: Chinese dialects. [The Chinese language.]
魚返善雄：シナ語——市河三喜，服部四郎，高津春繁監修：『世界言語概說』下卷

0474 Osada, Natsuki: Chūgoku shominzoku no gengo.—*KGR* 10:2, 1959, 41–79./ 57–61: Chinese dialects. [Languages of the nationalities in China—A historical and linguistico-geographical study.]
長田夏樹：中國諸民族の言語

0475 T'ien, Ju-k'ang: *The Chinese of Sarawak: A study of social culture.*—London: The London School of Economics and Political Science, 1953, 2nd print., 88 p.; 11–15: Dialect groups of Kwangtung and Fukien, map./ Monograph on Social Anthropology, 12.

0476 Tung, T'ung-ho: *Languages of China.* —Taipei: China Culture Publishing Foundation, 1953, 14 p.; 1 map.

0477 Tung, T'ung-ho: Chung-kuo yü-yen.— *Chung-kuo wen-hua lun chi* (1) (Taipei: Chung-hua wen-hua, 1954), 83–103; *Tung T'ung-ho . . . hsüan chi* (0110), 353–365. [Languages of China.]
董同龢：中國語言——『中國文化論集 （一）』

0478 U.S. Office of Strategic Services: *Notes on main dialects of southeast China.*— Washington, D.C.: U.S. Office of Strategic Services, 1944, 4 leaves, fold map./ R & A No. 2478.

0479 Voegelin, C.F. & Voegelin, F.M. (ed.): Languages of the world: Sino-Tibetan.— *AL* 6:3, 1964; 7:3–6, 1965./ 7:4, 1965, 19–77: Chinese dialects.

0480 Wang, Li: *Han-yü chiang-hua.*—Shanghai: Wen-hua chiao-yü, 1955, 76 p./ 12–17: Dialects: classification, etc. [Lectures on the Chinese language.]
王力：漢語講話

0481 Wang, Yü-te: Chūgoku no hōgen.— *Gengo* (0111), 407–446. [Dialects of China.]
王育德：中國の方言

5.2. Classification of Chinese Dialects (0482–0486)

0482 Chung, Ching-wen & Mao, K'un: Kuan-yü Chung-kuo fang-yen chih fen-lei te t'ao-lun.—*KHMC* 1:6, 1925, 21–23. [A discussion on the classification of Chinese dialects.]
鍾敬文，毛坤：關於中國方言之分類的 討論

0483 Huang, Chia-chiao; Chan, Po-hui & Ch'en, Shih-min: Yu-kuan Han-yü fang-yen fen-ch'ü te i-hsieh wen-ti.—*HMTH* 1963:4, 117–128. [Some problems concerning the areal classification of Chinese dialects.]
黃家教，詹伯慧，陳世民：有關漢語方 言分區的一些問題

0484 Iachontov, S.E.: Klassifikatsiia dialektov kitaiskogo iazyka.—*Issledovaniia po filologii stran Azii i Afriki* (Leningrad: Izdatel'stvo Leningradskogo U., 1966), 121–128. [Classification of Chinese dialects.]

0485 Möllendorff, Paul Georg von: *Classification des dialectes Chinois.*—Ningpo: Imprimerie de la Mission Catholique, 1899, 34 p./ Imprimé pour l'Exposition Universelle de Paris 1900 par ordre de l'inspecteur-général des douanes.

0486 Serdiuchenko, G.P.: K voprosu o klassifikatsii narodov i iazykov kitaiia.— *Sovetskoe Vostokovedenie* 4, 1957, 117–124. [On the classification of peoples and languages of China.]

5.3. History of Chinese Dialects (0487–0493)

0487 Chang, Kun: Tonal developments among Chinese dialects.—*BIHP* 46, 1975, 636–709.

0488 Chao, Yuen Ren: *Mandarin primer.*— Cambridge, Mass.: Harvard U. Press, 1948, viii, 335 p./ 5–8: Growth of modern dialects; *Lg* 25, 1949, 210–215, Charles F. Hockett.

0489 Kennedy, George A.: Dialect development.—*Synoptica, Wennti* 1, 1952 (July); *Selected works of George A. Kennedy* (Ed. by Li, Tien-yi; New Haven: Far Eastern Publications, 1964), 151–174./ Compares Archaic Chinese, Ancient Chinese, Wu, Cantonese, and Mandarin dialects.

0490 Lin, Yü-t'ang: Min Yüeh fang-yen chih lai-yüan.—*Kung-hsien* 9, 1928, 7–14; *CSTY* 8:85–87, 1929, 3–10, *Yü-yenhsüeh lun-ts'ung* (0105), 200–212. [The origin of the Min and Yüeh dialects.]
林語堂：閩粵方言之來源

0491 Wang, Yü-te: Chūgoku godai hōgen no bunretsu nendai no gengo-nendaigakuteki shitan.—*GK* 38, 1960, 33–105; 103–105: E.S. [A lexico-statistic estimation of the time-depths of the five main Chinese dialects.]/ Peking, Soochow, Cantonese, Hakka, Amoy; *RBS* 6, 1960, 383, Li Fang-kuei.
王育德：中國五大方言の分裂年代の言語年代學的試探

0492 Yang, Hsi-ling: Wo-kuo fang-yin chih fen-ch'i hsien-hsiang chi ch'i ch'eng-yin.—*Jen-wen hsüeh-pao* 1, 1970, 153–165. [The phenomenon of Chinese dialect diversity and its causes.]
楊喜齡：我國方音之紛歧現象及其成因

0493 Yüan, Chia-hua: Han-yü fang-yen fa-chan te li-shih niao-k'an.—*Han-yü fang-yen kai-yao* (0146), Chap. III. [A bird's-eye view of the development of Chinese dialects.]
袁家驊：漢語方言發展的歷史鳥瞰

5.4. Sociocultural Aspects of Chinese Dialects (0494–0506)

0494 Chao, Yüan-jen: Fan-ch'ieh yü pa chung.—*BIHP* 2:3, 1931, 312–354. [Eight varieties of language based on the principle of *fan-ch'ieh*.]/ Peiping, Changchow, Kunshan, Soochow, Canton, Foochow.
趙元任：反切語八種

0495 Chao, Yuen Ren: Interlingual and interdialectal borrowings in Chinese.—*Studies in general and Oriental linguistics: Presented to Shirō Hattori on the occasion of his sixtieth birthday* (Ed. by Jakobson, Roman & Kawamoto, Shigeo; Tokyo: TEC Company, 1970), 39–51; *Aspects of Chinese sociolinguistics* (0098), 184–200.
〔趙元任：中外借詞跟中國方言之間的借詞〕

0496 Ch'en, Yüan-t'an: Yeh t'an Kuo-yü yü fang-yen.—*Chung-hua tsa-chih* 126, 1974, 48–52. [Additional remarks on the National Language and dialects.]
陳原譚：也談國語與方言

0497 Cheng, Susie S.: Chinese dialect literature.—*JCLTA* 12, 63–75./ Cantonese, Hakka, N. Min, S. Min, Swatow, Wu.

0498 Fang, Ch'ing: Ts'ung hsien-tai Han-yü fang-yen te wen-pai i-tu ho hsin-lao i-tu k'an P'u-t'ung-hua tui fang-yen te ying-hsiang.—*WTKK* 1963:8, 4–5. [The influences of the Common Language upon modern Chinese dialects as seen from the differences in pronunciations between the literary and colloquial readings and between the younger and older speakers.]
方青：從現代漢語方言的文白異讀和新老異讀看普通話對方言的影響

0499 Fang, Ch'ing: Ku-jen t'an fang-yen yü P'u-t'ung-hua te chi-ko li-tzu.—*WTKK* 1963:9, 8–9. [Some examples of discussions on dialects and the Common Language by ancient scholars.]
方青：古人談方言與普通話的幾個例子

0500 Li, Charles N. & Thompson, Sandra A.: Chinese dialect variation and language reform.—*Languages and their status* (Ed. by Shopen, Timothy; Cambridge, Mass.: Winthrop Publishers, 1979), 295–335.

0501 Li, Ch'en-tung: Lun fang-yen yü wen-hsüeh te kuan-hsi.—*CKYWT* 6:6, 1960, 7–15. [On the relationship between dialects and literature.]
李辰冬：論方言與文學的關係

0502 Ōuchida, Saburō: Futsūwa no hōgen kyoyō ni tsuite.—*CBKK* 14, 1973, 9–15. [On the sanctioned dialect words in the Common Language.]
大內田三郎：普通話の方言許容について

0503 Sung, Margaret M.Y.: Chinese language and culture: A study of homonyms, lucky word and taboos.—*JCL* 7, 1979, 15–28; C.S./ Examples mainly taken from the Taiwanese dialect.
〔嚴棉：漢語語言與文化：同音詞，吉利話與禁忌之研究〕

0504 T'ien, Chung-chi: Kuan-yü fang-yen wen-hsüeh.—*Hsin Chung-hua* 12:15, 1949, 24–26. [Concerning dialect literature.]

田仲濟：關於方言文學

0505 Wang, Liao-i: Man-t'an fang-yen wen-hsüeh.—*Kuan-ch'a* 5:11, 1948, 14–15. [A casual discussion on dialect literature.]

王了一：漫談方言文學

0506 Wang, Peter Chin-tang: A note on dialectal tolerance and non-standard features.—*JCLTA* 6, 1971, 103–113.

5.5. General Studies on Chinese Dialects (0507–0554)

5.5.1. General (0507–0513)

0507 Egerod, Søren: Dialectology (0121).

0508 Forrest, R.A.D.: *The Chinese language.*—London: Faber and Faber, 1948, 352 p.; 1965, 2nd rev. ed., 372 p./ maps./ Chap. X-XI. Modern dialects; *YCHP* 36, 1949, 317–325, Yü Min; *AOH* 4, 1955, 297–301, B. Csongor; *TP* 40:1–2, 1959, 207–210, Willem A. Grootaers; *BSOAS* 30, 1967, 473, G.B. Downer.

俞敏評

0509 Hashimoto, Mantarō J.: Language diffusion on the Asian continent: problems of typological diversity in Sino-Tibetan.—*CAAAL* 3, 1976, 49–65./ Typological characteristics of modern Chinese dialects and other Sino-Tibetan languages.

0510 Ho, Chung-ying: Chung-kuo fang-yen-hsüeh kai-lun (0127). [Introduction to Chinese dialectology.]

何仲英：中國方言學概論

0511 Ho, Chung-ying: *Hsün-ku-hsüeh yin-lun.*—Shanghai: Shang-wu, 1934, 2, 108 p./ 77–108: Modern dialects. [Introduction to Chinese semasiology.]

何仲英：訓詁學引論

0512 Yüan, Chia-hua et al: *Han-yü fang-yen kai-yao* (0146). [Outline of Chinese dialects.]

袁家驊等：漢語方言概要

0513 Yüan, Chia-hua: *Dialekty kitaiskogo iazyka.*—Moscow: Nauka, 1965, 54 p. [Dialects of the Chinese language.]/ A summary of (0146).

5.5.2. Multidialectal Dictionaries (0514–0525)

0514 Chou, Fa-kao et al.: *Han-tzu ku-chin yin-hui.*—Hong Kong: The Chinese University of Hong Kong, 1973, xxi, 433, 47 p./ *JCL* 6:2, 1978, 330–335, William C. Lin. [A pronouncing dictionary of Chinese characters in Archaic and Ancient Chinese, Mandarin, and Cantonese.]

周法高等：漢字古今音彙

0515 Chung-kuo wen-tzu kai-ko yen-chiu wei-yüan-hui mi-shu ch'u p'in-yin fang-an kung-tso tsu: *Ch'üan-kuo chu-yao fang-yen-ch'ü fang-yin tui-chao piao.*—Peking: Chung-hua, 1954, 124 p. [A chart showing the corresponding dialect pronunciations of the important dialect regions in China.]

中國文字改革研究委員會 秘書處拼音方案工作組：全國主要方言區方音對照表

0516 Giles, Herbert Allen: *A Chinese-English dictionary.*—Shanghai: Kelly & Walsh; London: Bernard Quaritch, 3 vols., xlvi, 1415 p.; Shanghai: Kelly & Walsh, 1909–1912, rev. & enl. ed., 3 vols., xviii, 1711, 84 p.; New York: Paragon Book Gallery, 1964, repr., 2 vols.; Taipei: Ch'eng-wen, 1967, repr., xviii, 84, 1711 p./ Dialect pronunciations are given in Cantonese, Hakka, Foochow, Wenchow, Ningpo, Peking, Hankow, Yangchow, Szechwan, Korean, Japanese, Vietnamese by E.H. Parker. For evaluation and criticism, see B. Karlgren's *Études* (0518), 13–19; *Chung-kuo yin-yün-hsüeh yen-chiu* (0519), 13–19.

0517   Hsü, Yün-ch'iao: *Nan-yang Hua-yü li su tz'u-tien.*—Singapore: Shih-chieh, 1961, 2, 138 p. [Dictionary of the idioms used by the overseas Chinese in the South Seas.]/ Cantonese, Hakka, Ch'aochou, Amoy.

許雲樵：南洋華語俚俗辭典

0518   Karlgren, B.: *Études sur la phonologie chinoise.*—Uppsala: K.W. Appelberg and Leiden: E.J. Brill, 1915–1926, 898 p./ Chap. XVIII. Dictionary of 26 dialects.

0519   Karlgren, B. Transl. by Chao, Yüan-jen; Lo, Ch'ang-p'ei & Li, Fang-kuei: *Chung-kuo yin-yün-hsüeh yen-chiu.*—Shanghai: Shang-wu, 1940, xliii, 731 p., 1 map; Taipei: Shang-wu, 1962, repr./ Chap. XVIII. Dialect dictionary; *TSTH* 53, 1942, 12–141, Chou Fa-kao; *YCHP* 30, 1946, 296–299, Lu Chih-wei. [Études sur la phonologie chinoise.] (0518)

高本漢著，趙元任，羅常培，李方桂合譯：中國音韻學研究 / 周法高評，陸志韋評

0520   Lamasse, Henri: *Sin kouo wen, ou nouveau manuel de la langue chinoise écrite, traduit et expliqué en français et romanisé selon les principaux dielectes.* Hong Kong: Nazareth, 1922, 2nd ed., xxi, 607, 250 p. (Appendices, index, etc.)./ Dialect pronunciations: Szechwan, Peking, Tcheli (Hokienfou), Canton, Shanghai, Manchuria.

〔新國文〕

0521   Ni, Hai-shu: *Pei-fang-yin Chiang-nan-yin Kuang-chou-yin tui-chao tzu-hui.*—Shanghai: Tung-fang shu-tien, 1951, 131 p. [Comparative syllabary of northern Mandarin, Wu, and Cantonese.]

倪海曙：北方音江南音廣州音對照字彙

0522   Pei-ching ta-hsüeh Chung-kuo yü-yen wen-hsüeh-hsi Yü-yen-hsüeh chiao-yen shih (comp.): *Han-yü fang-yin tzu-hui.*—Peking: Wen-tzu kai-ko, 1962, xiii, 272 p./ *CKYW* 1963:2, 176–182, Shih Wen-t'ao; *Orbis* 15, 1966, 110, Paul Yang; *Lg* 45, 1969, 687–697, Anatole Lyovin. [Syllabary of dialect pronunciations of Chinese characters.]/17 localities: Peking, Chinan, Sian, T'aiyuan, Hankow, Ch'eng-tu, Yangchow, Soochow, Wenchow, Ch'angsha, Shuangfeng, Nanch'ang, Mei-hsien, Canton, Amoy, Ch'aochou, Foo-chow. The phonology of each locality is given at the beginning of the book.

北京大學中國語言文學系語言學教研室編：漢語方音字滙 / 施文濤評

0523   Pei-ching ta-hsüeh Chung-kuo yü-yen wen-hsüeh-hsi Yü-yen-hsüeh chiao-yen shih (comp.): *Han-yü fang-yen tz'u-hui.*—Peking: Wen-tzu kai-ko, 1964, xxvi, 460 p./ *CKYW* 1965:1, 60–64, Hsü Pao-hua; *TYGH* 48:1, 1965, 144–146, Tōdō Akiyasu; *Orbis* 15, 1966, 110, Paul Yang. [Lexicon of Chinese dialects.]/18 locali-ties: Peking, Chinan, Shenyang, Sian, Ch'engtu, K'unming, Hofei, Yangchow, Soochow, Wenchow, Ch'angsha, Nan-ch'ang, Meihsien, Canton, Yangchiang, Amoy, Ch'aochou, Foochow. The phono-logy of each locality is given at the be-ginning of the book.

北京大學中國語言文學系語言學教研室編：漢語方言詞滙 / 許寶華評，藤堂明保評

0524   Savina, François-Marie: *Guide linguis-tique de l'Indochine française.*—Hong Kong: Nazareth, 1939, 2 vols., xvii, 1198 p.; *Supplement,* 107 p./ Including Canton-ese, Hoklo (S. Min) and Mandarin dia-lects.

0525   Williams, Samuel Wells: *A syllabic dictionary of the Chinese language arrang-ed according to the Wu-fang yüan yin, with the pronunciation of the characters as heard in Peking, Canton, Amoy, and Shanghai.*—Shanghai: American Presby-terian Mission Press, 1874, lxxxiv, 1254 p.; 1903, repr.

〔衛三畏廉士：漢英韻府〕

5.5.3.   Phonetics and Phonology (0526–0543)

0526   Chang, Kun: Phonological aspects of Chinese dialectology.—*CHHP* 9:1–2, 1971, 192–215; C.S.

0527   Chao, Yüan-jen: Fang-yen-hsing pien-t'ai yü-yin san li.—*BIHP* 5, 1935, 24–53. [Three examples of the dialectal nature of speech defects.]
趙元任：方言性變態語音三例

0528   Chao, Yüan-jen: Chung-kuo fang-yen tang-chung pao-fa-yin te chung-lei.—*BIHP* 5, 1935, 515–520. [Types of plosives in Chinese dialects.]/ Ten types.
趙元任：中國方言當中爆發音的種類

0529   Chao, Yuen Ren: The morphemic status of certain Chinese tones.—*TICOJ* 4, 1959, 44–48.

0530   Chen, Matthew Y.: An areal study of nasalization in Chinese.—*JCL* 3:1, 1975, 16–59, 1 map./ Linguistic data are taken from Chinese dialects.

0531   Chung-kuo k'o-hsüeh-yüan Yü-yen yen-chiu so: Han-yü fang-yin te chi-ko wen-t'i.—*FPT* 1, 1958, 149–174. [Some problems concerning Chinese dialect pronunciations.]/ Compares certain initials, finals and tones of main dialect groups.
中國科學院語言研究所：漢語方音的幾個問題

0532   Gotō, Asatarō: Chung-kuo ju-sheng chih ti-li te yen-chiu.—*LNHP* 2:1, 1931, 19–34. [A study of the geographical distribution of the *ju* tone in Chinese.]
後藤朝太郎：中國入聲之地理的研究

0533   Hashimoto, Mantarō: Chūgokugo no tokushoku—On'in to hōgen.—*Gengo* 3:8, 1974, 2–15. [Characteristics of Chinese—phonemes and dialects.]
橋本萬太郎：中國語の特色——音韻と方言

0534   Liao, Chiu-chung: *The propagation of sound change: A case study in Chinese*

dialects.—Berkeley: U. of California, 1976, v, 263 p./ Unpubl. doc. diss.; *DAI* 38:763–764–A; UM 77–15,761.
〔廖秋忠〕

0535   Liu, Ming-shu: Ch'ü-wei te Ch'in Shu Min san ti fang-yin fang-yen.—*Li-shih yü k'ao-ku* 2, 1937, 14–26. [Interesting dialect sounds and dialect vocabulary of the Ch'in (Shensi), Shu (Szechwan) and Min (Fukien) areas.]
劉銘恕：趣味的秦蜀閩三地方音方言

0536   Matsumoto, Kazuo & Wang, Yü-te: Chūgokugo shohōgen no onkei.—*Chugoku gogaku jiten* (0093), 162–172. [Phonetic systems of Chinese dialects.]/ Peking, Soochow, Cantonese, South Min.
松本一男，王育德：中國語諸方言の音系

0537   Nagao, Mitsuyuki: Ikutsuka no Chūgokugo hōgen ni okeru seichō taikei to akusento taikei no mondaiten—nionsetsugo o chūshin ni.—*FDKR* 27:2, 1975, 71–79. [Problems concerning the tones and stresses in certain Chinese dialects—focusing on disyllabic words.]
長尾光之：いくつかの中國語方言における聲調體系とアクセント體系の問題點——二音節語を中心に

0538   Rai, Tsutomu: Chūgokugo no hōgen.—*OJKK* 13, 1960, 59–84. [Dialects of China.]/ Comparing initials of six dialect groups; *RBS* 6, 1960, 385, A. Rygaloff.
賴惟勤：中國語の方言

0539   Tung, T'ung-ho: *Han-yü yin-yün-hsüeh.*—Taipei: Wang Shou-ching [Mrs. Tung] and Kuang-wen, 1968, 2, 3, 330 p./ Chap. III. Modern dialect phonology: Mandarin, Soochow, Cantonese, Hakka, Foochow, Amoy. [Chinese phonology.]
董同龢：漢語音韻學

0540   Wang, Li: *Han-yü yin-yün-hsüeh.*—Peking: Chung-hua, 1957, 4, 2, 10, 682 p./ Chap. VII. Phonetic systems of modern Chinese dialects: Mandarin, Wu, Min, Yüeh, Hakka. [Chinese phonology.]
王力：漢語音韻學

0541 Yang, Hsi-ling: Wo kuo fang-yin chih fen-ch'i hsien-hsiang chi ch'i ch'eng-yin (0492). [The phenomenon of Chinese dialect diversity and its causes.]

楊喜齡：我國方音之分歧現象及其成因

0542 Yü-yen yen-chiu-so: Han-yü fang-yin te chi-ko wen-t'i.—*FPT* 1, 1958, 149–174. [Some phonetic problems of Chinese dialects.]/ Initials, finals, tones.

語言研究所：漢語方音的幾個問題

0543 Yüan, Chia-hua: Fang-yin yen-chiu.—*Han-yü fang-yen kai-yao* (0146), Chap. XII:1. [The study of dialect sounds.]

袁家驊：方音研究

5.5.4. Vocabulary and Grammar (0544–0554)

0544 Arendt, Carl: *Handbuch der nordchinesischen Umgangssprache*. Vol. I.—Stuttgart & Berlin: W. Spemann, 1891, xxi, 535 p., dialect map, table./ *TP* 3, 1892, 196–199, G. Schlegel. Notes on phonetics and grammar of principal dialects, such as Peking, Hangchow, Shanghai, Ningpo, Foochow, Amoy, Swatow, Canton, and Hakka.

0545 Hsü, Pao-hua: Lüeh shuo fang-yen ho P'u-t'ung-hua kou-tz'u te i-t'ung.—*CKYW* 1965:5, 356–362, 366./ *RBS* 11, 1965, 431, V. Alleton. [A sketch of the differences and similarities in word formation in the dialects and the Common Language.]/ A comparative study.

許寶華：略說方言和普通話構詞的異同

0546 Kim, Young-kee: Chunggukŏ bangŏn ŭi ŭmun chĕgye sang pigyo yŭngu.—*Sung Kyun Kwan University Journal* 10, 1965, 97–128; E.S. [A comparative study of the phonetic systems of Chinese dialects.]

金永基： 中國語方言의音韻體系上比較研究

0547 Kōsaka, Jun'ichi: Hōgen gohō zakki.—*AGK* 3, 1952, 6–20. [Miscellaneous notes on dialect grammar.]

香坂順一：方言語法雜記

0548 Kōsaka, Jun'ichi: Rinkai hōgen no ichi tokuchō—zai ni kansuru ichi kōsatsu.—*JBK* 3:7, 1952, 80–100. [A distinctive feature of Chinese coastal dialects—an observation of *zai*.]

香坂順一：臨海方言の一特徵——『在』に關する一考察

0549 Matsumoto, Kazuo: Nanpō hōgen no ninshō daimeishi ni tsuite.—*CGGG* 1958: 7, 5–11. [Personal pronouns in Southern Chinese dialects.]/ Cantonese, Amoy and Hakka.

松本一男： 南方方言の人稱代名詞について

0550 Nagamochi, Tokuichi: *Shumi no Sinago*.—Tokyo: Taizanbō, 1943, 6, 227 p. [Interesting Chinese language.]/ A comparative study of Peking, Shanghai and Canton dialects.

永持德一：趣味の支那語

0551 Parker, Edward Harper: The comparative study of the Chinese dialects.—*JRASNC* 12, 1878, 19–50./ *ChinRec* 10, 1879, 47–59, C. C. Baldwin.

0552 Sun, Ch'ang-hsü: *Han-yü tz'u-hui*.—Ch'angch'un: Chi-lin jen-min, 1958, 6, 26, 493 p.; illus., maps, tab./ *CKYW* 1957:8, 43, Lao Chün-fang; *RBS* 3, 1957, 591, J. Chmielewski. [Chinese lexicon.]/ Chap. 19. Dialect vocabulary; Chap. 33. Sound changes in dialects.

孫常叙：漢語詞彙／勞君方評

0553 Yüan, Chia-hua: Fang-yen tz'u-hui.—*Han-yü fang-yen kai-yao* (0146), Chap. XII:2. [Dialect lexicon.]

袁家驊：方言詞滙

0554 Yüan, Chia-hua: Fang-yen yü-fa.—*Han-yü fang-yen kai-yao* (0146), Chap. XII:3. [Dialect grammar.]

袁家驊：方言語法

6. NORTHERN MANDARIN DIALECTS (0555–0886)

6.1. Northern Mandarin Dialects in General (0555–0574)

6.1.1. General Studies (0555–0560)

0555 Eun, Boo-ki: Chunggukŏ kwanhwa wa bangŏn ŭi kochal.—*Chunkuk Hakpo* 11, 1970, 63–72. [A study on the Mandarin dialects.]

殷富基：中國語官話와方言의考察

0556 Forke, Alfred: A comparative study of northern Chinese dialects.—*CR* 21, 1895, 181–203.

0557 Hashimoto, Mantarō *Hoppō shohōgen no hikaku kenkyū*.—Tokyo: Tokyo U., 1956, 456 p., maps, sonograms./ Unpubl. M.A. thesis. [A comparative study of northern Chinese dialects.]

橋本萬太郎：北方諸方言の比較研究

0558 Shih, Ts'un-chih: Lun pei-fang-hua-te yu-yüeh-hsing.—*Kai-tsao tsa-chih* 1, 1946, 58–64; 2, 1947, 30–34. [On the superiority of northern dialects.]

史存直：論北方話的優越性

0559 Stimson, Hugh: Mandarin dialects: A problem in classification.—*JCLTA* 1:3, 1966, 92–98.

0560 Yüan, Chia-hua: Pei-fang hua.—*Han-yü fang-yen kai-yao* (0146), Chap. IV. [Northern Mandarin dialects.]

袁家驊：北方話

6.1.2. Phonetics and Phonology (0561–0569)

0561 Cheng, Chin-ch'üan: Kuan-hua fang-yen te sheng-tiao cheng-hsing ken lien-tiao pien-hua.—*TLTC* 33:4, 1966, 6–12. [Tonal distinctive features and tone sandhi in Mandarin dialects.]/ Shenyang, Sian, Ch'engtu.

鄭錦全：官話方言的聲調徵性跟連調變化

0562 Giet, Franz: Phonetics of North-China dialects: A study of their diffusion.—*MS* 11, 1946, 233–267, 11 maps; Taipei: Mei Ya, [1971], repr./ *BSL* 45, 1949, 278, Paul Demiéville.

0563 Giet, Franz: *Zur Tonität nordchinesischer Mundarten.*—Wien-Mödling: Verlag der Missionsdruckerei St. Gabriel, 1950, xx, 184 p., 54 pl., 11 maps in pocket; New York: Johnson Reprint Co., 1966, repr./ *Muséon* 63, 1950, 316–319, L. Grootaers; *Afrika und Übersee* 36, 1951, 67–88, O. von Essen; *Zphon* 5, 1951, 131–132, W.A. Grootaers; *Lg* 27, 1951, 449–451, Li Fang-kuei; *Anthropos* 46, 1951, 1020–1031, S. Wurm.

0564 Lyovin, Anatole: *Comparative phonology of Mandarin dialects.*—Berkeley: U. of California, 1972, ix, 718 p./ Unpubl. doc. diss.

0565 Ni, Hai-shu: *Pei-fang-yin Chiang-nan-yin Kuang-chou-yin tui-chao tzu-hui* (0521). [Comparative syllabary of northern Mandarin, Wu, and Cantonese.]

倪海曙：北方音江南音廣州音對照字彙

0566 Pai, Ti-chou: Pei-yin ju-sheng yen-pien k'ao.—*NSTH* 2:2, 1931, 1–42, tab./ *NGBK* 60, 1966, 45–100, Keiya Toshinobu. [A study of the evolution of the *ju* tone in northern Mandarin dialects.]

白滌洲：北音入聲演變考 / 慶谷壽信評

0567 Ting, Fang-hao: Pei-fang-hua ho Chiang-nan-hua te fa-yin.—*Hsin wen-tzu chou-k'an* 1951:55, 4–5; 56, 4; 57, 4; 58, 4; 59, 4. [The pronunciations of northern Mandarin and Wu dialects.]

丁方豪：北方話和江南話的發音

0568 Yang, Nai-szu: Pei-fang-hua cho-shang pien ch'ü lai-yüan shih-t'an.—*HSYK* 1958:2, 72–77. [On the origin of the 'Ancient voiced *shang* tone becoming *ch'ü* tone' in northern Mandarin dialects.]

楊耐思：北方話『濁上變去』來源試探

0569 Yü-yen yen-chiu-so: Kuan-hua ch'ü fang-yen chien-t'uan yin fen-ho te ch'ing-k'uang.—*FPT* 1, 1958, 141–148. [Survey of the distribution of 'sharp' and 'round' sounds (initials) in Mandarin-speaking areas.]

語言研究所：官話區方言尖團音分合的情況

6.1.3. Vocabulary (0570–0574)

0570 Chiang, Ch'eng: Pei-fang-hua, Chiang-nan-hua yü-tz'u pien i.—*YWCS* 1952:1, 17; 2, 23–24; 3, 21–22; 4, 16–17; 5, 26–27; 6, 25–26; 7, 22–23; 8, 29–30./ *YWCS* 1953:7, 38–39, Chao Ch'ien. [Lexical differences between northern and southern (Wu) dialects.]
江成：北方話、江南話語詞辨異 / 趙前評

0571 Ch'uan, Wen: Hsiao-hsüeh chiao-k'o-shu chung te pei-fang t'u-yü fang-yen chieh-shih.—*Kuang-tung chiao-yü yü wen-hua* 1951:3, 34. [Explanations of northern patois and dialect words found in textbooks of primary schools.]
川文：小學教科書中的北方土語方言解釋

0572 Hoppōgo Kenkyūkai: Saikin no Chūgoku bungaku ni arawareta Hoppōgo goi.—*CGGG* 1955:2, 21–24; 1955:4, 10–23; 1955:5, 20–22; 1955:6, 15–20. [Northern Chinese dialect vocabulary as appearing in recent Chinese literature.]
北方語研究會：最近の中國文學に現われた北方語語彙

0573 Jen, Ming: *Pei-fang t'u-yü tz'u-tien.*—Shanghai: Ch'un-ming, 1953, xxii, 116 p./ *YWCS* 1954:4, 38–39, Ts'en Kang; *Orbis* 2, 1953, 169, W.A. Grootaers. [Dictionary of northern dialect words.]
任明：北方土語辭典 / 岑崗評

0574 Kanagae, Nobumitsu: Saikin no Chūgoku bungaku ni awareta hoppō togo no kenkyū.—*Sōgō kenkyū hōkoku shūroku* (Showa 28 nendo), 1954, 277–282. [A study of northern dialect words appearing in recent Chinese literature.]
鐘ク江信光：最近の中國文學に現われた北方土語の研究——「（昭和28年度）總合研究報告集錄」

6.2. Peking Dialect (0575–0744)
6.2.1. General Studies (0575–0604)

6.2.1.1. Peking Dialect and Common Language (0575–0583)

0575 Chang, Ching-su: Pei-p'ing shih-nei yü-yen chih chien-t'ao.—*SCPL* 4:2, 1936, 8–11. [A thorough discussion of speech in the city of Peking.]
張景蘇：北平市內語言之檢討

0576 Hsien, Chou: Pei-ching t'u-yü ping pu shih P'u-t'ung-hua.—*P'u-t'ung-hua lun-chi* (0112), 159–160. [The patois of Peking is not the Common Language.]
先舟：北京土語并不是普通話

0577 Li, Tsu-pai: Piao-chun-yü te ts'e-yüan ti Pei-p'ing.—*Chiang-hsi chiao-yü yüeh-k'an* 23, 1936, 136–138. [Peiping: the place of origin of the standard language.]
李祖白：標準語的策源地北平

0578 Matsumoto, Kazuo & Wang, Yü-te: Pekingo to tōnan hōgen.—*Chūgoku gogaku jiten* (0093), 1031–1035. [Peking and southeastern dialects.]
松本一男，王育德：北京語と東南方言

0579 Ōhara, Nobukazu: Pekingo to kyōtsūgo.—*Dōshisha gaikoku bungaku kenkyū* 13, 1976, 45–61. [The Peking dialect and the Common Language.]
大原信一：北京語と共通語

0580 Sakamoto, Ichirō: Pekingo to Kōnango.—*Chūgoku gogaku jiten* (0093), 1029–1031. [The Peking dialect and dialects south of the Yangtze River.]
坂本一郎：北京語と江南語

0581 T'ang, Hung: *Pei-ching-hua yü Han-yü p'in-yin.*—Hong Kong: Shang-hai shu-chü, 1974, 2, 101 p. [The Peking dialect and the Pinyin system.]/ 57–96: Basic vocabulary of the Peking dialect.
唐宏：北京話與漢語拼音

0582 Tōdō, Akiyasu: Minzoku kyōtsūgo—Pekingo.—*CGGG* 1956:6, 3–10. [The common language of the nationalities of China—the Peking dialect.]/ A historical survey.
藤堂明保：民族共通語——北京語

0583 Tung, T'ung-ho: Kuo-yü yü Pei-ching-hua.—*TLTC* 1:10, 1950, 12–13; *Tung T'ung-ho . . . hsüan chi* (0110), 367–369. [The National Language and the Peking dialect.]

董同龢：國語與北京話

6.2.1.2. Historical Development (0584–0593)

0584 Ch'en, Wen-pin: Pei-ching-hua to-yin-tz'u fa-chan te ch'ü-shih ho su-tu.—*CKYW* 1958:4, 197–198. [The trend and speed in the development of polysyllabic words in the Peking dialect.]

陳文彬：北京話多音詞發展的趨勢和遠度

0585 Hsieh, Hsin-i: *The development of Middle Chinese entering tone in Pekinese.* --Berkeley: U. of California, 1971, iii, 184 p./ Unpubl. doc. diss.

0586 Kusaka, Tsuneo: Chūgoku kinsei hoppō on'inshi no ichi mondai—Pekin hōgen seirui taikei no seiritsu.—*JBGH* 91, 1973, 67–84; E.S. [On the initial consonantal system of the modern Peking dialect—With special reference to the merging period of *chien-yin* (尖音) and *t'uan-yin* (團音).]

日下恆夫：中國近世北方音韻史の一問題——北京方言聲類體系の成立

0587 Kusaka, Tsuneo: Shindai hokuon no inrui—Gendai Pekin hōgenkei no seiritsu.—*KSCB* 6, 1976, 15–31. [The rhymes of the Peking dialect during the Ch'ing period—The formation of the modern Peking dialect.]

日下恆夫：清代北音の韻類——現代北京方言系の成立

0588 Osada, Natsuki: Pekin bungoon no kigen ni tsuite.—*CGKK* 1953:2, 1–5; map. [On the origin of literary readings in the Peking dialect.]

長田夏樹：北京文語音の起源に就いて

0589 Ōta, Tatsuo: Shindai Pekingo gohō kenkyū no shiryō ni tsuite.—*KGR* 2:1, 1951, 13–30. [Materials for the study of the grammar of the Peking dialect during the Ch'ing dynasty.]/ Sino-Korean materials.

太田辰夫：清代北京語語法研究の資料について

0590 Pashkov, B.K.: Drevneishie dialekty kitaiskogo iazyka i istoricheskaia davnost' pekingskogo narechiia.—*Problemy Vostokovedeniia* 1960:3, 163–173; 172–173: E.S. [The most ancient Chinese dialects and the age of the Peking dialect.]

0591 Stimson, Hugh M.: Ancient Chinese -p, -t, -k endings in the Peking dialect.—*Lg* 38, 1962, 376–384.

0592 Stimson, Hugh M.: More on Peking archaisms.—*TP* 58, 1972, 127–186./ Gives 18 words.

0593 Tōdō, Akiyasu: Development of Mandarin from 14 c. to 19 c.—*AAs* 6, 1968, 31–40.

6.2.1.3. Sociocultural Aspects (0594–0604)

0594 Chao, Chen-chi: Pei-ching-yü chung chih Man-yü ch'eng-fen.—*Hua-nien chou-k'an* 3:48, 1934, 949–951. [Manchu loan words in the Peking dialect.]

趙振紀：北平語中之滿語成分

0595 Ch'en, Tzu-shih (comp.): *Pei-p'ing hsieh-hou-yü tz'u-tien.*—Taipei: Ta Chung-kuo t'u-shu kung-szu, 1969, 342 p. [A dictionary of *hsieh-hou-yü* in the Peking dialect.]/ With explanatory notes on Peking colloquialism.

陳子實編：北平諧後語辭典（兼北平口語註釋）

0596 Ch'i, T'ieh-hen: Pei-ching te ch'iao-p'i-huar.—*KYHK* 1:7, 1929, 73–74; 1:8, 1929, 96; 1:12, 1929, 157–162. [Witticisms in the Peking dialect.]

齊鐵恨：北京的俏皮話儿

0597 Ch'i, T'ieh-hen: *Pei-p'ing te ch'iao-p'i-huar* (1).—Taipei: Chung-kuo yü-wen yüeh-k'an she, 1973, 2, 186 p. [Witticisms in the Peiping dialect.]/ With notes on the dialect words of Peking.

齊鐵恨：北平的俏皮話兒

0598 Fukuchi, Shigeko: Pekingo ni okeru shinzoku meishō no ichi yōhō—Shinzoku kankei ga nai baai no taikeiteki yōhō.—*CGGG* 1974:1, 8–19. [One of the uses of kinship terms in the Peking dialect—The systematic use of kinship terms among non-related persons.]
福地滋子： 北京語における親族名稱の一用法—— 親族關係がない場合の體系的用法

0599 Jabłoński, Witold: *Les 'siao-ha (i-eu) l-yu' de Pékin: un essai sur le poésie populaire en Chine.*—Krakow: Polska Akademja Umiejętności, 1935, 193, iii p.

〔 小孩兒語 〕

0600 Stimson, Hugh M.: A tabu word in the Peking dialect.—*Lg* 42, 1966, 285–294.

0601 Suzue, Mantarō & Shimomizu, Kenji: *Pekin Kanwa zokugen shūkai.*—Tokyo: Ōsakayago shoten, 1925, vi, 149 p. [Pekinese proverbs collected and annotated.]
鈴江萬太郎，下水憲次： 北京官話俗諺集解

0602 Teboul, M.: Sur une famille d'expressions proverbiales du dialecte de Pékin.—*BEFEO* 62, 1975, 487–503.

0603 Tung, Tso-pin: Pei-ching ch'eng-li fang-yen-hua te ti-ming.—*KYAO* 70, 1924, 1–4. [Dialectalized place names in the city of Peking.]
董作賓：北京城裏方言化的地名

0604 Vitale, Guido: *Pekinese rhymes. First collected and edited with notes and translation.*—Peking: Pei-t'ang Press, 1896, xvii, 160 p.

6.2.2. Phonetics and Phonology (0605–0668)
6.2.2.1. General (0605–0635)

0605 Alekséev, V.M.: Resul'taty foneticheskikh nabliudenii nad pekinskim dialektom.—*IAN* 4, 1910, 935–942. [Results of phonetic observations of the Peking dialect.]

0606 Chang, Ching: T'an Pei-ching-hua te yin-wei.—*CKYW* 1957:2, 13–15. [A discussion of the phonemes of the Peking dialect.]
張靜：談北京話的音位

0607 Chao, Yüan-jen: Pei-p'ing yin-hsi te hsing-chih.—*KYCK* 289, 1937, Apr. 24. [The nature of the Peiping phonetic system.]
趙元任：北平音系的性質

0608 Deniker, Géorge: *Le mécanisme phonologique du parler de Pékin.*—Peking: A. Nachbaur, 1925, 68 p., pl., tab./ Précédé de deux notes sur les alphabets et sur les méthodes phonologiques.

0609 Frei, Henri: Les phonèmes de Pékin.—*Bulletin de la Maison Franco-Japonaise* 8, 1936, 123–134.

0610 Fu, Mao-chi: Pei-ching-hua chiu-ching hsü-yao to-shao p'in-yin tzu-mu?—*CKYW* 1953:11, 3–6. [After all, how many Pinyin phonetic symbols are needed for the Peking dialect?]
傅懋勣 ： 北京話究竟需要多少拼音字母？

0611 Fu, Mao-chi: Pei-ching-hua te yin-wei ho p'in-yin tzu-mu.—*CKYW* 1956:5, 3–12. [The phonemes of the Peking dialect and Pinyin phonetic symbols.]
傅懋勣：北京話的音位和拼音字母

0612 Germain, Robert: Essai de description phonétique du dialecte de Pékin.—*La Chine* 47, 1923, 975–996; 50, 1923, 1229–1236.

0613 Guernier, R. C.: *Notes sur la prononciation de la langue mandarine de Pékin.*—Bourge-la-Reine, 1912, 19 p.

0614 Hartman, Lawton M.: The segmental phonemes of the Peiping dialect.—*Lg* 20, 1944, 28–42; *Readings in linguistics* (0104), 116–123.

0615   Hattori, Shirō: Pekingo no on'in taikei ni tsuite.—*GK* 25, 1954, 78–79. [The phonological system of the Peking dialect.] /A review of Hartman's article (0614).
服部四郎： 北京語の音韻體系について

0616   Hirayama, Hisao: Pekingo no on'in-ron ni kansuru nisan no mondai.—*GK* 35, 1959, 31–51. [Some problems concerning Pekinese phonology.]
平山久雄： 北京語の音韻論に關する二三の問題

0617   Hockett, Charles F.: Peiping phonology.—*JAOS* 67, 1947, 253–267; *Readings in linguistics* (0104), 217–228.

0618   Hsü, Shih-jung: Pei-ching yü-yin yin-wei.—*P'u-t'ung-hua yü-yin chiang-hua* (0234), 120–128. [Phonemes of the Peking dialect.]
徐世榮：北京語音音位

0619   Hsü, Shih-jung: Pei-ching yü-yin yin-wei chien shu.—*YWHH* 1957:8, 22–24. [A short description of Peking phonemes.]
徐世榮：北京語音音位簡述

0620   Kratochvíl, Paul: Syllabic volume as acoustic correlate of perceptual prominence in the Peking dialect.—*Chi-Lin* 5, 1969, 1–17.

0621   Li, Jung: Pei-ching yü-yin kai-yao.—*Han-yü fang-yen tiao-ch'a shou-ts'e* (0219), 31–75. [An outline of Peking phonetics.]
李榮：北京語音概要

0622   Liu, Fu: Pei-p'ing fang-yin hsi-shu piao.—*KHCK* 3:3, 1932, 535–540, 1 tab. [A table of the analytical numbers of the Peiping dialect.]
劉復：北平方音析數表

0623   Liu, Tse-hsien: Pei-ching-hua li chiu-ching yu to-shao yin-chieh.—*CKYW* 1957:2, 1–8; 3, 17–23. [How many syllables are there in the Peking dialect?]
劉澤先：北京話裏究竟有多少音節

0624   Lu, Chih-wei: Kuan-yü Pei-ching-hua yü-yin hsi-t'ung te i-hsieh wen-t'i.—*Hsien-tai Han-yü kuei-fan wen-t'i hsüeh-shu hui-i wen-chien hui-pien* (0103), 48–68. [Some problems concerning the phonetic system of the Peking dialect.]
陸志韋： 關於北京話語音系統的一些問題

0625   Mulder, J.W.F.: *Sets and relations in phonology—An axiomatic approach to the description of speech.*—Oxford: Clarendon Press, 1968, xv, 259 p./ Includes a complete description of the phonology of the Peking dialect; *Lg* 46, 1970, 671–687, Charles-James N. Bailey; *CGGG* 1969:8, 1–10, Ōkōchi Yasunori.
大河內康憲評

0626   Nagashima, Eiichirō: Gendai Pekingo no onseigakuteki kōsatsu.—*JBGH* 16, 1957, 196–216. [A phonetic study of the modern Peking dialect.]
永島榮一郎： 現代北京語の音聲學的考察

0627   Nasu, Kiyoshi: Pekin goon nidai.—*BGRS* 3, 1955, 1–12. [Two topics on the sounds of the Peking dialect.]
那須清：北京語音二題

0628   Nasu, Kiyoshi: Pekingo no onsetsu.—*BGRS* 7, 1960, 1–15. [A study of syllables in the Peking dialect.]
那須清：北京語の音節

0629   Rygaloff, Alexis: La phonologie du pékinois.—*TP* 43, 1955, 183–264./ *RBS* 1, 1955, 276, M. Soymié.

0630   Shih, Ts'un-chih: Pei-ching-hua yin-wei wen-t'i shang-ch'üeh.—*CKYW* 1957:2, 9–12. [A discussion on the problems of phonemes in the Peking dialect.]
史存直：北京話音位問題商榷

0631   Sung, Yüan-chia: P'ing Ha-te-men ho Huo-k'ai-t'e tui Pei-ching yü-yin te fen-hsi.—*CKYW* 1965:3, 169–178. [A critique of Hartman's and Hockett's analyses of Peking phonology.] (0614) and (0617).
宋元嘉： 評哈忒門和霍凱特對北京語音的分析

0632 Tōdō, Akiyasu: Pekingo no on'in.—*Chūgoku gogaku jiten* (0093), 19–35. [The phonemes of the Peking dialect.]
藤堂明保：北京語の音韻

0633 Tōdō, Akiyasu. Transl. by Wang, William S-Y. et al.: The phonemes of the Peking dialect.—*POLA* 4, 1963, 1–18. [Pekingo no on'in.] (0632)

0634 Tōdō, Akiyasu: *Chūgokugo on'inron.* —Tokyo: Kōnan shoin, 1957, iv, 358 p./ 31–52: Peking phonology; *CGGG* 1957: 3, 19–20, Rai Tsutomu. [Chinese phonology.]
藤堂明保：中國語音韻論 / 賴惟勤評

0635 Wang, Ch'in: *Pei-ching yü-yin ch'ang-shih.*—Ch'angsha: Hu-nan jen-min, 1957, 127 p./ *CKYW* 1957:6, 45, Mao K'ai. [Fundamentals of Peking phonetics.]
王勤：北京語音常識 / 茅開評

6.2.2.2. Initials (0636–0641)

0636 Ballard, William L.: The Pekingese palatals: A conundrum?.—*AAGB* 12, 1976, 1–10.

0637 Chao, Yuen Ren: The voiced velar fricative as an initial in Mandarin.—*Maître Phonétique* 3:89, 1948, 2–3.

0638 Hirayama, Hisao: Pekingo [v-] no on'inronteki kaishaku—'Dōka no gensoku' tekiyō no ichi rei.—*Gendai gengogaku* (Tokyo, 1972), 57–70. [A phonetic interpretation of the [v-] consonant in the Peking dialect—An example of the application of the 'principle of assimilation'.]
平山久雄：北京語〔v-〕の音韻論的解釋──「同化の原則」適用の一例──『現代言語學』（服部四郎先生定年退官記念論文集）

0639 Kanō, Mitsunori: Pekingo no [m], [n], [l], [z] seibo no inpeiji.—*CGGG* 224, 1977, 1–8. [Chinese characters belonging to the *yin-p'ing* tone with initials [m], [n], [1], and [z].]
狩野充德：北京語の〔m〕，〔n〕，〔l〕，〔z〕聲母の陰平字

0640 Obręska-Jabłońska, Antonina: Secondary voicing of consonants in the Pekinese dialect.—*BPTJ* 8, 1948, 41–56.

0641 Obręska-Jabłońska, Antonina: A new type of Pekinese consonant group, a contribution to the assimilation processes of the suffix *-erl* in Pekinese.—*RO* 17, 1952, 173–179.

6.2.2.3. Finals (0642–0645)

0642 Chang, Hsün-ju: *Pei-p'ing yin-hsi shih-san che.*—Peiping: Kuo-yü t'ui-hsing wei-yüan hui & Chung-kuo ta tz'u-tien pien-tsuan ch'u, 1937, 13 chüan, cii, 322 p.; Taipei: T'ien-i, 1973, repr. [Thirteen rhyme groups of the Peiping dialect.]
張洵如：北平音系十三轍

0643 Lo, Ch'ang-p'ei: *Pei-ching su ch'ü pai-chung che yün.*—Peking: Lai-hsün-ko shu-tien, 1950, xii, 73 p. [Rhymes from 100 popular Pekinese plays.]
羅常培：北京俗曲百種摘韻

0644 Lo, Chi-kuang: Pei-ching-hua i ho](〔) te yin-wei wen-t'i.—*CKYW* 1961:1, 33–34. [The phonemic problem concerning the i and 1 (〔) in the Peking dialect.]
羅季光：北京話 i 和 1（〔）的音位問題

0645 Wang, Fu-shih: Pei-ching-hua yün-mu te chi-ko wen-t'i.—*CKYW* 1963:2, 115–124. [Some problems concerning finals in the Peking dialect.]
王輔世：北京話韻母的幾個問題

6.2.2.4. Tones (0646–0668)

0646 Chang, Hsün-ju: Pei-ching-hua li ch'ing-sheng te kung-yung.—*CKYW* 1956:5, 30, 40. [The function of the neutral tone in the Peking dialect.]
張洵如：北京話裏輕聲的功用

0647 Chang, Wei-kang: Pei-p'ing-yin ju-sheng te yen-hua ho lien-yin te pien-hua. —*Wen-hsüeh* (Canton) 1, 1947, 19–28. [Development and sandhi of the *ju* tone in the Peiping dialect.]
張爲綱：北平音入聲的演化和連音的變化

0648 Forrest, R.A.D.: The *ju-sheng* tone in Pekingese.—*BSOAS* 13, 1950, 443–447.

0649 Hattori, Shirō: Pekin hōgen no shisei no on'inronteki bunseki.—*GnK* 5, 1974, 97–102. [Phonological analysis of the four tones of Pekinese.]
服部四郎： 北京方言の四聲の音韻論的分析

0650 Hirai, Katsutoshi: Pekingo no keisei onsetsu ni okeru onsei henka no jikken onseigakuteki bunseki.—*CGGG* 1970:12, 9–12. [Acoustic analysis of phonetic features found in neutral tone syllables of the Peking dialect.]
平井勝利： 北京語の輕聲音節における音聲變化の實驗音聲學的分析

0651 Hirayama, Hisao: Pekingo no seichō taikei—toku-ni daisansei no kaishaku o megutte.—*GnK* 5, 1974, 85–96. [The tonemic system of Pekinese—Mainly interpretation of the 3rd tone.]
平山久雄： 北京語の聲調體系——とくに第三聲の解釋をめぐって

0652 Hirayama, Hisao: Pekingo ni okeru sei nisshō joseika no jōken ni tsuite.—*CGGG* 1961:10, 9–12; 12, 6–10. [On the conditions for the change of Ancient *ju* tone carried by syllables with voiceless initial in modern Pekinese.]
平山久雄： 北京語に清入聲舒聲化の條件について

0653 Hsü, Shih-jung: Shih-lun Pei-ching yü-yin te sheng-tiao yin-wei.—*CKYW* 1957: 6, 23–24. [A preliminary discussion of the tonemes in the Peking dialect.]
徐世榮：試論北京語音的聲調音位

0654 Hsü, Shih-jung: Pei-ching-hua li te liang lei t'e-shu pien-tiao.—*CKYW* 1960: 2, 73. [Two kinds of special tone sandhi in the Peking dialect.]
徐世榮：北京話裏的兩類特殊變調

0655 Karapet'iants, A.M.: Izuchenie tona i intonatsii pekinskogo dialekta.—*Phonetica*

12, 1965, 160–164; E.S.; *Ocherki po fonologii vostochnykh iazykov* (Ed. by Elizarenkov, T. Ia.; Moscow: Nauka, 1975), 217–239, 7 fig. [A study of tone and intonation in the Peking dialect.]

0656 Kratochvíl, Paul: Disyllabic stress patterns in the Peking dialect.—*AO* 32, 1964, 383–402./ *RBS* 10, 1964, 259, A. Rygaloff.

0657 Kratochvíl, Paul: On the phonology of Peking stress.—*TPS* 1967, 154–178.

0658 Kratochvíl, Paul: Stress shift mechanism and its role in the Peking dialect.—*Modern Asian Studies* 8:4, 1974, 433–458.

0659 Matsumoto, Akira: Pekingo akusento ni kansuru ichi kōsatsu.—*CGGG* 1960:7, 1–7. [An investigation of accents in the Peking dialect.]
松本昭： 北京語アクセントに關する一考察

0660 Matsumoto, Akira: Futatabi Pekingo akusento ni tsuite.—*CGGG* 1961:5–6, 2–6. [Another discussion of accents in the Peking dialect.]
松本昭： 再び北京語アクセントについて

0661 Nasu, Kiyoshi: Pekingo seichō no ichi kansatsu.—*CGGG* 1957:10, 1–17. [An observation of the tones of the Peking dialect.]
那須清：北京語聲調の一觀察

0662 Setoguchi, Ritsuko: Futsūwa no keisei to Pekingo no keisei.—*CGGG* 225, 1978, 1–8. [The neutral tone in the Common Language and in the Peking dialect.]
瀨戶口律子： 普通話の輕聲と北京語の輕聲

0663 Stimson, Hugh M.: Stress in Peking phonotactics.—*MS* 26, 1967, 202–212.

0664 Švarný, Oldřich: Pekinese tones—Proposal for a new approach.—*Phonetica Pragensia* 3, 1972, 257–259.

0665 Ueda, Kinjirō: Chūko Kango no nisshō no hensen to Pekingo no haon no genzō. —*CGGG* 1956:7, 9–18; 8, 16–19. [The change of the Ancient *ju* tone and the phenomenon of double readings in the Peking dialect.]
上田金次郎：中古漢語の入聲の變遷と北京語の破音の現象

0666 Vissière, Arnold Jacques Antoine: De la chute du ton montant dans la langue de Pékin.—*TP* 5, 1904, 448–460.

0667 Wang, Lien-tseng: Recherches expérimentales sur les tons du pékinois.— *Archives Néerlandaises de Phonétique Expérimentale* 13, 1937, 1–40; 14, 1938, 1–48.

0668 Wang, William S-Y: Tone 3 in Pekinese.—*Journal of Speech and Hearing Research* 10:3, 1967, 629–636.

6.2.3. Vacabulary and Grammar (0669–0711)

6.2.3.1. Vocabulary (0669–0685)

0669 Chang, Hsün-ju: *Pei-ching-hua ch'ing-sheng tz'u-hui.*—Peking: Chung-hua, 1957, 154 p./ *CKYW* 1957:12, 47, Ni Chi-yü; *RBS* 3, 1957, 590, P. Kratochvíl; *Orbis* 15, 1966, 113, Paul Yang. [A lexicon of neutral-tone words in the Peking dialect.]
張洵如：北京話輕聲詞滙／倪寄予評

0670 Ch'eng, K'ang: Man t'an Pei-p'ing yü-hui te sou-chi ho cheng-li.—*KWYK* 69, 1948, 11–15. [On the collection and arrangement of the vocabulary of the Pei-ping dialect.]
程亢：漫談北平語滙的搜集和整理

0671 Chin, Shou-shen: *Pei-ching-hua yü-hui.* —Peking: Shang-wu, 1961, 37, 214 p.; 1964, rev. ed., xxxix, 266 p. [Vocabulary of the Peking dialect.]
金受申：北京話語滙

0672 Fu, Tung-hua: Pei-ching-hua ch'ang-yung tz'u k'ao.—*YWCS* 1957:9, 40–42; 10, 42–44; 11, 45–47; 12, 47–50. [A study on commonly-used words in the Peking dialect.]
傅東華：北京話常用詞考

0673 Fu, Tung-hua: *Pei-ching-yin i-tu-tzu te ch'u-pu t'an-t'ao.*—Peking: Wen-tzu kai-ko, 1958, 2, 44 p. [A preliminary study of polyphonic characters in the Peking dialect.]
傅東華：北京音異讀字的初步探討

0674 Hani, Shin'ichi: Pekin togo no kenkyū. —*SK* 2, 1926, 91–97. [A study of the patois of Peking.]
羽仁新一：北京土語の研究

0675 Hatano, Tarō: *Pekin Kanwa jōgen yōrei* kaidai sakuin.—*YSDR* 27:3, 1977, 157–167. [A bibliographical introduction and index to *Pekin Kanwa jōgen yōrei* (0726).]
波多野大郎：『北京官話常言用例』解題索引

0676 Hirayama, Hisao: I-pa no pa, chih-chia no chih no Pekin-on no yurai.—*CGGG* 1960:3, 1–3. [The origin of Peking pronunciations for the *pa* in *i-pa* and the *chih* in *chih-chia*.]
平山久雄：尾巴の巴，指甲の指の北京音の由來

0677 Hirayama, Hisao: Ch'ih no Pekin'on no yurai.—*CGGG* 1960:5, 14–15. [The origin of the Peking pronunciation for 喫.]
平山久雄：『喫』の北京音の由來

0678 Hsü, Shih-jung: Pei-ching-hua li te t'u tz'u ho t'u yin.—*CKYW* 1957:3, 24–27. [The Local words and local pronunciations in the Peking dialect.]
徐世榮：北京話裏的土詞和土音

0679 Huang, Tien-ch'eng: Pei-ching-hua.— *YWCS* 1954:3, 4–8; 1954:4, 6. [The Peking dialect.]
黃典誠：北京話

0680 Liu, K'ai-ming: Tui Pei-ching-hua li te t'u tz'u ho t'u yin te i-chien.—*CKYW* 1957:11, 48. [My personal opinion concerning the article "Pei-ching-hua li te t'u tz'u ho t'u yin." (0679).]

劉凱鳴： 對『 北京話裏的土詞和土音 』 的意見

0681 Lu, Chih-wei: *Pei-ching-hua tan-yin-tz'u tz'u-hui.*—Peking: Jen-min, 1951; Peking: K'o-hsüeh, 1956, rev. ed., 13, 302 p./ *YCHP* 40, 1951, 259–264, Yü Min; *Orbis* 2:1, 1953, 170–172, Willem A. Grootaers. [A lexicon of the monosyllabic words in Pekinese.]

陸志韋： 北京話單音詞詞彙 / 俞敏評

0682 Ozaki, Minoru: *Yü-yen tzu-erh chi* goi sakuin (shokō).—*MSBGKT* 9, 1965, 1–90. [Index to the vocabulary of the *Yü-yen tzu-erh chi* (first draft).] / See Wade & Hillier (0731).

尾崎實： 『 語言自邇集 』 語彙索引（ 初稿 ）

0683 Pei-p'ing jen: Pei-p'ing-hua ti-i-chiang.—*CHCK* 37:7, 1932, 85–87. [First lesson on the Peiping dialect.]

北平人： 北平話第一講

0684 Sakai, Ken'ichi: Chūgokugo no hyōgen—Pekingo no goi.—*Gakusō* 7, 1966, 85–98. [Expressions of the Chinese language—The vocabulary of the Peking dialect.]

坂井健一： 中國語の表現——北京語の語彙

0685 Stent, George Carter: *A Chinese and English vocabulary in the Pekinese dialect.*—Shanghai: American Presbyterian Mission Press, 1898, 3rd ed., rev. by Donald MacGillivray, vii, 788 p.

6.2.3.2. Morphology (0686–0696)

0686 Chang, Hsün-ju: *Pei-p'ing yin-hsi hsiao-che pien.*—Shanghai: K'ai-ming, 1949, xlviii, 126 p. ['Erh' finals in the Peking dialect.]

張洵如： 北平音系小轍編

0687 Chao, Yuen Ren: A note on *Lia,[3] Sa,[1]* etc.—*HJAS* 1, 1936, 33–38.

0688 Ch'en, Chih-wen: Kuan-yü Pei-ching-hua li erh-hua te lai-yüan.—*CKYW* 1965: 5, 369–370, 412./ *CKYW* 1966:1, 67–68, Shang Ching; *RBS* 11, 1965, 404, K. Kaden. [The origin of erization in the Peking dialect.]

陳治文： 關於北京話裏兒化的來源 / 尚靜評

0689 Hirai, Katsutoshi: Pekingo ni okeru jika inbo no onka ni tsuite—toku-ni seichō to-no kankei kara.—*CGGG* 1969:12, 1–7. [The phonetic value of retroflex finals in the Peking dialect—With special reference to tones.]

平井勝利： 北京語における兒化韻母の音價について—— 特に聲調との關係から

0690 Hockett, Charles F.: Peiping morphophonemics.—*Lg* 26, 1950, 63–85; *Readings in linguistics* (0104), 315–328.

0691 Kusaka, Tsuneo: Pekingo ni okeru nin no seisei.—*KSBR* 26:2, 1977, 1–18. [The formation of *nin* in the Peking dialect.]

日下恒夫： 北京語におけるninの生成

0692 Li, Shan: Pei-ching-hua li te i-ko ch'ien-ju-yin -li-.—*CKYW* 1952:7, 37. [The inserted syllable (i.e. infix) *-li-* in the Peking dialect.]

力山： 北京話裏的一個嵌入音 -li-

0693 Lu, Chih-wei: *Han-yü te kou-tz'u-fa.*—Peking: K'o-hsüeh, 1951, 4, 155 p.; 1964, rev. ed., vi, 148 p. [Chinese morphology.] / Based on Peking dialect.

陸志韋： 漢語的構詞法

0694 Nagao, Mitsuyuki: Pekingo jūfuku keishiki akusento no seiritsu ni tsuite.—*Shūkan Tōyōgaku* 16, 1966, 88–99. [On the formation of accent in the reduplicative patterns of the Peking dialect.]

長尾光之： 北京語重複形式アクセントの成立について

0695 Nasu, Kiyoshi: Ken-erh to Ko-erh.—
CGGG 35, 1955, 43–44. [*Ken-erh* 'root'
and *ko-erh* 'song'.]
那須清：『 根兒 』と『 歌兒 』

0696 Tōdō, Akiyasu: Pekingo r-ka no hon-
shitsu.—*CGGG* 1960:4, 6–9. [The nature
of erization in the Peking dialect.]
藤堂明保：北京語 r 化の本質

6.2.3.3. Syntax (0697–0711)

0697 Chao, Yuen Ren: *Mandarin primer*
(0488), 37–59: Grammar.

0698 Chao, Yuen Ren. Transl. by Li, Jung:
Kuo-yü yü-fa kang-yao.—*Hsin chien-she*
4:1, 1951, 41–43; 2, 42–44; 3, 34–37;
Peking: K'ai-ming, 1952, vii, 60 p.;
Peking: Chung-kuo ch'ing-nien, 1953,
repr., with a new title: *Pei-ching k'ou-yü
yü-fa.* [A grammar of the Peking colloquial.]/ A modified transl. of Chap. III
of the *Mandarin primer* (0488).
趙元任著，李榮譯： 國語語法綱要（ 單
行本改爲： ）北京口語語法

0699 Chao, Yuen Ren: *A grammar* of
spoken Chinese.—Berkeley & Los Angeles: U. of California Press, 1968, xxxi,
847 p./ *JCL* 1, 1973, 126–149, Li Ying-
che; *Lg* 46, 1970, 513–524, Paul Kratochvíl; *JAS* 26, 1966, 103–104, Wang
Fang-yu (review of 1965 preliminary ed.).
〔 趙元任：中國話的文法 〕

0700 Chao, Yuen Ren. Transl. by Lü, Shu-
hsiang: *Han-yü k'ou-yü yü-fa.*—Peking:
Shang-wu, 1979, 380 p. [A grammar of
spoken Chinese.] (0700)
趙元任著，呂叔湘譯：漢語口語語法

0701 Ch'en, Kang: Pei-ching-hua li lou ho le
te ch'ü-pieh.—*CKYW* 1957:12, 33–34.
[The difference between *lou* and *le* in the
Peking dialect.]
陳剛：北京話裏 lou 和 le 的區別

0702 Cherovenetskii, Tikhon D.: *Grammatika kitaiskogo razgovornogo iazyka. Pekinskii dialekt.*—Vladivostok, 1933, 132 p.
[Grammar of conversational Chinese.
Peking dialect.]

0703 Dragunov, A.A.: *Issledovaniia po
grammatike sovremennogo kitaiskogo
iazyka. I. Chasti Rechi.*—Moscow: Akademiia Nauk, 1952, 231 p./*AOH* 3, 1953,
328–329, B. Csongor; Cites dialect examples. [Studies in the grammar of Modern Chinese. Pt. I. Parts of speech.]

0704 Dragunov, A.A. Transl. by W. Lippert:
*Untersuchungen zur grammatik der
modern Chinesischen sprache* (Ostasiatis-
che Forschungen-Sonderreihe Monogra-
phien. Vol. I).—Berlin: Akademie Verlag, 1960, xii, 280 p./ Transl. of (0703);
Cites dialect examples (see 256–257:
Subject index).

0705 Edkins, Joseph: *A grammar of the
Chinese colloquial language, commonly
called the Mandarin dialect.*—Shanghai:
London Mission Press, 1857, viii, 264 p.;
Shanghai: Presbyterian Mission Press,
1864, 2nd ed., 279 p.

0706 Kratochvíl, Pavel: On verb-noun constructions in modern Peking dialect.—*AO*
30, 1962, 145–147.

0707 Kratochvíl, Pavel: The role of stress in
the syntactical analysis of modern Peking
dialect.—*AO* 30, 1962, 147–149.

0708 Tōdō, Akiyasu: Pekingo no gohō.—
Chūgoku gogaku jiten (0093), 36–63.
[Grammar of the Peking dialect.]
藤堂明保：北京語の語法

0709 Tōdō, Akiyasu: Pekingo no bunpō.—
CGGG 1956:10, 21–37. [Grammar of the
Peking dialect.]
藤堂明保：北京語の文法

0710 Ti, Chou: Pei-ching-hua chung chih
piao-shih-fa.—*CSTY* 8:85–87, 1929, 78–
81. [Methods of calculating time in the
Peking dialect.]
荻舟：北京語中之表時法

0711 Ushijima, Tokuji: Pekingo no 'sūryō hogo'.—*Torii Hisayasu sensei kakō kinen ronshū—Chūgoku no gengo to moji* (Tenri: Torii Hisayasu Kyōju Kakō Kinenkai, 1972), 103–119. [Numeral complements in Pekinese.]

牛島德次：北京語の『數量補語』──
『鳥居久靖先生華甲記念論集 ──中國
の言語と文字』

6.2.4. Contrastive Studies (0712–0720)
(See also Contrastive Studies under all other dialect groups)

0712 Bradley, Cornelius Beach: The tone-accents of two Chinese dialects.—*JAOS* 35, 1915, 199–206./ Cantonese and Pekinese.

0713 Frei, Henri: Monosyllabisme et polysyllabisme dans les emprunts linguistiques, avec un inventaire des phonèmes de Pékin et de Tokio.—*Bulletin de la Maison Franco-Japonaise* 8, 1936, 76–164.

0714 Li, Lin-nei Yeung: *An instrumental study of Mandarin and Cantonese tones.* —Canberra: Australian National U., 1971, ii, 344 p./ Unpubl. doc. diss.

0715 Mathews, William R.: A contrastive study of relative clauses in two Chinese dialects.—*CAAAL* 9, 1978, 57–76./ Mandarin and Cantonese.

0716 P'an, Hung-wen: Pei-ching yü T'ang-shan ti-ch'ü yü-yin pien-cheng.—*FPC* 5, 1958, 104–105. [A contrastive analysis of pronunciations of the Peking and T'ang-shan dialects.]

潘鴻文：北京與唐山地區語音辨正

0717 Pei-ching yü-yin Ch'ao-chou fang-yin Chu-yin hsin tzu-tien pien-chi wei-yüan-hui (comp.): *Pei-ching yü-yin Ch'ao-chou fang-yin hsin tzu-tien.*—Canton: Kuang-tung jen-min, 1957, 24, 666, 80, 14, 107, 7 p.; illus. [A new dictionary of Peking-Ch'aochou pronunciations.]

北京語音潮州方音注音新字典編輯委員
會編：北京語音潮州方音新字典

0718 Sprenger, Arnold Heinrich: *A contrastive study of the Peiping and German phonologies.*—Washington, D.C.: George-town U., 1965, iii, 211 p./ Unpubl. doc. diss.; *DA* 26:3321; UM 65–4123.

0719 Teng, Shou-hsin: Negation in Chinese: Mandarin and Amoy.—*JAOS* 98, 1978, 50–60.

0720 Tipton, Gary Prior: *A contrastive analysis of Mandarin and Cantonese phonologies.*—Bloomington: Indiana U., 1974, v, 299 p./ Unpubl. doc. diss.; *DAI* 35: 4491–A; UM 75–1766.

6.2.5. Textbooks (0721–0734)

0721 Anonymous: *Exercices de chinois parlé.*—Peking: Imprimerie des Lazaristes, 1903, xii, 340 p.; 1915, new ed., xii, 321 p.; 1928, xii, 373 p./ With vocabulary and appendices.

0722 Ducat, Charles M.: *An elementary manual of the Pekinese dialect.*—Rangoon: American Baptist Mission Press, 1898, iv, 24 p./ For the use of officers preparing for the preliminary examination.

0723 Edkins, Joseph: *Progressive lessons in the Chinese spoken language, with lists of common words and phrases, and an appendix containing the laws of tones in the Peking dialect.*—Shanghai: London Mission Press, 1862, v, 103, 63 p.

0724 Imbault-Huart, Camille: *Cours électique graduel et pratique de langue chinoise.*—Peking: Typographie du Pei-t'ang & Paris: E. Leroux, 1887–1889, 4 vols., I. xxvii, 291 p.; II. 354 p.; III. 451 p.; IV. 296 p./ Peking dialect.

〔京話指南〕

0725 Karlgren, B.: *A Mandarin phonetic reader in the Pekinese dialect.*—Stockholm: Kungl. Boktryckeriet. P.A. Nor-stedt & Söner, 1917, 187 p./ With an introduction to pronunciation and romanization.

0726 Koji, Shinpei & Mogi, Ichirō: *Pekin Kanwa jōgen yōrei.*—Tokyo: Bunkyūdō, 1905, 4, 2, 84, 71 p. [Common words and phrases in the Peking Mandarin dialect and their usages.]
小路眞平，茂木一郎： 北京官話常言用例

0727 Mateer, Calvin Wilson: *A course of Mandarin lessons, based on idiom.*— Shanghai: American Presbyterian Mission Press, 1892, xlix, 714 p.; 1898, rev. ed., lv, 3, 781 p.; 1903, 2nd rev. ed., lv, 3, 768 p., fold tab.; 1922, repr./ With a comparative chart of the sounds in five dialects: Peking, Nanking, Kiukiang, Tengchow, Weihsien.

0728 Ratau, J.R.: *Posobie k izuchiniiu sovremennogo kitaiskogo iazyka. Pekinskii dialekt.*—Vladivostok, 1929, 156, 18 p. [A textbook for learning the modern Chinese language. The Peking dialect.]

0729 Thom, Robert: *The Chinese speaker or extracts from works written in the Mandarin language, as spoken at Peking. Pt. I.*—Ningpo: Presbyterian Mission Press, 1846, 102 p.; Canton: Canton Customs Press, 1865 repr.; Shanghai: Tien-shih-chai, 1880, 83 d.p./ Extract from the *Chia pao ch'üan chi* 家寶全集; Addenda: Extract from *Hung lou meng* 紅樓夢 Chap. VI.
〔華英說部撮要〕

0730 Vissière, Arnold Jacques Antoine: *Premières leçons de chinois, langue mandarine de Pékin.*—Leiden: E.J. Brill, 1909, x, 185 p.; 1914, 2nd ed., ix, 192 p.

0731 Wade, Thomas Francis & Hillier, Walter Caine: *Yü-yen tzŭ êrh chi: A progressive course designed to assist the student of colloquial Chinese as spoken in the capital and the metropolitan department.*—Shanghai: Inspectorate General of Customs, London: W.H. Allen & Co., 1886, 2nd ed., 3 vols., xxviii, 349; 523; 245 p. Shanghai: Kelly & Walsh, 1903, 3rd ed., 2 vols., 155; 248 p./ *CR* 16, 1888, 214–

225, H.A. Giles; for a vocabulary index, see Ozaki Minoru (0682).
〔 語言自邇集 〕

0732 Wu, Ch'i-t'ai & Cheng, Yung-pang: *Kuan-hua chih-nan.*—Shanghai: Mei-hua shu-kuan, 1882, 3 chüan; Tokyo: Yanagi Ryūtarō, 1908, 4, 6, 2, 211 p. [Guide to the Mandarin dialect.]
吳啓太，鄭永邦：官話指南

0733 Wu, Ch'i-t'ai & Cheng, Yung-pang. Transl. by Boucher, Henri: *Koan-hoa tche-nan. Boussole du langage mandarin.* —Shanghai: Imprimerie de la Mission Catholique, 1893, 2nd. ed., 2 vols., I. vi, 247 p.; II. ii, 232 p.; 1906, 4th ed., vi, 482 p. [Kuan-hua chih-nan.] (0732)

0734 Wu, Ch'i-t'ai & Cheng, Yung-pang. Transl. by Hopkins, L.C.: *The guide to Kuan-hua. A translation of the Kuan-hua chih-nan with an essay on tone and accent in Pekinese and a glossary of phrases.* —Shanghai: Kelly & Walsh, 1889, 230 p.; 1900, 3rd. & rev. ed., 193 p./ *CR* 18:2, 1890, 129, E.J. Eitel. [Kuan-hua chih-nan.] (0732)

6.2.6. Dictionaries (0735–0744)

0735 Chen, Janey: *A practical English-Chinese pronouncing dictionary: English, Chinese characters, romanized Mandarin and Cantonese.*—Rutland: C. E. Tuttle, 1970, xxix, 601 p.

0736 Giles, Herbert Allen: *A dictionary of colloquial idioms in the Mandarin dialect.* —Shanghai: A.H. de Carvalho, 1873, 3, 65 p.

0737 Hillier, Walter Caine: *An English-Chinese dictionary of the Peking colloquial.*—Shanghai: American Presbyterian Mission Press, 1910, viii, 712, 4 p.; London: Paul, Trench, Trübner, 1945, rev. & enl. ed. by Trelawny Backhouse & Sidney Barton, viii, 1030 p.; London: Routledge & K. Paul, 1953, repr.

0738 Lim, Yaw-tjiang: *A Mandarin dictionary (Chinese-Malay-English) and Peking syllabary.*—Shanghai: Commercial Press, 1922, v, iv, 370, 56 p.

0739 MacGillivray, Donald: *A Mandarin romanized dictionary of Chinese.*—Shanghai: Presbyterian Mission Press, 1907, 975 p.; Shanghai & London: Kegan Paul, 1930, 9th ed., x, 1145, 43 p.

0740 MacWeigh, Jean: *Dictionnaire phonétique chinois-français.*—Peking: Imprimerie des Lazaristes, 1893, x, 623 p.; 1906, rev. ed., xv, 734 p.

0741 Seidel, A.: *Systematisches Wörterbuch der nordchinesischen Umgangssprache (Peking-Dialekt).*—Oldenburg & Leipzig: A. Schwartz, 1901, 16, 208 p.

0742 Stent, George Carter: *A Chinese and English vocabulary in the Pekinese dialect.*—Shanghai: Customs Press, 1871, ix, 677 p.; 1877, 2nd ed., xii, 720 p.; Shanghai: American Presbyterian Mission Press, 1898, 3rd ed., rev. by Donald MacGillivray, vii, 788 p.
〔 漢英合璧相連字典 〕

0743 Wade, Thomas Francis: *An index to Dr. Williams' syllabic dictionary.*—Hong Kong & Shanghai: Kelly and Walsh, 1879, iv, 124 p.

0744 Williams, Samuel Wells: *Ying Hwá yun-fú lih-kiái. An English and Chinese vocabulary in the court dialect.*—Macao: Office of the Chinese Depository, 1844, lxxxviii, 440 p.
〔 英華韻府例解 〕

6.3. Hopei (0745–0776)

6.3.1. General Studies (0745–0750)

0745 An, Ju-p'an: Ho-pei fang-yen tz'u-hui li shih.—*FPC* 8, 1961, 73–106. [Dialect vocabulary of Hopei province explained with examples.]
安汝磐：河北方言詞滙例釋

0746 Chung-kuo k'o-hsüeh-yüan Ho-pei-sheng fen-yüan Yü-yen wen-hsüeh yen-chiu-so: Ho-pei-sheng fang-yen tz'u-hui tiao-ch'a cheng-li kung-tso te shou-huo.—*CKYW* 1960:12, 428–430. [Results of works on the survey and arrangement of dialect vocabulary of Hopei province.]
中國科學院河北省分院語言文學研究所：河北省方言詞滙調查整理工作的收獲

0747 Fujiwara, Teruzō: Seichō no hensen ni tsuite—Kahoku hōgen o chūshin toshite.—*AGDR* 18:2, 1970, 255–265. [The change of tones—With special reference to the dialects of Hopei province.]
藤原輝三：聲調の變遷について――河北方言を中心として

0748 Ho-pei Pei-ching shih-fan hsüeh-yüan & Chung-kuo k'o-hsüeh-yüan Ho-pei-sheng fen-yüan Yü-wen yen-chiu-so: *Ho-pei fang-yen kai-k'uang.*—Tientsin: Ho-pei jen-min, 1961, 2, 6, 80 p.; illus.; 24 maps./ *Orbis* 16, 1966, 111–112, Paul Yang Fu-mien. [General survey of Hopei dialects.]
河北北京師範學院，中國科學院河北省分院語文研究所：河北方言概況

0749 Hsiao, Hui: Tsan ch'ien, tsan fen yü shan-yao-tan.—*Kuang-tung chiao-yü yü wen-hua* 3:4, 1951, 33. [Dialect words *tsan ch'ien, tsan fen,* and *shan-yao-tan* explained.]
小蕙：『攢錢』，『攢糞』與『山葯蛋』

0750 Li, Hsing-chien: Ho-pei fang-yen chung te ku tz'u yü.—*CKYW* 1979:3, 227–231. [Archaic words in the dialects of Hopei province.]
李行健：河北方言中的古詞語

6.3.2. Northern Peking (Jehol) (0751–0755)

0751 Mullie, Joseph L-M.: Phonetische Untersuchungen Über die nordpekinesischen Sprachlaute.—*Anthropos* 8, 1913, 436–466.

0752 Mullie, Joseph L-M.: Une characteristique phonologique du dialect chinois de la Mongolie centrale.—*TP* 23, 1924, 67–81; 81–82: Comment by B. Karlgren.

0753 Mullie, Joseph L-M.: *Het Chineesch taaleigen, Indleiding tot de gesprokene taal, Nord-Pekineese dialect.*—Peiping, 1930–1933, 3 vols., xxxiii, 509; 607; 400 p./Linguistische Anthropos-Bibliothek, 5: 7.; *CCS* 6:12, 1933, 1082–1083, Anonymous.

0754 Mullie, Joseph L-M. Transl. by Versichel, A. Omer: *The structural principles of the Chinese language.*—Peiping: The Bureau of Engraving and Printing and Lazarist Press, 2 vols., 1932–1937, xxxiii, 566; 696 p./ *CCS* 6:2, 1933, 181–182, F. C. Dietz.

0755 Mullie, Joseph L-M.: *Korte Chinese spraakkunst van de gesproken taal (Noord-Pekinees dialect).*—Utrecht: Het Spectrum, 1947, iv, 273 p./ *Missiewerk* 27, 1948, 117–122, J. Wils.

6.3.3. Paoting (0756–0757)

0756 Yang, Fu-mien: Hōtei Tōryo hōgen no seichō.—*CGGG* 1960:97, 9–13. [Tones of the Tunglü dialect, Paoting.]
楊福綿：保定東閭方言の聲調

0757 Yang, Paul Fu-mien: Some characteristics of the Tunglü dialect.—*TICOJ* 8, 1963, 55–57.

6.3.4. Tientsin (0758–0760)

0758 Li, Shih-yü: T'ien-chin fang-yen tz'u-hui li-shih.—*FPC* 2, 1958, 9–19. [Examples of the vocabulary of the Tientsin dialect.]
李世瑜：天津方言詞彙例釋

0759 Nan-k'ai ta-hsüeh: *T'ien-chin fang-yen hsiao ts'u-tien.*—Tientsin: Nan-k'ai tahsüeh, 1950 [not seen]. [A pocket dictionary of the Tientsin dialect.]
南開大學：天津方言小詞典

0760 Wang, Chia-chün: T'ien-chin liu-hsing yü chung chih wai-lai-yü shih i.—*T'ien-chin wen-hua* 2, 1948, 9; 3, 1948, 9. [Explanations of loan-words in the colloquial speech of Tientsin.]
王家俊：天津流行語中之外來語釋義

6.3.5. Hochien (0761–0765)

0761 Chang, Hsün-ju: Ho-chien fang-yen i-luan.—*KYCK* 54, 1932, Oct. 1; 56, 1932, Oct. 15; 57, 1932, Oct. 22. [A slice of the Hochien dialect.]
張洵如：河間方言一臠

0762 Couvreur, Séraphin: *Langue Mandarine: Guide de la conversation français-anglais-chinois, contenant un vocabulaire et des dialogues familiers.*—Hokienfu: Imprimerie de la Mission Catholique, 1899, 4th ed., x, 222 p.; 1926, 11th ed., 452 p./ Mandarin Language: Guide to conversation in French, English and Chinese, containing vocabulary and familiar dialogues.

0763 Wieger, Léon: *Koan-hoa jou-men. Cours pratique de chinois parlé à l'usage des missionnaires du Tcheli S.E. Sons et tons usuels du Hokienfou.*—Ho Kien Fou: Imprimerie de la Mission Catholique, 1892, 4 pts./ *CCS* 5:11, 1932, Henri Bernard.
〔官話入門〕

0764 Wieger, Léon: *Rudiments de parler chinois, dialecte du* 河間府 *Ho Kien Fou.* 1er volume: *Introduction, méchanisme, phraséologie.*—Ho Kien Fou: Imprimerie de la Mission Catholique, 1895, 1513 p.; 1912, 3rd ed., title changed to: *Chinois parlé, manuel Koan-hoa du Nord, non-Pékinois,* 1146 p.

0765 Wieger, Léon: *Rudiments de parler chinois, dialecte du Ho Kien Fou.* Vol. V-VI: *Narrations populaires.*—Ho Kien Fou: Imprimerie de la Mission Catholique, 1893; 1903, rev. ed., 785 p.

6.3.6.   Other Localities (0766–0769)

0766   Anonymous: Ch'ang-li-hua te chi-ko yü-fa t'e-tien.—*CKYW* 1959:10, 493–496. [Some special grammatical features of the Ch'angli dialect.]
無名氏：昌黎話的幾個語法特點

0767   Ch'ang-li-hsien hsien-chih pien-tsuan wei-yüan-hui & Chung-kuo k'o-hsüeh-yüan Yü-yen yen-chiu-so fang-yen tsu: *Ch'ang-li fang-yen chih.*—Peking: K'o-hsüeh, 1960, iv, 283 p., 12 maps./ *RBS* 6, 1960, 386, Li Fang-kuei; *CKYW* 1960:12, 447–449, Wang Fu-t'ang; *Orbis* 15, 1966, 113–114, Paul Yang. [A survey of the Ch'angli dialect.]
昌黎縣縣志編纂委員會，中國科學院語言研究所方言組：昌黎方言志 / 王福堂評

0768   Jen, Tan & Li, Liu-shun: Cheng-chou fang-yen tiao-ch'a pao-kao.—*K'ai-feng shih-fan hsüeh-yüan hsüeh-sheng k'o-hsüeh hsi-tso* 1957:1, 45–61. [A report on the dialect survey in the city of Cheng-chou.]
任丹，李流順：鄭州方言調查報告

0769   Yang, Nai-szu & Shen, Shih-ying: Kao-ch'eng fang-yen li te men.—*CKYW* 1958: 6, 278. [The *men* (suffix) in the Kaoch'eng dialect.]
楊耐思，沈士英：藁城方言裏的『們』

6.3.7.   Contrastive Studies (0770–0776)

0770   Chao, Yüan-jen: Ting-hsien fang-yin kai Kuo-yin te chu-i-tien.—*KYCK* 243, 1936, May 30. [Points for attention to be paid to when converting Tinghsien dialect pronunciations to National Language pronunciations.]
趙元任：定縣方音改國音的注意點

0771   Chih, Ko: Ho-pei Wei-hsien-hua ho P'u-t'ung-hua te ch'a-pieh.—*FPC* 6, 1959, 112–118. [The differences between the Weihsien dialect of Hopei and the Common Language.]
止戈：河北魏縣話和普通話的差別

0772   Hou, Ching-i, Pa, Sang & Tien, Fu: Tui Shuo T'ien-chin-hua te jen tsen-yang hsüeh-hsi P'u-t'ung-hua i-wen te i-chien. —*CKYW* 1956:10, 51. [Some opinions concerning Li Shih-yü's article (0774).]
侯精一，巴桑，殿福：對『說天津話的人怎樣學習普通話』一文的意見

0773   Huang, Ch'i: T'ien-chin-jen jung-i hsüeh-hao P'u-t'ung-hua.—*FPC* 2, 1958, 1–8. [Easiness of a Tientsin dialect speaker in learning the Common Language.]
黃綺：天津人容易學好普通話

0774   Li, Shih-yü: Shuo T'ien-chin-hua te jen tsen-yang hsüeh-hsi P'u-t'ung-hua. — *CKYW* 1956:4, 24–27. [How a speaker of the Tientsin dialect should learn the Common Language.]
李世瑜：說天津話的人怎樣學習普通話

0775   Liu, Kuang-hua & Wei, Li: Shih-chia-chuang fang-yin yü Pei-ching-yin te tui-ying kuei-lü.—*FPC* 2, 1958, 19–21. [The rules of correspondence in the pronunciations of the Shihchiachuang dialect and the Peking dialect.]
劉光華，魏立：石家莊方音與北京音的對應規律

0776   P'ang, An-fu: Ho-pei Wan-hsien-hua ho P'u-t'ung-hua te ch'a-pieh.—*FPC* 6, 1959, 110–112. [The differences between the Wanhsien dialect of Hopei and the Common Language.]
龐安福：河北完縣話和普通話的差別

6.4.   Northeastern Provinces (0777–0794)

6.4.1.   General Studies (0777–0782)

0777   Chin, Kuei-shih: Tung-pei Huang-hai yen-an chi-ko ti-fang te yü-yin wen-t'i.—*CLTH* 1959:4, 57–63. / *CGGG* 1960:8, 16, Hirayama Hisao. [Phonetic problems of the dialects spoken along the coastal areas of the northeast.]
金貴士：東北黃海沿岸幾個地方的語音問題 / 平山久雄評介

0778 Chou, Hsiao-jo: Tung-pei ju-shengte yen-pien.—*KYCK* 41, 1932, July 2. [The development of the *ju* tone in northeastern dialects.]
周孝若：東北入聲的演變

0779 Fu, Wei: Tung-pei yin ho Pei-ching-yin te erh-hua-yün.—*YWCS* 1957:4, 28. [Northeastern dialects and the erization in Pekinese.]
傅爲：東北音和北京音的『兒化韵』

0780 Fang, Mao: Tung-pei fang-yen tz'u-hui li shih.—*FPC* 2, 1958, 96–109. [Explanations of dialect words of the northeast.]
方矛：東北方言詞滙例釋

0781 Hayashi, Yukimitsu: Tōhoku no hōon ni tsuite.—*CGGG* 1947:9, [not seen]. [On the dialects of the northeast.]
林雪光：東北の方音について

0782 Hayashi, Yukimitsu: Tōhoku hōon no ichi kōsatsu.—*Kōbe Gaikokugo Daigaku kaigaku kinen ronbunshū* (Kobe; Kōbe Gaikokugo Daigaku, 1949) 49–63. [An observation on the dialect sounds of northeast China.]
林雪光：東北方音の一考察──『神戶外國語大學開學記念論文集』

6.4.2. Various Localities (0783–0787)

0783 Chi-lin ta-hsüeh Chung-wen-hsi fang-yen tiao-ch'a hsiao-tsu: T'ung-hua yin-hsi.—*CLTH* 1959:4, 35–62. [Phonetic system of the T'unghua dialect.]
吉林大學中文系方言調查小組：通化音系

0784 Katō, Toyotaka: 1941-nen-goro no Harubinshi Fukaden ni okeru tokushu goi.—*CGGG* 1971:6, 1–5; 1971:7, 1–7; 1971:8, 1–10. [Vulgar words used at Fuchiatien, Harbin, around 1941.]
加藤豐隆：1941年頃の哈爾濱市傳家甸における特殊語彙

0785 Liao-ning ta-hsüeh Chung-kuo yü-yen wen-hsüeh-hsi yü-yen chiao-yen shih: Liao-ning yü-yin shuo-lüeh.—*CKYW* 1963:2, 104–114. [A brief discussion on the phonetics of Liaoning.]
遼寧大學中國語言文學系語言教研室：遼寧語音說略

0786 N.L.: Liao-hsi ti-ch'ü yü-yen chung te yin-pien.—*YWCS* 1955:11, 29–30. [Sound changes in the dialects of western Liaoning.]
N. L.：遼西地區語言中的音變

0787 Tu, Shu-t'ien: Shen-yang t'u-hua hui-chi chu-shih.—*STYK* 22, 1935, 192–211; 26, 1936, 197–206. [Collection and explanation of the dialect vocabulary of Shenyang.]
杜書田：瀋陽土話滙集注釋

6.4.3. Contrastive Studies (0788–0794)

0788 Azuma, Toranzō: Chūgoku hyōjungoon to Ryōtō hōon ni tsuite.—*OSGK* 113, 1963, 16–20; 16:E.S. [On the pronunciations of Standard Chinese and the Liaotung dialect.]
東寅三：中國標準語音と遼東方音について

0789 Chang, Hsiang-ch'en: Liao-ning Hsin-min fang-yin yü Pei-ching yü-yin te pi-chiao.—*FPC* 3, 1958, 53–61. [Comparison of the pronunciations of the Hsinmin dialect of Liaoning with Pekinese.]
張相臣：遼寧新民方音與北京語音的比較

0790 Hei-lung-chiang-sheng Chiao-yü-t'ing P'u-t'ung-hua t'ui-kuang-k'o: Hei-lung-chiang-sheng yü-yin yü P'u-t'ung-hua yü-yin te ch'u-pu tui-chao.—*Hei-lung-chiang chiao-yü* 1957:3, 28–30. [A preliminary phonetic comparison between the dialects of Heilungchiang and the Common Language.]
黑龍江省教育廳普通話推廣科：黑龍江省語音與普通話語音的初步對照

0791 Ho, Ai-jen: Tung-pei Sung-hua-chiang liu-yü yü-yin t'ung Pei-ching yü-yin pi-chiao yu na-hsieh hsien-chu ch'a-i.—*YWCS* 1956:1, 29–32. [What the salient phonetic differences between the dialects spoken along the Sunghua River N.E. and the Peking dialect are.]

何靄人：東北松花江流域語音同北京語音比較有哪些顯著差異

0792 Shang, Yün-ch'uan: Liao-yang-yin ho Pei-ching-yin te pi-chiao.—*FPC* 7, 1959, 18–20. [Comparison of Liaoyang pronunciation and Pekinese.]

尚允川：遼陽音和北京音的比較

0793 Sung, Hsüeh: Liao-ning (chiu-ko ti-ch'ü) yü Pei-ching sheng-tiao tui-ying kuan-hsi.—*FPC* 7, 1959, 14–18. [Tonal correspondences between Liaoning (9 areas) and Pekinese.]

宋學：遼寧（九個地區）與北京聲調對應關係

0794 Zhou, Ning: Tung-pei nan-pu tu-yin yü pei-fang P'u-t'ung-hua tu-yin te pu-t'ung.—*YWCS* 1955: 3, 36–38. [The differences between pronunciations of the southern regions of the Northeast and the Common Language.]

Zhou Ning: 東北南部讀音與北方普通話讀音的不同

6.5. Shantung, Northern Kiangsu and Honan (0795–0886)

6.5.1. Shantung (0795–0855)

6.5.1.1. General Studies (0795–0802)

0795 Abe, Tadashi: *Santōshō Shinago no kenkyū.*—Tsingtao: Shubigunmin seifubu, 1920 [not seen]. [Research on the Chinese language spoken in Shantung province.]/ Weihsien dialect.

安悟貞：山東省支那語の研究

0796 Chou, Kan-t'ing: Shan-tung jeng tai ku-yin te t'u-yü.—*CTYK* 1:8, 1931, 735–739. [Dialects in Shantung province still preserving ancient pronunciations.]

周幹庭：山東仍帶古音的土語

0797 Chou, Kan-t'ing: Shan-tung t'u-yü yen-chiu.—*CTCK* 6, 1935, 95–134; 7, 1935, 127–145. [A study on the dialects of Shantung province.]

周幹庭：山東土語研究

0798 Ch'ü, Wan-li: Ch'i Lu fang-yen tsa k'ao.—*Shih-tai ch'ing-nien* 1:1, 1936, 21–23. [Miscellaneous studies on the dialects of Ch'i and Lu (Shantung province).]

屈萬里：齊魯方言雜考

0799 Miller, Roy A.: *Studies in the Lu dialect.*—New York: Columbia U., 1950, 74 p./ Unpubl. M.A. thesis.

0800 T'ang, Ping-cheng: Ch'i-tung ku yü che lu.—*Chih-yen* 17, 1935, May. [Selected archaic words of eastern Shantung.]

湯炳正：齊東古語摘錄

0801 Ting, Wei-fen: Ch'i-tung yü.—*Shan-tung sheng-li t'u-shu-kuan chi-k'an* 1:1, 1931, 169–182. [The dialect of eastern Shantung.]

丁惟汾：齊東語

0802 Umehara, Keiun: Santō no hōgen ni tsuite.—*CGGG* 1947:5 [not seen]. [On the dialects of Shantung.]

梅原慧運：山東の方言について

6.5.1.2. Phonetics and Phonology (0803–0810)

0803 Arisaka, Hideyo: Santōkei no ichi hōon ni tsuite.—*Hōgen* 7:1, 1938, 22–37; *Kokugo on'inshi no kenkyū* (0097), 375–390. [A dialect of Shantung.]

有坂秀世：山東系の一方音について

0804 Bröring, Theodor: Experimental-phonetische Untersuchung über Laut und Ton Südschantung.—*Vox* 1925, 6–7.

0805 Bröring, Theodor: *Laut und Ton in Süd-Schantung, mit Anhang: Die töne in Nordostschantung, Peking, Sötschuän, Shanghai, Amoy und Canton.*—Hamburg: L. Friederichsen, 1927, 63 p., fold map. / Veröffentlichungen Seminar für Sprache und Kultur Chinas an der Hamburgischen Universität, 2.

〔卞志一：山東音聲〕

0806 Giet, Franz: Die Töne in Süd-Shantung besprochen und dargestellt von P. Franz Giet, S.V.D.—*Beiträge zur Einführung ins Chinesische Studium,* 1937, 9 p.

0807 Giet, Franz: Die Töne des Südschantung-Dialekts in Wortverbindungen.—*Beiträge zur Einführung ins Chinesische Studium,* 1939, 108 p., tab.

0808 Hsieh, Hsiu-wen: Hsien hua Lu-nan fang-yin.—*Shan-tung wen-hsien* 2:3, 1976, 120–122. [A chat on the dialect pronunciation of southern Shantung.]
謝秀文：閒話魯南方音

0809 Jo, Ping: Lu-nan fang-yin te t'e-tien.—*FPC* 2, 1958, 29–30. [Phonetic characteristics of the dialects of southern Shantung.]
若氷：魯南方音的特點

0810 Yang, Feng: Shan-tung fang-yin piencheng chü-li.—*FPC* 6, 1959, 1–13. [Examples of the conversion of the dialect sounds of Shantung into standard pronunciation.]
楊峯：山東方音辨正舉例

6.5.1.3. Vocabulary and Grammar (0811–0814)

0811 Jen, Chün-tse: Lu-hsi fang-yen tz'u-hui.—*FPC* 3, 1958, 35–46; 6, 1959, 22–61. [Dialect vocabulary of western Shantung.]
任均澤：魯西方言詞滙

0812 Kubota, Kyūsaku: Santō goishū.—*Shinago* 4:3–7, 1935 [not seen]. [Dialect vocabulary of Shantung.]
久保田久作：山東語彙集

0813 Mittler, Theodor: *Chinesische grammatik. Einführung in die Umgangssprache, mit besonderer Berücksichtigung der Shantungsprache.*—Yenchoufu: Verlag der Katholischen Mission, 1927, xxxvii, 515 p.

0814 Nagao, Mitsuyuki: Tan'onsetsugo to nionsetsugo no suryō chōsa (joron)—Ro hōgen to gendaigo no baai.—*Shūkan Tōyōgaku* 29, 1973, 227–240. [Toward statistical research of monosyllabic and disyllabic words (Introduction)—The cases of the Lu dialect and modern Chinese.]
長尾光之：單音節語と二音節語の數量調查（序論）── 魯方言と現代語の場合

6.5.1.4. Anch'iu (0815–0817)

0815 Chou, Kan-t'ing: *An-ch'iu t'u-yü chih.*—Tsinan: Ch'i-lu ta-hsüeh Kuo-hsüeh yen-chiu-so, 1939, 82 p. [A record of Anch'iu patois.]
周幹庭：安邱土語誌

0816 Ts'ao, Cheng-i: An-ch'iu fang-yen tz'u-hui.—*FPC* 8, 1961, 54–63. [Vocabulary of the Anch'iu dialect.]
曹正一：安丘方言詞滙

0817 Ts'ao, Cheng-i: Shan-tung An-ch'iu fang-yen tsai tz'u-hui yü-fa shang te i-hsieh t'e-tien.—*FPC* 8, 1961, 64–72. [Some special lexical and grammatical features of the Anch'iu dialect of Shantung.]
曹正一：山東安丘方言在詞滙語法上的一些特點

6.5.1.5. Chiaohsien (0818–0823)

0818 Chang, Ch'ün-yen: Chiao-chou fang-yen.—*Chiao-chou chih* (1845, rev. ed.), Chüan 5:3–4; *Chung-kuo fang-chih so-lu fang-yen hui-pien* (0454), 8:247–250. [The Chiaochou dialect.]
張群鴈：膠州方言──『膠州志』

0819 Chao, Ch'i, et al.: Chiao-ao fang-yen.—*Chiao-ao chih, min-she chih II* (1928 ed.), 63–70; *Chung-kuo fang-chih so-lu fang-yen hui-pien* (0454), 8: 239–245. [The Chiaoao dialect.]
趙琪等：膠澳方言──『膠澳志，民社志二』

0820 Ch'en, P'ei-lan: *Kuang-yün* ju-sheng tsai Chiao-tung-yü chung te yen-pien.—*KYCK* 47, 1932, Aug. 13. [The development of the *ju* tone of *Kuang-yün* in the Chiaotung dialect.]

陳培蘭：『廣韻』入聲在膠東語中的演變

0821 Ch'ien, Tseng-i: Chiao-tung fang-yin kai-k'uang.—*STTH* 1959:4, 110–129. [A sketch of the Chiaotung dialect.]

錢曾怡：膠東方音概況

0822 Kallgren, Gerty: Notes on the Kiao-hsien dialect.—*BMFEA* 27, 1955, 11–40. / *RBS* 1, 1955, 277, H.F. Simon.

0823 K'uang, Ch'ao, et al.: Chiao-hsien fang-yen.—*Tseng-hsiu Chiao chih* (Chiaohsien: Ta-t'ung yin-shua-she, 1931), Chüan 10: 5–13; *Chung-kuo fang-chih so-lu fang-yen hui-pien* (0454) 8: 131–146. [The Chiaohsien dialect.]

匡超等：膠縣方言----『增修膠志』

6.5.1.6. Various Localities (0824–0839)

0824 Anonymous: Tzu-ch'uan t'u-yü tz'u-tien.—*Liao-chai ch'üan chi* (Taipei: Chin-hsüeh shu-chü, 1970), 3 p. [Vocabulary of the Tzuch'uan dialect, Shantung.]

無名氏：淄川土語辭典 ──『聊齋全集』

0825 Ch'en, Shun-cheng: *Jung-ch'eng fang-yen yin-hsi.*—Taipei: San-jen-hsing, 1974, 66 p., tab. [Phonetics and phonology of the Jungch'eng dialect, Shantung.]

陳舜政：榮成方言音系

0826 Ch'ien, Tseng-i: Chi-nan-hua te pien-tiao ho ch'ing-sheng.—*STTH* 1963:1, 86–97. [Tone sandhi and the neutral tone in the Chinan (Tsinan) dialect.]

錢曾怡：濟南話的變調和輕聲

0827 Hsüeh, Feng-sheng: The P'ing-tu dialect as a variant of Mandarin.—*CHHP* 10:1, 1973, 74–89; C.S.

〔薛鳳生：論平度方言之官話成分〕

0828 Hsüeh, Ju-hua, et al.: Ch'iu-hsien fang-yen.—*Ch'iu-hsieh chih* (Chinan(?),

1935), last chüan: 1–7; *Chung-kuo fang-chih so-lu fang-yen hui-pien* (0454), 8: 117–129. [The Ch'iuhsien dialect.]

薛儒華等：邱縣方言──『邱縣志』

0829 Liu, Jen-ch'ien, et al.: Lin-hsü fang-yen.—*Lin-hsü hsü-chih* (Tsingtao: Chün-te-ch'ang nan-chih yin-shua-chü, 1931), Chüan 18:41–70; *Chung-kuo fang-chih so-lu fang-yen hui-pien* (0454), 8:149–207. [The Linhsü dialect.]

劉仞千等：臨朐方言──『臨朐續志』

0830 Mei, Ch'i-hsi, et al.: Tung-p'ing fang-yen.—*Tung-p'ing chou-chih* (1878 ed.), Chüan 2, 16–18; *Chung-kuo fang-chih so-lu fang-yen hui-pien* (0454), 8:3–7. [The Tungp'ing dialect.]

梅啓熙等：東平方言──『東平州志』

0831 Pai, Ti-chou: Shan-tung Yang-ku ju-sheng chih pien tu.—*KYCK* 117, 1933, Dec. 26. [The change of readings in the *ju* tone of Yangku.]

白滌洲：山東陽谷入聲之變讀

0832 Sakamoto, Ichirō: Sokuboku hōgen on'in goi.—*SK* 54, 1940, 67–127. [The pronunciation and vocabulary of the Chimo dialect.]

坂本一郎：卽墨方言音韻語彙

0833 Shan-tung ta-hsüeh Chung-wen-hsi She-hui shih-chien fang-yen tiao-ch'a hsiao-tsu: Yen-t'ai fang-yen pao-kao.—*STTH* 1963:3, 21–51. [A report on the Yent'ai dialect.]

山東大學中文系社會實踐方言調查小組：煙台方言報告

0834 Tien, Lu: Chü-nan fang-yen.—*FPC* 6, 1959, 14–21. [The Chünan dialect.]

奠陸：莒南方言

0835 Tung, Tsun-chang: Shan-tung Shou-kuang fang-yen li te i-hsieh yü-yin, yü-fa hsien-hsiang.—*CKYW* 1957:5, back cover. [Some phonetic and grammatical phenomena in the Shoukuang dialect, Shantung.]

董遵章：山東壽光方言裏的一些語音語法現象

0836 Wang, Meng-hsü, et al.: Lin-i fang-yen.—*Lin-i-hsien hsü-chih* (Chinan: T'ien-ch'eng-ch'ien-chi nan-chih-tien, 1936), Chüan 4:6; *Chung-kuo fang-chih so-lu fang-yen hui-pien* (0454), 8:115–116.

王孟戌等： 臨邑方言——『 臨邑縣續志 』

0837 Wang, P'ei-hsü, et al.: Lai-yang fang-yen.—*Lai-yang hsien-chih* (Chinan (?), 1935), Chüan 3:2, 31–41; *Chung-kuo fang-chih so-lu fang-yen hui-pien* (0454), 8:26–44. [The Laiyang dialect.]

王丕煦：萊陽方言——『萊陽縣志 』

0838 Yü, Ch'ing-p'an, et al.: Mou-p'ing fang-yen.—*Mou-p'ing hsien-chih* (Chinan: Shan-tung yin-shua-chü, 1936), Chüan 10:46–80; *Chung-kuo fang-chih so-lu fang-yen hui-pien* (0454), 8:47–106. [The Moup'ing dialect.]

于清泮等： 牟平方言——『 牟平縣志 』

0839 Yüan, Shao-ang, et al.: Chi-ning fang-yen p'ien.—*Chi-ning hsien-chih* (1927), Chüan 4, 23–31; *Chung-kuo fang-chih so-lu fang-yen hui-pien* (0454), 8:23–25. [The Chining dialect.]

袁紹昂等：濟寧方言篇——『濟寧縣志 』

6.5.1.7. Dictionaries (0840–0844)

0840 Anonymous: *Deutsch-Chinesisches Taschen-Lexikon, mit besonderer Berücksichtigung der Schantung-Sprache.*—Yenchoufu: Katholische Mission, 1908, iv, 658 p.

0841 Bousack, Christian: *Chinesische Wortkunde. Neue Methode der Chinesischen Sprache durch die Wortquell-Rechschreibung tonrein sprechen zu lernen. Spezialausgabe für Shantung.*—Münster: Aschendorff, 1957, x, 106 p./ Veröffentlichungen des Inst. für Mission wissenschaft der Westfälischen Wilhelms-Univ. 5.

0842 Bröring, Theodor: *Deutsch-Chinesisches Hand-Wörterbuch, mit besonderer Berücksichtigung der Schantung-Sprache.*—Yen-choufu: Verlag der Kath. Mission, 1906–1907, 2 vols., ix, 1171 p.; 1917, 2nd ed., xviii, 1091, 16 p.

0843 Stangier, Joseph & Jörgens, Otto: *Chinesisch-Deutches Taschen-Wörterbuch.*—Tsingtao: Druck & Verlag der Missiondruckerei, 1941, ix, 857 p./ Mandarin and Shantung dialect pronunciations.

0844 Welzel, A.: *Deutsch-Chinesisches Taschenwörterbuch, mit Aussprache-bezeichnung der Chinesischen Wörter unter besonderer Berüksichtigung des Schantungdialektes.*—Tsingtao: Deutsche Druckerei, 1902, vi, 148, 5 p.

6.5.1.8. Contrastive Studies (0845–0855)

0845 Azuma, Torazō: Futsūwa to Santō hōon no taiō kankei.—Yokohama: The Author, 1963, 18 p.; map. / Mimeogr. [On the phonetic correspondences between the Common Language and the Shantung dialects.]

東寅三： 普通話と山東方音の對應關係

0846 Chang, Chao-yü & Kao, Wen-ta: Chinan-yin ho Pei-ching-yin te pi-chiao.—*FPT* 1, 1958, 103–139. [Comparison of Chinan and Peking pronunciations.]

張兆鈺，高文達： 濟南音和北京音的比較

0847 Kao, Wen-ta: Shang-tung ko-ti fang-yin yü Pei-ching yü-yin tsai sheng-mu yün-mu fang-mien te i-hsieh pi-chiao.—*FPC* 3, 1958, 30–32. [Some comparisons of initials and finals in the dialects of different areas of Shantung with the Common Language.]

高文達： 山東各地方音與北京語音在聲母韵母方面的一些比較

0848 Kao, Wen-ta: Shan-tung Ning-yang yin yü Pei-ching yin.—*FPC* 3, 1958, 32–35. [The pronunciations of the Ningyang dialect of Shantung and the Peking dialect.]

高文達：山東寧陽音與北京音

0849 Kao, Wen-ta: Shan-tung Huang-hsien fang-yin yü Pei-ching yü-yin te tui-ying.—*FPC* 8, 1961, 33–39. [Phonetic correspondences between the Huanghsien dialect of Shantung and the Peking dialect.]
高文達：山東黃縣方音與北京語音的對應

0850 Pao, Ming-wei: *Lu-hsi-nan-jen tsen-yang hsüeh-hsi P'u-t'ung-hua.*—Chinan: Shan-tung jen-min, 1957, 52 p. [How dialect speakers from southwest Shantung should learn the Common Language.]
鮑明煒：魯西南人怎樣學習普通語

0851 Tai, Lei: P'ing-tu fang-yin yü P'u-t'ung-hua yü-yin te i-t'ung chi ch'i tui-ying kuei-lü.—*FPC* 2, 1958, 22–29. [Phonetic differences and correspondences between the P'ingtu dialect and the Common Language.]
戴磊：平度方音與普通話語音的異同及其對應規律

0852 Ting, Chih-k'un: Chu-ch'eng-hua yü piao-chun-yü yü-yin te hsi-t'ung pi chao.—*Shan-tung ta-hsüeh hsüeh-sheng k'o-hsüeh lun-wen chi-k'an* 1956: 1:4, 1–30. [A systematic phonetic comparison of the Chuch'eng dialect and the Standard Language.]
丁志坤：諸城話與標準語語音的系統比照

0853 Ts'ao, Cheng-i: Shan-tung An-ch'iu fang-yin ho Pei-ching yü-yin.—*FPC* 8, 1961, 39–54. [The pronunciations of the Anch'iu dialect of Shantung and the Peking dialect.]
曹正一：山東安丘方音和北京語音

0854 Wu, Lang: *Chi-nan-hua ho P'u-t'ung-hua yu na-hsieh pu-t'ung te ti-fang.*—Chinan: Shan-tung jen-min, 1957, 37 p. [What are the differences between the Chinan dialect and the Common Language?]
吳朗：濟南話和普通話有哪些不同的地方

0855 Yang, Feng: Lu hsi-nan sheng-tiao yü Pei-ching sheng-tiao te tui-ying ch'ing-

k'uang.—*FPC* 2, 1958, 30–33. [Tonal correspondences between the dialects of southwestern Shantung and the Peking dialect.]
楊峰：魯西南聲調與北京聲調的對應情況

6.5.2. Northern Kiangsu (0856–0859)

0856 Chang, Che-sheng: Mo, p'u-ho, mei.—*CKYW* 1979:4, 310–312. [The words *mo, p'u-ho* and *mei* in the Hsüchou dialect.]
張喆生：抹，蒲合，每

0857 Chiang, Hsi-wen: Kan-yü fang-yen te jen-ch'eng tai-tz'u.—*CKYW* 1957:8, 27, 19. [Personal pronouns in the Kanyü dialect.]
蔣希文：贛榆方言的人稱代詞

0858 Chiang, Hsi-wen: Kan-yü fang-yen te sheng-mu.—*CKYW* 1961:9, 25–29. [The initials in the Kanyü dialect.]
蔣希文：贛榆方言的聲母

0859 Chiang, Hsi-wen: Kan-yü-hua erh-hua-tz'u te t'e-shu tso-yung.—*CKYW* 1962:6, 276–278./ *RBS* 8, 1962, 522, S.N. Cartier. [Special function of the *-erh* suffix in the Kanyü dialect.]
蔣希文：贛榆話兒化詞的特殊作用

6.5.3. Honan (0860–0886)

6.5.3.1. General Studies (0860–0864)

0860 Ch'i, Chih: Ho-nan fang-yen chung te *u*.—*KYCK* 29, 1932, April 2. [The vowel *u* in the Honan dialect.]
憨之：河南方言中的 *u*

0861 Ho-nan T'ung-chih kuan: Ho-nan fang-yen tiao-ch'a.—*Ho-nan chiao-yü yüeh-k'an* 5:7, 1935, 1–39. [On the dialect survey of Honan province.]
河南通志館：河南方言調查

0862 Jen, Chün-tse: Ho-nan fang-yen tz'u-hui.—*FPC* 3, 1958, 16–29; 6, 1959, 102–109. [Dialect vocabulary of Honan.]
任均澤：河南方言詞滙

0863 Shih, Tsung-chou: Chi Sung fang-yen shih li.—*Hsüeh-ts'ui* 6:2, 1964, 25; 6:3, 1964, 21–24; 6:6, 1964, 24–26; 7:1, 1964, 24; 7:4, 1965, 24–26; 8:1, 1965, 25–26; also reprinted in *Chung-kuo wen-tzu lun-ts'ung* (Taipei: Chung-hua ts'ung-shu, 1978), 315–452. [Explanation of dialect words of Chihsien and K'aifeng.]
史宗周：杞宋方言釋例──『中國文字論叢』

0864 Tu, Tzu-chin: Ho-nan su-yü lu.—*K'ai-feng nü-shih hsiao-k'an* 6, 1937, 31–40. [A record of popular sayings of Honan.]
杜子勁：河南俗語錄

6.5.3.2. Chungho (0865–0866)

0865 Ho, Wei: Chung-ho fang-yen chung te pəʔ, kuəʔ, kəʔ.—*CKYW* 1959:6, 272–274. [The functions of *pəʔ*, *kuəʔ*, and *kəʔ* in the Chungho dialect.]
賀巍：中和方言中的『呸』、『喟』、『圪』

0866 Ho, Wei: Chung-ho fang-yen te tai-tz'u.—*CKYW* 1962:1, 50–53. [Pronouns in the Chungho dialect.]
賀巍：中和方言的代詞

6.5.3.3. Huochia (0867–0868)

0867 Ho, Wei: Huo-chia fang-yen yün-mu pien-hua te kung-yung chü li.—*CKYW* 1965:4, 299–303./ *RBS* 11, 1965, 405, A. Lucas. [Morphological functions of sound changes occurring in finals of the Huochia dialect.]
賀巍：獲嘉方言韻母變化的功用舉例

0868 Ho, Wei: Huo-chia fang-yen te lien-tu pien-tiao.—*FY* 1979:2, 122–136. [Tone sandhi in the Huochia dialect.]
賀巍：獲嘉方言的連讀變調

6.5.3.4. K'aifeng (0869–0870)

0869 Chou, Meng-che; Wu, Hung-hsü & Wang, Ching-chu'an: K'ai-feng-shih fang-yen tiao-ch'a pao-kao.—*K'ai-feng-shih-*

fan hsüeh-yüan hsüeh-sheng k'o-hsüeh hsi-tso 1957:1, 36–44. [A report on the dialect survey of K'aifeng City.]
周孟哲，吳宏緒，王鏡川：開封市方言調查報告

0870 Tōdō, Akiyasu: 17-seiki no Kaifū hōgen.—*Chūbun Gakkaihō* 7, 1956 [not seen]. [The dialect of K'aifeng in the 17th century.]
藤堂明保：17世紀の開封方言

6.5.3.5. Loyang (0871–0874)

0871 Chao, Yüeh-p'eng: Lo-yang-hua ch'ien-shuo.—*FPC* 2, 1958, 35–69. [A simple introduction to the Loyang dialect.]
趙月朋：洛陽話淺說

0872 Chao, Yüeh-p'eng: Lo-yang fang-yen chung te i-hsieh yü-fa hsien-hsiang. — *CKYW* 1958:7, 342–343. [Some grammatical phenomena in the Loyang dialect.]
趙月朋：洛陽方言中的一些語法現象

0873 Chao, Yüeh-p'eng: Lo-yang fang-yen tz'u-hui.—*FPC* 6, 1959, 68–102. [Loyang dialect vocabulary.]
趙月朋：洛陽方言詞滙

0874 Mather, Richard B.: A note on the dialect of Lo-yang and Nanking during the Six dynasties (0411).

6.5.3.6. Other Localities (0875–0880)

0875 Chang, Ch'i-huan; Ch'en, T'ien-fu & Ch'eng, I: Shang-ch'iu shih fang-yen k'ao.—*K'ai-feng shih yüan hsüeh-pao* 1960:7, 1–41. [A study on the Shangch'iu dialect.]
張啓煥，陳天福，程儀：商丘市方言考

0876 Hsü, Wei-yü: Teng-chou fang-yen k'ao.—*Yü-yen yü wen-hsüeh*, 1937, 133–140. [A study on the dialect of Tengchou.]
許維遹：登州方言考

0877 Wang, John C. & Hsüeh, Feng-sheng: The Lin-ch'i dialect and its relation to Mandarin.—*JAOS* 93, 1973, 136–145.
〔臨淇〕

0878 Wang, Li: San-pai-nien ch'ien Ho-nan Ning-ling fang-yin k'ao.—*KHLT* 1:2, 1927, 287–292. [The dialect pronunciation of Ningling, Honan three hundred years ago.]
王力：三百年前河南寧陵方音考

0879 Liu, William W.: Dialect features and communication problems in Linxian.—*JCL* 7:1, 1979, 29–43; C. S.
〔劉維漢：林縣方言特點分析〕

0880 Yang, Shih-feng & Ching, Yün-ching: Ling-pao fang-yen.—*CHHP* 9, 1–2, 1971, 106–147; E.S. [The Lingpao dialect.]
楊時逢，荊允敬：靈寶方言

6.5.3.7. Contrastive Studies (0881–0886)

0881 Hsü, Ch'eng-chün: Wen-hsien t'u-hua yü P'u-t'ung-hua chien-shuo.—*FPC* 5, 1958, 113–118. [Brief discussion of the Wenhsien dialect and the Common Language.]
徐承俊：溫縣土話與普通話簡說

0882 Huang, P'ei-hsü: Ho-nan-sheng Suihsien yü-yin ho Pei-ching yü-yin te pi-chiao.—*FPC* 6, 1959, 62–67. [A comparison of pronunciations of the Suihsien dialect, Honan province, and Pekinese.]
黃培需：河南省睢縣語音和北京語音的比較

0883 Ku, Pen-cheng: Shih t'an Ho-nan Hsiang-ch'eng fang-yen ho Pei-ching yü-yin te ch'a-i.—*FPC* 3, 1958, 1–13. [A tentative discussion of the phonetic differences between the Hsiangch'eng dialect and Pekinese.]
古本正：試談河南襄城方音和北京語音的差異

0884 Li, Ts'un-chü: Ho-nan fang-yin yü Pei-ching yü-yin te pi-chiao.—*FPC* 2, 1958, 34. [A phonetic comparison of the dialects of Honan with the Peking dialect.]
李存聚：河南方音與北京語音的比較

0885 Ma, P'ei-chih: Ling-pao fang-yin yü Pei-ching yü-yin te tui-ying.—*FPC* 2, 1958, 70–75. [The phonetic correspondences between the Lingpao dialect and Pekinese.]
馬培芝：靈寶方音與北京語音的對應

0886 Wang, Sung-mao: Ho-nan Che-ch'eng-yin-yü Pei-ching-yin te tui-ying kuan-hsi.—*FPC* 3, 1958, 13–16. [The phonetic correspondences between the Chech'eng dialect of Honan and Pekinese.]
王松茂：河南柘城音與北京音的對應關係

7. NORTHWESTERN MANDARIN DIALECTS (0887–0959)

7.1. Northwestern Mandarin in General (0887–0891)

0887 Dow, Francis D. M.: Nasalization: A traditional characteristic in Northwestern dialects.—*JCL* 2:2, 1974, 180–185.

0888 Hoppōgo Kenkyūkai: *Chūgoku seihoku hōgen shiryō.*—Tokyo: Tōkyō Gaigokugo Daigaku, 1956, 59 p. Mimeogr. [Materials on Northwestern Mandarin dialects.]
北方語研究會：中國西北方言資料

0889 Kanagae, Nobumitsu & Shimamura, Shūji:Seihoku hōgen no goi.—*Chūgoku gogaku jiten* (0093), 853–910. [Vocabulary of Northwestern Mandarin dialects.]
鐘ヶ江信光，島村修治：西北方言の語彙

0890 Nomura, Masayoshi: Hoku-Shi Sansei oyobi Mōkyō ni okeru Shinago hōgen'on no bunpu ni tsuite.—*Teikoku Gakushiin Tōa shominzoku chōsashitsu hōkokukai kiroku* 11, 1943, 30 p., 9 maps. [The geographical distribution of Chinese dialect sounds in northern China, Shansi and Inner Mongolia.]
野村正良： 北支山西及蒙疆に於ける支那語方言音の分布に就いて──『帝國學士院東亞諸民族調査室報告會記錄 』

0891 Novgorodskii, Iu. V.: *Foneticheskii ocherk severo-zapadnykh dialektov kidaiskogo iazyka.*—Moscow: Institut Narodov Azii Akademii Nauk SSSR, 1963. / Unpubl. doc. diss. [A study of the phonetics of the Northwestern dialects of the Chinese language.]

7.2. Hopei (formerly Chahar) (0892–0898)

0892 Grootaers, Willem A.: Une courte exploration linquistique dans le Chahar (Chine du Nord) avec un projet de ques-tionnaire dialectal.—*BSL* 46, 1950, 123–143.

0893 Grootaers, Willem A.: Linguistic geography of the 宣化 Hsüan-hua region (察哈爾 Chahar Province).—*BIHP* 29, 1958, 59–86; 10 maps./ *RBS* 4, 1958, 604, N.G.D. Malmqvist.

0894 Hashimoto, Mantarō: Chūgokugo Sūrei Shōgi hōgen'on jii.—*AAGB* 10, 1975, 144–164. [A syllabary of the Ch'ungli and Shangi dialects of Chinese.]
橋本萬太郎： 中國語崇禮、尙義方言音字彙

0895 Léva, René: *Particules du dialecte de Chahar.*—Siwantze: Scheut Language School, 1941, 343 p.

0896 Léva, René: *Dialecte du Chansi-Nord (Tchahar): liste alphabétique d'expressions avec traduction française.* — Peiping: Scheut Language School, 1944–1945, 2 vols., xxiv, 619 p.

0897 Nomura, Masayoshi: Chūgokugo Chaharu nanbu hōgen ni okeru bion no owaru inrui.—*Kindaichi hakushi koki kinen ronbunshū* (Tokyo, 1953), 969–991. [The nasal finals in the southern Chahar dialect.]
野村正良： 中國語察哈爾南部方言における鼻音に終る韻類── 『 金田一博士古稀紀念論文集 』

0898 Nomura, Masayoshi: Chōkako hōgen oyobi Hōtō hōgen ni okeru seirui — iwayuru seihoku shohōgen to-no hikaku.—*NGBK* 10:4, 1955, 1–62; 143: E.S. [Initials in the Changchiak'ou and Paot'ou dialects—A comparative study with the so-called Northwestern dialects.]
野村正良： 張家口方言及包頭方言に於ける聲類── いわゆる西北諸方言との比較

7.3. Shansi (0899–0925)
7.3.1. General Studies (0899–0904)

0899 Feng, Kuo-jui: Kuan-hsi fang-yen chin shih.—*Kuo-feng* 6:7–8, 1935, 43–54; 6:9–10, 1935, 19–30; 7:1, 1935, 28–39. [Dialect words of Shansi, Shensi and Kansu in Yang Hsiung's *Fang-yen,* with new explanations.]

馮國瑞：關西方言今釋

0900 Hashimoto, Mantarō J.: Shingo sho-hōgen no hikaku kenkyū.—*AAGB* 12, 1976, 11–58; 13, 1977, 77–127; 14, 1977, 72–132. [A comparative study of the Chin dialects of Chinese.]

橋本萬太郎：晉語諸方言の比較研究

0901 Kuraishi, Takeshirō: Shinnan no hōgen shiryō.—*Morohashi hakushi koki shukuga kinen ronbunshū* (Tokyo: Taishūkan, 1953), 289–306. [Dialect materials from southern Shansi.]

倉石武四郎：晉南の方言資料――『諸橋博士古稀祝賀記念論文集』

0902 Liu, Wen-chin: Ch'in-chung fang-yen. —*CSTY* 8:85–87, 1929, 64–77. [The dialects of central Shensi.]

劉文錦：秦中方言

0903 Serruys, Paul L.-M.: Les cérémonies du marriage. Usages populaires et textes dialectaux du sud de la préfecture de Tat'oung (Chansi).—*Folklore Studies* 3:1, 1944, 73–154; 3:2, 1944, 77–129./ *Journal of American Folklore* 61, 1948, 323, R. C. Rudolph.

0904 Ts'ui, Ying-k'o: Shan-hsi Wen-hsi-hsien chih fang-yen.—*CSTY* 9:106, 1929, 9–11. [The dialect of Wenhsi district, Shansi.]

崔盈科：山西聞喜縣之方言

7.3.2. Phonology (0905–0913)

0905 Chao, Ping-hsüan: Chin-chung-hua fu-yin yün-wei te hsiao-shih.—*FPC* 3, 1958, 46–49. [On the extinction of final con-sonants in the central Shansi dialects].

趙秉璇：晉中話輔音韵尾的消失

0906 Grootaers, Willem A.: Différences phonétiques dans les dialects chinois, un exemple d'évolution linguistique locale dans les parlers de Tat'ong (Chansi-Nord).—*MS* 11, 1946, 207–231. / *BSL* 45, 1949, 273–277, Paul Demiéville.

0907 Hashimoto, Mantarō: Shingo no maeba kuchibiru hasatsu-masatsuon.—*THG* 22, 1961, 131–144. / *RBS* 7, 1961, 444, Li Fang-kuei. [Labiodental affricates and fricatives in the Chin dialects.]

橋本萬太郎：晉語の唇齒破擦摩擦音

0908 Liu, Wen-ping: Ju-sheng yen-chiu yü T'ai-yüan p'en-ti-jen chih tu ju-sheng mu-lu.—*SWYK* 3:1, 1941, 53–72. [A study of the *ju* tone and a list of the pronunciations of *ju* tone words by the inhabitants of the T'aiyüan Basin, Shansi.]

劉文炳：入聲研究與太原盆地人之讀入聲目錄

0909 Liu, Yao-li: Shan-hsi chung-pu wu pi-yin chih ku yün pieh-tu-yin k'ao-cheng.— *SWYK* 4, 1944, 173–176. [Research on the alternate readings of ancient rhymes which became denasalized in the dialects of central Shansi.]

劉耀黎：山西中部無鼻音之古韵別讀音考証

0910 Nomura, Masayoshi: Sansei shohōgen ni okeru mei, dei, jō, gi bo no tōon.—*GK* 19–20, 1951, 43–50; 199: E.S. [Initials *m-, n-, gn-,* and *ng-* in the Shansi dialects.]

野村正良：山西諸方言に於ける『明』、『泥』、『娘』、『疑』母の頭音

0911 Siulin: Chin-nan fang-yen te chi-ko li tzu.—*YWCS* 1955:8, 34. / *YWCS* 1955: 10, 46, Ts'ao Kuang-ch'ü. [Several examples of the dialect pronunciations in southern Shansi.]

Siulin: 晉南方音的幾個例子 / 曹廣衢評

0912 Ti, Chou: Ch'in-yin t'an so.—*KYCK* 98, 1933, Aug. 12; 99, 1933, Aug. 19. [A discussion of the dialect pronunciations in Shansi.]

荻舟：秦音談瑣

0913 Wang, Li-ta: T'ai-yüan fang-yen chung te wen-pai i-tu hsien-hsiang.—*CKYW* 1958:1, 29–30. [The phenomenon of different pronunciations between the literary and colloquial readings in the T'aiyüan dialect.]

王立達：太原方言中的『文白異讀』現象

7.3.3. Vocabulary and Grammar (0914–0920)

0914 Chao, Ping-hsüan: Chin-chung-hua ch'ien *l* tz'u hui-shih.—*CKYW* 1979:6, 455–458. [Notes on words with inserted *l* in the dialects of central Shansi.]

趙秉璇：晉中話嵌 l 詞滙釋

0915 Frei, Henri: The ergative construction in Chinese: theory of Pekinese pa 3 把.—*GK* 31, 1956, 22–50; 32, 83–115. / *RBS* 2, 1956, 398, A. Rygaloff.

0916 Grootaers, Willem A: Initial "pə" in a Shansi dialect: A problem of grammar.—*TP* 42, 1953, 36–69. / *CGGG* 1956:7, 19–23, Sogō Teiji.

十河悌次評介

0917 Grootaers, W.A.: H. Frei-shi no 把 no bunseki.—*CGGG* 1958:6, 3–8, 16. [H. Frei's analysis of 把.]

Grootaers: T. Frei 氏の『把』の分析

0918 T'ien, Hsi-ch'eng: Yün-ch'eng-hua te jen-ch'eng tai-tz'u.—*CKYW* 1962:8–9, 411. [Personal pronouns in the Yünch'eng dialect.]

田希誠：運城話的人稱代詞

0919 Wang, Hsün: Chin tung-nan fang-yen chung te kə?.—*CKYW* 1959:3, 130. [The kə? in the dialects of southeastern Shansi.]

王迅：晉東南方言中的『吃 *kə?*』

0920 Wang, Li-ta: T'ai-yüan fang-yen tz'u-hui te chi-ko t'e-tien ho jo-kan hsü-tz'u te yung-fa.—*CKYW* 1961:2, 26–28. [Some special lexical features and the use of various particles in the T'aiyüan dialect.]

王立達： 太原方言詞滙的幾個特點和若干虛詞的用法

7.3.4. Contrastive Studies (0921–0925)

0921 Hu, Shuang-pao: Shan-hsi Wen-shui-hua ho P'u-t'ung-hua yü-yin yü-hui te pi-chiao.—*FPC* 7, 1959, 21–39. [Phonetic and lexical comparison between the Wen-shui dialect of Shansi and the Common Language.]

胡雙寶： 山西文水話和普通話語音語滙的比較

0922 T'ien, Hsi-ch'eng: Chin tung-nan yü-yin ho Pei-ching yü-yin te ch'a-pieh.—*YWCS* 1956:6, 43–46; 1956:7, 41–44; Corrigenda: 1956:11, 45. [The phonetic differences between the dialects of southeastern Shansi and the Peking dialect.]

田希誠： 晉東南語音和北京語音的差別

0923 Wang, Li-ta. T'ai-yüan-jen hsüeh-hsi P'u-t'ung-hua ying-kai chu-i te chi-ko wen-ti.—*CKYW* 1956:8, 35–36. [Some problems for a speaker of the T'aiyüan dialect to be aware of when learning the Common Language.]

王立達： 太原人學習普通話應該注意的幾個問題

0924 Wang, Li-ta: T'ai-yüan fang-yin chung te ju-sheng yü P'u-t'ung-hua te tui-ying kuan-hsi.—*FPC* 3, 1958, 50–53. [The correspondences between the *ju* tone of the T'aiyüan dialect and that of the Common Language.]

王立達： 太原方音中的入聲與普通話的對應關係

0925 Wang, Li-ta: Shan-hsi fang-yin chung te sheng-tiao yü P'u-t'ung-hua te tui-ying kuan-hsi.—*FPC* 5, 1958, 106–111. [Tonal correspondences between the Shansi dialects and the Common Language.]

王立達： 山西方音中的聲調與普通話的對應關係

7.4. Shensi, Kansu, Mongolia and Sinkiang (0926–0959)

7.4.1. Shensi and Kansu (0926–0948)

7.4.1.1. General Studies (0926–0931)

0926   Chao, Chün: Kan-su yin lüeh.—*Kan-su shih-fan ta-hsüeh hsüeh-pao* 1960:5, 96–100. [A short description of dialect pronunciations in Kansu.]

趙浚：甘肅音略

0927   Liu, Wen-chin: Kuan-chung Han-tai fang-yen chih yen-chiu.—*CSTY* 8:85–87, 1929, 104–111. [A study on the central Shensi dialects of the Han dynasty.]

劉文錦：關中漢代方言之研究

0928   Pai, Ti-chou: Kuan-chung sheng-tiao shih-yen lu.—*BIHP* 4, 1934, 447–488. [An experimental study of the tones in central Shensi.]

白滌洲：關中聲調實驗錄

0929   Pai, Ti-chou: Kuan-chung ju-sheng chih pien-hua.—*BIHPEV* 1, 1933–1935, 997–1092. [The change of the *ju* tone in central Shensi.]

白滌洲：關中入聲之變化

0930   Pai, Ti-chou: Kuan-chung ju-sheng pien-tu te yüan-yin ho ch'eng-hsü.—*KHCK* 6:1, 1936, 25–44. [The cause and process of *ju* tone changes in the dialects of central Shensi.]

白滌洲：關中入聲變讀的原因和程序

0931   Pai, Ti-chou. Ed. by Yü, Shih-ch'ang: *Kuan-chung fang-yin tiao-ch'a pao-kao.*—Peking: K'o-hsüeh, 1954, [iii], 273 p. [Report on a survey of the dialect pronunciations in Shensi.]

白滌洲遺稿，喻世長整理：關中方音：調查報告

7.4.1.2. Lanchow (0932–0934)

0932   Huang, Po-jung; Chao, Chün, et al.: Lan-chou fang-yen kai-shuo.—*Kan-su Shih-fan ta-hsüeh hsüeh-pao* 1960:1, 71–122. [An outline of the Lanchow dialect.]

黃伯榮，趙浚等：蘭州方言概說

0933   Lan-chou ta-hsüeh Chung-wen-hsi yü-yen yen-chiu hsiao-tsu: Lan-chou fang-yen.—*Lan-chou ta-hsüeh hsüeh-pao* 2, 1963, 81–141. [The Lanchow dialect.]

蘭州大學中文系語言研究小組：蘭州方言

0934   Yang, Kuo-chu: Lan-chou-jen k'ou-yü chung ch'ang-chien chih 'ho-yin'.—*Hsin hsi-pei* 6:8, 1943, 111–112. [The 'fused sound' often occuring in the colloquial speech of Lanchow dialect speakers.]

楊國柱：蘭州人口語中常見之『合音』

7.4.1.3. Shanghsien (0935–0937)

0935   Chang, Ch'eng-ts'ai: Shang-hsien fang-yen te jen-ch'eng tai-tz'u.—*CKYW* 1958:3, 127–128. [Personal pronouns in the Shanghsien dialect.]

張成材：商縣方言的人稱代詞

0936   Chang, Ch'eng-ts'ai: Shang-hsien fang-yen tung-tz'u wan-ch'eng-t'i te nei-pu ch'ü-che.—*CKYW* 1958:6, 279–280. [On the internal verbal inflections of perfective tense in the Shanghsien dialect.]

張成材：商縣方言動詞完成體的內部屈折

0937   Chang, Ch'eng-ts'ai: Kuan-yü Shang-hsien fang-yen tz'u te piao yin.—*CKYW* 1965:6, 496. [Phonetic transcription of the Shanghsien dialect.]

張成材：關於商縣方言詞的標音

7.4.1.4. Sian (0938–0940)

0938   Hsü, Shu-sheng: Hsi-an fang-yen te i-hsieh t'e-shu yü-fa hsien-hsiang.—*CKYW* 1958:9, 432–433. [Certain special grammatical phenomena in the Sian dialect.]

許樹聲：西安方言的一些特殊語法現象

0939   Sakamoto, Ichirō: Seian hōgen ni tsuite.—*SK* 63, 1942, 83–109. [The Sian dialect.]

坂本一郎：西安方言に就いて

0940 Sun, Fu-ch'üan: Hsi-an fang-yen te pien-tiao.—*CKYW* 1961:1, 28–29. [Tone sandhi in the Sian dialect.]

孫福全：西安方言的變調

7.4.1.5. Other Localities (0941–0943)

0941 Hsüeh, Po-an: Han-chung fang-yen chi-yao.—*Ch'unsun* 1:2, 1929, 72–74; 2:1, 1930, 124–125. [A summary of the phonetics in the Hanchung dialect.]

薛博盦：漢中方言記要

0942 Li, Chin-hsi: *Shan-pei Kuan-chung liang fang-yen fen-lei tz'u-hui.*—Peking: Shih-fan ta-hsüeh, 1951, 62 p. [A classified vocabulary of the dialects of northern Shensi and Kuanchung.]

黎錦熙：陝北關中兩方言分類詞彙

0943 Liu, Wen-chin: Chi Hsien-yang fang-yin.—*BIHP* 3, 1932, 415–436. [Phonetics of the Hsienyang dialect.]

劉文錦：記咸陽方言

7.4.1.6. Contrastive Studies (0944–0948)

0944 Chang, Ch'eng-ts'ai: Shang-hsien fang-yin ho Pei-ching yü-yin te ch'a-pieh.— *FPC* 2, 1958, 90–95. [Phonetic differences between the Shanghsien dialect and Pekinese.]

張成材：商縣方音和北京語音的差別

0945 Chang, Ch'eng-ts'ai: Ts'ung Hsi-an-yin ken Pei-ching-yin te ch'a-pieh t'an-tao Hsi-an-jen tsen-yang hsüeh-hsi piao-chun-yin.—*FPC* 7, 1959, 1–14. [How a Sian speaker should learn the standard pronunciation from the standpoint of phonetic differences between the Sian dialect and Pekinese.]

張成材：從西安音跟北京音的差別談到西安人怎樣學習標準音

0946 Chao, Lin-sen: Hsi-an fang-yen ken P'u-t'ung-hua te yü-yin tui-ying kuei-lü.— *FPC* 2, 1958, 77–99. [Rules of phonetic correspondences between the Sian dialect and the Common Language.]

趙林森：西安方言跟普通話的語音對應規律

0947 Hsüeh, Sheng-min: *Shan-pei-jen tsen-yang hsüeh-hsi P'u-t'ung-hua.*—Sian: Shan-hsi jen-min, 1959 [not seen]. [How a person from northern Shensi should learn the Common Language.]

薛生民：陝北人怎樣學習普通話

0948 Tu, Yeh-p'ing: Ling-t'ai fang-yin yü Pei-ching yü-yin te tui-ying kuan-hsi.— *FPC* 5, 1958, 111–112. [Phonetic correspondences between the Lingt'ai dialect and the Peking dialect.]

杜也平：靈台方音與北京語音的對應關係

7.4.2. Mongolia and Sinkiang (0949–0959)
7.4.2.1. General Studies (0949–0954)

0949 Chang, P'ei-chung: Nei Meng hsi-pu-ch'ü fang-yen yü-yin ch'u-t'an.—*FPC* 3, 1958, 70–72. [Preliminary research on the sounds of the dialects spoken in western Inner Mongolia.]

張培中：內蒙西部區方言語音初探

0950 Ch'ui: Kuan-yü Nei Meng hsi-pu fang-yen tz'u.—*YYWH* 1959:2, 31; 1959: 3, 32. [Dialect vocabulary of western Inner Mongolia.]

鎚：關於內蒙西部方言詞

0951 Liu, Chung-sheng: Hsin-chiang te Han-yü yü-yin ho Pei-ching yü-yin yu shen-ma ch'a-pieh.—*FPC* 3, 1958, 61–70. [What are the phonetic differences between the Chinese spoken in Sinkiang and Pekinese.]

劉象生：新疆的漢語語音和北京語音有什麼差別

0952 Mullie, Joseph L-M.: Une characteristique phonétique du dialecte Chinois de la Mongolie centrale.—*TP* 23, 1924, 67–81. /*TP* 23, 1924, 81–82, B. Karlgren.

0953 Nei Meng-ku Chiao-yü t'ing Fang-yen tiao-ch'a kung-tso tsu: Wu-lan-hao-t'e yü-yin chien chieh.—*YYWH* 1958:2, 19–20. [A short introduction to the phonetics of the Ulanhot dialect, Inner Mongolia.]

內蒙古教育廳方言調查工作組：烏蘭浩特語音簡介

0954   Yang, Hsiao-min: Wu-lu-mu-ch'i Han-yü fang-yen chung te t'e-shu yü-fa hsien-hsiang.—*Hsin-chiang ta-hsüeh lun-wen chi* 1963:1, 9–12. [Special grammatical phenomena in the Chinese dialect of Urumchi.]
楊曉敏： 烏魯木齊漢語方言中的特殊語法現象

7.4.2.2.   Contrastive Studies (0955–0959)

0955   Chang, Ch'ing-ch'ang: Nei Meng-ku tzǔ-chih-ch'ü Han-yü fang-yin yü P'u-t'ung-hua yü-yin tui-ying kuei-lü.—*Nei Meng-ku ta-hsüeh hsüeh-pao* 1959:1, 75–103. [Rules of phonetic correspondences between the Chinese dialects spoken in the autonomous districts of Inner Mongolia and the Common Language.]
張清常： 內蒙古自治區漢語方言與普通話語音對應規律

0956   Chang, P'ei-chung: Nei Meng hsi-pu-ch'ü-jen tsen-yang hsüeh-hsi P'u-tung-hua.—*YYWH* 1959:1, 27–31; 1959:3, 30–31; 1959:4, 30–31; 1959:5, 30–31. [How a person from western Inner Mongolia should learn the Common Language.]
張培中： 內蒙西部區人怎樣學習普通話

0957   Hu, Hsin: Lüeh t'an Je-ho yü-yin ho Pei-ching yü-yin te ch'a-pieh.—*YWCS* 1956:3, 57–59. [A short discussion on the phonetic differences of the Jehol dialect and the Peking dialect.]
胡新： 略談熱河語音和北京語音的差別

0958   Sui, Shu-hua: Tsai Hu-ho-hao-t'e chiao hsüeh P'u-t'ung-hua yü-yin te t'i-hui.—*FPC* 3, 1958, 72–74. [Teaching Common Language pronunciation at Huhehot.]
隋樹華： 在呼和浩特教學普通話語音的體會

0959   Wen, Jui-hua: Sui-yüan-yin yü Kuo-yin.—*Sui-yüan lü p'ing hsüeh-hui hsüeh-k'an* 6:2, 1935, 41–46; 6:4–5, 1935, 20–23. [The dialect pronunciation of Suiyüan and standard pronunciation.]
文瑞華：綏遠音與國音

8. EASTERN MANDARIN DIALECTS (0960–1009)

8.1. Kiangsu (0960–0993)

8.1.1. General Studies (0960–0961)

0960 Kōsaka, Jun'ichi: Gekō Kanwa no seikaku (1)—Goi no men kara mita. — *SBGK* 2, 1962, 60–80. [The characteristics of Eastern Mandarin—as seen from its vocabulary.]
香坂順一：下江官話の性格㈠——語彙の面からみた

0961 Satō, Akira: Chūkoon to Kōsoshō hōgen—Kanwakei hōgen o chūshin toshite.—*Shūkan Tōyōgaku* 34, 1975, 1–21. [Ancient Chinese phonology and the dialects of Kiangsu—focusing on the Mandarin dialects.]
佐藤昭：中古音と江蘇省方言-——官話系方言を中心として

8.1.2. Nanking (0962–0972)

0962 Chao, Yüan-jen: Nan-ching yin-hsi.—*K'o-hsüeh* 13, 1929, 1005–1036. [Phonetic system of the Nanking dialect.]
趙元任：南京音系

0963 Chiang, Ming: Nan-ching-hua chung te 'A-li-AB'.—*CKYW* 1957:10, 47. [The 'A-li-AB' phrase pattern in the Nanking dialect.]
蔣明：南京話中的『A裏AB』

0964 Chu, Chin-chiang: Chin-ling fang-yen k'ao.—*Hsiao-hsüeh yen-chiu* 1936, 113–124. [A study on the Nanking dialect.]
朱錦江：金陵方言考

0965 Chu, Chün: Chin-ling fang-yen hsü k'ao.—*Szu-wen* 1:5, 1940, 19. [Continuation of a study on the Nanking dialect.]
朱濬：金陵方言續考

0966 Hemeling, Karl Ernst Georg: *The Nanking Kuan Hua.*—Shanghai: Statistical Department of the Inspectorate General of Customs, 1902, 107 p.; Leipzig: Otto Harrassowitz, 1907, vii, 107 p./ *BEFEO* 3, 1903, 486–491, Paul Pelliot.

0967 Kühnert, Franz: Einige bemerkungen über die Shēng im Chinesischen und den Nanking-dialect.—*WZKM* 7, 1893, 302–310.

0968 Kühnert, Franz: *Die Chinesische sprache zu Nanking.*—Vienna: F. Tempsky, 1894, 38 p., 2 tab.

0969 Kühnert, Franz: *Syllabar des Nanking-Dialectes oder der correcten Aussprache* (正音) *sammt Vocabular zum Studium der Hochchinesischen Umgangssprache.*—Vienna: Alfred Hölder, 1898, vii, 472 p.

0970 Kusaka, Tsuneo: Shindai Nankin Kanwa hōgen no ippan.—*KSCB* 5, 1974, 20–47. [One aspect of the Nanking Mandarin dialect during the Ch'ing dynasty.]/ A study of the *Kuan-hua chih-nan* (0732).
日下恒夫：清代南京官話方言の一斑

0971 Mather, Richard B.: A note on the dialect of Lo-yang and Nanking during the Six dynasties (0411).

0972 Nan-ching ta-hsüeh Chung-wen-hsi fang-yen tiao-ch'a tsu: Nan-ching fang-yin chung chi-ko wen-t'i te tiao-ch'a.—*FPC* 8, 1961, 1–32. [A survey of several problems in the phonetics of the Nanking dialect.]
南京大學中文系方言調查組：南京方音中幾個問題的調查

8.1.3. Yangchow (0973–0978)

0973 Liu, Lin: Tsai t'an t'ao-hsi.—*CKYW* 1959:6, 271. [Another discussion on the word *t'ao-hsi* in the Yangchow dialect.] (See 0975).
劉琳：再談『討喜』

0974   Liu, P'ei-lun: Yang-chou fang-yen li te ch'eng-tu fu-tz'u man ho hsi.—*CKYW* 1958:1, 25–26. [The adverbs of degree *man* and *hsi* in the Yangchow dialect.]
劉培倫：揚州方言裏的程度副詞『蠻』和『稀』

0975   Liu, P'ei-lun: Yang-chou-hua li te t'ao-hsi.—*CKYW* 1958:11, 535. [The word *t'ao-hsi* in the Yangchow dialect.]
劉培倫：揚州話裏的『討喜』

0976   Parker, Edward Harper: The dialect of Yangchow.—*CR* 12, 1884 9–17.

0977   Wang, Nien-fang: Yang-chou fang-yen. —*FPT* 2, 1959, 1–38. [The Yangchow dialect.]
王年芳：揚州方言

0978   Wang, Shih-hua: *Yang-chou-hua yin-hsi.*—Peking: K'o-hsüeh, 1959, 72 p. [The phonetic system of the Yangchow dialect.]
王世華：揚州話音系

8.1.4.   Nant'ung (0979–0981)

0979   Hsü, T'ieh-sheng: Lüeh t'an Chiang-su Nan-t'ung chuan-ch'ü fang-yin te sheng-mu.—*FPC* 5, 1958, 21–25. [A short discussion on the finals of the dialects spoken in Nant'ung Special Administrative District, Kiangsu.]
徐鐵生：略談江蘇南通專區方音的聲母

0980   I, Tso-lin: Nan-t'ung yü-yin tzu-mu shuo-ming shu.—*Chung-hua chiao-yü chieh* 11:2, 1921, 1–16. [An explanation of the phonetic alphabet of the Nant'ung dialect.]
易作霖：南通語音字母說明書

0981   Sun, Chin-piao: *Nan-t'ung fang-yen shu-cheng.*—Nant'ung: Han-lin shu-chü, 1913, 4 chüan; Nagoya: Saika shorin, n.d., repr., 332 p., 1 portr. [Commentaries on the Nant'ung dialect.]/ Classified vocabulary and phrases.
孫錦標：南通方言疏證

8.1.5.   T'aihsing (0982–0983)

0982   Li, Jen-chien: T'ai-hsing fang-yen chung tung-tz'u te hou-fu ch'eng-fen. —*CKYW* 1957:5, 16–20. [Verbal suffixes in the T'aihsing dialect.]
李人鑑：泰興方言中動詞的後附成分

0983   Li, Jen-chien: T'ai-hsing fang-yen li te na-tzu-chü.—*CKYW* 1962: 8–9, 399–408./ *RBS* 8, 1962, 497, S.N. Cartier. [Sentences with the word *na* in the T'aihsing dialect.]
李人鑑：泰興方言裏的『拿』字句

8.1.6.   Tanyang (0984–0985)

0984   Lü, Hsiang [Lü Shu-hsiang]: Tan-yang-hua li te lien-tz'u pien-tiao.—*CWYH* 7, 1947, 225–238; E.S.; *Lü Shu-hsiang chiao-shou yen-yü-hsüeh lun-wen chi* (Tokyo: Teikoku shoin, 1951), 40–57. [Tone sandhi in the Tanyang dialect.]
呂湘：丹陽話裏的聯詞變調——『呂叔湘教授言語學論文集』

0985   Rai, Tsutomu: Tan'yō hōgen to Nihon Kanjion to-no seichō ni tsuite.—*OJKK* 5, 1954, 65–90. [On the tones of the Tanyang dialect and the Japanese readings of Chinese characters.]
賴惟勤：丹陽方言と日本漢字音との聲調について

8.1.7.   Other Localities (0986–0990)

0986   Ch'ien, Wen-chin: Shu-yang fang-yen k'ao.—*Chung-yang ta-hsüeh pan-yüeh-k'an* 1:6, 1930, 765–772. [A study on the Shuyang dialect.]
錢文晉：沭陽方言考

0987   Pao, Ming-wei: *Lei-yin tzu-hui* yü Yen-ch'eng fang-yen.—*CKYW* 1979:3, 221–226. [The *Lei-yin tzu-hui* and the Yen-ch'eng dialect.]
鮑明煒：『類音字滙』與鹽城方言

0988   Ting, Pang-hsin: Ju-kao fang-yen te yin-yün.—*BIHP* 36, 1966, 573–633, tab.; E.S. [The phonetic system of the Jukao dialect.]
丁邦新：如皋方言的音韻

0989 Yeh, Te-chün: Huai-an fang-yen lu.— *Min-su* 45, 1929, 32–34. [The Huaian dialect.]

葉德均：淮安方言錄

0990 Yü, Yang: T'ai-chou-hua li te wen-pai i-tu.—*CKYW* 1961:5, 41–43, 29. [The difference between the literary and colloquial readings in the T'aichou dialect.]

俞揚：泰州話裏的文白異讀

8.1.8. Contrastive Studies (0991–0993)

0991 Chiang-su-sheng Shang-hai-shih fang-yen tiao-ch'a chih-tao tsu, et al. (ed.): *Ju-kao-jen hsüeh-hsi P'u-t'ung-hua shou-ts'e.*—Shanghai: Shang-hai chiao-yü, 1959, ii, 96 p. [A handbook for Jukao dialect speakers in learning the Common Language.]

江蘇省上海市方言調查指導組主編 ·
復 旦 大 學 方 言 調 查 工 作 組 編
如皋人學習普通話手冊

0992 Chiang-su-sheng Shang-hai-shih fang-yen tiao-ch'a chih-tao tsu, et al. (ed.): *Nan-t'ung-jen hsüeh-hsi P'u-t'ung-hua shou-ts'e.*—Shanghai: Shang-hai chiao-yü, 1959, ii, 112 p. [A handbook for Nant'ung dialect speakers in learning the Common Language.]

江蘇省上海市方言調查指導組主編 ·
復 旦 大 學 方 言 調 查 工 作 組 編
南通人學習普通話手冊

0993 Hsing, Ju-nan: Chiang-yin fang-yen yü Pei-ching yin-hsi te pi-chiao.—*FPC* 5, 1958, 12–21. [A phonological comparison of the Chiang-yin dialect and Pekinese.]

邢儒南：江陰方言與北京音系的比較

8.2. Anhwei (0994–1009)
8.2.1. General (0994–0995)

0994 Liu, T'e-ju: Huai-pei fang-yin.—*FPC* 7, 1959, 42–50. [Dialect sounds of the northern area of the Huai River.]

劉特如：淮北方音

0995 Meng, Ch'ing-hui: *An-hui fang-yin pien-cheng.*—Hofei: An-hui jen-min, 1961, v, 166 p. [Identification and correction of the dialect sounds of Anhwei.]

孟慶惠：安徽方音辨正

8.2.2. Hofei (0996–0997)

0996 Chou, Ching-shao: Ho-fei she-chien-ch'ien yüan-yin *i* yün pien-cheng.—*Ho-fei shih-fan hsüeh-yüan hsüeh-pao* 1959: 1, 105–107. [Identification of the apical front vowel *i* in the Hofei dialect.]

周景紹：合肥舌尖前元音 i 韻辨正

0997 Li, Ch'ing-fu: Ho-fei fang-yen k'ao.— *Hsüeh-feng* 6:4, 1936, 1–10. [A study on the Hofei dialect.]

李慶富：合肥方言考

8.2.3. Other Localities (0998–1002)

0998 Fang, Chin: Wu-hu-hsien Fang-ts'un-hua chi-yin.—*CKYW* 1966:2, 137–146. [Phonetics of the Fangts'un dialect, Wuhu prefecture.]

方進：蕪湖縣方村話記音

0999 Hao, Ning: An-ch'ing-jen tsen-yang hsüeh-hsi Pei-ching yü-yin.—*FPC* 3, 1958, 75–78. [How a speaker of an An-ch'ing (Anking) dialect should learn the pronunciation of the Peking dialect.]

郝凝：安慶人怎樣學習北京語音

1000 Hu, Yün-yü [Hu, P'u-an]: Ching-hsien fang-yen k'ao cheng.—*Kuo-hsüeh hui-pien* Vol. 2, 6, 11, 1924–1925. Later reprinted in one volume: Shanghai: Kuo-hsüeh yen-chiu she [not seen]. [A study on the Chinghsien dialect.]

胡韞玉〔胡樸安〕：涇縣方言考證

1001 Huang, Chia-chung: An-hui Shou-hsien fang-yen chung te chi-ko chi-tu ho huan-tu te tiao.—*CKYW* 1960:6, 259. [Several 'fast reading' and 'slow reading' tones in the Shouhsien dialect of Anhwei.]

黃家忠：安徽壽縣方言中的幾個『急讀』
和『緩讀』的調

1002 Huang, Ch'i: An-ch'ing fang-yen ku tz'u li cheng.—*Ho-pei ta-hsüeh hsüeh-pao* 1961:1, 125–145. [Proof of the existence of ancient words in the Anch'ing dialect.]
黃綺：安慶方言古詞例証

8.2.4.   Hweichow Dialects (1003–1009)
8.2.4.1.   General Studies (1003–1007)

1003 Chao, Yüan-jen: Chi-ch'i Ling-pei yin-hsi.—*BIHP* 34, 1962, 27–30./ *RBS* 8, 1962, 471, P. Kratochvíl. [The phonology of Lingpei, Chich'i.]
趙元任：績溪嶺北音系

1004 Chao, Yüan-jen & Yang, Shih-feng: Chi-ch'i Ling-pei fang-yen.—*BIHP* 36, 1965, 11–113. [The dialects of Lingpei, Chich'i.]/ *RBS* 11, 1965, 407, F.K. Li.
趙元任，楊時逢：績溪嶺北方言

1005 Ho-fei shih-fan hsüeh-yüan Fang-yen tiao-ch'a kung-tso tsu: She-hsien fang-yen tz'u-hui yü-fa t'e-tien kai-shu.—*Ho-fei shih-fan hsüeh-yüan hsüeh-pao* 1961:1, 32–45. [A general description of the special lexical and grammatical features of the Shehsien dialect.]
合肥師範學院方言調查工作組： 歙縣方言詞滙語法特點概述

1006 Lo, Hsin-t'ien [Lo Ch'ang-p'ei]: Hui-chou fang-yen te chi-ko yao-tien.—*KYCK* 152, 1934, Aug. 25. [Some essential points concerning the Hweichow dialect.]
羅莘田〔羅常培〕： 徽州方言的幾個要點

1007 Wei, Chien-kung, et al.: I-hsien fang-yin tiao-ch'a lu.—*KHCK* 4:4, 1935, 35–85. [Phonetic survey of the dialect of Yih-sien, Anhwei province.]
魏建功等：黟縣方音調查錄

8.2.4.2.   Contrastive Studies (1008–1009)

1008 An-hui-sheng fang-yen tiao-ch'a chih-tao tsu, et al. (ed.): *She-hsien-jen hsüeh-hsi P'u-t'ung-hua shou-ts'e.*—Hofei: An-hui jen-min, 1960, ii, 116 p. [A handbook for Shehsien dialect speakers in learning the Common Language.]
安徽省方言調查指導組主編
歙 縣 文 教 局，合 肥 師 範 ⎱ ： 歙縣人
學院方言調查工 作 組 合 編
學習普通話手冊

1009 An-hui-sheng fang-yen tiao-ch'a chih-tao tsu, et al. (ed.): *Hsiu-ning-jen hsüeh-hsi P'u-t'ung-hua shou-ts'e.*—Hofei: An-hui jen-min, 1961, ii, 126 p. [A handbook for Hsiuning dialect speakers in learning the Common Language.]
安徽省方言調查指導組主編
休寧縣文教局，合 肥 師 範 ⎱ ： 休寧人
學院方言調查工 作 組 合 編
學普通話手冊

9. SOUTHWESTERN MANDARIN DIALECTS (1010–1120)
9.1. Hupei (1010–1035)
9.1.1. General Studies (1010–1014)

1010 Chao, Yüan-jen; Ting, Sheng-shu; Yang, Shih-feng; Wu, Tsung-chi & Tung, T'ung-ho: *Hu-pei fang-yen tiao-ch'a pao-kao.*—Shanghai: Shang-wu, 1948, vii, 1574 p., 66 maps; Taipei: T'ai-lien kuo-feng ch'u-pan-she, 1972, repr./ *Orbis* I, 1952, 210–211, W. A. Grootaers. [Report on a survey of the Hupeh dialects.]
趙元任，丁聲樹，楊時逢，吳宗濟，董同龢：湖北方言調查報告

1011 De Nino, Generoso: *Piccolo vocabolario Cinese-Italiano.*—Peking: Lazaristes, 1923, vii, 325 p.

1012 Hu, Cheng-hua: Yeh t'an Hu-pei hua. —*Hu-pei wen-hsien* 45, 1977, 74–77. [Another discussion on the Hupei dialects.]
胡正華：也談湖北話

1013 Keiya, Toshinobu: Onsetsu kōsei to on'in henka—Kohoku hōgen ni okeru nisshō inbi no shōshitsu no katei.—*NGBK* 43, 1967, 17–49; E.S. [Syllabic structure and phonetic change—The extinction of final consonants for the words *ju* tone in the dialects of Hupei.]
慶谷壽信：音節構成と音韻變化──湖北方言における入聲韻尾消失の過程

1014 Landi, F.: *Piccolo dizionario Italiano-Cinese.*—Shanghai: T'ou-Sè-wè, 1939, x, 655 p./ Hupei dialects.
〔義華字典〕

9.1.2. Hankow (1015–1022)

1015 Anonymous. Preface by Kōsaka, Jun'ichi: *Hsieh-pen Hu-pei Kuan-hua.*—Nagoya: Saika shorin, 1968, [47] d.p. [Hupei Mandarin conversations.]/ Written during the Ch'ing dynasty. Character text without phonetic transcription. Hankow dialect.
無名氏，香坂順一序：寫本湖北官話

1016 Ara, Motoi: Kankōgo ni tsuite.—*Shina-gogakuhō* 1, 1936, 6–22. [The Hankow dialect.]/ Phonetics, vocabulary, sentences.
荒基：漢口語に就いて

1017 Chiang, Ching-fu: *Han-k'ou-yü tzu tso* (Japanese: *Kankōgo jisa*).—Hankow: Szu-ming-t'ang & Tokyo: Tōkaidō, 1935, 3, 5, 6, 236 p. [The Hankow dialect self-taught.]
江矜夫：漢口語自佐

1018 Grosvenor, M. Donald: *A colloquial English-Chinese pocket dictionary in the Hankow dialect.*—Shanghai: Presbyterian Mission Press, 1925, iii, 269 p.

1019 Haenisch, Erich: *Viertausend Deutsch-Chinesische Sprachmuster.* — Hankow: Wei Hsin Printing Office, 1909, 130 p.

1020 Hatano, Tarō: Hoppōwa seinan hōgen ni tsuite—jii gohō o chūshin ni.—*YSDR* 20:1, 1968, 58–85. [The Southwestern Mandarin dialects—a focus on their vocabulary and grammar.]/ Hankow dialect.
波多野太郎：北方語西南方言について──詞彙語法を中心に

1021 Ingle, James Addison: *Hankow syllabary, with references to Giles' dictionary.*—Hankow: N.B.S.C. Mission Press, 1899; 1915, 2nd ed., iv, 195 p.
〔漢音集字〕

1022 Parker, Edward Harper: The Hankow dialect.—*CR* 3, 1875, 308–312.

9.1.3. Hsishui (1023–1024)

1023 Chan, Po-hui: Hsi-shui-hua tung-tz'u t'i te piao-hsien fang-shih. — *CKYW* 1962:8–9, 409–410./ *RBS* 8, 1962, 498, S.N. Cartier. [The way of expressing verbal aspects in the Hsishui dialect.]
詹伯慧：浠水話動詞『體』的表現方式

1024 Liu, Tse: Tsai ta Wang Ch'u-p'ing hsien-sheng wen Hsi-shui fang-yen. — *WHTH* 1957:2, 137–138. [Another reply to Mr. Wang Ch'u-p'ing regarding the Hsishui dialect.]
劉賾：再答王楚屏先生問浠水方言

9.1.4.   Kuangchi (1025–1027)

1025   Ch'in, Chiung-ling: *Kuang-chi fang-yen tz'u-hui* te fan-li ho yang-kao.—*CKYW* 1965:6, 483–491./   *RBS* 11, 1965, 223, A. Lucas. [Introductory notes and sample entries from *Vocabulary of the Kuangchi dialect.*]
秦炯靈：『廣濟方言詞彙』的凡例和樣稿

1026   Liu, Tse: Kuang-chi fang-yin chih tiao-lei yü tiao-chih.—*WHTH* 1958:1, 83–87. [Tonal categories and tonal pitches in the Kuangchi dialect.]
劉賾：廣濟方音之調類與調值

1027   Liu, Tse: Kuang-chi fang-yen. — *WHTH* 1963:1, 81–86. [The Kuangchi dialect.]
劉賾：廣濟方言

9.1.5.   Other Localities (1028–1029)

1028   Chan, Po-hui & Li, Yüan-shou: O-nan P'u-ch'i-hua te yü-yin t'e-tien.—*WHTH* 1964:1, 111–132. [Special phonetic features of the P'uch'i dialect of southern Hupei.]
詹伯慧，李元授：鄂南蒲圻話的語音特點

1029   Chao, Yüan-jen: *Chung-hsiang fang-yen chi.*—Shanghai: Shang-wu, 1939, 160 p./   *TSCK* 2:3, 1940, 416–419, Chang Ching. [The Chunghsiang dialect.]
趙元任：鍾祥方言記 / 張敬評

9.1.6.   Contrastive Studies (1030–1035)

1030   Chan, Po-hui: *Wu-han-jen tsen-yang hsüeh-hsi P'u-t'ung-hua.*—Wuhan: Hu-pei jen-min, 1956, 90 p. [How a Wuhan dialect speaker should learn the Common Language.]
詹伯慧：武漢人怎樣學習普通話

1031   Chan, Po-hui: Kuang-chi fang-yin ho Pei-ching yü-yin te pi-chiao.—*WHTH* 1959:6, 32–55. [A comparison of the phonetics of the Kuangchi dialect and the Peking dialect.]
詹伯慧：廣濟方音和北京語音的比較

1032   Ch'en, Chi-wu: T'an Pei-ching yin yü Wu-han yin te ch'a-i.—*YWCS* 1955:9, 36–38; Addenda: 1959:11, 46. [The phonetic differences between the Peking and Wuhan dialects.]
陳激悟：談北京音與武漢音的差異

1033   Hu, Wei-hsin: Hu-pei Kuang-chi fang-yin ho Pei-ching yü-yin.—*FPC* 3, 1958, 86–93. [The pronunciations of the Kuang-chi dialect and the Peking dialect.]
胡維新：湖北廣濟方音和北京語音

1034   Liu, Hsing-ts'e, et al.: P'u-ch'i-jen tsen-yang hsüeh-hsi P'u-t'ung-hua. — *Hua-chung shih-fan hsüeh-yüan hsüeh-pao* 1960:2, 166–203. [How a P'uchi dialect speaker should learn the Common Language.]
劉興策等：蒲圻人怎樣學習普通話

1035   Yüan, Ting: Han-k'ou fang-yin ho Pei-ching yü-yin te tui-ying kuei-lü.—*FPC* 3, 1958, 79–85. [Rules for phonetic correspondences between the Hankow dialect and Pekinese.]
元丁：漢口方音和北京語音的對應規律

9.2.   Szechwan (1036–1094)

9.2.1.   General Studies (1036–1047)

1036   Amundsen, Edward: *Short cut to Western Mandarin, First hundred steps.* — Shanghai: Kelly & Walsh, 1910, xii, 69 p.; list of radicals./   Romanized.

1037   Gourdin, Édouard-François: *Premières études de la langue parlée dans l'ouest de la Chine.*—Hong Kong: Imprimerie de la Société des Missions Etrangères, 1896, iv, 291 p.; 1905, 2nd ed., with changed title: *Premières études de la langue mandarine parlée,* ii, 291 p./   Southern Szechwan dialect.

1038   Grainer, Adam: *Western Mandarin, or the spoken language of western China, with syllabic and English indexes.* — Shanghai: American Presbyterian Mission Press, 1900, vi, 803 p.
〔西蜀方言〕

1039 Hsü, Fu: Shu fang-yen chieh.—*Hsin p'ing-lun* 6:4, 1941, 17–20. [Szechwan dialect explained.]

徐復：蜀方言解

1040 Hsü, Te-an: Li Shih *Shu-yü* ting pu.—*Ta-hsüeh*, 2:5, 1943, 39–45. [Addenda and corrigenda to Li Shih's (fl. 1640's) *Shu-yü*.]

徐德庵：李實『蜀語』訂補

1041 Hsü, Te-an: Shu-yü cha-chi.—*KWYK* 57, 1947, 28–30. [Notes on the Szechwan dialect.]

徐德庵：蜀語札記

1042 Parker, Edward Harper: The dialect of eastern Sz Ch'uan.—*CR* 11, 1883, 112–120.

1043 Scott, N.C.: Szech'wanese. — *Maître Phonétique* 70, 1940, 28–30.

1044 Sun, Fu-Yüan: Shu fang-yen.—*Szu-ch'uan chiao-yü t'ung-hsün* 35, 1948, 12–15. [The Szechwan dialect.]

孫伏園：蜀方言

1045 Sun, Fu-yüan: Shu-yü.—*Szu-ch'uan chiao-yü t'ung-hsün* 39, 1948, 11–14. [The Szechwan dialect.]

孫伏園：蜀語

1046 Wang, Yü: Shu-yü.—*Chung-yang ta-hsüeh wen-i ts'ung-k'an* 1:1, 1933, 293–298. [The Szechwan dialect.]

王煜：蜀語

1047 Yü, Ch'e: Wo yeh t'an-t'an Szu-ch'uan fang-yen.—*SCWH* 37, 1965, 20. [I likewise discuss the Szechwan dialect.]

于車：我也談談四川方言

9.2.2. Phonetics and Phonology (1048–1056)

1048 Ch'ai, Jan-chih: Szu-ch'uan fang-yen chung erh-hua-tz'u te yin-pien.—*YWCS* 1956:8, 43–45. [Sound changes in erized words in the Szechwan dialects.]

柴然之：四川方言中『兒化詞』的音變

1049 Chang, Wei-szu: Hsien-tai Szu-ch'uan fang-yen chung chih ku-yin.—*Hsüeh-szu* 1:10, 1942, 15–19. [Old pronunciations found in the modern Szechwan dialects.]

張維思：現代四川方言中之古音

1050 Feng, Lü: Shu-yin lun lüeh.—*Wu-han ta-hsüeh Szu-ch'uan t'ung-hsüeh-hui hui-k'an* 1:2, 1934, 1–12. [A short discussion on the Szechwan dialect.]

馮履：蜀音論略

1051 Scott, N.C.: The monosyllable in Szechuanese.—*BSOS* 12, 1948, 197–213.

1052 Scott, N.C.: A phonological analysis of the Szechuanese monosyllable.—*BSOAS* 18, 1956, 556–560./ *RBS* 2, 1956, 373, M.A.K. Halliday.

1053 Szu-ch'uan ta-hsüeh: Szu-ch'uan fang-yen yin-hsi.—*SCTH* 1960:3, 1–123./ *CKYW* 1961:9, 44–49, 43, Shen Tzu-p'ing. [Phonetic system of the Szechwan dialect.]

四川大學：四川方言音系 / 沈子平評

1054 Yang, Hsin-an: *Hsien-tai Han-yü*. — Chungking: Ch'ung-ch'ing jen-min, 1956–1958, 4 vols./ Vol. I, Chap. 7–9: Phonology of the Szechwan dialect compared with Pekinese; Vol. II, Chap. 6: Szechwan vocabulary compared with Pekinese. [Modern Chinese.]

楊欣安：現代漢語

1055 Yang, Shih-feng: Szu-ch'uan fang-yen sheng-tiao fen-pu.—*BIHPEV* 4, 1960, 359–388./ *RBS* 7, 1961, 443, Li Fang-kuei. [Tonal distributions in the dialects of Szechwan.]

楊時逢：四川方言聲調分佈

1056 Yang, Shih-feng: Szu-ch'uan fang-yen yin-yün t'e-tien chi fen-ch'ü kai-shuo.—*BIE* 29, 1970, 107–130. [General remarks on the special phonological features and the divisions of the dialects of Szechwan.]

楊時逢：四川方言音韻特點及分區概說

9.2.3. Vocabulary (1057–1063)

1057 A. P.: *Szu-ch'uan fang-yen tz'u-hui* pu.
—*YWCS* 1955:11, 447–48; 1955:12,
25–27; 1956:1, 37–38. [Addenda to *Szu-
ch'uan fang-yen tz'u-hui* (1060).]
A.P.: 『四川方言詞滙』補

1058 Kōsaka, Jun'ichi: Seinan hōgen no goi.
—*Chūgoku gokaku jiten* (0093), 910–
919. [Vocabulary of Southwestern dialects.]
香坂順一：西南方言の語彙

1059 Liu, Feng: Szu-ch'uan-hua tou-tou ho
ka-ka te chieh-shih.—*YWCS* 1956:5, 53.
[Explanation of *tou-tou* and *ka-ka* in the
Szechwan dialects.]
柳鳳： 四川話『兜兜』和『嘎嘎』的解
釋

1060 Mao, Hsi-p'ang: Szu-ch'uan fang-yen
tz'u-hui.—*YWCS* 1955:6, 44–45; 7, 34;
8, 39–40; 9, 39–40; 10, 44. [Vocabulary
of the Szechwan dialects.]
毛西旁：四川方言詞滙

1061 P'ing, Tzu: Szu-ch'uan fang-yen chü
yü.—*SCWH* 35, 1965, 18–20. [A sampling from the Szechwan dialects.]
平子：四川方言舉隅

1062 Shan, Jung: Szu-ch'uan t'u-tzu 扨 ho
ch'i-ta.—*YWCS* 1958:5, 7. [Dialect character 扨 (dai) and others in Szechwan.]
山榕：四川土字『扨』和其他

1063 Ts'ao, Te-ming: Szu-ch'uan-hua te yin-
tao.—*CKYW* 1962:1, 49. [The word *yin-
tao* in the Szechwan dialects.]
曹德明：四川話的『陰到』

9.2.4. Grammar (1064–1065)

1064 Malmqvist, Göran: The syntax of
bound form in Sïch'uanese.—*BMFEA* 33,
1961, 125–199./ *RBS* 7, 1961, 451, Li
Fang-kuei.

1065 Yang, Hsin-an: Szu-ch'uan-hua li te i-
hsieh yü-fa hsien-hsiang.—*Yü-wen* 1959:

4, 38. [Some grammatical phenonemon a
in the Szechwan dialects.]
楊欣安：四川話裏的一些語法現象

9.2.5. Ch'engtu (1066–1072)

1066 Chang, Nien-chuang Ting: *A descriptive study of the tones in the Chengtu dialect (Szechwan, China) and the intonation
of certain types of sentences.*—Edinburgh:
U. of Edinburgh, 1954, 147 p./ Unpubl.
doc. diss.

1067 Chang, Nien-chuang Ting: Tones and
intonation in the Ch'engtu dialect. —
Phonetica 1958:2, 59–85./ *RBS* 4,
1958, 552, A. Duverger.

1068 Chen, Shang-ling: Ch'eng-tu yü-yin te
ch'u-pu yen-chiu.—*SCTH* 1958:1, 1–30,
tab., 36 p. [A preliminary study on the
phonetics of the Ch'engtu dialect.]
甄尚靈：成都語音的初步研究

1069 Malmqvist, Göran: Some observations
on the tone manifestations of a Ch'engtu
dialect.—*Studia Serica* 9:2, 1950, 55–70.

1070 Malmqvist, Göran: A note on two Szechuanese dialects.—*Studia Serica Bernhard Karlgren Dedicata* (Copenhagen:
Ejnar Munksgaard, 1959), 92–97./
Ch'engtu & Loshan dialects; *RBS* 5, 1959,
491, Li Fang-kuei.

1071 Malmqvist, Göran: Studies in Western
Mandarin phonology. — *BMFEA* 34,
1962, 129–192./ Ch'engtu, Loshan, and
Omei dialects; *RBS* 8, 1962, 467, P.
Kratochvíl.

1072 Yang, Shih-feng: Ch'eng-tu yin-hsi
lüeh chi.—*BIHP* 23, 1951, 289–302. [A
short description of the phonetic system of
the Ch'engtu dialect.]
楊時逢：成都音系略記

9.2.6. Chungking (1073–1076)

1073 Ch'ing, Ch'ing: Ch'ung-ch'ing fang-yen
chü yü. — *SCWH* 161, 1976, 80–82. [A
sampling from the Chungking dialect.]
青青：重慶方言舉隅

1074 Fan, Chi-yen: Ch'ung-ch'ing fang-yen ming-tz'u te ch'ung-tieh ho erh-hua. — *CKYW* 1962:12, 558–560./ *RBS* 8, 1962, 520, K. Kaden. [Reduplication and erization of nouns in the Chungking dialect.]
范繼淹：重慶方言名詞的重叠和兒化

1075 Fan, Chi-yen: Ch'ung-ch'ing fang-yen piao tung-liang te hsia-erh ho piao shih-liang te hsia-erh.—*CKYW* 1965:6, 494 p. / *RBS* 11, 1965, 244, S.N. Cartier. [*Hǝr* as verbal measure and *hǝr* as complement of time in the Chungking dialect.]
范繼淹：重慶方言表動量的『下兒』和表時量的『下兒』

1076 Fan, Chi-yen: Ch'ung-ch'ing fang-yen hsia tzu te fen-hua.—*FY* 1979:2, 88–92. [Differentiation of the word *hsia* in the Chungking dialect.]
范繼淹：重慶方言『下』字的分化

9.2.7. Omei (1077–1079)

1077 Ch'en, Shao-ling & Hao, Hsi-chiung: O-mei yin-hsi.—*SCTH* 1959:1, 1–66. [The phonetic system of the Omei dialect.]
陳紹齡，郝錫炯：峨嵋音系

1078 Malmqvist, Göran: A phonological description of some irregular phenomena in the dialect of Omei, Szechuan.—*Studia Serica* 9:2, 1950, 89–93.

1079 Malmqvist, Göran: Studies in Western Mandarin phonology (1071)./ Omei dialect included.

9.2.8. Other Localities (1080–1084)

1080 Li, Ling: Szu-ch'uan Chiung-lai-hua li te hou-chia ch'eng-fen erh ho erh-tzu.—*CKYW* 1959: 1, 35. [The suffixes *-erh* and *-erh-tzu* in the Chiunglai dialect of Szechuan.]
李齡： 四川邛崍話裏的後加成分『兒』和『兒子』

1081 Mao, I-po: Tzu-kung-shih fang-yen.—*SCWH* 32, 1965, 15–17. [The dialect in the city of Tzukung, Szechwan.]
毛一波：自貢市方言

1082 P'eng, P'ai: Szu-ch'uan Feng-chieh fang-yen fen-lei tz'u-hui.—*FPC* 7, 1959, 51–59. [Classified vocabulary of the Fengchieh dialect, Szechwan.]
彭湃：四川奉節方言分類詞滙

1083 T'u, Feng: Fang-yen. — *Yün-yang hsien-chih* (1936 ed.), Chüan 14 & 15; *Chung-kuo fang-chih so-lu fang-yen hui-pien* (0454), 3:222–405. [The Yünyang dialect.]
涂鳳：方言——『雲陽縣志』

1084 Yang, Shih-feng: Szu-ch'uan Li-chuang fang-yen lüehchi.—*BIHP* 27, 1956, 283–317./ *RBS* 3, 1957, 565, Li Fang-kuei. [A brief note on the dialect of Lichuang, Szechwan.]
楊時逢：四川李莊方言略記

9.2.9. Dictionaries (1085–1088)

1085 Buhot, Ed.: *Locutions modernes dialecte setchouanais.*—Hong Kong: Imprimerie de la Société des Missions-Etrangères de Paris, 1950, 2nd ed. 931 p.
〔漢法新詞句〕

1086 Gaztelu, J.: Petit *dictionnaire français-chinois de la langue mandarine parlée dans l'Ouest de la Chine.*—Hong Kong: Nazareth, 1928, 3rd ed., xxi, 677 p./ Szechwan dialect.

1087 Gaztelu, J.: *Lexique chinois-français de la langue mandarine parlée dans l'Ouest de la Chine.*—Hong Kong: Nazareth, 1935, 375, 119 p./ Szechwan dialect.

1088 Société des Missionnaires: *Dictionnaire chinois-français de la langue mandarine parlée dans l'Ouest de la Chine.*—Hong Kong: Imprimerie de la Société des Missions-Étrangères de Paris, 1893, xiv, 736 p.

9.2.10. Contrastive Studies (1089–1094)

1089 Ch'en, K'uei-miao: Shu-yü yü Kuo-yü chih pi-chiao yen-chiu.—*TWFW* 13:5, 1963, 11–16. [A comparative study of the Szechwan dialect and Mandarin.]
陳癸淼：蜀語與國語之比較研究

1090 Li, Yün-i: *Ch'ung-ch'ing-jen tsen-yang hsüeh-hsi piao-chun yin.*—Chungking: Ch'ung-ch'ing jen-min, 1956, iii, 91 p. [How a Chungking dialect speaker should learn the standard pronunciation.]

李運益：重慶人怎樣學習標準音

1091 Li, Yün-i & Su, Yün-chung: *Szu-ch'uan-jen tsen-yang hsüeh-hsi P'u-t'ung-hua.*—Chungking: Ch'ung-ch'ing jen-min, 1956, 54 p. [How a Szechwan dialect speaker should learn the Common Language.]

李運益，蘇運中： 四川人怎樣學習普通話

1092 T'ien, Yüan: Szu-ch'uan Chien-lo fang-yin ho Pei-ching yü-yin.—*FPC* 3, 1958, 91–95. [The dialect pronunciations of Chienlo, Szechwan and the Peking dialect.]

田元：四川犍樂方音和北京語音

1093 Tung, T'ung-ho: Ju-ho ts'ung Szu-ch'uan-hua hsüeh Kuo-yü.—*TSTH* 68, 1943, 7–9. [How to study Mandarin from the Szechwan dialect.]

董同龢：如何從四川話學習國語

1094 Yang, Chia-wen: Kuo-yin yü Ch'uan-yin.—*KYCK* 34, 1932, May 14. [Mandarin and Szechwan pronunciations.]

楊嘉文：國音與川音

9.3. Yunnan, Kweichow and Kwangsi (1095–1120)

9.3.1. Yunnan (1095–1107)
9.3.1.1. General Studies (1095–1100)

1095 Cordier, Georges: *Méthode pratique de la langue chinois (dialecte Yunnanais).* Hanoi: Imprimerie Tonkinois, 1928, 159 p.

1096 Enríquez, Colin Metcalfe Dallas: *Colloquial Yünnanese. A survey of Yünnanese language as spoken on parts of the north-east Burmese frontier.*—Calcutta & Simla: Thacker, Spink & Co., 1919, 4, 100 p.

1097 Hsü, Ch'eng-chün: Yün-nan-hua tien-ti.—*YWCS* 1955:6, 42–43./ *YWCS* 1955:10, 45, Wang Li-ko. [A sprinkling from the Yunnan dialects.]

徐承俊：雲南話點滴 / 王立革評

1098 Hsü, Ch'eng-chün: Yün-nan Yün-hsien t'u-hua tiao-ch'a pao-kao t'i-kang.—*FPC* 3, 1958, 101–104. [A summary report of a survey of the Yünhsien dialect, Yunnan.]

徐承俊：雲南雲縣土話調查報告提綱

1099 Yang, Shih-feng: Yün-nan fang-yen t'e-tien chi fen-ch'ü kai-shuo.—*BIHP* 35, 1964, 87–112./ *RBS* 10, 1964, 259, Li Fang-kuei. [General remarks on the special features and the divisions of dialects of Yunnan.]

楊時逢：雲南方言特點及分區概說

1100 Yang, Shih-feng: *Yün-nan fang-yen tiao-ch'a pao-kao.*—Taipei: Academia Sinica, 1969, 2 vols. viii, 1838 p.; 64 dialect maps. [Report on a survey of the dialects of Yunnan (Chinese section).]

楊時逢： 雲南方言調查報告（ 漢語部分）

9.3.1.2. Phonetics and Phonology (1101–1103)

1101 Nakata, Yoshikatsu: Unnanshō ni okeru inbo ai on ni kansuru ichi kōsatsu.—*Nagasaki Kenritsu Kokusai Keizai Daigaku Ronshū* 8:1, 1974, 77–93. [An examination of the final *ai* in Yunnan province.]

中田喜勝：雲南省に於ける韻母 ai 音に關する一考察

1102 Yang, Shih-feng: Yün-nan fang-yen sheng-tiao fen-pu.—*BIHP* 30, 1959, 119–142, 6 maps./ *RBS* 5, 1959, 495, Li Li Fang-kuei. [Tonal distributions in the dialects of Yunnan.]

楊時逢：雲南方言聲調分佈

1103 Yang, Shih-feng: K'un-ming yin-hsi.—*CYYK* 1, 1954, 337–372. [Phonetic system of the Kunming dialect.]

楊時逢：昆明音系

9.3.1.3. Vocabulary and Grammar (1104–1107)

1104 Bentley, Charles William: *Anglo-Chinese phrase book and vocabulary, Yunnanese dialect.*—Rangoon: American Baptist Mission Press, 1901, iv, 74 p.

1105 Li, Ju-han: Yün-nan fang-yen tz'u-hui. —*YWCS* 1955:12, 28–30. [Vocabulary of the Yunnan dialects.]
李孺韓：雲南方言詞滙

1106 P'eng, Kuo-chün: Yün-nan Ho-ch'ing-hua li te i-hsieh yü-yin yü-fa hsien-hsiang. —*CKYW* 1957:9, 30–31. [Some phonetic and grammatical phenomena in the Hoch'ing dialect, Yunnan.]
彭國鈞：雲南鶴慶話裏的一些語音語法現象

1107 Yang, Shih-feng: Yün-nan fang-yen chung te chi-ko chi ch'ang-yung te tz'u-hui.—*BIHP* 34, 1963, 589–616, 11 maps. / *RBS* 9, 1963, 536, N.G.D. Malmqvist.
楊時逢：雲南方言中幾個極常用的詞彙

9.3.2. Kweichow (1108–1110)

1108 Clarke, Samuel R.: Among the tribes of southwest China.—London: China Inland Mission, 1911./ 307–312: Vocabulary of the Kweiyang dialect.

1109 Sakamoto, Ichirō: Kiyō hōon ni tsuite. —*SK* 61, 1942, 133–158. [On the dialect sounds of Kweiyang.]
坂本一郎：貴陽方音に就いて

1110 Tu, Nai-keng: Kuei-yang fang-yen chung piao-shih ch'eng-tu te wan-le.— *CKYW* 1979:1, 43, 69. [The degree marker *-wan-le* in the Kweiyang dialect.]
杜乃庚：貴陽方言中表示程度的『完勒』

9.3.3. Kweilin, Kwangsi (1111–1113)

1111 Anonymous: *Short vocabulary of religious terms. Southwestern Mandarin—Kweilin.*—Hong Kong: St. Louis Industrial School, Salesian Press, n.d. 40 p./ English, Chinese characters, romanization.

1112 I, Hsi-wu: Kuei-lin-hua. — *YWCS* 1954:9, 15–16. [The Kweilin dialect.]
易熙吾：桂林話

1113 Yang, Huan-tien: Kuei-lin yü-yin. — *CKYW* 1964:6, 454–462, 444. [The phonetics of the Kweilin dialect.]
楊煥典：桂林語音

9.3.4. Contrastive Studies (1114–1120)

1114 Chao, Po-yü: *Kuei-chou-jen tseng-yang hsüeh-hsi P'u-t'ung-hua.* — Kweiyang: Kuei-chou jen-min, 1956 [not seen]. [How a Kweichow dialect speaker should learn the Common Language.]
趙伯愚：貴州人怎樣學習普通話

1115 Chiu, I: Tsen-yang pa Kuei-yang yin kai-wei piao-chun yin.—*T'ien-chin shih-fan hsüeh-yüan k'o-hsüeh lun-wen chi-k'an* 1957:1, 80–92. [How to convert the dialect pronunciation of Kweiyang into standard pronunciation.]
九一：怎樣把貴陽音改爲標準音

1116 Chou, Wen-yü: *Yün-nan-jen tsen-yang hsüeh Pei-ching yin.*—Kunming: Yün-nan jen-min, 1957, 75 p. [How a Yunnan dialect speaker should learn Peking pronunciations.]
周文煜：雲南人怎樣學北京音

1117 Kao, Kuang-yü: Shih t'an K'ung-ming-jen tseng-yang hsüeh-hsi P'u-t'ung-hua.— *FPC* 3, 1958, 105–109. [An attempt to show how a Kunming dialect speaker should learn the Common Language.]
高光宇：試談昆明人怎樣學習普通話

1118 Lo, Hsin-t'ien [Lo, Ch'ang-p'ei]: K'un-ming-hua ho Kuo-yü te i-t'ung.—*TFTC* 38:3, 1941, 41–44; *Wen-shih tsa-chih* 1:4, 1941, 9–14. [The differences and similarities in the Kunming dialect and the National Language.]
羅莘田：昆明話和國語的異同

1119 T'ung, Wei: Yün-nan-jen hsüeh-hsi P'u-t'ung-hua te chi-ko wen-t'i.—*FPC* 3, 1958, 93–101. [Some problems of speakers of the Yunnan dialects when learning the Common Language.]

童瑋：雲南人學習普通話的幾個問題

1120 Yün-nan-sheng Chiao-yü-chü: *Yün-nan fang-yin yü P'u-t'ung-hua yü-yin.*—Kunming: Yün-nan jen-min, 1979, 97 p. [The pronunciations of the Yunnan dialect and the Common Language.]

雲南省教育局：雲南方音與普通話語音

10. ISOLATED MANDARIN DIALECTS (1121–1168)

10.1. Dungan (1121–1164)

10.1.1. General Studies (1121–1128)

1121 Dragunov, A.A. & Dragunova K.: Über die Dunganische sprache.—*AO* 8, 1936, 34–48.

1122 Dragunov, A.A. & Dragunova E.N.: Dunganskii iazyk.—*UZIV* 6, 1938, 117–131. [The Dungan language.]

1123 Hashimoto, Mantarō: Jun'yango (Dungāngo) kenkyū no rekishi to genjō. — *CGGG* 1957:1, 13–18. [History and present state of studies on the Dungan language.]
橋本萬太郎：ジュンヤン語（ドウンガーン語）研究の歴史と現状

1124 Hashimoto, Mantarō: Tōkango kenkyū shūsei.—CGGG 1974:2, 20–32; 1975:1, 16–33. [Readings in Dunganese linguistics.]
橋本萬太郎：東干語研究集成

1125 Ianshansin, Iu: *Gan'suiskii i Shen'siiskii dialekty Dunganskogo iazyka.*—Frunze: Nauchno-Issledovatel'skii Institut Kirgizskogo Iazyka i Pis'mennosti, 1938, 22 p. [The Kansu and Shensi dialects of the Dungan language.]

1126 Kalimov, A.A.: K istorii izucheniia Dunganskogo iazyka.—*Trudy Instituta Iazyka i Literatury, Akademiia Nauk, Kirgizkoi, SSSR* 7, 1956, 129–133. [A note on the history of the Dungan language.]

1127 Kalimov, A.A.: Dunganskii iazyk. — *Iazyki Narodov SSSR* (Leningrad) 5, 1968, 475–478. [The Dungan language.]

1128 Rimsky-Korsakoff, Svetlana: Soviet Dungan: The Chinese language of central Asia—Alphabet, phonology, morphology. —*MS* 26, 1967, 352–421./ 409–417: Bibliography.

10.1.2. Orthography (1129–1136)

1129 Hashimoto, Mantarō: Jun'yango (Dungāngo) jibo no rekishi.—*CGGG* 1957:10, 9–15. [The history of the Dungan alphabet.]
橋本萬太郎：ジュンヤン語（ドウンガーン語）字母の歴史

1130 Hashimoto, Mantarō: Jun'yango no shin jibo to onsetsu, no tsuzurikata kisoku.—*CGGG* 1957:11, 12–24. [The new alphabet of the Dungan language and rules for syllabic spelling.]
橋本萬太郎：ジュンヤン語の新字母と音節の綴リ方規則

1131 Ianshansin, Iu.: *Orfografiia Dunganskogo iazyka.*—Frunze: Kirgizgosizdat, 1936, 18 p. [Orthography of the Dungan language.]

1132 Ianshansin, Iu.: *Osnovy orfografii Dunganskogo iazyka.*—Frunze: Nauchno-Issledovatel'skii Institut Kirgizskogo Iazyka i Pis'mennosti, 1960, 67 p. [The principles of the orthography of the Dungan language.]

1133 Ianshansin, Iu. & Polivanov, E. D.: *Voprosy orfografii Dunganskogo iazyka.*—Frunze: Nauchno-Issledovatel'skii Institut Kirgizskogo Iazyka i Pis'mennosti, 1937, 71 p. [Questions on the orthography of the Dungan language.]

1134 Stravanovich, G.: Novyi Dungansky alfavit.—*Sovetskaia Etnografiia* 1954:1, 164–165. [The new Dungan alphabet.]

1135 Tu, Sung-shou (transl.): Tung-kan-yü tz'u-erh shu-hsieh kuei-tse.—*P'in-yin* 1956:9, 9–13. [Orthographical rules for writing Dungan words.]
杜松壽譯：東干語詞兒書寫規則

1136 Tu, Sung-shou (transl.): Tung-kan-yü tz'u-erh lien-hsieh kuei-tse.—*P'in-yin wen-tzu hsieh-fa tzu-liao hsüan chi* (Peking, 1957), 226–235. [Rules for conjunctive writing of the words of the Dungan language.]
杜松壽譯： 東干語詞兒連寫規則 ──『拼音文字寫法資料選集』

10.1.3.　Phonetics and Phonology (1137–1144)

1137　Ianshansin, Iu.: *Tony i udareniia v Dunganskom iazyke.*—Frunze: Nauchno-Issledovatel'skii Institut Kirgizskogo Iazyka i Pis'mennosti, 1940, 80 p. [Tones and stresses in the Dungan language.]

1138　Imazov, M.X.: *Osnovy Dunganskoii fonetiki.*—Frunze: Mektep, 1972, 80 p. [Fundamentals of dungan phonetics.]

1139　Imazov, M.X.: *Fonetika Dunganskogo iazyka.*—Frunze: Ilim, 1975, 174 p. [Phonetics of the Dungan language.]

1140　Polivanov, E.D.: *Fonologicheskaia sistema Gan'suiskogo narechiia Dunganskogo iazyka.*—*Voprosy Orfografii Dunganskogo Iazyka* (Frunze, 1937), 30–40. [The phonological system of the Kansu dialect of the Dungan language.]

1141　Trubetskoy, N. S.: *Aus meiner phonologischen Kartothek, I: Das phonologische System der Dunganischen Sprache.*—*TCLP* 8, 1939, 22–26.

1142　Tsunvazo, Iu.: *Tony dvuslozhnykh sushchestvitel'nykh v Dunganskom iazyke.*— *IANK* 1, 1950, 84–91. [The tones of disyllabic nouns in the Dungan language.]

1143　Zavjalova, Olga I.: *Tony v Dunganskom iazyke.* — *Narody Azii i Afriki* 3, 1973, 109–119. [The tones of the Dungan language.]

1144　Zavjalova, Olga I.: *Some phonological aspects of the Dungan dialects.*—*CAAAL* 9, 1978, 1–15.

10.1.4.　Vocabulary and Dictionaries (1145–1146)

1145　Bugazov, Kh.: *Russkaia leksika v Dunganskom iazyke.*—Moscow: Moskovskii Gosudarstvennyi Universitet, 1954 [not seen]./ Unpubl. doc. diss. [Russian vocabulary in the Dungan language.]

1146　Kalimov, A.A. (ed.): *Russko-Dunganskii slovar.*—Frunze: Akademiia Nauk Kirgizskoi, Instituta Iazyka i Literatury

1959, 261 p. [Russian-Dungan dictionary (comp. by Iu. Ianshansin & L. Shinlo).]

10.1.5.　Grammar and Textbooks (1147–1164)

1147　Bugazov, Kh. & Iusurov, Kh.: *Rodnaia Rech' dlia 3–4 klassov.*—Frunze: Kirgizuchpedgiz, 1956, 134 p. [Mother tongue: A reader for the third and fourth classes.]

1148　Dragunov, A. A.: *Issledovaniia v oblasti Dunganskoi grammatiki, I. Kategoriia vida i vremeni v Dunganskom iazyke (Dialekt Gan'su).*—Moscow & Leningrad: Trudy Instituta Vostokokovedeniia Akademiia Nauk SSSR 20, 1940, 86 p. [Researches in Dungan grammar, I. Aspect tense in the Dungan language (Kansu dialect).]

1149　Ianshansin, Iu.: *Dunganskii iazyk: grammatika i pravopisanie dlia 3-4 klassov.*—Frunze: Kirgizuchpedgiz, 1956, 46 p. [Dungan language: Grammar and orthography for the third and fourth classes.]

1150　Ianshansin, Iu: *Kratkaia grammatika Dunganskogo iazyka.*—Frunze: Kirgizuchpedgiz, 1957, 80 p. [A short grammar of the Dungan language.]

1151　Kalimov, A. A.: *Grammaticheskiie osobennosti shchetnykh slov, shchetnykh suffiksov i edinits izmereniia v sovremennom Dunganskom iazyke.*—*KSIV* 12, 1955, 77–82. [Grammatical pecularities of numerative words, numerative suffixes, and units of measure in the modern Dungan language.]

1152　Kalimov, A.A. Transl. by P'eng Ch'u-nan: *Hsien-tai Tung-kan-yü te chi-suan tz'u-wei ho shu-liang tan-wei tz'u te yü-fa t'e-cheng.*—*CKYW* 1955:10, 37–39. [Grammatical peculiarities of numerative words, numerative suffixes, and units of measure in the modern Dungan language.] (1151).
卡里莫夫著，彭楚南譯：現代東干語的計算詞，計算詞尾和數量單位詞的語法特徵

1153 Kalimov, A.A.: Schetnye suffiksy v sovremennom Dunganskom iazyke. — *Voprosy grammatiki i istorii vostochnykh iazykov*. (Moscow & Leningrad: Akademiia Nauk, Instituta Vostokovedeniia, 1958), 82–101. [Numerative suffixes in the modern Dungan language.]

1154 Polivanov, E.D.: Dunganskii suffiks mnozhestvennogo chisla -*mw*.—*Stat'i po Obschemu iazykoznaniiu (Izbranny Raboty)* ed. by A.A. Leont'ev. Moscow: Izdatel'stvo NAUKA, 1968), 172–175. [The Dungan plural suffix -*mw*.]

1155 Polivanov, E.D.: Dungan plural suffix -*mw*.—*Selected works*s *Articles on general linguistics* (Comp. by A.A. Leont'ev, The Hague and Paris: Mouton, 1974), 163–166.

1156 Polivanov, E. D. & Ianshansin, Iu.: *Grammatika Dunganskogo iazyka.* — Frunze, 1936, 76 p. [Grammar of the Dungan language for the third and fourth classes.]

1157 Shinlo, L. & Sushanlo, M.: *Rodnaia rech' dlia 1–2 klassov.*—Frunze: Kirgizuchpedgiz, 1956, 114 p. [Mother tongue: A reader for the first and second classes.]

1158 Shivaza, Ia.: *Dunganskii iazyk: grammatika i pravopisanie dlia 1-2 klassov.*— Frunze: Kirgizuchpedgiz, 1956, 58 p. [Dungan language: grammar and orthography for the first and second classes.]

1159 Shivaza, Ia.: *Grammatika Dunganskogo iazyka, chast' II dlia 3 goda obucheniia.* —Frunze: Kirgizgosizdat, 1958, 218 p. [Grammar of the Dungan language: Part II. For third year instruction.]

1160 Tsunvazo, Iu.: Povtorenie v Dunganskom iazyke.—*VANK* 7, 1949, 67–73. [Reduplication in the Dungan language.]

1161 Tsunvazo, Iu.: K Voprosu o sredstvakh vyrazheniia otritsaniia v Dunganskom iazyke.—*VANK* 10, 1949, 100-106. [A note on means of expressing negation in the Dungan language.]

1162 Tsunvazo, Iu.: K voprosu o sposobakh slovoobrazovaniia v Dunganskom iazyke: O sposobakh obrazovaniia dvuslozhnykh sushchestvitel'nykh i o nekotorykh kriteriiakh differentsiatsii ikh ot slovosochetanii. —*IANK* 3–4, 1955, 74–88. [A note on methods of word-formation in Dungan: On methods of forming disyllabic nouns and on some criteria for differentiating them from noun phrases.]

1163 Tsunvazo, Iu.: O dvuslozhnykh sushchestvitel'nykh v sosvremennom Dunganskom Iazyke.—*VANK* 8, 1956, 53–66. [On disyllabic nouns in modern Dungan.]

1164 Tsunvazo, Iu.: O morfologicheskom sposobe slovoobrazovaniia narechii v Dunganskom iazyke.—*Trudy Instituta Iazykoznaiia Akademiia Nauk Kazakhskoi SSR* 3, 1963, 172–178. [On the morphological method for word-formation of adverbs in Dungan.]

10.2. Nanp'ing (1165–1166)

1165 Chow, Chung-yu Chen: *A study of the Nanping Mandarin dialect of Fukien.* — Ithaca: Cornell U., 1974, vi, 175 p./ Unpubl. doc. diss.; *DAI* 35:2965–A; UM 74–24, 273.

〔周陳重瑜〕

1166 P'an, Mao-ting; Li, Ju-lung; Liang, Yü-chang; Chang, Sheng-yü & Ch'en, Chang-t'ai: Fu-chien Han-yü fang-yen fen-ch'ü lüeh-shuo.—*CKYW* 1963:6, 475–495, 21 maps./ *RBS* 9, 1963, 500, S.N. Cartier, [A short discussion on divisions of the Chinese dialects of Fukien.]

潘茂鼎，李如龍，梁玉璋，張盛裕，陳章太：福建漢語方言分區略說

10.3. Hainan (1167–1168)

1167 Chan, Po-hui: Hai-nan-tao Chün-hua yü-yin kai-shu.—*YLT* 3, 1959, 127–149. [A general description of the phonetics of the 'Solders' speech' of Hainan Island.]

詹伯慧：海南島『軍話』語音概述

1168 Huang, Chia-chiao: Hai-nan Lin-kao te Su Tung-po-hua.—*Lan-chou ta-hsüeh hsüeh-pao* 1957:1, 69–76. [The so-called 'Su Tung-po's speech' of Linkao, Hainan Island.]

黃家教：海南臨高的『蘇東坡話』

11. WU DIALECTS (1169–1359)

11.1. Wu Dialects in General (1169–1195)

11.1.1. Historical Studies (1169–1175)

1169 Ballard, William L.: *Phonological history of Wu.*—Berkeley: U. of California, 1969, 176 p./ Unpubl. doc. diss.; 173–176: Bibliography; *DA* 30:4433-A; UM 70–6058.

1170 Ballard, William L.: Scenarios of change in Chinese dialectology.—*AL* 13, 1971, 125–157; maps./ The relationship between Wu, Hsiang and Min dialects.

1171 Ballard, William L.: The literary/colloquial distinction in Wu and Chu.—*CLAO* 5, 1979, 19–45.

1172 Hu, Ming-yang: Shang-hai-hua i-pai nien-lai te jo-kan pien-hua.—*CKYW* 1978:3, 199–205. [Some changes in the Shanghai dialect during the last one hundred years.]

胡明揚：上海話一百年來的若干變化

1173 Kōsaka, Jun'ichi: Mindai no Gogo—*Hakuan kyōki fuchū.*—*SBGK* 1, 1962, 39–55. [The Wu dialect of the Ming dynasty—From the *P'ai-an ching-ch'i fu-chu.*]

香坂順一：明代の吳語――『拍案驚奇附注』

1174 Nakamura, Kyūshirō: Kodai Shina no Gogo Goon ni tsuite.—*Shiratori hakushi kanreki kinen Tōyō shi ronsō* (Ed. by Ikeuchi Hiroshi; Tokyo: Iwanami shoten, 1925), 691–708. [The Wu dialect and Wu pronunciation in ancient China.]

中村久四郎：古代支那の吳語吳音に就いて――池內宏編輯：『白鳥博士還曆紀念東洋史論叢』

1175 Ōshima, Shōji: *Biwaki* no yōin ni han'eishita Genmatsu Go-hōgen.—*TYGH* 54:4, 1972, 1–32. [The Wu dialect during the later part of the Yüan dynasty as reflected in the rhymes of the *P'i-pa chi.*]

大島正二：『琵琶記』の用韻に反映した元末吳方言

11.1.2 General Studies (1176–1184)

1176 Chao, Yüan-jen: *Hsien-tai Wu-yü te yen-chiu.*—Peking: Ch'ing-hua hsüeh-hsiao Yen-chiu-yüan, 1928, xv, 135 p.; 1 map./ *Fang-chih yüeh-k'an* 7:10, 1934, 38, Anonymous; *Seikai meicho daijiten* (0096) 2, 304, Hirayama Hisao. [Studies in the modern Wu dialects.]/ Introduction in English.

趙元任：現代吳語的研究 / 平山久雄評介

1177 Chiang-su sheng ho Shang-hai shih fang-yen tiao-ch'a chih-tao-tsu, et al. (ed.): *Chiang-su sheng ho Shang-hai shih fang-yen kai-k'uang.*—Nanking: Chiang-su jen-min, 1960, v, 813 p.; 43 maps./ *CKYW* 1961:7, 38–45, 36, Shen Tzu-p'ing; *Orbis* 15, 1966, 117–118, Paul Yang. [General survey of the dialects of Kiangsu province and the city of Shanghai.]

江蘇省和上海市方言調查指導組編：江蘇省和上海市方言概況 / 沈子平評

1178 Ch'ien, Hsiao-pai: Ts'ung ko-yao chung yen-chiu Chiang-su fang-yen te i-t'ung.—*T'ai-pai pan yüeh-k'an* 1:8, 1935, 401–405. [A study of the differences in the dialects of Kiangsu from folk songs.]

錢小柏：從歌謠中研究江蘇方言的異同

1179 Hashimoto, Mantarō: Hsien-tai Wu-yü te lei-hsing-hsüeh.—*FY* 3, 1979, 196–200; E.S. [Typology of modern Wu dialects.]

橋本萬太郎：現代吳語的類型學

1180 Iwaki, Hideo: Nanki ni okeru gogo no kinō.—*NCGH* 5, 1953, 95–108. [On the function of the Wu dialect in Southern Drama.]

岩城秀夫：南戲に於ける吳語の機能

1181 Sakamoto, Ichirō: Kōnan heiya no hōgen ni tsuite.—*Kago Gekkan* 76, 1937, 22–27; 77, 79, 80, 81, 82. [The dialects on the plains south of the Yangtse River.]

坂本一郎：江南平野の方言に就いて

1182 Tōdō, Akiyasu: Gohōgen to Soshūgo.
—*Chūgokugo on'inron* (0634), 126–127.
[Wu dialects and the Soochow dialect.]/
Historical aspects.

藤堂明保：呉方言と蘇州語

1183 Wang, Tung: Wu-yü.—*Chih-yen* 6,
1935, 1–14. [The Wu dialects.]

汪東：吳語

1184 Yüan, Chia-hua: Wu fang-yen.—*Han-
yü fang-yen kai-yao* (0146), Chap. V.
[The Wu dialects.]

袁家驊：吳方言

**11.1.3.   Phonetics and Phonology (1185–
1189)**

1185 Chang, Kung-kuei: Cho-yin tzu te pien-
tu.—*YWCS* 1957:7, 41–46./   Referring
to Wu dialect pronunciations. [Sound
changes of voiced initials.]

張拱貴：濁音字的變讀

1186 Désirat, Michel: Quelques remarques
sur les systèmes tonaux des dialectes Wu.
—*CLAO* 3, 1978, 77–83.

1187 Kōno, Rokurō: Go hōon ni okeru
kansetsu ittō jūin no atsukai.—*Tōyō
Kenkyū* 53, 1979, 39–63. [Treatment of
the double-rhyme of the first division of
the *hsien* rhyme in the modern Wu dialect.]

河野六郎：吳方音における咸攝一等重
韻の扱い

1188 Sakamoto, Ichirō: Chūgokuon yakugo
to Chūgoku nanpō hōon.—*KSCB* 3,
1970,   47–58.   [Chinese   transliterated
words and southern Chinese dialect pronunciations.]

坂本一郎：中國音譯語と中國南方方音

1189 Wei, Chien-kung: *Wu ko* sheng yün lei.
—*KHMC* 1:1, 1925, 4–5; 1:10, 12–16;
1:11, 13–16; 1:12, 22–16; 2:13, 1926,
12–14; *KHMY* 1:2, 1926, 183–195.
[Types of initials and finals in *Wu folk
songs.*]

魏建功：『吳歌』聲韻類

**11.1.4.   Vocabulary and Grammar (1190–
1195)**

1190 Ko, I-ch'ing: Wu fang-yen chieh.—
CSTY 2:22, 1928, 255–263; 2:23, 1928,
289–296. [Wu dialect words explained.]

葛毅卿：吳方言解

1191 Mei, Tsu-lin: The etymology of the aspect marker [tsɿ] in the Wu dialect.—
CAAAL 9, 1978, 39–55; *JCL* 7:1, 1979,
1–14; C.S.

〔梅祖麟：吳語情貌詞『仔』的語原〕

1192 Miyata, Ichirō: Kōnango goi shūkai.—
MSBGK 2 & 4, 1963, 89 & 27 p./   *RBS*
9, 1963, 534, Anonymous. [A collection
and explanation of the vocabulary of dialects spoken in the regions south of the
Yangtze.]

宮田一郎：江南語語彙集解

1193 Miyata, Ichirō: Gendai bungaku saku-
hin ni mirareru Gogokei goi.—*MSBGK* 5,
1964, 39–54. [Vocabulary of Wu dialects
as   seen   from   contemporary   literary
works.]

宮田一郎：現代文學作品にみられる吳
語系語彙

1194 Mu, An: Wu-yü t'ung-su k'ao-shih.—
Min-sheng chou-k'an 22, 1936, 17; 23,
18; 24, 17–18; 25, 18; 27, 17–19; 28,
17–18; 29, 17–18; 30, 19; 31, 19–20;
32, 18–19. [A study on the popular vocabulary of the Wu dialects.]

木安：吳語通俗考釋

1195 Su,   Ch'ih: Chiang-nan-hua   tz'u-hui
chiu-shih-chiu.—*Chung-kuo   yü-wen* 7,
1940, 109. [99 dialect words from areas
south of the Yangtze River.]

蘇遲：江南話詞滙九十九

11.2.   Kiangsu (1196–1315)

11.2.1.   Shanghai (1196–1272)

11.2.1.1.   General Studies (1196–1198)

1196 Hashimoto, Mantarō J.: *A guide to the
Shanghai   dialect.*—Washington,   D.C.,
1971, iv, 350 p./   ERIC Microfilm
Series, #061851.

1197 Kageyama, Takashi: Shanhai ni okeru gengo.—*SK* 18, 1930, 673–703. [The dialects of Shanghai.]
影山巍：上海に於ける言語

1198 Sakamoto, Ichirō: Gendai no Shanhai-go ni tsuite.—*KGR* 2:4, 1951, 1–14. [On the present-day Shanghai dialect.]
坂本一郎：現代の上海語について

11.2.1.2. Phonetics and Phonology (1199–1213)

1199 Hsü, Pao-hua: Shang-hai-hua te tu-shu yin ho shuo-hua yin.—*YWCS* 1957:12, 45–46. [Literary and colloquial readings in the Shanghai dialect.]
許寶華：上海話的讀書音和說話音

1200 Hsü, Pao-hua & T'ang, Chen-chu: Shang-hai fang-yin te nei-pu ch'a-i.—*FTTH* 1962:1, 87–94. [The internal differences of the Shanghai dialect pronunciation.]
許寶華，湯珍珠：上海方音的內部差異

1201 Itō, Ryōkichi: Shanhaigoon gairyaku.—*Shinago Kenkyū* 1, 1938, 156–157. [An outline of the sound system of the Shanghai dialect.]
伊東良吉：上海語音概略

1202 Kühnert, Franz: Über einige Lautcomplexe des Shanghai-Dialeketes.—*Sitzungsberichte der Kais. Akademie der Wissenschafte* 116, 1888, 235–249; Vienna: F. Tempsky, 1888, 17 p.

1203 Mu, Kung: Shang-hai-hua te chien t'uan yin.—*YWCS* 1957:3, 37–40. [The 'sharp' and 'round' sounds in the Shanghai dialect.]
牧公：上海話的尖團音

1204 Rygaloff, Alexis: Absence de distinction tonale dans un dialecte chinois.—*BSL* 60, 1965, 173–179./ *RBS* 11, 1965, 406, F. K. Li.

1205 Sakamoto, Ichirō: Shanhaigo no dakuon ni tsuite.—*KSCB* 1, 1968, 22–25. [Voiced initials in the Shanghai dialect.]
坂本一郎：上海語の濁音について

1206 Shanghai Christian Vernacular Society (ed.): *Syllabary of the Shanghai vernacular.*—Shanghai: American Presbyterian Press, 1891. [not seen]

1207 Sherard, Michael Lewis: *Shanghai phonology.*—Ithaca: Cornell U., 1972, viii, 238 p./ 229–238: Bibliography; *DAI* 33:5157-A; UM 73–6669. Published doc. diss.
［滬語音韻論］

1208 Sherard, Michael: Syntactic constraints on tone sandhi in Shanghai.—*CAAAL* 10, 1979, 23–37.

1209 Silsby, John Alfred: *Shanghai syllabary, arranged in phonetic order.*—Shanghai: American Presbyterian Mission Press, 1897 (preface), viii, 42 p.; 1900, 2nd ed.

1210 Sokolov, M.V.: Eksperimental'noe issledovanie tonov Shankhaiskogo dialekta.—*Phonetica* 12, 1965, 197–200; E.S. [An experimental investigation of Shanghai dialect tones.]

1211 Sokolov, M.V.: Tonal'naia sistema Shankhaiskogo dialekta.—*Spornye Voprosy Stroia Kitaiskogo iazyka* (Moscow: Nauka, 1965), 62–73. [The tonemic system of the Shanghai dialect.]

1212 Walton, A. Ronald: *Phonological redundancy in Shanghai.*—Ithaca: China-Japan Program, Cornell U., 1976, vii, 140 p./ Cornell U. East Asia Papers, No. 11.

1213 Young, Elizabeth Jen: *The segmental phonemes of the Shanghai dialect.*—Washington, D.C.: Georgetown University, 1956, ii, 29 p./ Unpubl. M.S. diss. Thesis No. 1352.

11.2.1.3. Vocabulary (1214–1224)

1214 Chang, Hui-chih: Shang-hai-hua ch'ang-yung tz'u.—*YWCS* 57, 1957, 40–43. [Commonly-used words in the Shanghai dialect.]
張撝之：上海話常用詞

1215 Ch'en, Chih-liang: Shang-hai te fan-ch'ieh yü.—*SWYK* 1:10–11, 1941, 213–240. [The *fan-ch'ieh* language in the dialect of Shanghai.]

陳志良：上海的反切語

1216 Edkins, Joseph: *A vocabulary of the Shanghai dialect* (To accompany *A Grammar of the Shanghai dialect* [1228].—Shanghai: Presbyterian Mission Press, 1869, vi, 151 p.

1217 Lanning, G.: Names and nicknames of the Shanghai settlements.—*JRASNC* 51, 1920, 81–98.

1218 Miyata, Ichirō: Shanhai hōgen goi reikai (1 shū).—*SBGK* 2, 1962, 89–116. [Shanghai dialect vocabulary, collected and annotated (1).]

宮田一郎：上海方言語彙例解（一集）

1219 Shu, Feng: Shang-hai fang-yen tzu shih-ling.—*Chung-kuo yü-wen* 4, 1940, 56. [Dialect characters gleaned from the Shanghai dialect.]

舒鳳：上海方言字拾零

1220 Suenobu, Yasuo & Harada, Matsuzaburō: Shanhai hōgen ichi kōsatsu.—*KGR* 22:3, 1971, 41–83. [A study on the Shanghai dialect.]

末延保雄，原田松三郎：上海方言一考察

1221 Takeuchi, Minoru & Li, P'ei-chi: Shanhaigo ni okeru [d'a:] to [d'u:] ni tsuite.—*Panse* 11, 1951. [not seen]. [On [d'a:] and [d'u:] in the Shanghai dialect.]

竹内實，李培基：上海語における [d'a:] と [d'u:] について

1222 Tso, Ch'i: Shang-hai ch'ang-yung fang-yen tz'u li te i-hsieh sheng-p'i tzu.—*YWCS* 1957:8, 45–46. [Some unusual characters which are in commonly-used dialect words of Shanghai.]

左企：上海常用方言詞裏的一些生僻字

1223 Wang, Hsüan: Shang-hai-hua tang-chung te t'ou tzu.—*Chung-kuo yü-wen* 4, 1940, 54–55; *Chung-kuo yü-wen te hsin sheng* (0107), 330–334. [The word *t'ou* in the Shanghai dialect.]

王弦：上海話當中的『頭』字

1224 Wei, Chü-hsien: *piˀ se k'ao*.—*SWYK* 1:9, 1939, 57–60. [A study on the origin of the word *piˀ se*.]

衞聚賢：『瘟三』考

11.2.1.4. Grammar (1225–1229)

1225 Bourgeois, Albert: *Grammaire du dialecte de Chang-hai.*—Shanghai: T'ou-sè-wè, 1941, vii, 190 p.

1226 Bourgeois, A.: Shang-hai-hua wen-fa.—*Hsin yü-wen* 26, 1947, Sept. 17; 27, 1947, Sept. 24; 29, 1947, Oct. 8; 30, 1947, Oct. 15; 31, 1947, Oct. 22; 32, 1947, Oct. 29. [A grammar of the Shanghai dialect.]

Bourgeois: 上海話文法

1227 Bourgeois, A. Transl. by Miyamori, Tsuneko: *Shanhaigo gohō.*—*MSBGK* 11, 1968, 28 p.; 13, 1970, 47–110. [Grammar of the Shanghai dialect.]/ Japanese transl. of Bourgeois' *Leçons sur le dialecte de Chang-hai, cours moyen* (1231).

Bourgeois 著，宮森常子譯：上海語語法

1228 Edkins, Joseph: *A grammar of colloquial Chinese, as exhibited in the Shanghai dialect.*—Shanghai: London Mission Press, 1853, viii, 248 p.; Shanghai: Presbyterian Mission Press, 1868, 2nd ed., viii, 225 p./ See (1216).

1229 Rabouin, Paul: *Petite grammaire, avec appendice et table comparative des sons.*—Shanghai: T'ou-sè-wè, n.d., 2nd ed., xxvi, xii, 20 p./ Shanghai dialect, reprinted from his *Dictionnaire* (1269).

11.2.1.5. Textbooks (1230–1262)

1230 Anonymous: *T'ou-wo tse né. Boussole du langage Mandarin traduite et romanisée en dialecte de Changhai.*—Shanghai: T'ou-sè-wè, 1908, 138 d. p./ French transl. of the *Kuan-hua chih-nan* (0732) by James Ling, cf. *Orbis* 9:1, 1960, 176, Paul Yang Fu-mien.

〔土話指南〕

1231 Bourgeois, Albert: *Leçons sur le dialecte de Chang-hai, cours moyen.*—Shanghai: T'ou-sè-wè, 1939, vii, 399 p./ *Orbis* 9:1, 1960, 174–175, Paul Yang Fu-mien.

1232 Chiang, Yün: *Hu-yü chieh-t'i.*—Shanghai: Harada Shanhai shiten, 1927, 4, 156 p. [Shanghai dialect primer.]
蔣輯：滬語階梯

1233 Cooper, F.C.: *Short readings in the Shanghai vernacular.* — Shanghai:(?), 1914, 108 p.
〔滬語便讀〕

1234 Crofoot, Jay William & Rawlinson, F.: *Conversational exercises in the Shanghai dialect. A supplement to Dr. Pott's Lessons in the Shanghai dialect.*—Shanghai: Presbyterian Mission Press, 1915, 2, 24 d. p./ In Chinese with introduction in English. See Pott (1252).
〔滬語開路〕

1235 Davis, D.H.: *Shanghai dialect exercises in romanized and character with key to pronunciation and English index.*—Shanghai: T'usewei Press, 1910, xiv, 278 p.

1236 Ho, Charles & Foe, George: *Shanghai dialect in four weeks.*—Shanghai: Chi Ming Book Co., 1940, 102, 5, 9, 9 p.; map of Shanghai, illus.

1237 Hu, Pei-sheng: *Poketto hitsukei jitsuyō Shanhai kaiwa.*—Shanghai: Shōsuidō shoten, 1910, 2, 2, 7, 170 p. [A practical handbook for Shanghai dialect conversation.]
湖北生：ポケット必携實用上海會話

1238 Huang, Tsai-chiang: *Poketto Shanhaigo.*—Shanghai: San-t'ung shu-chü, 1942. [not seen]. [A handbook for the Shanghai dialect.]
黃在江：ポケット上海語

1239 Inaba, Teiichirō: *Shanhaitgo shinan.*—Tokyo: Bunkyūdō, 1936, 1, 12, 92, (Japanese-Shanghai dictionary) 67 p. [A guide to the Shanghai dialect.]
稲葉鼎一郎：上海語指南

1240 Kageyama, Takashi: *Jistuyō sokusei Shanhaigo.*—Tokyo: Bunkyūdō, 1937; 1942, rev. ed., 3, 11, 208 p.; map of Shanghai. [Practical and intensive course in the Shanghai dialect.]
影山巍：實用速成上海語

1241 Kageyama, Takashi: *Gendai Shanhaigo.*—Tokyo: Bunkyūdō, 1936; 1944, 11th ed., 4, 2, 2, 6, 26, 143, 36 p.; map. [Contemporary Shanghai dialect.]/ With appendix: Shanghai idioms.
影山巍：現代上海語

1242 Kita, Seiji: *Jistuyō Shanhaigo.*—Tokyo: Shun'yōdō, 1933, 2, 8, 185 p.; map of Shanghai, illus. [Practical Shanghai dialect.]/ Basic vocabulary, daily conversation, idioms.
喜多青磁：實用上海語

1243 Lin, Chen: *Shang-hai chih-nan.* — Shanghai: Shang-wu, 1930, 23rd ed., 9 chüan; Chüan 9: A sketch of the Shanghai dialect (10 p.). [A guide to Shanghai.]
林震：上海指南　卷九：滬方言記要

1244 Lyon, D.: *Lessons for beginners in the Shanghai dialect, systematically arranged.*—Shanghai: (?), 1890 (preface), 2, 137 p.

1245 MacGowan, John: *A collection of phrases in the Shanghai dialect, systematically arranged.*—Shanghai: Presbyterian Mission Press, 1862, iii, 4, 193 p.

1246 McIntosh, Gilbert: *Useful phrases in the Shanghai dialect, with index, vocabulary and other helps.*—Shanghai: American Presbyterian Mission Press, 1906, iv, 109 p.; 1922, 5th ed., 121 p.

1247 McIntosh, Gilbert: *Conversations usuelles.*—Zi-ka-wei: Lithographie de T'ou-sè-wè, 1921, 97 p.

1248 Obata, Gabun: *Kogo shinryō.*—Shanghai: Tso-hsin she, 1907; Shanghai: Tung-Ya t'ung-wen shu-yüan, 1926, rev. ed. [not seen]. [A bridge to the Shanghai dialect.]
御幡雅文：滬語津梁

1249 Obata, Gabun: *Kogo binshō.*—Shanghai: Nihondō, 1924. [not seen]. [Easy lessons on the Shanghai dialect.]

御幡雅文：滬語便商

1250 Ōkawa, Yosaku: *Katsuyō Shanhaigo.*—Shanghai: Shiseidō shoten, 1925, 2nd ed., 8, 5, 218 p. [Shanghai dialect for practical use.]/ Classified vocabulary, common conversation, commercial conversation.

大川與朔：活用上海語

1251 Parker, R.A.: *Lessons in the Shanghai dialect, in romanized and character with key to pronunciation.*—Shanghai: Municipal Council, 1923, iii, 220, (glossary) 44 p.; tab.

〔滬語彙編〕

1252 Pott, Francis Lister Hawks: *Lessons in the Shanghai dialect.*—Shanghai: American Presbyterian Mission Press, 1907, vii, 99 p.; 1913, rev. ed., viii, 151 p.; Shanghai: Mei Hua Press, 1939, rev. ed., xii, 174 p./ See Crofoot & Rawlinson (1234).

1253 Pott, Francis Lister Hawks. Transl. & romanized by Bourgeois, A.: *Leçons sur la dialecte de Changhai.*—Shanghai: Imprimerie de la Mission Catholique, 1922; 1939, 399 p./ French translation of (1252).

1254 Pott, F.L. Hawks. Transl. by Slovodchikova, L.A.: *Uchenik Shankhaiskago narechiia.*—Shanghai: Tipografiia Grafik, 1936, vii, 240 p. [Lessons in the Shanghai dialect (1252).]

1255 Sakamoto, Ichirō: Shanhaigo kaiwa.—*Shinago zasshi* 1:10, 1941, 100–103; 1:11, 100–103; 1:12, 90–93; 2:1, 1942, 100–103; 2:2, 80–83; 2:3, 74–77; 2:4, 69–73; 2:5, 75–79; 2:6, 77–82; 2:7, 95–100; 2:8, 91–95; 2:9, 90–94; 2:10, 49–54; 2:11, 94–97; 2:12, 86–90; 3:1, 1943. [not seen]. [Shanghai dialect conversation.]

坂本一郎：上海語會話

1256 Scharfenberg, W.A.: *Standard five year course of study in the Chinese language.* Unit I, II, III.—Shanghai:(?), 1932–1933, 2 vols./ In Mandarin with Shanghai dialect equivalents.

1257 Silsby, John Alfred: *Introduction to the study of the Shanghai vernacular.*—Shanghai: American Presbyterian Mission Press, 1911, 2 pts., 32, 21 p.

1258 Sugie, Bōzō: *Kaisei zōho Shanhaigo dokuannai.*—Shanghai: Nihondō, 1904; 1916, rev. ed.; 1923, 13th ed. [not seen]. [The Shanghai dialect self-taught, rev. & enl. ed.]

杉江房造：改正增補上海語獨案內

1259 Ting, Cho: *Chung-Jih hui-hua chi.*—Shanghai: Ch'iu-chin shu-wu, 1938, 4th ed., 4, 3, 14, 9, 241 p. [Chinese-Japanese conversation.] / Mandarin-Japanese-Shanghai dialect, with *kana* phonetic transcription.

丁卓：中日會話集

1260 Wang, Chung-hsien: *Shang-hai su-yü t'u-shuo.*—Shanghai: She-hui, 1935, 597 p.; Soochow: Li-hsing, 1948, repr. (?). [not seen]. [Shanghai vernacular illustrated.]

汪仲賢：上海俗語圖說

1261 Wang, T'ing-chüeh: *Tseng-pu shih-yung Shang-hai-yü.*—Shanghai: Mei-shu kung-i ch'u-pan she, 1932, 8th ed., 2, 2, 2, 2, 2, 5, 226 p. [Revised practical Shanghai dialect.]/ Vocabulary, conversation. Chinese text only.

王廷珏：增補實用上海語

1262 Yates, M.T.: *First lessons in Chinese.*—Shanghai: American Presbyterian Mission Press, 1904, rev. ed., xiv, 151 p./ Shanghai dialect.

11.2.1.6. Dictionaries (1263–1272)

1263 Bourgeois, Albert: *Dictionnaire français-chinois dialecte de Shanghai.* — Shanghai: T'ou-sè-wè, 1950, xxiv, 893 p./ *Orbis* 9:1, 1960, 175, Paul Yang Fu-mien.

1264 Davis, D.H. & Silsby, John Alfred: *Shanghai vernacular Chinese and English dictionary.*—Shanghai: American Presbyterian Mission Press, 1900, xx, 188 p.

1265 Davis, D.H. & Silsby, John Alfred: *Chinese-English pocket dictionary, with Mandarin and Shanghai pronunciation and references to the dictionaries of Williams and Giles.*—Shanghai: T'ou-sè-wè, 1911, 236 p.

1266 Lapparent, Joseph de & Doherty, W.: *Petit dictionnaire chinois-français (dialects de Chang-hai).* — Shanghai: Imprimerie de la Mission Catholique, T'ou-sè-wè, 1911, vi, 160 p.; tab.; 1915, rev. ed. Ière Partie: *Caractères par classifiques et par nombre de traits,* vii, 219 p.; IIe Partie: *Expressions de langage par ordre de sons,* 421 p.

〔華法字彙（上海土話）〕

1267 Lapparent, Joseph de: *Petit dictionnaire chinois-français, mandarin et dialecte de Chang-hai.*—Shanghai: Imprimerie de la Mission Catholique, 1929, 2nd ed., rev. & enl., 2 pts., viii, 235; 473 p.

〔孔道明：華法字彙（官話，上海土話）〕

1268 Pétillon, Corentin: *Petit dictionnaire français-chinois (dialecte de Chang-hai).*—Shanghai: Imprimerie de la Mission Catholique, 1905, v, 568 p./ *TP* 6, 1905, 249–250, Ed. Chavannes.

〔法華字彙（上海土話）〕

1269 Rabouin, Paul: *Dictionnaire français-chinois dialecte de Changhai, Songkiang, etc.*—Shanghai: T'ou-sè-wè, 1894–1896, 2 vols., I. iv, xxvi, 680 p.; II. 634, xiii, 20 p./ With a short grammar, an appendix showing the dialect differences of Soochow and other localities, and a comparative phonetic table of Sungchiang dialect and Mandarin. See (1229).

1270 Shanghai Christian Vernacular Society: *An English-Chinese vocabulary of the Shanghai dialect.*—Shanghai: American Presbyterian Mission Press, 1913, 2nd ed., vii, 593 p./ With appendix of new terms, comp. by Ada Haven Mateer, rev. by P. Parker.

1271 Silsby, John Alfred: *Complete Shanghai syllabary with an index to Davis and Silsby's Shanghai vernacular dictionary with Mandarin pronunciation of each character.*—Shanghai: American Presbyterian Mission Press, 1907, vii, 150 p.

1272 Yen, Fu-sun: *Shang-hai su-yü ta tz'u-tien.*—Shanghai: Yün-hsüan ch'u-pan-she, 1924, 2, 3, 3, 166 p. [A comprehensive dictionary of the Shanghai dialect.]

嚴芙孫：上海俗語大辭典

11.2.2. Changchow (1273–1276)

1273 Chao, Yüan-jen: Ch'ang-chou yin-shih te yüeh-tiao shih-ch'i li.—*BIHPEV* 4, 1961, 467–471. [Seventeen examples of melodies for chanting poetry in the Changchow dialect.]

趙元任：常州吟詩的樂調十七例

1274 Chao, Yuen Ren: The Changchow dialect.—*JAOS* 90, 1970, 45–56; *Aspects of Chinese sociolinguistics* (0098), 48–71.

1275 Ch'en, Sung-mao: Ch'ang-chou fang-yen hsiao chih.—*Hsia-men t'u-shu-kuan sheng* 3:7–9, 1936, 10–11. [Brief notes on the Changchow dialect.]

陳松茂：常州方言小識

1276 Chwang, Wang Schu-yün: *Die Frage im Dialekt von Tschang-dschou. Eine experimental-phonet. Untersuchung.*—Charlottenburg, 1935, 83 p.

11.2.3. Soochow (1277–1294)

11.2.3.1. Phonetics and Phonology (1277–1285)

1277 Chang, Chia-mao: Su-chou fang-yen shang-sheng ho yin-ch'ü te lien-tu pien-tiao.—*FY* 4, 1979, 304–306. [Sandhi of *shang-sheng* and *yin-ch'ü* tones in the Soochow dialect.]

張家茂：蘇州方言上聲和陰去的連讀變調

1278 Kuraishi, Takeshirō & Takada, Hisahiko: Soshūgo no onsetsu ni tsuite.— *Teikoku Gakushiin Kiji* 5:2–3, 1947. [not seen]. [On the syllables of the Soochow dialect.]

倉石武四郎，高田久彦： 蘇州語の音節に就て

1279 Liao, Hsü-tung: *Su-chou yü-yin.* — Nanking: Chiang-su jen-min, 1958, 120 p. [The phonetics of the Soochow dialect.]

廖序東：蘇州語音

1280 Osada, Natsuki: Soshūgo on'in taikei no sho tokuchō ni tsuite.—*CGKR* 1, 1953, 35–50./ *Lg* 30, 1954, 429, Roy A. Miller. [On some characteristics of the phonological system of the Soochow dialect.]

長田夏樹： 蘇州語音韻體系の諸特徴について

1281 Sakamoto, Ichirō: Soshū hōgen jion oyobi seichō.—*SK* 52, 1939, 1–112. [The pronunciations and tones of the Soochow dialect.]

坂本一郎：蘇州方言字音及音聲調

1282 Suenobu, Yasuo: Soshū hōgen no tanji seichō—Pitch-indicator ni yoru kansatsu. —*KGR* 24:4, 1973, 1–31. [Tones of monosyllabic words in the Soochow dialect—as seen from the pitch-indicator.]

末延保雄： 蘇州方言の單字聲調──
ピッチ・インディケーターによる觀察

1283 Tōdō, Akiyasu: Soshūgo no on'inron. —*Chūgokugo on'inron* (0634), 52–63. [Phonology of the Soochow dialect.]

藤堂明保：蘇州語の音韻論

1284 Yeh, Hsiang-ling: Su-chou fang-yen te lien-tu pien-tiao.—*FY* 1979:1, 30–46. [Tone sandhi in the Soochow dialect.]

葉祥苓：蘇州方言的連讀變調

1285 Yeh, Hsiang-ling: Tsai lun Su-chou fang-yen shang-sheng ho yin-ch'ü te lien-tu pien-tiao.—*FY* 1979:4, 306–308. [Once more concerning the sandhi of *shang-sheng* and *yin-ch'ü* tones in the Soochow dialect.]/ A discussion with

Chang Chia-mao (1277).

葉祥苓： 再論蘇州方言上聲和陰去的連讀變調

11.2.3.2. Vocabulary (1286–1291)

1286 Osada, Natsuki, et al.: *Soshūgo hatsuon jiten.*—Kobe: Kōbeshi Gaikokugo daigaku Chūgokugaku Kenkyūshitsu, 1953, 222 p./ Mimeogr. [A dictionary of Soochow dialect pronunciation.]

長田夏樹等：蘇州語發音字典

1287 Sakamoto, Ichirō: Soshū hōgen ni tsuite.—Appendix to *SK* 46, 1937, 70 p. [On the Soochow dialect.]/ Pronunciation and vocabulary.

坂本一郎：蘇州方言に就いて

1288 Su, Jen: Su-chou-hua yen-chiu.— *Chung-kuo yü-wen* 7, 1940, 109–110. [A study on the Soochow dialect.]

蘇人：蘇州話研究

1289 Suenobu, Yasuo: *Hyōdan* ni miru Soshū hōgen.—*KGR* 23:3, 1972, 25–46; 24:3, 1973, 53–68. [The Soochow dialect as found in the *P'ing-t'an*.]/ Popular literature.

末延保雄：『評彈』にみる蘇州方言

1290 Takakura, Shōzō: Shoshūwa yaku kō. —*THGHK* 13:1, 1942, 123–159; 13:3, 1943, 129–144; *Shina oyobi Shinago* 4:11, 1942; 5:2, 1943; 5:4; 5:5. [not seen]. [Soochow texts with Kuan-hua translation.]

高倉正三：蘇州話釋稿

1291 Yoshida, Megumu: *Setsumon tsūkun teisei no Soshūgo no goi.*—The Author, 1954, 11 p./ Mimeogr. [Soochow vocabulary as found in the *Shuo-wen t'ung-hsün ting-sheng* (by Chu Chün-sheng).]

吉田惠：『說文通訓定聲』の蘇州語の語彙

11.2.3.3. Grammar (1292–1294)

1292 Chao, Yüan-jen: Pei-ching Su-chou Ch'ang-chou yü-chu-tz'u te yen-chiu.— *CHHP* 3:2, 1926, 865–918. [Studies in the particles of Peking, Soochow and Changchow.]

趙元任：北京蘇州常州語助詞的研究

1293 Chin, Yu-ching: Su-chou, I-wu shu-tz'u te yü-yin t'e-tien.—*CKYW* 1961:5, 33–40. [Special phonetic features of numerals in the Soochow and Iwu dialects.]

金有景：蘇州、義烏數詞的語音特點

1294 Chin, Yu-ching: Su-chou fang-yen te fang-wei chih-shih-tz'u.—*CKYW* 1962:4, 188. [Directional demonstratives in the Soochow dialect.]

金有景：蘇州方言的方位指示詞

11.2.4. Wuchiang (1295–1296)

1295 Yeh, Hsiang-ling: Wu-chiang fang-yen yen-chiu.—*FPC* 5, 1958, 1–8. [A study on the Wuchiang dialect.]

葉祥苓：吳江方言研究

1296 Yeh, Hsiang-ling: Wu-chiang fang-yen te sheng-tiao.—*FPC* 5, 1958, 8–11. [Tones of the Wuchiang dialect.]

葉祥苓：吳江方言的聲調

11.2.5. Wuhsi (1297–1298)

1297 Chao, Yüan-jen: Wu-hsi fang-yin k'uan-shih yin-piao ts'ao-an.—*KYAO* 2:20, 1936, 1–2. [A draft for a broad phonetic notation of the Wuhsi dialect.]

趙元任：無錫方音寬式音標草案

1298 Ch'en, Ch'i-sheng: Ts'ung yin-wei kuan-tien k'an Wu-hsi-hua te tiao-lei hua-fen.—*Hua-tung shih-ta hsüeh-pao* 1960:1, 93–99. [Tonal divisions of the Wuhsi dialect from a phonemic point of view.]

陳祺生：從音位觀點看無錫話的調類劃分

11.2.6. Other Localities (1299–1303)

1299 Chang, Hui-ying: Ch'ung-ming fang-yen te lien-tu pien-tiao.—*FY* 4, 1979, 284–302. [Tone sandhi in the Ch'ungming dialect.]

張惠英：崇明方言的連讀變調

1300 Chao, Hui-hsien: Tung-yang yü-yin ch'u-pu yen-chiu.—*YWCS* 1956:9, 45–47; 11, 42–45; 12, 38–42. [A preliminary study on the phonetics of the Tungyang dialect.]

趙輝賢：東陽語音初步研究

1301 Huang, Yen-p'ei: Ch'uan-sha fang-yen shu.—*Jen-wen yüeh-k'an* 5:4, 1934, 1–10. [An account of the Ch'uansha dialect.]

黃炎培：川沙方言述

1302 Ko, Yu-p'u: Jun-tung ku-hsiang chih-yen lu.—*Hsia-men t'u-shu-kuan sheng* 4:4–6, 1937 (March). [not seen]. [The patois of eastern Chenchiang.]

葛幼圃：潤東故鄉質言錄

1303 Ting, Pei: Jikei (K'un-shan-hua kuei-ch'ü).—*YWCS* 1958:11, 42–43. [The word *jikei* in the K'unshan dialect.]

定北：Jikei（昆山話『歸去』）

11.2.7. Contrastive Studies (1304–1315)

1304 Chang, Kung-kuei: Chiang-su-jen tsen-yang hsüeh-hsi P'u-t'ung-hua.—*Chiang-su chiao-yü* 1956:13–14, 15–18. [How a person from Kiangsu province should learn the Common Language.]

張拱貴：江蘇人怎樣學習普通話

1305 Chang, Kung-kuei: Chiang-su-jen tsen-yang hsüeh-hsi Pei-ching yü-yin.—*CKYW* 1956:6, 15–18./ *CKYW* 1957:3, 23, Kao Chih-yung & Hsü T'ieh-sheng; *CKYW* 1957:3, 48, Chang Kung-kuei (Reply). [How a person from Kiangsu province should learn the Peking pronunciation.]

張拱貴：江蘇人怎樣學習北京語音 / 高志用，徐鐵生評

1306 Chiang, Ch'eng: T'an nan-fang-jen hsüeh-hsi Pei-ching sheng-tiao te wen-t'i.—*CKYW* 1955:7, 7–9; *Han-tsu te kung-t'ung yü ho piao-chun yin* (Peking: Chung-hua, 1956), 148–154. [Discussion on the problems southern dialect speakers have when learning the tones of the Peking dialect.]

江成：談南方人學習北京聲調的問題

——『漢族的共同語和標準音』

1307   Chiang-su sheng Shang-hai shih fang-yen tiao-ch'a chih-tao tsu, et al. (ed.): *Shang-hai-jen hsüeh-hsi P'u-t'ung-hua shou-ts'e.*—Shanghai: Hsin chih-shih, 1958, vi, 112 p. [A handbook for Shang-hai dialect speakers in learning the Common Language.]

江蘇省上海市方言調查指導組主編 復旦大學方言調查工作組編 : 上海人學習普通話手冊

1308   Chiang-su sheng Shang-hai shih fang-yen tiao-ch'a chih-tao tsu, et al. (ed.): *Chia-ting-jen hsüeh-hsi P'u-t'ung-hua shou-ts'e.*—Shanghai: Shang-hai chiao-yü, 1959, ii, 90 p. [A handbook for Chiating dialect speakers in learning the Common Language.]

江蘇省上海市方言調查指導組主編 復旦大學方言調查工作組編 : 嘉定人學習普通話手冊

1309   Chiang-su sheng Shang-hai shih fang-yen tiao-ch'a chih-tao tsu, et al. (ed.): *Ch'uan-sha-jen hsüeh-hsi P'u-t'ung-hua shou-ts'e.*—Shanghai: Shang-hai chiao-yü, 1959, ii, 102 p. [A handbook for Ch'uan-sha dialect speakers in learning the Common Language.]

江蘇省上海市方言調查指導組主編 復旦大學方言調查工作組編 : 川沙人學習普通話手冊

1310   Chiang-su sheng Shang-hai shih fang-yen tiao-ch'a chih-tao tsu, et al. (ed.): *Hai-men-jen, Ch'ung-ming-jen, Ch'i-tung-jen hsüeh-hsi P'u-t'ung-hua shou-ts'e.*—Shanghai: Shang-hai chiao-yü, 1959, ii, 96 p. [A handbook for Haimen, Ch'ung-ming and Ch'itung dialect speakers in learning the Common Language.]

江蘇省上海市方言調查指導組主編 復旦大學方言調查工作組編 : 海門人、崇明人、啟東人學習普通話手冊

1311   Chiang-su sheng Shang-hai shih fang-yen tiao-ch'a chih-tao tsu, et al. (ed.): *Sung-chiang-jen hsüeh-hsi P'u-t'ung-hua shou-ts'e.*—Shanghai: Shang-hai chiao-yü, 1959, ii, 91 p. [A handbook for Sung-chiang dialect speakers in learning the

Common Language.]

江蘇省上海市方言調查指導組主編 復旦大學方言調查工作組編 : 松江人學習普通話手冊

1312   Liao, Hsü-tung: Su-chou-yin ho Pei-ching-yin te i-t'ung.—*YWCS* 1958:3, 36–39; 4, 35–40. [The phonetic differences and similarities of the Soochow dialect and the Peking dialect.]

廖序東 : 蘇州音和北京音的異同

1313   Wang, Li: *Chiang-Che-jen tsen-yang hsüeh-hsi P'u-t'ung-hua.*—Peking: Wen-hua chiao-yü, 1955, 72 p./ *CKYW* 1956:4, 43, Chan Po-hui. [How Kiangsu and Chekiang dialect speakers should learn the Common Language.]

王力 : 江浙人怎樣學習普通話 / 詹伯慧 評

1314   Yeh, Tzu-hsiung & Hsü, Mei-chen: Shang-hai-jen hsüeh-hsi P'u-t'ung-hua sheng-tiao te i-hsieh pan-fa.—*WTKK* 1959:1, 11–12. [Methods for Shanghai dialect speakers to learn the tones of the Common Language.]

葉子雄，徐美貞 : 上海人學習普通話聲調的一些辦法

1315   Yu, Tun-ming: Shang-hai-jen tsen-yang chang-wo ai ho an yün.—*YWCS* 1958:7, 43. [How a Shanghai dialect speaker should master the finals *ai* and *an* of the Common Language.]

尤敦明 : 上海人怎樣掌握 ai 和 an 韻

11.3.   Chekiang (1316–1359)

11.3.1.   Ningpo (1316–1323)

1316   Chün, Ch'in: Ts'ung Ning-po ti-ch'ü te kei k'an yü-yen te fa-chan.—*YWCS* 1958: 3, 51. [Linguistic development as seen from the word *kei* in the Ningpo dialect.]

君勤 : 從寧波地區的『給』看語言的發展

1317   Möllendorff, Paul Georg von: *The Ningpo syllabary.*—Shanghai: American Presbyterian Mission Press, 1901, xi, 241 p.

1318 Möllendorff, Paul Georg von. Ed. by Sheppard, G.W.: *Ningpo colloquial handbook.*—Shanghai: American Presbyterian Mission Press, 1910, xi, 282 p.

1319 Morrison, William T.: *An Anglo-Chinese vocabulary of the Ningpo dialect.*—Shanghai: American Presbyterian Mission Press, 1876, xv, 559 p.

1320 Parker, Edward Harper: The Ningpo dialect.—*CR* 13, 1885, 138–160.

1321 Rose, Philip John: *Phonology of the Ningpo dialect of Chinese.*—Manchester: U. of Manchester, 1974, 2, 97 p./ Unpubl. M.A. thesis.

1322 Shih, Wen-t'ao: Ning-po fang-yen pen tzu k'ao.—*FY* 3, 1979, 161–170. [Research on standard form characters in the Ningpo dialect.]/ An etymological study.
施文濤：寧波方言本字考

1323 Streenevassa, P.: *A manual for youth and students. Or Chinese vocabulary and dialogues. Containing an easy introduction to the Chinese language. Ningpo dialect.*—Chusan, 1846 (preface), 282 p.

11.3.2. T'anghsi (1324–1326)

1324 Kennedy, George A.: Voiced gutturals in Tangsic.—*Lg* 28, 1952, 457–464; *Selected works of George A. Kennedy* (Ed. by Li Tien-yi, New Haven: Far Eastern Publications, 1964), 183–198.

1325 Kennedy, George A. Transl. by Li, T'ien-i: T'ang-hsi-hua li te chuo-hou-yin.—*TLTC* 7:4, 1953, 6–11. [Voiced gutturals in Tangsic (1324).]
金守拙著，李田意譯：塘棲話裏的濁喉音

1326 Kennedy, George A.: Two tone patterns in Tangsic.—*Lg* 29, 1953, 367–373; *Selected works of George A. Kennedy* (1324), 213–225.

11.3.3. Wenchow (1327–1334)

1327 Chang, Kun: Wenchow historical phonology.—*BIE* 32, 1971, 13–76; C.S.
〔張琨：溫州方言的音韻歷史〕

1328 Cheng, Chang Shang-fang: Wen-chou yin-hsi.—*CKYW* 1964:1, 28–60, 75./ *RBS* 10, 1964, 468, M. Désirat. [The phonetic system of Wenchow.]
鄭張尚芳：溫州音系

1329 Cheng, Chang Shang-fang: Wen-chou fang-yen te lien-tu pien-tiao.—*CKYW* 1964:2, 106–152./ *RBS* 10, 1964, 469, M. Désirat. [Tone sandhi in Wenchow dialect.]
鄭張尚芳：溫州方言的連讀變調

1330 Cheng, Chang Shang-fang: Wen-chou fang-yen te erh wei.—*FY* 3, 1979, 207–230. [The suffix *erh* in the Wenchou dialect.]
鄭張尚芳：溫州方言的『兒』尾

1331 Fu, Tso-chih: Wen-chou fang-yen te hsing-jung-tz'u ch'ung-tieh. — *CKYW* 1962:3, 128–131./ *RBS* 8, 1962, 521, S.N. Cartier. [Adjectival reduplications in the Wenchou dialect.]
傅佐之：溫州方言的形容詞重疊

1332 Montgomery, P.H.S.: *Introduction to the Wênchow dialect.*—Shanghai: Kelly & Walsh, 1893, 294 p.

1333 Parker, Edward Harper: The Wenchow dialect.—*CR* 12, 1884, 162–175; 377–389.

1334 Yang, Ch'ien-ming: P'ing *Han-yü fang-yen tz'u-hui* Wen-chou pu-fen.—*FY* 4, 1979, 309–314. [A review of the Wenchou vocabulary recorded in the *Han-yü fang-yen tz'u-hui* (0523).]
楊乾明：評『漢語方言詞滙』溫州部分

11.3.4. Wenling (1335–1340)

1335 Hang-chou ta-hsüeh Chung-wen-hsi fang-yen tiao-ch'a tsu: Wen-ling fang-yen.—*Hang-chou ta-hsüeh hsüeh-pao* 1959: 3, 151–205. [The Wenling dialect.]
杭州大學中文系方言調查組：溫嶺方言

1336 Li, Jung: Wen-ling fang-yen yü-yin fen-hsi.—*CKYW* 1966:1, 1–9. [Phonetic analysis of the Wenling dialect.]

李榮：溫嶺方言語音分析

1337 Li, Jung: Wen-ling fang-yen te pien-yin.—*CKYW* 1978:2, 96–103. [Tonal suppletion in the Wenling dialect.]

李榮：溫嶺方言的變音

1338 Li, Jung: Wen-ling fang-yen te lien-tu pien-tiao.—*FY* 1979:1, 1–29. [Tone sandhi in the Wenling dialect.]

李榮：溫嶺方言的連讀變調

1339 Ts'ao, Kuang-ch'ü: Wen-ling-hua ju-sheng pien-tiao t'ung yü-fa te kuan-hsi.—*CKYW* 1958:7, 340–341. [The relationship between *ju* tone sandhi and grammar in the Wenling dialect.]

曹廣衢：溫嶺話入聲變調同語法的關係

1340 Ts'ao, Kuang-ch'ü: Che-chiang Wen-ling-hua t'ou te yung-fa yen-chiu.—*CKYW* 1959:2, 78–79, 88. [A study of the use of the word *t'ou* in the Wenling dialect of Chechiang.]

曹廣衢：浙江溫嶺話『頭』的用法研究

11.3.5. Hangchow (1341–1343)

1341 Anonymous: *Sound-table of the Hangchow dialect.*—Shao-hsing: C.M.S., 1902, iv, 25 p.; 1908, 2nd ed., 26 p.; Note by Henry W. Moule.

1342 Moule, G.E.: *Hangchow primer. Translation and notes.*—London: Society for Promoting Christian Knowledge, sold at the Depositories, 1876, 34 p.

1343 Moule, George Evans: *Hang-chou t'u-hua ch'u hsüeh.*—Shao-hsing, 1903, 12 d. p., 183 p.

〔杭州土話初學〕

11.3.6. Other Localities (1344–1355)

1344 Ch'en, Ch'eng-yung: P'ing-yang fang-yen chi-lüeh.—*FY* 1979:1, 47–74. [A sketch of the P'ingyang dialect.]

陳承融：平陽方言記略

1345 Chin, Yu-ching: I-wu-hua li hsien shan liang she san-teng tzu te fen-pieh.—*CKYW* 1964:1, 61. [The difference between the *hsien* and *shan* rhyme groups in their third Division in the Iwu dialect.]

金有景：義烏話裏『咸』『山』兩攝三等字的分別

1346 Fan, Kung-yüan: Che-chiang Hsiang-shan fang-yen k'ao.—*Jen-wen yüeh-k'an* 7:2, 1936, 1–9; 7:3, 9–18; 7:4, 19–28. [A study on the Hsiangshan dialect, Che-kiang.]

樊恭垣：浙江象山方言考

1347 Fu, Kuo-t'ung: Wu-i-hua li te i-hsieh yü-yin yü-fa hsien-hsiang.—*CKYW* 1961: 9, 30–31. [Some phonetic and grammatical phenomena in the Wui dialect.]

傅國通：武義話裏的一些語音語法現象

1348 Hsiang, Shih-yüan: T'ai-chou fang-yen k'ao.—*WLHP* 3:2, 1937, 1–26. [A study on the Taichow dialect.]

項士元：台州方言考

1349 Hsieh, Te-hsien: *Lu Hsün tso-p'in chung te Shao-hsing fang-yen chu-shih.*—Hangchow: Che-chiang jen-min, 1977, 110 p. [Explanatory notes on the Shao-hsing dialect found in Lu Hsün's works.]

謝德銑：魯迅作品中的紹興方言注釋

1350 Hu, Ming-yang: Hai-yen T'ung-yüan fang-yen te tai-tz'u.—*CKYW* 1957:6, 17–22. [Pronouns in the T'ungyüan dialect, Haiyen district.]

胡明揚：海鹽通圓方言的代詞

1351 Hu, Ming-yang: Hai-yen T'ung-yüan fang-yen chung pien-tiao ch'ün te yü-fa i-i.—*CKYW* 1959:8, 372–376. [Grammatical meanings of tone sandhi groups in the T'ungyüan dialect, Haiyen district.]

胡明揚：海鹽通圓方言中變調羣的語法意義

1352 Nakano, Miyoko: *Nihon kigo* ni yoru jūroku seiki Teikai onkei no suitei (Oyobi Muromachi makki kokugoon ni kansuru jakkan no mondai).—*THG* 28, 1964, 101–120. [A reconstruction of the phonetic system of the Tinghai dialect in the 16th century, based on *Jih-pen chi-yü* transcriptions and some problems relating to the Japanese sound system during the late Muromachi period.]
中野美代子：『日本寄語』による16世紀定海音系の推定 ──および室町末期國語音に關する若干の問題

1353 Rudlang, W.D.: T'ai-chow romanization.—*ChinRec* 35, 1904, 89–91.

1354 Wang, Ching-liu: Huang-yen-hua chien shih.—*YWCS* 1956:3, 59–63; 5, 44–47. [A short note on the Huangyen dialect.]
王敬騮：黃嚴話撿拾

1355 Wang, Fu-t'ang: Shao-hsing-hua chi-yin.—*YLT* 3, 1959, 73–126. [A phonetic description of the Shaohsing dialect.]
王福堂：紹興話記音

11.3.7. Contrastive Studies (1356–1359)

1356 Han, T'ao: Ning-po fang-yin ho Kuo-yin pi-chiao te cha-chi.—*Chung-hua chiao-yü chieh* 11:2, 1921, 1–6. [Comparative notes on the pronunciations of the Ningpo dialect and Mandarin.]
寒濤：寧波方音和國音比較的劄記

1357 K'o, Ch'iao: Hsien-chü fang-yin ho Pei-ching yü-yin te tui-ying kuan-hsi.—*FPC* 5, 1958, 98–103. [Phonetic correspondences between the Hsienchü dialect and Pekinese.]
柯喬：仙居方音和北京語音的對應關係

1358 Yen, P'in-jen: Wen-chou yü-yin ho Pei-ching yü-yin te tui-ying kuan-hsi—sheng-mu te tui-ying kuan-hsi.—*Wen-chou shih-fan hsüeh-yüan hsüeh-pao* 1963:1, 86–122. [The phonetic correspondences between the Wenchow dialect and the Peking dialect—Initials.]
顏品仁：溫州語音和北京語音的對應關係──聲母的對應關係

1359 Yüeh, Chai: Chin-hua fang-yin yü Pei-ching yü-yin te tui-chao.—*FPC* 5, 1958, 25–98. [Phonetic correspondences between the Chinhua dialect and Pekinese.]
約齋：金華方音與北京語音的對照

12. HSIANG DIALECTS (1360–1384)

12.1. Hsiang Dialects in General (1360–1365)

1360 I, Jen: Ch'u-yü yen-chiu.—*Hai-wang* 7:1, 1934, 22; 7:2, 44; 7:3, 64; 7:4, 86; 7:5, 106; 7:6, 125; 7:7, 140; 7:8, 157; 7:9. 172; 7:10, 183; 7:11, 1935, 216; 7:12, 245; 7:13, 263; 7:15, 297; 7:16, 313; 7:17, 330; 7:18, 345–346; 7:19, 361; 7:20, 377–378; 7:21, 391–392; 7:22, 410–411; 7:23, 422; 7:24, 440–441; 7:25, 458; 7:26, 472; 7:27, 487–488; 7:28, 506–507; 7:29, 519; 7:30, 535; 7:32, 587–588; 7:33, 603–604; 7:34, 621; 7:35, 635; 7:36, 654–655; 8:2, 30; 8:3, 56–57; 8:4, 74; 8:5, 90–91; 8:6, 107–110; 8:7, 121–122; 8:8, 138; 8:9, 154. [A study of the Ch'u dialect.]
異人：楚語研究

1361 Kōsaka, Jun'ichi: Konan hōgen to sono shūhen—Hōgen no haba to fukasa.—*CGGG* 1962:11, 2–10. [The Hunan dialects and nearby environs—The width and depth of a dialect.]
香坂順一： 湖南方言とその周邊──方言のはばと深さ

1362 Tsuji, Nobuhisa: Konan shohōgen no bunrui to bunpu—zendaku seibo no henka ni motozuku shohoteki kokoromi. —*CGGG* 226, 1979, 1–12; maps. [Classification and distribution of the Hunan dialects—a preliminary attempt based on the shift of the *ch'üan-cho* initials.]
辻伸久： 湖南諸方言の分類と分布──全濁聲母變化に基く初步的試み

1363 Yang, Shih-feng: Hu-nan fang-yen sheng-tiao fen-pu.—*BIHP* 29, 1957, 31–57./ *RBS* 4, 1958, 551, A. Rygaloff. [Tonal distribution in the dialects of Hunan.]
楊時逢：湖南方言聲調分佈

1364 Yang, Shih-feng: Hu-nan fang-yen chi ch'ang-yung te yü-hui.—*Ch'ing-chu Li Chi hsien-sheng 70-sui lun-wen chi* (Taipei: Ch'in-hua hsüeh-pao she, 1967) II, 831–888. [The most commonly used vocabulary of the Hunan dialects.]
楊時逢 : 湖南方言極常用的語彙 ──
『慶祝李濟先生七十歲論文集』（下冊）

1365 Yüan, Chia-hua: Hsiang fang-yen.—*Han-yü fang-yen kai-yao* (0146), Chap. VI. [The Hsiang dialects.]
袁家驊：湘方言

12.2. Ch'angsha (1366–1370)

1366 Chao, Yüan-jen & Li, Chin-hsi: Ch'ang-sha fang-yin tzu-mu.—*KYCK* 239, 1936, May 2. [A phonetic alphabet for the Ch'angsha dialect.]
趙元任，黎錦熙：長沙方音字母

1367 Firth, J.R. & Rogers, B.B.: The structure of the Chinese monosyllable in a Hunanese dialect (Changsha).—*BSOS* 8, 1937, 1055–1074; *Papers in linguistics 1943–1951* (by J.R. Firth; London: Oxford U. Press, 1957), 76–91.

1368 Ming, Yüan: Ko ho Ch'ang-sha fang-yen.—*YWCS* 1958:5, 43. [The word *ko* and the Ch'angsha dialect.]
鳴遠：『個』和長沙方言

1369 Yang, Shih-feng: Ch'ang-sha yin-hsi.—*BIPH* 27, 1956, 135–173./ *RBS* 2, 1956, 372, M.A.K. Halliday. [The phonetic system of the Ch'angsha dialect.]
楊時逢：長沙音系

1370 Yang, Shu-ta: Ch'ang-sha fang-yen k'ao (chi hsü k'ao).—*Min-to tsa-chih* 6:5, 1925, 1–5; *T'ai-p'ing yang* 4:4, 1932, 1–10; *CHHP* 11:1, 1936, 205–219; *Chi-wei-chü hsiao-hsüeh chin-shih lun-ts'ung* (Peking: K'o-hsüeh, 1955, rev. ed.), 155–189./ *YLT* 5, 1963, 71–98, Wu Hsiao-ju. [A study on the Ch'angsha dialect (and Addenda).]
楊樹達 : 長沙方言考（及續考）──
『積微居小學金石論叢 』/ 吳小如評

12.3. Shuangfeng (1371–1373)

1371 Hsiang, Hsi: Hu-nan Shuang-feng-hsien fang-yen.—*YLT* 4, 1960, 134–171. [The Shuangfeng dialect of Hunan.]
向熹：湖南雙峯縣方言

1372 Wang, William S-Y. & Cheng, Chin-chuan: Implementation of phonological change: the Shuang-feng case.—*Papers from the sixth regional meeting of the Chicago Linguistics Society*, 1970, 552–559; also in *POLA* 2:10.

1373 Yüan, Chia-hua: Shuang-feng yin-hsi. —*Han-yü fang-yen kai-yao* (0146), 110–122. [The Shuangfeng phonetic system.]
袁家驊：雙峯音系

12.4. Yüehyang (1374–1375)

1374 Akimoto, Ichirō: Konanshō Gakuyō fukin no hōgen ni tsuite.—*CGKK* 1954: 11, 12–18. [The dialect spoken near Yüehyang, Hunan.]/ Consonants.
秋元一郎：湖南省岳陽附近の方言につ
いて

1375 Liu, Ching-hsüan: Yüeh-yang nan hsiang te t'u-yin.—*FPC* 4, 1958, 53–56. [The dialect pronunciations in southern Yüehyang.]
劉涇選：岳陽南鄉的土音

12.5. Other Localities (1376–1380)

1376 Chou, Ling-wu: Hsin-hua-hua yü P'u-t'ung-hua te ch'a-pieh.—*FPC* 4, 1958, 16–20. [The differences between the Hsinhua dialect and the Common Language.]
周另吾：新化話與普通話的差別

1377 Dragunova, E.N. & Dragunov, A.A.: K latinizatsii dialektov tsentral'nogo Kitaia. Dialekty Siantan' i Siansian (Khunan').—*IAN* 27, 1932, 239–269./ [The romanization of central Chinese dialects. Hsiangt'an and Hsianghsiang dialects (Hunan).]
〔湘潭、湘鄉〕

1378 Lou, Po-p'ing: Liu-yang fang-yen chung te zi wei.—*CKYW* 1958:10, 486–

487. [The *zi* suffix in the Liuyang dialect.]
裴伯平：瀏陽方言中的 zi 尾

1379 T'ang, Tso-fan: Hu-nan Tung-k'ou-hsien Huang-ch'iao-chen fang-yen.—*YLT* 4, 1960, 83–133. [The Huangch'iaochen dialect of Tungk'ou Prefecture, Hunan.]
唐作藩：湖南洞口縣黃橋鎮方言

1380 Yang, Nai-szu: Lin-hsiang fang-yen te tung-tz'u pu-tsu-yü.—*CKYW* 1957:9, 28–29. [The verbal complements in the Linhsiang dialect.]
楊耐思：臨湘方言的動詞補足語

12.6. Contrastive Studies (1381–1384)

1381 Li, Yü-en: Ch'ang-sha-jen tsen-yang hsüeh-hsi P'u-t'ung-hua.—*FPC* 4, 1958, 10–16. [How a Ch'angsha dialect speaker should learn the Common Language.]
李遇恩：長沙人怎樣學習普通話

1382 Lo, Tso-han: *Ch'ang-te T'ao-yüan-jen tsen-yang hsüeh-hsi P'u-t'ung-hua.*— Changsha: Hu-nan jen-min, 1957, 158 p. [How Ch'angte and T'aoyüan dialect speakers should learn the Common Language.]
羅祚韓：常德桃源人怎樣學習普通話

1383 Wan, Yü-hsiang: Hsiang-hsi Yung-shun, Sang-chih, Ta-yung, Lung-shan, Pao-ching, Ku-chang liu-ko-hsien te fang-yin yü P'u-t'ung-hua yü-yin te tui-ying pi-chiao.—*FPC* 4, 1958, 21–53. [Phonetic comparisons of the Common Language with the dialects in six prefectures of western Hunan—Yungshun, Sangchih, Tayung, Lungshan, Paoching, Kuchang.]
萬玉祥：湘西永順、桑植、大庸、龍山、保靖、古丈六個縣的方音與普通話語音的對應比較

1384 Yang, Tao-ching: Hu-nan Lin-hsiang fang-yin yü Pei-ching yü-yin te pi-chiao. --*FPC* 4, 1958, 56–59. [A phonetic comparison of the Linhsiang dialect of Hunan and Pekinese.]
楊道經：湖南臨湘方音與北京語音的比較

13. KAN AND HAKKA DIALECTS (1385–1520)

13.1. Kan Dialects (1385–1400)

13.1.1. General Studies (1385–1386)

1385 Yang, Shih-feng: Chiang-hsi fang-yen sheng-tiao te tiao-lei.—*BIHP* 43, 1971, 403–432. [The tone classes of the Kiangsi dialect.]

楊時逢：江西方言聲調的調類

1386 Yüan, Chia-hua: Kan fang-yen.—*Han-yü fang-yen kai-yao* (0146), Chap. VII. [The Kan dialects.]

袁家驊：贛方言

13.1.2. Nanch'ang (1387–1390)

1387 Chang, Wei-kang: Nan-ch'ang-hua te sheng-tiao pien-hua ho shih-yen yen-chiu. —*Chung-shan ta-hsüeh yen-chiu-yüan wen-k'o yen-chiu-so chi-k'an* 1, 1943, 86–90. [An experimental study on tone-sandhi of the Nanch'ang dialect.]

張爲綱：南昌話的聲調變化和實驗研究

1388 Hsiung, Cheng-hui: Nan-ch'ang fang-yen te tzu wei.—*FY* 3, 1979, 201–206. [The suffix *tzu* in the Nanch'ang dialect.]

熊正輝：南昌方言的『子』尾

1389 Hsiung, Cheng-hui: Nan-ch'ang fang-yen te sheng-tiao chi ch'i yen-pien.—*FY* 4, 1979, 275–283. [The tonal system of the Nanch'ang dialect and its development.]

熊正輝：南昌方言的聲調及其演變

1390 Yang, Shih-feng: Nan-ch'ang yin-hsi.—*BIHP* 39, 1969, 125–204. [The phonetic system of the Nanch'ang dialect.]

楊時逢：南昌音系

13.1.3. Other Localities (1391–1398)

1391 Chang, Wei-kang: T'ai-ho t'ou ting erh-mu te liang-chung t'e-pieh pien-hua chih yen-chiu.—*Chung-shan hsüeh-pao* 1:8, 1943, 78–82. [A study on the special changes of the *t'ou* and *ting* initials in the T'aiho dialect.]

張爲綱：泰和『透』、『定』二母的兩種特別變化之研究

1392 Chin, Yu-ching: Chiang-hsi Kuang-feng-hua hsiao-she tzu te tu-yin.—*CKYW* 1961:10–11, 97. [The readings of characters in the Kuangfeng dialect which belonged to the *hsiao* rhyme group.]

金有景：江西廣豐話『效』攝字的讀音

1393 Condax, Iovanna Delano: *Phonology of Lung-Yen Chinese: A synchronic and diachronic analysis of a Kiangsi dialect based on 3,700 character readings and selected colloquial forms.*—Princeton: Princeton U., 1973, ix, 169 p., 2 maps./ Unpubl. doc. diss.; *DAI* 34:5140–41–A; UM 74–2319.

1394 Hsü, Fu: Hsün-yang fang-yen hsiao chi. —*Tai-tan* 1, 1935, 45–51. [A short note on the Hsünyang dialect.]

徐復：潯陽方言小記

1395 Lo, Chang-p'ei: *Lin-ch'uan yin-hsi.*—Changsha: Shang-wu, 1940, viii, 237 p.; Peking: K'o-hsüeh, 1958, vi, 240 p.; 239–240: E.S./ *Minzokugaku kenkyū* 1:6, 1943, 83–89, Nomura Masayoshi. [Phonetics and phonology of the Lin-ch'uan dialect.]

羅常培：臨川音系 / 野村正良評

1396 Wang, Lien: Chi-an yü-yin kai-shu.— *Ching-kang-shan ta-hsüeh hsüeh-pao* (*Tsung-ho-pan*) 1960:1, 130–171. [An outline of Chian phonetics.]

王練：吉安語音概述

1397 Yang, Shih-feng: Kan-hsien yin-hsi.— *Tsung-t'ung Chiang-kung shih-shih chou-nien chi-nien lun-wen chi* (Taipei: Academia Sinica, 1976), 1187–1202. [Phonetic system of the Kanhsien dialect.]

楊時逢：贛縣音系 ——『總統蔣公逝世周年紀念論文集』

1398 Yen, Hsüeh-chün: Fen-i fang-yin shu lüeh.—*Chung-shan ta-hsüeh shih-fan hsüeh-yüan chi-k'an* 1:1, 1943, 247–262. [A short description of the Feni dialect.]

嚴學宭：分宜方音述略

13.1.4. Contrastive Studies (1399–1400)

1399 Hu, Ching-hsiu: Nan-ch'ang fang-yin yü Pei-ching yü-yin tui-ying kuan-hsi te t'an-so.—*FPC* 4, 1958, 60–72. [An inquiry into the phonetic correspondences between the Nanch'ang dialect and Pekinese.]

胡經修：南昌方音與北京語音對應關係的探索

1400 Wang, Kuang-lü: T'an-t'an Chiang-hsi-jen tsen-yang hsüeh P'u-tung-hua.—*Chiao-yü kung-tso* 1956:13, 8–9. [How a Kiangsi dialect speaker should learn the Common Language.]

王光閭：談談江西人怎樣學普通話

13.2. Hakka Dialects (1401–1520)

13.2.1. History of the Hakkas (1401–1414)

1401 Chang, Fen-ch'ien: K'o-chia min-hsi chih yen-hua.—*TWWH* 13:4, 1962, 49–87. [The origin and growth of the Hakkas.]

張奮前：客家民系之演化

1402 Ch'en, Yün-tung: *K'o-chia-jen.*—Taipei: Lien-ya, 1979, 2nd ed., 16, 11, 406 p. [The Hakkas.]/ Origin, language, and culture.

陳運棟：客家人

1403 Gaimushō Jōhōbu: *Kanton Hakka minzoku no kenkyū.*—Tokyo: Gaimushō, 1932, 29 p. [A study on the Hakka people of Kwangtung.]

外務省情報部：廣東客家民族の研究

1404 Hsiang-kang Ch'ung-cheng tsung-hui (comp.): *Ch'ung-cheng tsung-hui san-shih chou-nien chi-nien t'e-k'an.*—Hong Kong: Ch'ung-cheng tsung-hui, 1950, 4, 28 (photographs), 1, 106, 58, 74, 2, 4. [Thirty years of the Tsung Tsin Association.]/ Including the Hakka dialects.

香港崇正總會編：崇正總會三十週年紀念特刊

1405 Hsieh, Shu-hsin (ed.): *Chung-yüan wen-hua ts'ung-shu* (Ti-i chi).—Miaoli: Miao-yu Chung-yüan tsa-chih-she, 1965, 31, 48, 104, 32, 50, 60 p. [Series on the culture of the Central Plateau (Ser. 1).]/ Hakka language, customs, history, literature, etc.

謝樹新：中原文化叢書（第一集）

1406 Hsieh, T'ing-yü: Origin and migration of the Hakkas.—*Chinese Social and Political Science Review* 13:3, 1929, 202–227; map.

〔謝廷玉〕

1407 Jao, Ying-ch'i: Han-tsu te chu-liu—K'o-chia min-hsi.—*Chung-yüan wen-hua yü T'ai-wan* (Taipei: T'ai-pei wen-hsien wei-yüan-hui, 1971), 313–329; 2 maps. [The main stream of the Han race—The Hakkas.]

饒穎奇：漢族的主流──客家民系──『中原文化與臺灣』

1408 Kuo, Shou-hua: *K'o-tsu yüan-liu hsin chih.*—Taipei: The Author, 1964, rev. ed., 2, 6, 88; 2 maps. [A new record of the origin and development of the Hakkas.]

郭壽華：客族源流新志

1409 Lo, Hsiang-lin: *K'o-chia yen-chiu tao-lun.*—Hsingning: Hsi-shan shu-ts'ang, 1933, 12, 2, 4, 2, 292, 2, 4, 1 p.; E. foreword. [An introduction to the study of the Hakkas.]/ Ethnic, historical and cultural aspects of the Hakkas.

羅香林：客家研究導論

1410 Lo, Hsiang-lin. Transl. by Arimoto, Takeshi: *Hakka kenkyū dōron.*—Taipei: Yoshimura shōkai (printer), 1942, 2 vols., 130; 183 p. [An introduction to the study of the Hakkas (1409).]

羅香林著，有元剛譯：客家研究導論

1411 Nakagawa, Manabu: Studies on the history of the Hakkas: Reconsidered.—*Developing Economies* 13:2, 1975, 208–223.

1412 P'eng, A-mu: Hakka no kenkyū.—*SK* 21, 1930, 77–183; 23, 1930, 113–217. [A study on the Hakkas.]/ Language and culture.

彭阿木：客家の研究

1413 Ting, Ti-hao: K'o-chia yen-chiu.— *Min-ta Chung-kuo wen-hsüeh-hsi ts'ung-k'an* 1:1, 1934, 49–57. [A study on the Hakkas.]

丁迪豪：客家研究

1414 Vaillant, L.: Contribution à l'étude anthropologique des chinois Hakka de la province de Moncay (Tonkin).—*L'Anthropologie* 30, 1920, 83–109.

13.2.2. Sociocultural Aspects (1415–1424)

1415 Char, Tin-yuke [Hsieh, T'ing-yü]: *The Hakka Chinese, their origin and folk songs,* with translation by C. H. Kwok [Kuo, Ch'ang-ch'eng].—San Francisco: Jade Mountains Press, 1969, vi, 69 p.

1416 Chin, K'ai: Lüeh-t'an K'o-chia te min-chien wen-hsüeh.—*Fang-yen wen-hsüeh* (Ti-i chi; Hong Kong: Hsin min-chu, 1949), 71–85. [A short discussion on Hakka popular literature (Vol. I).]

金凱：略談客家的民間文學 ——『方言文學（第一集）』

1417 Cohen, Myron L.: The Hakka or 'guest people': Dialect as a sociocultural variable in southeastern China.—*Ethnohistory* 15, 1968, 237–292.

1418 Hayashi, Morimichi: Hakka gengo to bungei ni kansuru ichi kōsatsu.—*Kita Kyūshū Daigaku Ronbunshū* 6, 1956, 129–162. [Some observations on the language and literature of the Hakkas.]/ Origin, people, language, literature, folk songs, etc.

林盛道：客家の言語と文芸に關する一考察

1419 Hayashi, Morimichi: Hakka no chiiki shakai to sono rigan.—*Kita Kyūshū Daigaku Gaikokugo Gakubu Kiyō* 18, 1969, 1–18. [Hakka provincial societies and their proverbs.]

林盛道：客家の地域社會とその俚諺

1420 Herrmann, F.: Zur Volkskunde der Hakka in Kuangtung.—*Sinica* 12, 1937, 18–38.

1421 Li, Yih-yuan: The dynamics of the dialect groups among the Chinese in Sarawak.—*Ch'ing-chu Li Chi hsien-sheng ch'i-shih sui lun-wen chi* (Taipei: Ch'ing-hua hsüeh-pao she, 1965–1967, 2 vols.), 211–217./ *RBS* 11, 1965, 410, A. Lucas./ Hakka, Foochow, Hokkien, Cantonese, Ch'aochou, etc.

〔李亦園〕『慶祝李濟先生七十歲論文集』

1422 P'eng, A-mu: Hakka ketsugogo ni tsuite.—*SK* 30, 1933, 213–273. [On the *hsieh-hou-yü* in the Hakka dialect.]

彭阿木：客家歇後語に就いて

1423 Yang, Paul Fu-mien: A sociolinguistic profile of the Hakka dialect.—*Languages and Linguistics* 1:1, 1966, 8–16; *Languages and Linguistics: Working Papers* 1, 1970, 117–124.

1424 Yang, Paul Fu-mien: *An ethno-linguistic survey of Hakka.*—Washington, D.C.: Georgetown U., 1967, viii, 178 p.; 7 maps, illus.; 173–175: Bibliography./ Unpubl. doc. diss. *DA* 28:3171–A; UM 68–1922.

13.2.3. Historical Studies (1425–1427)

1425 Hirayama, Hisao: Hakka Tōen hōgen seichō chōchi naiteki saikō.—*Chūgoku no gengo to moji* (see 0711), 209–228. [Internal reconstruction of tonemes in the Hakka dialect of T'aoyüan, Taiwan.]

平山久雄：客家桃園方言聲調調值內的再構——『中國の言語と文字』

1426 O'Connor, Kevin A.: Proto-Hakka.—*AAGB* 11, 1976, 1–64.

1427 Wang, Yü-te: Hakkago no gengo-nendaigakuteki kōsatsu.—*Gendai gengogaku* (Tokyo: Sanseidō, 1972), 559–578. [A glottochronological study of the Hakka dialect.]

王育德：客家語の言語年代學的考察——『現代言語學』（服部四郎先生定年退官記念論集）

13.2.4. General Studies (1428–1440)

1428 Chang, Ping-lin: *Ling-wai san-chou yü.* —Appended to the *Hsin Fang-yen* (0457). [Hakka dialect spoken in the Huichou, Chiayingchou and Ch'aochou districts.]

章炳麟：嶺外三州語

1429 Ch'en, Chen-ai: Mei-hsien fang-yen tsai Hua-yü shang te i-hua hsien-hsiang. —*NYHP* 25:1, 1970, 1–31. [The phenomenon of dissimilation in the Meihsien Hakka dialect of the Chinese language.]

陳眞愛： 梅縣方言在華語上的異化現象

1430 Chu, Hsi-tsu & Tseng, Yün-ch'ien: Shen-ch'a K'o fang-yen pao-kao shu.— *CSTHW* 1:4, 1933, 21–23. [A report on the survey of the Hakka dialect.]

朱希祖，曾運乾：審查客方言報告書

1431 Hashimoto, Mantarō J.: *The Hakka dialect: A linguistic study of its phonology, syntax, and lexicon.*—Cambridge: Cambridge U. Press, 1973, xxvi, 580 p.; map./ Princeton-Cambridge studies in Chinese linguistics, #5; *CGGG* 1973:12, 30, 18, Wen Tai-k'uei; *AAGB* 9, 1973, 213–214, Paul Yang Fu-mien; *General Linguistics* 14, 1974, 213–220, Geoffrey Sampson; *MS* 31, 1974–1975, 636–638, Paul Yang Fu-mien; *CLAO* 2, 1977, 81–91, Laurent Sagart.

溫戴奎評；楊福綿評

1432 Ishida, Takeo: Hakkago kenkyū nōto. —*CGGG* 21, 1948, 3–4. [Notes on the study of the Hakka dialect.]

石田武夫：客家語研究ノート

1433 Ku, Chih: Shu K'o fang-yen chih yen-chiu che.—*CSTY* 8:85–87, 1929, 54–56. [Researchers of the Hakka dialect.]

古直：述客方言之研究者

1434 Lo, Hui-yün: *K'o fang-yen.*—Canton: Chung-shan ta-hsüeh, 1922, 12 chüan; Taipei: Ku-t'ing shu-wu, 1972, repr., 10 chüan, 526 p.; 1 portr. [The Hakka dialect.]/ Classified vocabulary with etymological notes.

羅翽雲：客方言

1435 Tōdō, Akiyasu: Haku hōgen.—*Chūgokugo on'inron* (0634), 132–133. [The Hakka dialect.]

藤堂明保：客方言

1436 Tōdō, Akiyasu: Hakkago.—*Ajia rekishi jiten* (0095) 7, 384. [The Hakka dialect.]

藤堂明保：客家語

1437 Tseng, Hsing-li: *K'o fang-yen* pa.— *Wen-hsüeh tsa-chih* 2, 1933, 10–12. [Postscript to *K'o fang-yen* (1434).]

曾星笠：『客方言』跋

1438 Wen, Chung-ho, et al.: Fang-yen.— *Kuang-hsü Chia-ying-chou chih* (1898 ed.), Chüan 7:1–90. [Dialects.]

溫仲和等：方言 ——『光緒嘉應州志』

1439 Yang, Paul Fu-mien: Elements of Hakka dialectology.—*MS* 26, 1967, 305–351; map.

1440 Yüan, Chia-hua: K'o-chia fang-yen.— *Han-yü fang-yen kai-yao* (0146), Chap. VIII.

袁家驊：客家方言

13.2.5. Szuhsien (1441–1461)

13.2.5.1. Phonetics and Phonology (1441–1452)

1441 Bollini, Robert J.: *The phonemics of Hakka, a Sino-Tibetan language.*—Washington, D.C.: Georgetown U., 1960, 181 p./ Unpubl. M.A. thesis.

1442 Hashimoto, Mantarō J.: Hakkago Shiken hōgen no on'in taikei ni tsuite.— *Chūgoku Gogaku Kenkyūkai Dai-8-kai Zenkoku Taikai Annai* (Tokyo: Chūgoku Gogaku Kenkyūkai, 1957), 7. [On the phonological system of the Szuhsien dialect of Hakka.]

橋本萬太郎： 客家語四縣方言の音韻體系について ——『中國語學研究會第8回全大會案內』

1443 Hashimoto, Mantarō: Hakka phonemics: The phonetics of Moi-yan (梅縣) dialect and its phonemic system.—*GK* 35, 1958, 52–85./ *RBS* 4, 1958, 553, Li Fang-kuei.

1444 Hashimoto, Mantarō J.: Hakkago on'inron—Baiken Hōkō hōgen no onso taikei ni tsuite.—*CGGG* 1958:10, 8–9. [Hakka phonology—The phonemic system of the Paok'ang village of Meihsien.]
橋本萬太郎：客家語音韻論——梅縣寶坑方言の音素體系について

1445 Hayashi, Morimichi: Hakkago no tokushoku.—*Chūgoku gogaku jiten* (0093), 172–178. [Special features of the Hakka dialect.]
林盛道：客家語の特色

1446 Hu, Ching-fu: *K'o-yin hui-pien.*—(?): Ch'ien yeh shu-tien, 1931, 4, 165 p. [Hakka syllabary.]
胡景福：客音彙編

1447 Ishida, Takeo: Nisshō to kankei go—Hakka ni tsuite-no oboegaki.—*HKR* 13, 1963, 1–18. [The *ju* tone and related words—A note on the Hakka dialect.]
石田武夫：入聲と關係語——客家についての覺書

1448 Ishida, Takeo: Hakka hōgen ni okeru nisshō no shōchōsei to Chūgokugo no ongakusei.—*HKR* 17, 1965, 1–13. [The symbolic nature of the *ju* tone of the Hakka dialect and the musicality of the Chinese language.]
石田武夫：客家方言における入聲の象徵性と中國語の音樂性

1449 Kanamaru, Kunizō: Hakkago on'in ryakujutsu.—*CGGG* 1965:3, 19–27. [A brief description of Hakka phonology.]
金丸邦三：客家語音韵略述

1450 Kollecker, C.A.: *Anhang zum Chinesisch-Deutschen Wörterbuch von Werner Rüdenberg enthaltend die 6400 Schriftzeichen mit ihren Aussprache und Tonbezeichungen in der Kantoner und Hakka-Mundart.*—Hamburg: L. Friederichsen & Co., 1925, 75 p.

1451 Parker, Edward Harper: Syllabary of the Hakka language or dialect.—*CR* 8, 1880, 205–217./ *CR* 8, 1880, 316–318, Ch. Piton.

1452 Vömel, Johann Heinrich: Der Hakka-dialekt (Lautlehre, silbenlehre und betonungslehre).—*TP* 14, 1913, 597–696.

13.2.5.2. Vocabulary (1453–1457)

1453 Hashimoto, Mantarō: *Hakkago kiso goishū.*—Tokyo: Ajia-Afurika Gengo Bunka Kenkyūjo, 1972, 118 p. [Collected basic vocabulary of the Hakka dialect.]/ Phonetic system of Meihsien, Szuhsien, Hailu; classified vocabulary.
橋本萬太郎：客家語基礎語彙集

1454 Hashimoto, Mantarō: *Hakkago kiso goishū sakuin.*—Tokyo: Ajia-Afurika Gengo Bunka Kenkyūjo, 1973, 101 p. [Index to the *Collected basic vocabulary of the Hakka dialect* (1453).]/ With an English index.
橋本萬太郎：客家語基礎語彙集索引

1455 Hayashi, Morimichi: Hakkago no goi. —*Chūgoku gogaku jiten* (0093), 1036–1038. [Vocabulary of the Hakka dialect.]
林盛道：客家語の語彙

1456 Ho, Keng-feng: Kuang-tung tung-pei-pu K'o-chia fang-yen tz'u-hui tien-ti.—*FPC* 4, 1958, 90–91. [Some words of the Hakka dialect spoken in the northeastern part of Kwangtung.]
何耿豐：廣東東北部客家方言詞滙點滴

1457 Li, Ying-ch'uan: Mei-hsien fang-yen te i-hsieh tz'u-hui.—*FPC* 4, 1958, 85–87. [Some vocabulary of the Meihsien dialect.]
李映川：梅縣方言的一些詞滙

13.2.5.3. Grammar (1458–1461)

1458 Li, Tso-nan: K'o-chia-hua te chi-ko yü-fa t'e-tien.—*YWCS* 1957:1, 44–46. [Some special grammatical features of the Hakka dialect.]
李作南：客家話的幾個語法特點

1459 Li, Tso-nan: K'o-chia fang-yen te tai-tz'u.—*CKYW* 1965:3, 224–231, 205./ *RBS* 11, 1965, 433, S.N. Cartier. [Pronouns of the Hakka dialect.]
李作南：客家方言的代詞

1460 Lin, Yün-lai: Mei-hsien fang-yen ming-tz'u tai-tz'u tung-tz'u te i-hsieh kou-tz'u t'e-tien. — *CKYW* 1959:11, 30–31. [Some morphological features of nouns, pronouns, and verbs in the Meihsien dialect.]

林運來：梅縣方言名詞、代詞、動詞的一些構詞特點

1461 Nan, T'ai: K'o-chia-hua jen-ch'eng ling-shu tai-tz'u te yung-fa.—*CKYW* 1957:11, 31–32. [The usage of possessive pronouns in the Hakka dialect.]

南台：客家話人稱領屬代詞的用法

13.2.6. P'ingyüan (1462–1463)

1462 Lin, Yü-hsin: P'ing-yüan-hua te ming-tz'u kou-tz'u-fa.—*CKYW* 1957:11, 31–32. [Word formation of nouns in the P'ingyüan dialect.]

林雨新：平遠話的名詞構詞法

1463 Lin, Yü-hsin: P'ing-yüan-hua li te i-chung t'e-shu ko-shih.—*CKYW* 1958:10, 488. [A special phrase pattern formed with the words for 'pus' and 'blood' in the P'ingyüan dialect.]

林雨新：平遠話裏的一種特殊格式

13.2.7. Tap'u (1464–1465)

1464 Ho, Keng-yung: Ta-p'u K'o-chia-hua te hou-chui.—*CKYW* 1965:6, 492–493./ *RBS* 11, 1965, 434, A. Lucas. [Suffixes of the Hakka dialect at Tap'u.]

何耿鏞：大埔客家話的後綴

1465 Wen, T'ing-ching: Ta-p'u-hsien hsin-chih fang-yen chih erh p'ien (shih ch'in-shu, shih ch'ung yü niao shou).—*YWC* 1:2, 1936, 353–363. [Two sections of dialect records at Tap'u (kinship terms and insects, fish, birds, and animals).]

温廷敬：大埔縣新志方言之二篇（釋親屬，釋蟲魚鳥獸）

13.2.8. Haifeng and Lufeng (1466–1468)

1466 Hashimoto, Mantarō: Hakkago (Kairiku) hōgen—Sono onso no bunseki.— *CGGG* 1959:2, 3–10. [The Hakka (Hai-

lu) dialect: A phonemic analysis.]

橋本萬太郎：客家語（海陸）方言——其の音素の分析

1467 Schaank, S.H.: *Het Loeh-foeng dialect.*—Leiden: E.J. Brill, 1897, 2, 226 p.

1468 Schaank, Simon H. Transl. by Lindauer, Bennett M.: *The Lu-feng dialect of Hakka.*—Tokyo: Institute for the Study of Languages and Cultures of Asia and Africa, 1979, 262 p./ Writing and Language Reference Materials, 5; translation of (1467).

13.2.9. Sathewkok (1469–1471)

1469 Henne, Henry: Sathewkok Hakka Phonology.—*Norsk Tidsskrift for Sprogvidenskap* 20, 1964, 109–161, 8 tab./ *RBS* 11, 1965, 409, N. G. D. Malmqvist.

1470 Henne, Henry: An annotated syllabary of Sathewkok Hakka.—*AcOr* 28: 1–2, 1964, 61–127.

1471 Henne, Henry: A sketch of Sathewkok Hakka grammatical structure.—*ALH* 10, 1966, 69–108.

13.2.10. Taiwan (1472–1475)

1472 Yang, Paul Fu-mien: A preliminary study of the Jaop'ing Hakka dialect spoken in Hsinchu, Taiwan.—*TICOJ* 6, 1961, 27–37.

1473 Yang, Paul Fu-mien: *The Jaoping dialect: A descriptive and comparative study of a Hakka variety spoken in Taiwan.*—Tokyo: U. of Tokyo, 1963, 55 p./ Unpubl. M.A. thesis.

1474 Yang, Shih-feng: *T'ai-wan T'ao-yüan K'o-chia fang-yen.*—Taipei: Academia Sinica, 1957, v, 451 p./ *RBS* 3, 1957, 566, Li Fang-kuei. [The Hakka dialect of T'aoyüan, Taiwan.]

楊時逢：台灣桃園客家方言

1475 Yang, Shih-feng: T'ai-wan Mei-nung K'o-chia fang-yen.—*BIHP* 42, 1971, 405–466. [The Hakka dialect of Meinung, Taiwan.]

楊時逢：臺灣美濃客家方言

13.2.11.   Other Localities (1476–1482)

1476   Egerod, Søren: A sampling of Chung-sha Hakka.—*Studia . . . Karlgren dedicata* (0102), 36–54./ *RBS* 5, 1959, 494, J. Chmielewski.

1477   Haudricourt, André G.: Note sur les dialectes de la région de Moncay.—*BEFEO* 50, 1960, 173–177./ Including Hakka dialect.

1478   Li, Fu-ts'ai: Yüeh-tung T'ao-yüan-hua te t'e-shu pien-tiao kuei-lü.—*CKYW* 1959:8, 377–379. [Rules for special tone sandhi in the T'aoyüan dialect of eastern Kwangtung.]
李富才：粤東桃源話的特殊變調規律

1479   Ling, Tz'u-fang: Lung-nan-hua li te i-hsieh yü-fa hsien-hsiang.—*CKYW* 1957:11, 29–30. [Some grammatical phenomena in the Lungnan dialect.]
凌慈房：龍南話裏的一些語法現象

1480   Lo, Chao-chin: *Jui-chin fang-yen.*—Taipei: National Taiwan Normal U., 1977, 216 p.; map./ Unpubl. M.A. thesis. [The Juichin Hakka dialect of Kiangsi.]
羅肇錦：瑞金方言

1481   Sagart, Laurent: *Phonologie d'un dialecte Hakka des Noveaux Territoires de Hong Kong: Sunghimtong.*—Paris: U. of Paris 7, 1977, 355 p./ Unpubl. doc. diss.
〔崇謙堂〕

1482   Tung, T'ung-ho: Hua-yang Liang-shui-ching K'o-chia-hua chi-yin.—*BIHP* 19, 1948, 81–201; *Tung T'ung-ho . . . hsüan chi* (0110), 153–273. [The phonetic system of a Hakka dialect spoken in Liang-shuiching, Huayang district, Szechwan.]
董同龢：華陽涼水井客家話記音

13.2.12.   Contrastive Studies (1483–1488)

1483   Ho, Chiung: I Mei-hsien fang-yen wei tai-piao te K'o-chia-hua yü Pei-ching yü-yin te tui-ying kuei-lü.—*FPC* 4, 1958, 73–85. [Rules for phonetic correspondences between the Meihsien dialect and Pekinese.]
何炯：以梅縣方言爲代表的客家話與北京語音的對應規律

1484   Jao, Ping-ts'ai: *K'o-chia-jen tsen-yang hsüeh-hsi P'u-t'ung-hua.*—Canton: Kuang-tung jen-min, 1957, ii, 120 p./ *CKYW* 1958:1, 45, Hsü Ling-fang. [How a Hakka dialect speaker should learn the Common Language.]
饒秉才：客家人怎樣學習普通話 / 許令芳評

1485   Kuang-tung-sheng fang-yen tiao-ch'a chih-tao tsu: *K'o-chia-jen hsüeh-hsi P'u-t'ung-hua shou-ts'e.*—Canton: Kuang-tung jen-min, 1958, 88 p.; illus. [A handbook for Hakka dialect speakers in learning the Common Language.]
廣東省方言調查指導組：客家人學習普通話手冊

1486   Li, Tso-nan: K'o-chia-hua ho P'u-t'ung-hua tsai tz'u-hui shang te chu-yao ch'a-pieh.—*YWCS* 1956:5, 41–43./ *YWCS* 1956:7, 44–45, Ch'en Sung-yüan & P'ang Hung-ch'i. [The chief lexical differences between the Hakka dialect and the Common Language.]
李作南：客家話和普通話在詞滙上的主要差別 / 陳嵩元，龐鴻祺評

1487   Li, Tso-nan: Pei-ching yü-yin ho Kuang-tung tung-pei-pu K'o-chia fang-yin tsai sheng yün tiao shang te pi-chiao.—*FPC* 4, 1958, 88–90. [A comparison of initials, finals, and tones of the Hakka dialect spoken in the northeastern part of Kwangtung with the Peking dialect.]
李作南：北京語音和廣東東北部客家方音在聲韻調上的比較

1488   Yü, Min: K'o-chia-jen hsüeh Kuo-yin te ts'o-wu ch'ing-hsiang.—*Kuo-yü t'ung-hsün* 1, 1947, 5–7. [Erroneous tendencies of Hakka speakers in learning Mandarin pronunciation.]
俞敏：客家人學國音的錯誤傾向

13.2.13. Textbooks (1489–1509)

1489 Ball, James Dyer: *Easy sentences in the Hakka dialect, with a vocabulary.*—Hong Kong: Kelly & Walsh, 1896, 2nd ed., xvi, 57 p./ 31–57: English-Hakka vocabulary.

1490 Ball, James Dyer: *Hakka made easy.* Pt. I.—Hong Kong: Kelly & Walsh, 1896, xv, 63 p.; 1913, repr.

1491 Chabanel Language Institute: *The new Hakka reader.* Book I-II.—Hsinchu: Chabanel Language Institute, 1962, 2 vols., 2, 114; 118 p.; 1 map.
〔新客話課本〕

1492 Chabanel Language Institute: *The new Hakka reader. Romanized edition.* Book I-II.—Hsinchu: Chabanel Language Institute, 1962, 2, 112; 2, 118 p.
〔新客話課本：羅馬字注音〕

1493 Chien, Hsiang-jung: *Hyōjun Kantongo ten.*—Taipei: Taiwan Keisatsu Kyōkai, 1935, 2, 8, 380 p. [A handbook for the Standard Hakka dialect.]/ Szuhsien dialect. Pronunciation, grammar, conversation, proverbs, basic vocabulary.
菅向榮：標準廣東語典

1494 Chong, Peter: *Hakka for beginners.*—Singapore: Peter Chong & Co., 1954, 50 p.
〔客話易解〕

1495 Downs, J.: *Beginning Hakka.*—Hong Kong: Stanley Maryknoll House, 1953, xviii, 269 p.
〔客話讀本〕

1496 Drought, James M.: *Introduction to Hakka.*—Hong Kong: Nazareth Press, 1926, 298 p./ 163–230: Grammatical notes; 239–298: Vocabulary.

1497 Harkin, George F.: *Hakka one.*—Taichung: Maryknoll Language School, 1976, xviii, 359 p.; 2 maps./ Miaoli dialect.
〔客家〕

1498 Kōno, Tōkisu: *Kantongo no kenkyū.*—Hsinchu: Shinchikushū Keisatsu Bunko, 1933, 10, 252 p. [A study on the Hakka dialect.]
河野登喜壽：廣東語之研究

1499 Lee, Toong-hin: *Hakka lessons for Malayan students.*—Kuala Lumpur: Charles Grenier & Son, 1955, 276 p.
〔客話入門〕

1500 Liu, K'o-ming: *Kantongo shūsei.*—Taipei: Shinkōdō, 1919, 4, 5, 158 p. [Collection of Hakka dialect words.]/ Szuhsien dialect. Pronunciation, grammar, conversation.
劉克明：廣東語集成

1501 Mercer, Bernard: *Hakka-Chinese lessons.*—London: The Sheldon Press, 1930, 190 p./ *BSOS* 6, 1930–1932, 253–254, W. Bernard Paton.

1502 Quinn, Raymond P.: *Introduction to Hakka.* Vol. II. *Sermon-study.*—Kaying: The Maryknoll Press, 1937(?), 171 p./ *CCS* 10:2, 1937, 175, Anonymous.

1503 Rey, Charles: *Conversations chinoises prises sur le vif avec notes grammaticales, langage Hac-ka.*—Hong Kong: Nazareth, 1939, x, 736 p.; *Supplément,* 147 p./ *Orbis* 9:1, 1960, 176–177, Paul Yang Fu-mien.

1504 Shiba, Yoshitarō: *Kantongo kaiwa hen.*—Taipei: Taiwan Nichinichi Shinpōsha, 1915; 1920, 4th ed., 3, 4, 2, 3, 3, 2, 282 p. [Japanese-Hakka conversations.]
志波吉太郎：廣東語會話篇

1505 Taipei Language Institute: *Speak Hakkanese. Pronunciation drills.*—Taipei: Language Institute, 1967, 29 p.
〔台北語文學院：客語會話、客語發音〕

1506 Taipei Language Institute: *Speak Hakkanese.* Book I.—Taipei: Taipei Language Institute, 1967, 181 p.
〔台北語文學院：客語會話〕

1507 Takayama, Kizen: *Kōhan jitsuyō Kantongo tokuhon.*—Taipei: Nikkōdō, 1944, 3, 3, 205 p. [A comprehensive and practical Hakka dialect reader.]/ Szuhsien dialect. Hakka-Japanese conversations.

昌山喜全：廣粕實用廣東語讀本

1508 Tjen, Fo-sang: *Eenvoudig leerboekje voor het Hakka-Chineesch.*—Muntok: Bankatinwinning, 1926, 54 p.; 1930, 2nd print.

1509 Ven, Canisius van de: *Leerboek voor het praktisch gebruik van het Hakka-dialekt.*—Peking: Drukkerij der Lazaristen, 1938, xxi, 250 p.

［客話指南］

13.2.14. Dictionaries (1510–1520)

1510 China Inland Mission (ed.): *A combined index of Chinese words with Hakka pronunciations.*—London: China Inland Mission, 1957, 137 p./ *JRAS* 1958, G.B. Downer.

1511 MacIver, Donald: *A Hakka index to the Chinese-English dictionary of Herbert A. Giles and to the Syllabic dictionary of S. Wells Williams.*—Shanghai: American Presbyterian Mission Press, 1904, 150, 5 p. See (0516) & (0525).

1512 MacIver, Donald: *A Hakka syllabary.*—Shanghai: American Presbyterian Mission Press, 1909, ii, 184, 4 p.

［客音彙編］

1513 MacIver, Donald: *An English-Chinese dictionary in the vernacular of the Hakka people in the Canton province.*—Shanghai: American Presbyterian Mission Press, 1905, ix, 1221 p.

1514 MacIver, Donald: *A Chinese-English dictionary, Hakka dialect as spoken in Kwangtung province.*—Shanghai: American Presbyterian Mission Press, 1926, rev. & enl. by M. C. MacKenzie, 1142 p.; Taipei. Ku Ting Book Store, 1970, repr.

1515 Marsecano, Guerrino & García, Otilio: *English-Hakka dictionary.*—Taichung: Kuang-ch'i, 1959, x, 620 p./ *Orbis* 15, 1966, 138, Paul Yang Fu-mien.

［滿思謙，吉愛慈：英客字典］

1516 Rey, Charles: *Dictionnaire chinois-français dialecte Hac-ka.*—Hong Kong: Imprimerie de la Société des Missions Étrangères, 1901, xxxix, 360 p.; *Vocabulaire français-chinois,* 77 p.

1517 Rey, Charles: *Dictionnaire chinois-français dialecte Hac-ka.*—Hong Kong: Nazareth, 1901, xxxix, 360, 79 p.; 1926, rev. & enl., xl, 1444 p./ *Orbis* 9:1, 1960, 176, Paul Yang Fu-mien.

1518 Sallé, Robert: *Index syllabaire Hakka.*—Kuanhsi: Catholic Mission, 1954, 149 p.

［陸若伯：客語字典］

1519 Stadt, P. A. van de: *Hakka woordenboek.*—'S-gravenhage: Martinus Nijhoff, 1912, xxxi, 412 p.

1520 Taiwan Sōtokufu: *Kantongo jiten.*—Taipei: Taiwan Sōtokufu, 1932, 5, 1554 p. [Japanese-Hakka dictionary.]/ Cheng-p'ing dialect of Szuhsien.

臺灣總督府：廣東語辭典

14. YÜEH DIALECTS (1521–1860)

14.1. Yüeh Dialects in General (1521–1559)

14.1.1. Historical Studies (1521–1530)

1521 Boltz, William G.: Notes on dating the Cantonese dentilabialization of Middle Chinese gutturals.—*JAOS* 98, 1978, 99–100.

1522 Ch'en, Che-san: Min Yüeh fang-yen chih lai-yüan chi ch'i so pao-ts'un te ku yin ku yü.—*YSYK* 47:2, 1978, 21–23. [The origin of the Min and Yüeh dialects and the old pronunciations and words they preserved.]

陳哲三：閩粵方言之來源及其所保存的古音古語

1523 Hashimoto, Oi-kan Yue: Two features of Proto-Yue initials.—*Chi-Lin* 9, 1972, 20–41.

1524 K'ung, Chung-nan: *Kuang-tung su-yü k'ao.*—Canton: Fu-lun-she, 1933, 71 p./ Another title: *Kuang-tung fang-yen.* [A study on Cantonese vernacular speech.]/ Classified vocabulary with etymological notes.

孔仲南：廣東俗語考（廣東方言）

1525 Lin, Lien-hsien: Yüeh-yü shih su.— *Shou Lo Hsiang-lin chiao-shou lun-wen chi* (Hong Kong: Dept. of Chinese, Hong Kong U., 1970), 229–243. [Cantonese dialect idioms explained.]/ Etymological study.

林蓮仙：粵語釋俗——『壽羅香林教授論文集』

1526 Lin, Yü-t'ang: Min Yüeh fang-yen chih lai-yüan (0490). [The origin of the Min and Yüeh dialects.]

林語堂：閩粵方言之來源

1527 McCoy, William John, Jr.: *Szeyap data for a first approximation of Proto-Cantonese.*—Ithaca: Cornell U., 1966, viii, 208 p., *Appendix,* 105 p./ Unpubl. doc. diss.; 201–208: Bibilography; *DA* 27: 1805–A; UM 66–11,038.

1528 Ou, Ching-huan: Yüeh-yü pen yin i k'ao.—*Wen-shih hsüeh-pao* 3, 1966, 73–78; 4, 1967, 77–79; 5, 1968, 103–105. [A study on the original sounds and meanings of Cantonese words.]

區靜寰：粵語本音義考

1529 Su, Wen-cho: Yüeh-tung fang-yen k'ao. —*TFWH* 1:1, 1942, 62–64; 1:3, 1942, 48–51; 2:5, 1943, 70–73. [A study on the dialect of eastern Kwangtung.]

蘇文擢：粵東方言考

1530 Tsuji, Nobuhisa: Murmured initials in Yue Chinese and Proto-Yue voiced obstruents: The case of Cenxi dialect, Guangxi province.—*GK* 72, 1977, 29–46.

〔辻伸久〕〔廣西岑溪〕

14.1.2. General Studies (1531–1542)

1531 Chang, Wei-kang: Kuang-tung yü-yen te fen-lei.—*Kuang-tung chiao-yü yü wen-hua* 2:2, 1950, 9–10. [The classification of the languages of Kwangtung.]

張爲綱：廣東語言的分類

1532 Hao, Chih: Kuang-tung te t'u-yü.— *Ch'u-pan chou-k'an* 78, 1934, 2–3. [Patois of Kwangtung.]

郝志：廣東的土語

1533 Hashimoto, Anne Yue: The Liang-Yue dialect materials.—*Chi-Lin* 6, 1970, 35–51; map.

1534 Huang, Tien-ch'eng: Kuang-fu-hua.— *YWCS* 1954:5, 10–13; 6, 10–13. [The dialect of Canton.]

黃典誠：廣府話

1535 Kōsaka, Jun'ichi: Kantongo no kenkyū —Morison kara Chō Gen-jin e.—*JBK* 3:3, 1952, 35–63. [The study of Cantonese—From Morrison to Chao Yuen Ren.]

香坂順一：廣東語の研究——モリソンから趙元任へ

1536 Noguchi, Masayuki: Kōshū hōgen ni tsuite.—*DBDK* 12, 1974, 203–229. [A study of the Kuangchou (Canton) dialect.]

野口正之：廣州方言について

1537 Tōdō, Akiyasu: Etsuhōgen to Kantongo.—*Chūgokugo on'inron* (0634), 127–
130. [The Yüeh dialects and Cantonese.]/
Historico-descriptive.

藤堂明保：粤方言と廣東語

1538 Ts'en, Ch'i-hsiang: Fang-yen.—*Kuang-
tung nien-chien,* Vol. I, 1942, Pt. 1, Chap.
3, 41–52. [Dialects.]

岑麒祥：方言──『廣東年鑑』

1539 Tsou, Lu: Kuang-tung yü-yen shuo
lüeh.—*TSTH* 26, 1941, 4. [A short note
on the languages of Kwantung.]

鄒魯：廣東語言說略

1540 Wang, Li: Liang Yüeh yin shuo.—
CHHP 5:1, 1928, 1519–1565. [A study
of the phonetic systems of the dialects
spoken in Kwangtung and Kwangsi.]/
Kwangtung, Popai, Yülin, and Hakka.

王力：兩粤音說

1541 Wang, Li: *Kuang-chou-hua ch'ien shuo.*
—Peking: Wen-tzu kai-ko, 1957, ii, 108
p./ *CKYW* 1957:8, 44–45, Li Shan;
1958:3, 123–126, Li Wei. [An easy introduction to the Kuangchou (Canton)
dialect.]

王力：廣州話淺說／力山評；李未評

1542 Yüan, Chia-hua: Yüeh fang-yen.—
Han-yü fang-yen kai-yao (0146), Chap.
IX. [The Yüeh dialects.]

袁家驊：粤方言

14.1.3. Sociocultural Aspects (1543–1559)

1543 Aubazac, Louis: *Proverbes de la langue
Cantonnaise recueillis çà et là.*—Hong
Kong: Imprimerie de Nazareth, 1918, iv,
176 p./ *Orbis* 9:1, 1960, 178, Paul Yang
Fu-mien.

1544 Boltz, William G.: Canton: the Seville
of China.—*Romance Philology* 21, 1967–
1968, 171–174./ The "Cantonese" language of China in the Americas.

1545 Ch'en, Tun: Ou-hua te Kuang-chou
fang-yen.—*CSTY* 8:85–87, 1929, 48.
[Europeanized Cantonese.]

陳鈍：歐化的廣州方言

1546 Fabre, Alfred: *Film de la vie chinoise,
proverbes et locutions.*—Hong Kong:
Nazareth, 1937, xviii, 694 p./ *Orbis* 9:1,
1960, 178, Paul Yang Fu-mien.

1547 Kehl, Frank: Chinese nicknaming be-
haviour: sociolinguistic pilot study.—*JOS*
9:1, 1971, 149–172./ Examples taken
from Cantonese.

1548 Lin, Lien-hsien: Hsiang-kang Chung-
kuo-jen te yü-yen hsien-hsiang kai-k'uang.
—*CCHP* 3:2, 1964, 132–161. [Spoken
language phenomena of the Chinese in
Hong Kong.]/ A survey of Chinese dialects spoken in Hong Kong: Cantonese,
Ch'aochou, Amoy, Hakka, Szeyap, Shanghai, Mandarin.

林蓮仙：香港中國人的語言現象概況

1549 Liu, Wan-chang: Kuang-chou te chin-
chi yü.—*KYAO* 3:11, 1937, 7–8. [Lin-
guistic tabu in Canton.]

劉萬章：廣州的禁忌語

1550 Mei, Shou: Kuang-tung-jen te chi-hui.
—*Yüeh-pao* 1:5, 1937, 1096. [Tabu of
the Cantonese people.]

梅瘦：廣東人的忌諱

1551 Parker, Edward Harper: Canton plants.
—*CR* 15, 1886–1887, 104–119, 379./
List of Cantonese plant names.

1552 Playfair, G.M.H.: Notes on Parker's
Canton plants.—*CR* 15, 1886–1887,
178–179./ See (1551).

1553 Tse, John Kwock-ping: Maŋ⌐ kuŋ⌐
wa⌐: A game language of Cantonese.
—*Studies in English Literature and Linguistics* 1979, 97–106.

〔謝國平〕

1554 Ts'en, Ch'i-hsiang: Ts'ung Kuang-tung
fang-yen chung t'i-ch'a yü-yen te chiao-
liu ho fa-chan.—*CKYW* 1953:4, 9–12.
[Some observations on the contact and
development of languages from a study of
Cantonese dialects.]

岑麒祥：從廣東方言中體察語言的交流
和發展

1555 T'sou, Benjamin K.: Asymmetric bilingualism: a sociolinguistic study of Cantonese emigrants.—*JCLTA* 8:3, 1973, 134–144.

1556 Tsou, Chia-yen [T'sou, Benjamin K.]: Shuang-ch'ung yü-yen yü wen-hua t'ung-hua—I-ko chien-li she-hui yü-yen-hsüeh li-lun te li cheng.—*Tou-sou* 13, 1976, 47–59. [Bilingualism and cultural assimilation—Towards a theory of the sociology of language.]/ Based on (1555).
鄒嘉彥： 雙重語言與文化同化──一個建立社會語言學理論的例證

1557 T'sou, Benjamin K.: Sound symbolism and some socio-historical linguistic implications of linguistic diversity in Sino-Tibetan languages.—*CLAO* 3, 1978, 67–76./ Cites sound symbolism in Cantonese.

1558 Whitaker, K.P.K.: Cantonese version of a mock disputation.—*AM* 11, 1965, 233–239.

1559 Yang, Ch'eng-chih: *Kuang-tung jen-min yü wen-hua.*—Canton: Kuo-li Chung-shan ta-hsüeh Yen-chiu-yüan Wen-k'o yen-chiu-so, 1943, 108 p. [The people and culture of Kwangtung.]
楊成志：廣東人民與文化

14.1.4. Phonetics and Phonology (1560–1610)
14.1.4.1. General Studies (1560–1582)

1560 Blatchford, Charles H.: *Cantonese phonology and some phonological problems of Cantonese speakers in learning English.*—Washington, D.C.: Georgetown U., 1962, 25 p./ Unpubl. M.S. thesis.

1561 Chan, Jachin Yin-man: *Distribution of Cantonese phonemes.*—Baton Rouge: Louisiana State U., 1967, vi, 135 p./ Unpubl. doc. diss.; *DA* 28:1805-A; UM 67-11,648.

1562 Ch'en, Li: Kuang-chou yin-shuo.—*Tung-shu-chi* (1892 ed.), 27–29. [On the sounds of Cantonese.]/ Compared with other dialects and Ancient Chinese.
陳澧：廣州音說──『東塾集』

1563 Cheng, Teresa: The phonological system of Cantonese.—*POLA* 2:5, 1968. C1–C85.

1564 Chou, K'ang-hsieh (ed.): *Kuang-chou yin shuo chi tzu i chü li.*—Hong Kong: Ch'ung-wen shu-tien, 1971, 1, 51 p.; tab. [Three articles on the pronunciations and meanings of characters in Cantonese.]
周康燮編：廣州音說及字義舉例

1565 Fujitsuka, Shōichi: Kantongo zen-onpyō.—*AGK* 8, 1955, 24 p. [A syllabary of Cantonese.]
藤塚將一： 廣東語全音表（粵語等韻圖）

1566 Fujitsuka, Shōichi: Kantongo no hatsuon to on'in bunrui no kenkyū.—*AGK* 8, 1955, 15 p. [A study of the classification of Cantonese phonetics and phonology.]
藤塚將一： 廣東語の發音と音韻分類の研究

1567 Hashimoto, Oi-Kan Yue: A note on D. Jones & K.T. Woo's *A Cantonese phonetic reader.*—*ONK* 15, 1971, 79–94./ A critico-analytical review of (1570).

1568 Hashimoto, Oi-kan Yue: *Studies in Yüe dialects, I: Phonology of Cantonese.*—Cambridge: Cambridge U. Press, 1972, xxiii, 755 p.; 5 maps in pocket; 676–693: Annotated bibliography./ *BSOAS* 35, 1972, 695, Hugh D.R. Baker; *THG* 46, 1973, 158–163, Shimizu Shigeru; *HKCW* 5:1, 1972, 293–297, Miao Chin-an; *AAGB* 7, 1974, 237–240, Nakajima Motoki; *Linguistics* 149, 1975, 112–121, A.A. Moskalev.
清水茂評；繆錦安評；中鳩幹起評

1569 Huang, Hsi-ling [Wong, Sik-ling]: *Yüeh yin yün hui.*—Shanghai: Chung-hua, 1940; Hong Kong: Chung-hua, 1954; 1978, repr., 77, 46 p.; E. Introduction. [A Chinese syllabary pronounced according to the dialect of Canton.]
黃錫凌：粵音韻彙

1570 Jones, Daniel & Woo, Kwing-tong: *A Cantonese phonetic reader.*—London: U. of London Press, 1912, xxiii, 95 p./ With an introduction by Daniel Jones. *Supplement, the text in Chinese writing.*—Ibid., 1916, 41 p./ *BIHP* 2, 1932, 515–521, Liu Hsüeh-chün (rev. of the *Supplement*).

劉學濬：勘誤

1571 Jones, Daniel & Woo, Kwing-tong. Transl. by Ogaeri, Yoshio: *Kantongo no hatsuon.*—Tokyo: Bunkyūdō, 1942, ii, 10, 18, 95, 6 p. [A Cantonese phonetic reader (1570).]

魚返善雄譯：廣東語の發音

1572 Kao, Diana L.: *Structure of the syllable in Cantonese.*—The Hague & Paris: Mouton, 1971, 189 p./ *Janua Linguarum, Series Practica*, 78; *Lg* 49:4, 1973, 954–961, Anatole Lyovin; *ZDMG* 125, 1975, 234, Kamil Sedláček.

1573 Lin, Lien-hsien: Yüeh-yin yü *Kuang-yün* pi-chiao piao ch'u-ni (Yün-yin chih pu).—*CCHP* 4:2, 1965, 174–239. [A preliminary comparative table of Cantonese phonology and *Kuang-yün* (phonetic section.]

林蓮仙：粵音與『廣韵』比較表初擬（韵音之部）

1574 Lin, Lien-hsien: *Yüeh-tu fan-ch'ieh yin-piao liang-yung cheng-yin piao.*—Hong Kong: The Chinese Literary Society, Chinese U. of Hong Kong, 1975, 76 p. [A standard phonetics table for Cantonese (Fan-ch'ieh and I.P.A.)]/ A revised version of (1573).

林蓮仙：粵讀反切音標兩用正音表

1575 Lockhart, J.H. Stewart: Canton syllabary.—*CR* 10, 1882, 312–326.

1576 Matsumoto, Kazuo: Kantongo no on-kei.—*Chūgoku gogaku jiten* (0093), 166–168. [Phonetic system of Cantonese.]

松本一男：廣東語の音系

1577 Parker, Edward Harper: Canton syllabary.—*CR* 8, 1880, 363–382.

1578 Rai, Tsutomu: Kantongo no on'inron ni tsuite.—*CGGG* 1958:1, 3–5. [On the phonology of Cantonese.]

賴惟勤：廣東語の音韻論について

1579 Seers, O.: Chinese phonetics: Observation made on the sounds of the Cantonese dialect of Chinese.—*Maître Phonétique* 1908, 30–34.

1580 Ts'en, Ch'i-hsiang: Étude expérimentale sur les articulations des sons du dialecte cantonnais.—*YWC* 1:2, 1936, 11–41.

〔岑麒祥：粵語發音實驗錄〕

1581 Ts'en, Ch'i-hsiang: Kuang-chou yin-hsi kai-shu.—*Kuang-tung chien-she,* 1–2, 1946, 1–9. [Summary of the phonetic system of Cantonese.]

岑麒祥：廣州音系概述

1582 Wei, Tseng-shan: *Kuang-chou-hua t'ung-yin tzu piao.*—Hong Kong: Wen-fang ch'u-pan-she, 1953, 62 p. [Syllabary of Cantonese homophones.]

魏曾山：廣州話同音字表

14.1.4.2. Initials (1583–1586)

1583 Cheng, Chao-lin: Pekingo yori mita Kantongo no seibo.—*CBKK* 2, 1962, 12–18. [Cantonese initials compared with Pekinese.]

鄭兆麟：北京語より見た廣東語の聲母

1584 Hashimoto, Mantarō: Etsugo no soku-men masatsuon.—*CGGG* 1961:2, 10–13. [The voiceless lateral initials of the Cantonese dialects.]

橋本萬太郎：粵語の側面摩擦音

1585 Matsumoto, Kazuo: Seibo no men kara mita Kantongo to Fukkengo.—*CGGG* 1959:1, 3–7, 17. [The Cantonese and Fukien dialects as seen from their initials.]

松本一男：聲母の面から見た廣東語と福建語

1586 Shan, Chou-yao: Kuang-chou-hua ling sheng-mu tzu yü ŋ sheng-mu tzu tsai sheng-tiao shang te ch'ü-pieh.—*YWTC* 1, 1979, 27–28. [Tonal differences between words with zero initial and ŋ- initial in Cantonese.]
單周堯：廣州話零聲母字與 ŋ 聲母字在聲調上的區別

14.1.4.3. Finals (1587–1592)

1587 Cheng, Chao-lin: Pekingo yori mita Kantongo no inbo.—*CBKK* 3, 1963, 43–48; 4, 1964, 30–35; 5, 1965, 17–23. [The finals of Cantonese as compared with Pekinese.]
鄭兆麟： 北京語より見た廣東語の韻母

1588 Hashimoto, Anne Yue & Hashimoto, Mantarō J.: Phonological redundancy and Cantonese vowels.—*GK* 53, 1968, 101–111.

1589 Light, Timothy: The Cantonese final: An exercise in indigenous analysis.—*JCL* 5:1, 1977, 75–102.

1590 Rai, Tsutomu: Kantongo no kaion ni tsuite.—*CGKK* 1954:9, 1–8. [On the medial vowels in Cantonese.]
賴惟勤：廣州方言の介音について

1591 Rygaloff, Alexis: Remarques sur le vocalisme du cantonnais.—*Langages et techniques*, Tome I, *Approche linguistique* (Ed. by Jacques Barrau, et al.; Paris: Klincksieck, 1972), 221–224.

1592 Shimizu, Shigeru: Kantongo no /e/.—*SPhon.*—3, 1963–1964, 7–16. [The vowel /e/ in Cantonese.]
清水茂：廣東語の/e/

14.1.4.4. Tones (1593–1610)

1593 Bradley, Cornelius B.: The tone-accents of two dialects of Chinese (0712)./ Cantonese and Pekinese.

1594 Chan, Yuen-yuen Angela: *A perceptual study of tones in Cantonese.*—London: University College, 1971, 237 p./ Unpubl. doc. diss.

1595 Ch'an, Chan-sin: Rules for the use of various tones in Cantonese.—*CR* 24, 1900, 209–226.

1596 Ch'en, San-su: Kuang-chou-hua te shang-ju ho chung-ju.—*HKCK* 7:3, 1952, 389–396. [The upper and middle *ju* tone in the Cantonese dialect.]
陳三蘇：廣州話的上入和中入

1597 Cheng, Chao-lin: Pekingo yori mita Kantongo no seichō.—*CBKK* 6, 1966, 43–46. [Tones of Cantonese as compared with Pekinese.]
鄭兆麟： 北京語より見た廣東語の聲調

1598 Fok, Chan Yuen-yuen: *A perceptual study of tones in Cantonese.*—Hong Kong: U. of Hong Kong, 1974, viii, 191 p.; 186–191: Bibliography.
〔霍陳婉媛〕

1599 Huang, Parker: *Cantonese sounds and tones.*—New Haven: Far Eastern Publications, Yale U., 1965, 69 p.

1600 Kōsaka, Jun'ichi: Kantongo no hensei.—*CGGG* 1960:7, 8–15. [Tone sandhi in Cantonese.]
香坂順一：廣東語の變聲

1601 Lin, Lien-hsien: Lun Yüeh-yü te ju-sheng-tiao.—*CCHP* 3:1, 1963, 23–45. [On the *ju* tone of Cantonese.]
林蓮仙：論粵語的入聲調

1602 Lo, Hsin-t'ien: Kuan-yü Kuang-chou-hua ju-sheng te t'ao-lun.—*KYCK* 41, 1932, July 2. [A discussion on the *ju* tone of Cantonese.]
羅莘田：關於廣州話入聲的討論

1603 Tse, Kwock-ping: *The upper even tone in Cantonese: An instrumental investigation.*—Taipei: National Taiwan Normal U., 1973, iv, 66 p./ Unpubl. M.A. thesis.
〔謝國平〕

1604 Tse, Kwock-ping: Tone acquisition in Cantonese: A longitudinal case study.— *Journal of Child Language* 5, 1978, 191–204.

1605 Ts'en, Ch'i-hsiang: Ju-sheng fei sheng shuo.—*TSYK* 2:7, 1942, 8–11. [On the non-tonal status of *ju* tones.]/ Uses Cantonese as an example.

岑麒祥：入聲非聲說

1606 Tsung, Fu-pang: Kuan-yü Kuang-chou-hua yin-p'ing-tiao te fen-hua wen-t'i.— *CKYW* 1964:5, 376–389./ *RBS* 10, 1964, 470, A. Rygaloff. [Problems concerning the split of the *yin-p'ing* tone in Cantonese.]

宗福邦：關於廣州話陰平調的分化問題

1607 Vance, Timothy J.: Tonal distinction in Cantonese.—*Phonetica* 34:2, 1974, 92–107; G.S., F.S.

1608 Vance, Timothy J.: An experimental investigation of tones and intonation in Cantonese.—*Phonetica* 33:5, 1976, 368–392.

1609 Whitaker, Katherine Po Kan: *Characterization of the Cantonese dialect with special reference to its modified tones.*— London: School of Oriental and African Studies, 1952. [not seen.]/ Unpubl. doc. diss.

1610 Whitaker, K.P.K.: A study on the modified tones in spoken Cantonese.— *AM* 5, 1955, 9–36; 184–207./ *RBS* 1, 1955, 278, A. Rygaloff; 2, 1956, 374, A. Rygaloff.

14.1.5. Vocabulary (1611–1622)

1611 Anonymous: *A Chinese phonetic vocabulary.*—Hong Kong: The London Missionary Society Press, 1855, 31 d.p./ Contains all the most common characters, with their sounds in the Cantonese dialect.

〔初學粵音切要〕

1612 Baronsfeather, C.G.S.: *English-Cantonese. Medical dispensary vocabulary from Chalmer's English and Cantonese dictionary and other sources.*—Pakhoi: C.M.S. Mission Press, 1914, 2, [37] p.

1613 Bauer, Robert S.: Alveolarization in Cantonese: A case of lexical diffusion.— *JCL* 7:1, 1979, 132–141.

1614 Ch'en, Hui-ying: Kuang-chou fang-yen te chi-tsu tz'u-hui.—*FPC* 1, 1958, 55–58. [Several groups of vocabulary in the Cantonese dialect.]

陳慧英：廣州方言的幾組詞彙

1615 Cheng, Chao-lin: Pekingo yori mita Kantongo no goi.—*CBKK* 7, 1967, 1–8. [Vocabulary of Cantonese as compared with Pekinese.]

鄭兆麟：北京語より見た廣東語の語彙

1616 Ch'iao, Yen-nung: *Kuang-chou-hua k'ou-yü tz'u te yen-chiu.*—Hong Kong: Hua-ch'iao yü-wen, 1966, xvii, 322 p. [A study of Cantonese colloquial expressions.]/ Classified.

喬硯農：廣州話口語詞的研究

1617 Jen, I-ch'i: Kuang-chou-hua fu-yin tz'u te fen ho sheng-lüeh tso-yung.—*Chung-kuo yü-wen te hsin sheng* (0107), 508–510. [The functions of separation or combination and abbreviation of polysyllabic words in Cantonese.]

任以奇：廣州話複音辭的分合省略作用

1618 Liu, Chin: Kuang-tung-hua fang-yen tz'u-hui. — *YWCS* 1955:12, 22–24; 1956:1, 35–36; 2, 45–48. [Vocabulary of the Cantonese dialect.]

劉進：廣東話方言詞滙

1619 Lo, Cheng-p'ing: Kuang-chou fang-yen tz'u-hui t'an yüan.—*CKYW* 1960:3, 129–134. [On the origin of Cantonese dialect vocabulary.]

羅正平：廣州方言詞滙探源

1620 Matsumoto, Kazuo: Kantongo no goi ni tsuite no jakkan no kōsatsu.—*CGGG* 1956:2, 5–13. [Some observations on the vocabulary of Cantonese.]

松本一男：廣東語の語彙についての若干の考察

1621 Parker, Edward Harper: New Cantonese words.—*CR* 8, 1880, 18–22.

1622 Thompson, Robert Wallace: Some words in Cantonese.—*JRASHK* 6, 1966, 160–165.

14.1.6. Grammar (1623–1644)

1623 Castañeda, Benjamin: *Gramática elemental de la lengua China, dialecto Cantonés.*—Hong Kong: Typ. de De Sousa, 1869, 137 p.

1624 Chan, Po-hui: Yüeh fang-yen chung te hsü-tz'u ts'an, fan, tsy, mai, t'im.—*CKYW* 1958:3, 119–122. [The particles *ts'an, fan, tsy, mai, t'im* in Cantonese.]
詹伯慧：粵方言中的虛詞『親、翻、住、埋、添』

1625 Chang, Hung-nien: Yüeh-yü chung ch'ang chien te wei-tz'u tz'u-wei.—*HKCW* 3:2, 1970, 459–488. [Some commonly seen predicative suffixes in Cantonese.]
張洪年：粵語中常見的謂詞詞尾

1626 Chang, Lien-ch'iang: Kuang-chou-hua liang-tz'u te yü-fa t'e-tien.—*CKYW* 1961: 1, 30–32. [Special grammatical features of quantitatives in Cantonese.]
張鍊強：廣州話量詞的語法特點

1627 Ch'en, Hui-ying: T'an-t'an Kuang-chou-hua te hsing-jung-tz'u.—*CKYW* 1979:6, 451–454. [A discussion of Cantonese adjectives.]
陳慧英：談談廣州話的形容詞

1628 Ch'en, San-su: Min Yüeh fang-yen chung hsing-jung-tz'u te ch'en tzu.—*Hsinan yen-chiu* 1, 1940, 75–94. [Inserted characters in adjectives of the Min and Yüeh dialects.]
陳三蘇：閩粵方言中形容詞的襯字

1629 Cheng, Chao-lin: Pekingo yori mita Kantongo no gohō.—*CBKK* 8, 1968, 30–35; 9, 1969. [not seen]. [Cantonese grammar as compared with Pekinese.]
鄭兆麟：北京語より見た廣東語の語法

1630 Feng, Liang: Kuan-yü Kuang-chou-hua li te ta.—*CKYW* 1965:6, 496. [On the verb *ta* 'to hit' in the Cantonese dialect.]
馮亮：關於廣州話裏的『打』

1631 Huang, Po-jung: Kuang-chou fang-yen yü-fa te chi-ko t'e-tien.—*FPC* 1, 1958, 58–60. [Some special grammatical features of the Cantonese dialect.]
黃伯榮：廣州方言語法的幾個特點

1632 Huang, Po-jung: Kuang-chou-hua pu-yü pin-yü te tz'u-hsü.—*CKYW* 1959:6, 275–276. [The word order of verb complements and objects in Cantonese.]
陳伯榮：廣州話補語賓語的詞序

1633 Kam, Tak Him: Derivation by tone change in Cantonese.—*JCL* 5:2, 1977, 186–210.

1634 Killingley, Siew Yue: *The grammatical hierarchy of Malayan Cantonese.*—London: School of Oriental and African Studies, 1972, 418 p./ Unpubl. doc. diss.

1635 Kōsaka, Jun'ichi: Gohō no anteisei—Kantongo ko o chūshin ni shite.—*JBK* 4:8, 1953, 43–56. [Grammatical stability in Chinese—Focusing on *ko* in Cantonese.]
香坂順一： 語法的安定性──廣州語『個』を中心にして

1636 Kōsaka, Jun'ichi: Rinkai hōgen no ichi tokuchō (0548). [A distinctive feature of Chinese coastal dialects.]/ With Cantonese examples.
香坂順一：臨海方言の一特徵

1637 Kōsaka, Jun'ichi: Kantongo goki-joshi shikō.—*CGGG* 1959:1, 8–17. [A preliminary study of Cantonese intonational particles.]
香坂順一：廣東語語氣助詞試稿

1638 Kwok, Helen: *A study of the Cantonese verb.*—Hong Kong: U. of Hong Kong, 1971, vi, 177 p./ Centre of Asian Studies, Occasional Papers and Monographs, 5.
〔郭張凱倫〕

1639 Lin, Lien-hsien: Yüeh-yü tung-tz'u tz'u-wei hsü-tzu yung-fa te t'an-t'ao.—*CCHP* 2:2, 1963, 181–191. [The use of certain cenematic particles as verbal suffixes in Cantonese.]

林蓮仙：粵語動詞詞尾虛字用法的探討

1640 Lobscheid, W.: *Grammar of the Chinese language.*—Hong Kong: Office of the Daily Press, 1864, 2 parts; Pt. I, xxxvii, 110 p.; Pt. II, v, 178 p./ A grammar of spoken Cantonese and the written (literary) language.

1641 Shimizu, Shigeru: Etsu hōgen sōhingo no shijo.—*Chūgoku no gengo to moji* (see 0711), 193–208. [The word order of double objects in Cantonese dialects.]

清水茂：粵方言雙賓語の詞序──『中國の言語と文字』

1642 T'sou, Benjamin K.: *A basic Cantonese grammar.*—San Diego: Dept. of Linguistics, U. of San Diego, 1972, prelim. ed., iii, 137 p.

1643 T'sou, Benjamin K.: Homorganic nasal/stop alternations in Cantonese.—*Studies in Tai and Mon-Khmer phonetics and phonology* (Ed. by Theraphan L. Thongkum, et al.; Bangkok: Chulalongkorn Univ. Press, 1979), 290–312.

1644 Yau, Shun-chiu: *Le système de la négative en cantonnais.*—Paris: Université de Paris VII, 1974, 268 p./ Unpubl. doc. diss.

〔游順釗〕

14.1.7. Contrastive Studies (1645–1671)
(See also 6.2.4.)

1645 Browning, Larry K.: *The Cantonese dialect with special reference to contrasts with Mandarin as an approach to determining dialect relatedness.*—Washington, D. C.: Georgetown U., 1974, iii, 181 p./ Unpubl. doc. diss.; *DAI* 35:3727-A; UM 74–26,430.

1646 Chalmers, John: List of characters used in spelling in the concise dictionary of Dr. Chalmers, with their pronunciations in Pekinese and Cantonese.—*CR* 15, 1886–1887, 158–163.

1647 Chang, Tzu-p'ing: Yüeh-yin yü K'o-yin chih pi-chiao.—*Chiang-nan shih-ti ts'ung-k'ao* 1, 1942, 39 p. [Pronunciations of Cantonese and Hakka compared.]

張資平：粵音與客音之比較

1648 Ch'en, Hui-ying & Pai, Wan-ju: Kuang-chou-yin ho Pei-ching-yin te pi-chiao.—*FPT* 1, 1958, 5–101. [A comparison of Cantonese and Pekinese sounds.]

陳慧英，白婉如：廣州音和北京音的比較

1649 Ch'iao, Yen-nung: *Kuang-chou-yin lei-t'ui fa.*—Hong Kong: Hua-ch'iao yü-wen, 1964, 44 p. [Methods of converting Cantonese sounds to Mandarin.]

喬硯農：廣州音類推法

1650 Fang, Shu-chen: Ying-yü ho Kuang-chou-hua yü-yin pi-chiao fen-hsi.—*Hsi-fang yü-wen* 1:2, 1957, 172–180. [A comparative analysis of English and Cantonese phonetics.]

方淑珍：英語和廣州話語音比較分析

1651 Hsieh, Kuo-p'ing: I i-ch'i yen-chiu Kuang-tung-jen hsüeh-hsi kuo-yü shih sheng-tiao fang-mien so tsao-yü chih k'un-nan.—*Chiao-yü yü wen-hua* 422, 1974, 62–66. [An instrumental study of the difficulties encountered by a Cantonese in learning Mandarin tones.]

謝國平：以儀器研究廣東人學習國語時聲調方面所遭遇之困難

1652 Huang, Po-jung: *Kuang-chou-jen tsen-yang hsüeh-hsi P'u-t'ung-hua.*—Canton: Kuang-tung jen-min, 1957, iii, 102 p. [How a speaker of Cantonese should learn the Common Language.]

黃伯榮：廣州人怎樣學習普通話

1653 Huang, Po-jung: Kuang-chou-hua ho P'u-t'ung-hua te yü-yin pi-chiao.—*FPC* 1, 1958, 1–54. [A phonetic comparison of the Cantonese dialect and the Common Language.]

黃伯榮：廣州話和普通話的語音比較

1654 Kao, Chih-teng: *Kuo-yü yü Kuang-tung-hua.*—Taipei: Cheng-yu, 1976, 110 p. [Mandarin and Cantonese.]/ Phonetics compared.

高志澄：國語與廣東話

1655 Kollecker, C.A.: *Anhang zum Chinesisch-Deutschen Wörterbuch von Werner Rüdenberg, enthaltend die 6400 Schriftzeichen mit ihren Aussprache-und Tonbezeichnungen in der Kantoner und Hakka-Mundart* (1450).

1656 Kōsaka, Jun'ichi: *Pekingo taishō Kantongo kenkyū.*—Taipei: Tōto shoseki, 1943, 4, 8, 686 p. [A study on the Cantonese dialect as compared with the Peking dialect.]

香坂順一：北京語對照廣東語研究

1657 Kōsaka, Jun'ichi: *Pekingo Kantongo taishō Kago tokuhon.*—Taipei: Takei shobō, 1944, 62 p. [A Chinese reader in the Peking dialect and Cantonese.]/ 25 lessons reprinted from the author's *Kantongo kenkyū* (1656), Pt. VII.

香坂順一：北京語廣東語對照華語讀本

1658 Kuang-tung-sheng fang-yen tiao-ch'a chih-tao tsu: *Szu-i-jen hsüeh-hsi P'u-t'ung-hua shou-ts'e.*—Canton: Kuang-tung jen-min, 1958, 99 p.; tab. [A handbook for Szeyap dialect speakers in learning the Common Language.]

廣東省方言調查指導組：四邑人學習普通話手冊

1659 Li, Shou-chih: Tsen-yang chang-wo Kuang-chou-yin ho Pei-ching-yin te tui-ying kuei-lü. — *Kuang-tung chiao-yü* 1956:7, 27–29. [How to master the rules of phonetic correspondence between the Cantonese and the Peking dialects.]

李瘦芝：怎樣掌握廣州音和北京音的對應規律

1660 Phoon, Mun-kwong: A comparative study of Ancient Chinese and Cantonese initials.—*Hsin-she hsüeh-pao* 3, 1969, 14 p.

［潘文光：中古漢語與粵語聲母比較研究］

1661 Shih, Jerome Jen-chung: *A contrastive study of the phonological structures of Mandarin and Cantonese.*—Hsinchuang: Fu Jen Catholic U., 1971, 66 p./ Unpubl. M.A. thesis.

［史仁仲］

1662 Shih, Nan-yü: *Kuang-tung-jen tsen-yang hsüeh chiang P'u-t'ung-hua.*—Hong Kong: Hung-yeh shu-chü, 1960, ix, 254 p. [How a Cantonese dialect speaker should learn to speak the Common Language.]

史南育：廣東人怎樣學講普通話

1663 Tai, Chung-chieh: Yüeh-yin yü Kuo-yin te pi-chiao.—*CTSY* 8:85–87, 1929, 40–46. [A comparison of the phonetics of Cantonese and Mandarin.]

戴仲傑：粵音與國音的比較

1664 Tipton, Gary Prior: *A contrastive analysis of Mandarin and Cantonese phonologies* (0720).

1665 Tipton, Gary: Non-cognate consonants of Mandarin and Cantonese.—*JCLTA* 10, 1975, 1–13./ A contrastive analysis.

1666 Tse, Sou-mei [Hsieh, Shou-mei]: English consonants and learning problems for Cantonese speakers.—*CTHP* 37–38, 1978, 81–96./ A contrastive analysis.

［謝壽眉］

1667 Tseng, Tzu-fan: *Kuang-chou-hua P'u-t'ung-hua tui-chao ch'ang-yung tz'u shou-ts'e.*—Hong Kong: Hsiang-kang P'u-t'ung-hua yen-hsi she, 1978, 40 p. [A handbook of Cantonese-Common Language commonly used vocabulary.]

曾子凡：廣州話普通話對照常用詞手冊

1668 Tseng, Tzu-fan: *Kuang-chou-hua P'u-t'ung-hua tui-chao k'ou-yü-tz'u hui-pien.*—Hong Kong: Hsiang-kang P'u-t'ung-hua yen-hsi she, 1979, 6, 76 p. [Collection of Cantonese-Common Language colloquial words.]

曾子凡：廣州話普通話對照口語詞滙編

1669 Wang, Liao-i: *Kuang-tung-jen hsüeh-hsi Kuo-yü fa.*—Canton: Hua-nan jen-min, 1951, iv, 153 p./ *CKYW* 1952:2, 33–34, Wang Chün. [Methods of learning Mandarin for Cantonese speakers.]

王了一： 廣東人學習國語法 / 王鎣評

1670 Wang, Li: *Kuang-tung-jen tsen-yang hsüeh-hsi P'u-t'ung-hua.*—Peking: Wen-hua chiao-yü, 1955, 167 p./ *CKYW* 1956:4, 43, Chan Po-hui. [How a speaker of the Cantonese dialect should learn the Common Language.]

王力： 廣東人怎樣學習普通話 / 詹伯慧評

1671 Whymant, A. Neville John: *Colloquial Chinese (Northern).*—London: Kegan Paul, Trench, Trübner, 1943, 3rd ed., v, 106 p.; 61–106: An English and Chinese vocabulary in the Pekinese and Cantonese dialects.

14.1.8. Textbooks (1672–1778)

1672 Anonymous: *Easy phrases in the Canton dialect of the Chinese language.*—Canton: The Canton Customs Press, 1866, 75 p.

1673 Anonymous (preface by Donald Bruce): *Easy phrases in the Canton dialect of the Chinese language.*—San Francisco: Bruce's Printing House, 1877, 4, 72 p.

［發客英華常語合璧］

1674 Anonymous: *Phrases usuaes dos dialectos de Cantão e Peking.*—Macao: Typographia Popular, 1884, 16, 45 p./ Cantonese texts extracted from J. Dyer Ball's *Cantonese made easy* (1675); Peking text ed. by Hsü Hua-fang; both in characters without romanization.

1675 Ball, James Dyer: *Cantonese made easy.*—Hong Kong: "China Mail" Office, 1888, 2nd ed., rev. & enl., lvi, 122 p.; Hong Kong: Kelly & Walsh, 1924, 4th ed., rev. & enl., lxxxix, 186 p./ Subtitle: A book of simple sentences in the Cantonese dialect, with free and literal trans-

lations, and directions for the rendering of English grammatical forms in Chinese.

1676 Ball, James Dyer: *The Cantonese made easy vocabulary.*—Hong Kong: Kelly & Walsh, 1908, 3rd ed., rev. & enl., 294 p./ Subtitle: A small dictionary used in the spoken language, with the classifiers indicated for each noun, and definitions of the different shades of meaning, as well as notes on the different uses of some of the words where ambiguity might otherwise arise./ English-Cantonese.

1677 Ball, James Dyer: *Readings in Cantonese colloquial.*—Hong Kong: Kelly & Walsh, 1894, xxxii, 171 p./ Subtitle: Being selections from books in the Cantonese vernacular, with free and literal translations of the Chinese character and romanized spelling.

1678 Baronsfeather, C.G.S.: *The A B C of Cantonese.*—Pakhoi: C.M.S. Hospital, 1912, 9 p.

1679 Bonney, Samuel W.: *Phrases in the Canton colloquial dialect, arranged according to the number of Chinese characters in a phrase. With an English translation.*—Canton: Office of the Chinese Repository, 1853, 98 p.

1680 Bonney, Samuel W.: *A vocabulary with colloquial phrases of the Canton dialect.*—Canton: Office of the Chinese Repository, 1854, 2, 216 p.

1681 Boyle, Elisabeth L.: *Cantonese: basic course.*—Washington, D. C.: Foreign Service Institute, 1970, 2 vols., xvi, 392; iii, 410 p./ *JAS* 31, 1972, 923–924, James Dew.

1682 Bridgman, Elijah Coleman: *A Chinese chrestomathy in the Canton dialect.*—Macao: S. Wells Williams, 1841, xxxvi, 693 p.; illus., 2 fold tab.

1683 Bruce, R.: *Cantonese lessons for Malayan students.*—Kuala Lumpur: Government of the Federation of Malaya, 1954, 240 p.

1684 Bruce, R.: *Cantonese.*—London: Teach Yourself Books, 1970, viii, 259 p.

1685 Bunkyōkyoku Gakumuka: *Nichi-Etsu kaiwa.*—Taipei: Taiwan Sōtokufu Bunkyōkyoku, 1938, 8, 352 p. [Japanese-Cantonese conversation.]
文教局學務課：日粵會話

1686 Caysac, Georges-Philippe: *Introduction a l'étude du dialecte cantonnais.*—Hong Kong: Nazareth, 1922, iii, 229 p.; 1926, rev. ed., iv, 314, 34 p.; Hong Kong: Catholic Truth Society, 1952, repr./ *Orbis* 9, 1960, 178, Paul Yang Fu-mien.

1687 Chan, Yeung-kwong [Ch'en, Yang-kuang]: *Cantonese for beginners.*—Hong Kong: Man Sang Printers, 1946, 71 p.; Hong Kong: Chung Yuen Printing Press, 1955, 4th ed., rev. & enl., xiii, 283 p.; 1974, repr.
［陳陽光：粵語初階］

1688 Chan, Yeung-kwong: *Everybody's Cantonese.* — Hong Kong: Man Sang Printers, 1949, xv, 264 p./ Combined progressive and beginner's course.
［陳陽光］

1689 Chang, Yüan-hsiang: *Kantongo no kaiwa.*—Osaka: Shōzankaku, 1942, 12, 250 p. [Cantonese conversation.]/ Classified; kana and romanization.
張源祥：廣東語の會話

1690 Chao, Jung-kuang: *Hsien-tai Yüeh-yü.*—Hong Kong: Kuang-wen t'u-shu kung-szu, 1972, 10, 40, 38, 267 p. [Modern Cantonese.]/ Spoken in Hong Kong; Chinese character text only.
趙榮光：現代粵語

1691 Chao, Yuen Ren: *Cantonese primer.*— Cambridge, Mass.: Harvard U. Press, 1947, vii, 242 p./ *HJAS* 10, 1947, 60–62, Li Fang-kuei; *Books Abroad* 22, 1948, 85, F. Frauchiger; *JA* 237, 1949, 159–160, E. Gaspardone; *AM* 1, 1949, 136, W[alter] S[imon]; *JRAS* 98, 1949,

K. P. K. Whitaker; *Lg* 27, 1951, 445–449, Yu T'ung.
［趙元任：粵語入門］

1692 Chao, Yuen Ren: *Character text for Cantonese primer.*—Cambridge, Mass.: Harvard U. Press, 1947, 112 p.

1693 Chapman, Tim: *A practical guide to Cantonese conversation.*—Hong Kong: The Author, 1973, 114 p.

1694 Ch'en, T'ieh-pi & Tanaka, Yoshitarō: *Nichi-Etsu-Ei kaiwa.*—Tokyo: Okamura shobō, 1942, 16, 290 p. [Japanese-Cantonese-English conversation.]/ See Chou T'ing-feng (1698).
陳鐵筆，田中與四太郎：日粵英會話

1695 Chiang, Ker-chiu: *Progressive Cantonese readers.*—Singapore: Chin Fen Book Store, 1946, 2 vols.; Book I, 99 p.; Book II, 86 p./ Subtitle: Learning Cantonese through self-taught word-for-word method, with characters, pronunciation, tones, and combinations.
［蔣克秋：粵語進階］

1696 Chinese Language School: *Character text for beginning Cantonese.*—Hong Kong: Chinese Language School, 1970, 2 vols., 178, 316 p.

1697 Chinese Language School: *Romanized text for beginning Cantonese.*—Hong Kong: Chinese Language School, 1970, 411 p.

1698 Chou, T'ing-feng (ed.): *Yüeh-Jih-Ying-yü ying-yung hui-hua ta-ch'üan.*—Hong Kong: Hui-t'ung shu-tien, 1971, 16, 290 p. [A complete collection of Chinese-Japanese-English practical conversation.]/ A reprint of Ch'en and Tanaka (1694).
周廷峯編：粵日英語應用會話大全

1699 Chuang, Shih-kuang: *Kuang-tung-hua chih-nan.*—Taipei: Wen-shih-che, 1977, vii, 208 p. [A guide to the Cantonese dialect.]
莊世光：廣東話指南

1700   Condit, I.M.: *English and Chinese reader with a dictionary.*—Shanghai: Hua-mei shu-kuan, 1880, 144 p.; *English and Chinese dictionary*: 134 p.; illus./ English and Cantonese, without romanization.

[英華字典連通語英語入門英華字典]

1701   Cowles, Roy T.: *Inductive course in Cantonese.*—Hong Kong: Kelly & Walsh, Book I, 1920, 2nd ed., 6, 225 p.; *Companion book* for Book I, 1915, v. p.; Book II, 1916, 183–397; *Companion book* for Book II, 1916, v. p.; Book III, 1918, 476 p.; *Companion book* for Book III, 1918, v. p.

1702   Daly, Charles: *Cantonese missionary handbook.*—Hong Kong: Catholic Truth Society, 1958, 2nd ed., iii, 336 p./ English, Cantonese romanization, and Chinese character text.

1703   Deloustal, Raymond: *Manuel de cantonnais.*—Hanoi: F.-H. Schneider, 1907, 4, xvi, 226, 3, 11, 2 p./ Subtitle: Comprenant un essai de grammaire avec exemples variés de nombreux exercices avec texte en caractères chinois et transcription d'après une adaptation du système quôc-ngū des vocabulaires après chaque leçon. Un choix de phrases progressives avec traduction libre et littérale.

1704   Devan, Thomas T.: *The beginner's first book in the Chinese language (Canton vernacular).*—Hong Kong: "China Mail" Office, 1847, vi, 161 p.

1705   Devan, Thomas T.: *The beginner's first book, or a vocabulary of the Canton dialect.*—Hong Kong: "China Mail" Office, 1858, rev. & enl. ed. by William Lobscheid, viii, 123 p.; Hong Kong: A. Shortrede & Co., 1861, 3rd ed., enl. by W. Lobscheid, 5, 3, 148 p.

1706   Egawa, Kingo: *Kantongo kaiwa.*—Tokyo: Ōsakayago shoten, 1941, 4, 4, 204 p. [Cantonese conversation.]/ Grammar, vocabulary, conversation.

江川金五：廣東語會話

1707   Fujitsuka, Shōichi: *Kantongo nyūmonsho.*—Nagoya: Saika shorin, 1970, 10, 474, 24 p. [Cantonese primer.]/ With I.P.A. transcription.

藤塚將一：廣東語入門書

1708   Fujitsuka, Shōichi: *Kantongo sokusei.*—Nagoya: Tenzan shoten, 1977, 173 p. [An intensive course in Cantonese.]

藤塚將一：廣東語速成

1709   Fukuya, Masao: *Nichi-Etsu kaiwa.*—Canton: Tung-fang jih-pao she, 1923, 14, 406 p. [Japanese-Cantonese conversations.]

福屋正男：日粵會話

1710   Fulton, A.A.: *Progressive and idiomatic sentences in Cantonese colloquial.*—Hong Kong: Kelly & Walsh, 1931, 2nd ed., 101 p.

1711   Gibson, O.: *Easy questions for beginners in English and Chinese.*—Foochow: M. E. Mission Press, 1879, iii, 109 p./ Cantonese text in Chinese characters only.

[初學問答]

1712   Gomes, Luís Gonzaga: *Nações elementares da língua Chinesa.*—Macao: Tipografia Soi Sang, 1958, 38 p.

1713   Hernisz, Stanislas: *A guide to conversation in the English and Chinese languages for the use of Americans and Chinese in California and elsewhere.*—Boston: John P. Jewett & Co., 1854, 2, viii, 41, 179 p./ Cantonese dialect.

1714   Hess, Emil: *Sprechen Sie Chinesisch? Chinesische Phraseologie nebst ausführlicher Grammatik. Dialekt von Canton.*—Leipzig: C.A. Koch, 1891, iv, 185 p.

[你嘸講唐話唔嘸 ?]

1715   Ho, Ch'an-shan: *Yüeh-yü chih-nan.*—(?): Ch'an-shan shu-chü, n.d., 91 p. The same book with another title: *Kuangchou-hua chih-nan.*—Canton (?): Fuhsing shu-chü, n.d., 100 p. [A guide to Cantonese.]/ Character text only.

何禪山：粵語指南（廣州話指南）

1716 Hobson, Benjamin: *Dialogues in the Canton vernacular.*—Canton (?), 1850, 44 p./ English & Chinese characters, without romanization.

1717 Hoh, Fuk-sz & Belt, Walter: *A pocket guide to Cantonese.*—Canton: Lingnan U., 1936, rev. & enl. ed., 96, 24 p.

〔 何福嗣，皮泰德：增訂粵語撮要 〕

1718 Hsü, Hsüeh-hang: *Hsin-pien Kuangtung sheng-ch'eng pai-hua.*—Bangkok: The Author, n.d., 247 p. [Newly edited vernacular of the Kwangtung provincial capital.]/ Classified vocabulary and conversation. Character text only.

許雪航：新編廣東省城白話

1719 Huang, Parker Po-fei & Kok, Gerard P.: *Speak Cantonese.*—New Haven: Institute of Far Eastern Languages, Yale U., 1958, xii, 432 p.; illus.

1720 Huang, Parker Po-fei & Kok, Gerard P.: *Speak Cantonese.*—New Haven: Far Eastern Publications, Yale U., *Book I,* 1963, xii, 365 p.; *Book II,* 1960, xiv, 460 p.; *Book III,* 1967, 305 p.; *Character text,* 1961, 342 p.; *Exercise book for Speak Cantonese, Book II,* 1963, 193 p.

1721 Kageyama, Takashi: *Jitsuyō sokusei Kantongo.* — Tokyo: Bunkyūdo, 1940; 1942, 2nd ed., ii, ix, x, 170 p. [Practical intensive Cantonese.]

影山巍：實用速成廣東語

1722 Kerr, John G.: *Select phrases in the Canton dialect.*—Hong Kong: Kelly & Walsh, n.d., 6th ed., rev., ii, 66 p.

1723 Kōsaka, Jun'ichi: *Nan-Shi kakyō kaiwa yōketsu.*—Tokyo: Gaigo gakuin shuppanbu, 1942, 1, 4, 285 p. [Japanese-Cantonese-Amoy conversation.]/ Pronunciation, grammar, basic conversation, practical conversation.

香坂順一：南支華僑會話要訣

1724 Kōsaka, Jun'ichi & Lin, Yao-po: *Kantongo kaiwa ten.*—Taipei: Tōto Shoseki, 1943, 4, 508 p. [A handbook of Cantonese conversation.]/ Pronunciation, grammar, simple conversation, classified conversation.

香坂順一，林耀波：廣東語會話典

1725 Kuang-chou-shih jen-min cheng-fu wenchiao-chü (comp.): *Kuang-chou-yin chihkung su-ch'eng shih-tzu chiao-ts'ai.*—Canton: Hua-nan jen-min, 1953, 118 p., 2 tab. [Teaching materials for Cantonese-speaking workers in learning Chinese characters.]/ Cantonese pronunciation in *chu-yin fu-hao* (注音符號).

廣州市人民政府文教局編： 廣州音職工速成識字教材

1726 Lagarrue, Julien: *Éléments de la langue chinoise, dialecte cantonnais. Notation Quôc Ngŭ, à l'usage des officiers, fonctionnaires et colons.*—Paris: Ernest Leroux, 1900, ix, 290 p.

1727 Lanctot, Benoni: *Chinese and English phrase book.*—San Francisco: A. Roman & Co. 1867, 2nd rev. & enl. ed., 88 p./ With the Chinese pronunciation indicated in English, specially adapted for the use of merchants, travellers and families.

〔 華英通語 〕

1728 Lau, Sidney: *Kwong-tung wah. Cantonese by radio—Elementary. Listeners' guides to accompany lessons 1 to 170 and Cantonese-English glossary.* Comp. & ed. by Beryl Cubbitt.—Hong Kong: Government Printer, 1965, v, 192 p.

1729 Lau, Sidney: *Kwong-tung wah. Cantonese by radio—Intermediate. Listeners' guides to accompany lessons 1 to 117.* Ed. by Irene Yuen.—Hong Kong: Government Printer, 1965, xii, 316 p.

1730 Lau, Sidney: *Elementary Cantonese.*—Hong Kong: Government Printer, 1972, 2 vols., 898 p.; 1978, 5th version.

〔 劉錫祥：初級粵語課本 〕

1731 Lau, Sidney: *A Cantonese-English and English-Cantonese glossary to accompany Elementary Cantonese (lessons 1-20).*—Hong Kong: Government Printer, 1973, iii, 226 p.

1732 Lau, Sidney: *Intermediate Cantonese.* —Hong Kong: Government Printer, 1972, 3rd version, 2 vols., lxi, 1011 p.

［劉錫祥：中級粵語課本］

1733 Lau, Sidney: *A Cantonese-English and English-Cantonese glossary to accompany Intermediate Cantonese.*—Hong Kong: Government Printer, 1973, iii, 252 p.

1734 Lau, Sidney: *Advanced Cantonese.*— Hong Kong: Government Printer, 1975–1976, rev. version, 2 vols., xxiii, 602 p.

［劉錫祥：高級粵語課本］

1735 Leblanc, Joseph Alexis Marie: *Cours de la langue chinoise parlée, dialecte cantonnais. 1re parties grammaire.*— Hanoi-Haiphong: Imprimerie d'Extrême-Orient, 1910, [v], 178, iii p.

1736 Lee, S. K.: *Cantonese simplified.*— Hong Kong: Graphic Press, n.d., x, 311 p./ Textbook for 'Cantonese by Radio'.

［李錫鈞］

1737 Lobscheid, W.: *Select phrases and reading lessons in the Canton dialect.*— Hong Kong: De Souza & Co, 1864, 69 p.; 1867, 2nd ed., i, 46 p.

1738 Mo, Chao-hsiung: *Yüeh-yü chiao-hsüeh yü tu-yin yen-chiu.*—Hong Kong: Hsiang-kang chiao-yü, 1960, [iv], 108 p. [A study on the pronunciation and teaching of Cantonese.]

莫朝雄：粵語教學與讀音研究

1739 Nagano, Seirai: *Nichi-Etsu kaiwa toku-hon.*—Taipei: Fukudai kōshi, 1939, 8, 166 p. [A reader for Japanese-Cantonese conversation.]/ Pronunciation, vocabulary, conversation.

長野政來：日粵會話讀本

1740 Nhật, La-quang: *Hoa ngũ' chỉ nam. Guide pour apprendre la langue cantonnaise (sans maître). Transcrite en anna-mite et en français avec la prononciation traduite en Quôc-ngu.*—Saigon: Imprimerie Tin duc thu xa, 1932, 4th ed., 124 p.

［華語指南］

1741 Nolasco da Silva, Pedro: *Bussola do dialecto Cantonese, adaptado para as es-colas Portuguezas de Macau.*—Macao: Guedes, 1912, 298 p./ Based on *Beginning Cantonese* by O.F. Wisner (1770).

［教話指南］

1742 Oakeley, R.H.: *Rules for speaking Cantonese.*—Kuala Lumpur: The Mala-yan Government, 1953, ii, 192 p./ As-sisted by Lum Mun-chak, et al.

1743 Okamoto, Kazuo: *Kantongo nyūmon.* —Tokyo: Bunkyūdō, 1944, 4, 253 p. [Beginner's Cantonese.]

崗本一雄：廣東語入門

1744 O'Melia, Thomas A.: *First year Can-tonese.*—Hong Kong: Catholic Truth So-ciety, 1938; 1954, 3rd ed., Pt. I, xxx, 306, v. p.; Pt. II, 92 p.; Pt. III, 263 p.; Pt. IV, 236 p.

1745 O'Melia, Thomas A.: *First year Can-tonese.*—Hong Kong: Catholic Truth So-ciety, 1965, rev. ed., 2 vols., iv, 394; 292 p./ A completely rev. ed. of (1744).

1746 Smith, J.F.: *Practical Cantonese.*— Hong Kong: Maryknoll Fathers, 1963 (?), 175 p./ Classified conversation.

［實用粵語］

1747 Stedman, T. Lathrop & Lee, K.P.: *A Chinese and English phrase book in the Canton dialect.*—New York: William R. Jenkins, 1888, iv, 186 p.; 1920, repr./ Dialogues on ordinary and familiar sub-jects for the use of the Chinese resident in America, and of Americans desirous of learning the Chinese language; with the pronunciation of each word indicated in Chinese and Roman characters.

［李桂攀：英語不求人］

1748 Su, Hsi-hung: *Yüeh-Ying yü-yen tui-chao tu-pen.*—Hong Kong: The Author, 1968, 117 p. [Cantonese-English reader.]/ Romanized and explained in English.

蘇錫鴻：粵英語言對照讀本

1749 Sung, Hok-p'ang [Sung, Hsüeh-p'eng]: *Cantonese conversations.*—Hong Kong: (?), 1934, 10, 260 p./ In Chinese characters, with English notes.

〔宋學鵬：廣州白話會話（附英文註釋）〕

1750 Tallandier, I.: *Le manuel de conversation franco-chinoise (dialecte cantonnais).*—Hong Kong: Imprimerie de la Société des Missions-Étrangères, 1927, 2nd ed., xii, 92 p.; Hong Kong: Catholic Truth Society, n.d., repr.

〔法漢談論廣東土語〕

1751 T'an, Chi-ch'iang: *Fen-lei t'ung-hsing Kuang-chou-hua chih-nan.*—Canton: Wu-kuei-t'ang, 1937, rev. ed., 115 p./ With a syllabary of *Pai-chia hsing* 百家姓. [Classified guide to Cantonese.]

譚季強：分類通行廣州話指南

1752 Teng, Chih-hsien: *Kuang-chou pai-hua chiao-chi li-i lüeh shuo.*—Canton (?), 1930, [iv], 28 p. [A short introduction to social intercourse and etiquette in Cantonese colloquial.]

鄧志賢：廣州白話交際禮儀略說

1753 To, Thien-tru: *Manuel de la langue cantonaise.*—Cholon: (?), 1952, xiii, 240 p.; Tokyo: (?), rev. & corr. by René de Berval, 250 p./ Romanized and explained in French.

1754 U.S. Army Language School: *Conversational Cantonese,* Book II.—Presidio of Monterey: U.S. Army Language School, 1951, 2 vols.

1755 U.S. Army Language School: *Chinese-Cantonese civil affair terms.*—Presidio of Monterey: U.S. Army Language School, 1951, 41 p.

1756 U.S. Army Language School: *Chinese-Cantonese.*—Presidio of Monterey: U.S. Army Language School, 1952, 6 vols.

1757 U.S. Army Language School: *Chinese-Cantonese, basic course.*—Presidio of Monterey: U.S. Army Language School, 1956, 97 p.

1758 U.S. Army Language School: *Chinese-Cantonese, refresher course, instructor's manual.*—Presidio of Monterey: U.S. Army Language School, 1960, 169 p.

1759 U.S. Dept. of Army: *Cantonese phrase book.*—Washington, D.C.: Government Printing Office, 1963, 128 p.

1760 U.S. War Department: *Cantonese, a guide to the spoken language.*—Washington, D.C.: U.S. War Department, 1943, 79 p.

1761 U.S. War Department: *Cantonese phrase book.*—Washington, D.C.: U.S. War Department, 1943, 135 p.

1762 Wang, Tzu-ming: *Shih-yung Kuang-chou-hua.*—Hong Kong: Wan-li, 1978, 3, 3, 198 p.; with cassette tape. [Practical Cantonese.]

王子明：實用廣州話

1763 Wells, Herbert Richmond: *Guide to Cantonese.*—Hong Kong: Wing Fat & Co., 1930, 2, 3, 205, 2 p./ Subtitle: New translation of L.C. Hopkins's translation of *Kuan-hua chih-nan,* assited by Fung Iu-ting./ See (0734).

〔威禮士，馮習亭：訂正粵音指南〕

1764 Wells, Herbert Richmond: *Commercial conversation in Cantonese and English.*—Hong Kong: Kae Shean Printing Co., 1931, [iv], 82, 52 p.

〔英粵商業雜話〕

1765 Wells, Herbert Richmond: *Cantonese for everyone, a simple introduction to Cantonese.*—Hong Kong: Kelly & Walsh, 1931, vi, 120 p.; 1941, together with *An English-Cantonese dictionary,* 301 p.

〔英粵通語〕

1766 Whitaker, K.P.K.: *1200 Chinese basic characters for students of Cantonese.*—London: Lund Humphries, 1953, xlii, 316 p./ An adaptation of W. Simon's National language version, with an introduction by W. Simon; *FEQ* 14:1, 1954, 93–96, S. Egerod.

〔中英對照平民千字課〕

1767 Whitaker, K.P.K.: *Cantonese sentence series.*—London: A. Probsthain, 1954, xii, 150 p.

1768 Whitaker, K.P.K.: *Structure drill in Cantonese. First fifty patterns.*—London: Lund Humphries, 1954, xxix, 101 p.; 1959, 2nd rev. ed.

1769 Williams, Samuel Wells: *Easy lessons in Chinese, or progressive exercises to facilitate the study of the language, especially adapted to the Canton dialect.*—Macao: Office of the Chinese Repository, 1842, ix, 238 p., tab.

〔 衞三畏：拾級大成 〕

1770 Wisner, O. F.: *Beginning Cantonese.*—Canton: China Baptist Publication Society, 1906, 32, (Chinese text) 68 d. p.

〔 教話指南 〕

1771 Wisner, O. F.: *Wisner's Cantonese romanized.*—Kongmoon: Maryknoll Language School, 1929 (?), 2 vols., 186 p.; *Supplementary notes*, 43 p.

1772 Wong, Le-hing [Huang, Lü-ch'ing]: *English and Chinese dialogues.*—Hong Kong: Empire Printing Press, 1927, 18th ed., [ix], 349 p.; portr./ Classified vocabulary and conversation.

〔 黃履卿：英語指南 〕

1773 Wong, Sik-ling [Huang, Hsi-ling]: *Cantonese conversation grammar.*—Hong Kong: Government Printer, 1963, Book I, Pt. I, xv, 147 p.; Book I, Pt. II, xv, 125 p.

〔 黃錫凌 〕

1774 Wong, Sik-ling: *Intermediate Cantonese conversation.* Book II. — Hong Kong: Government Printer, 1967, xiii, 249 p./ This is Book II of *Cantonese conversation grammar* (1773).

1775 Wu, T.C.: *Daily Cantonese.*—Hong Kong: Too Hung Engraving & Printing Co., 1965, 142 p.

〔 日用粵語 〕

1776 Yamashita, Noboru: *Kantongo kōza.*—Taipei: Taiwan Hōsō Kyōkai, 1938, 83 p.; 1940, rev. ed., 2 vols., 8, 125; 2, 138 p. [Radio Taiwan Cantonese course.]

山下昇：廣東語講座

1777 Yang, Liang: *Sokusei Kantongo kaiwa.*—Osaka: Kyōjinsha, 1939, 160 p. [Intensive Cantonese conversation.]

楊艮：速成廣東語會話

1778 Yuen, Y. C. [Yüan, Ying-ts'ai]: *A guide to Cantonese (self-taught).*—Kowloon: Bright Sun Printing Co., 1950, enl. ed., [v], 50 p.; 1960, 8th ed.

〔 袁英才：粵語指南 〕

14.1.9. Dictionaries (1779–1818)

1779 Anonymous: *An English and Cantonese pocket dictionary.*—Hong Kong: London Missionary Society Press, 1870, 146 p.

1780 Aubazac, Louis: *Dictionnaire français-chinois dialecte cantonnais.* — Hong Kong: Imprimerie de la Société des Mission Étrangères, 1902, xl, 333, xi p.; 1909, new ed., rev. & enl., xxvii, 469, x p./ *BEFEO* 3, 1903, 101–102, E. Huber; *TP* 10, 1909, 713–716, H. Cordier; *Orbis* 9:1, 1960, 178, Paul Yang Fu-mien.

〔 法粵字典 〕

1781 Aubazac, Louis: *Dictionnaire français-cantonnais.* — Hong Kong: Nazareth, 1909, rev. ed., xxvii, 469, x p./ *BEFEO* 3, 1903, 101, E. Huber; *TP* 10, 1909, 713–716, H. Cordier.

1782 Aubazac, Louis: *Liste des caractères les plus usuels de la langue cantonnais.*—Hong Kong: Imprimerie de la Société des Missions Étrangères, 1909, 46 p.

1783 Aubazac, Louis: *Dictionnaire cantonnais-français.*—Hong Kong: Imprimerie de la Société des Missions Étrangères, 1912, xix, 1116 p.; *Liste des caractères d'après l'ordre des clefs et le nombre des traits*, 139 p.

〔 粵法字典 〕

1784 Aubazac, Louis: *Lexique français-cantonnais des termes de religion.*—Hong Kong: Nazareth, 1918, 207 p.

1785 Chalmers, John: *An English and Cantonese dictionary, for the use of whose who to learn the spoken language of Canton province.*—Hong Kong: De Sousa & Co., 1878, 5th ed., xi, 258 p.

1786 Chalmers, John: *English and Cantonese dictionary.*—Hong Kong: Kelly & Walsh, 1907, rev. & enl. by T. Kirkman Dealy, 2 vols., vii, 822 p.
〔英粵字典〕

1787 Cheung, Oakman: *Oakman's Cantonese-English dictionary.*—Hong Kong: The Author, 1971, xix, 608 p.
〔蔣愛民：粵語分韻中英辭典〕

1788 Chiang, Ker-chiu [Chiang, K'o-ch'iu]: *A practical English-Cantonese dictionary.*—Singapore: Chin Fen Book Store, n.d., 460 p.
〔蔣克秋：實用英粵辭典〕

1789 Ch'iao, Yen-nung: *Kuang-chou-yin Kuo-yin Chung-wen tzu-tien.*—Hong Kong: Hua-ch'iao yü-wen, 1963, 6, 668, 18 p.; illus. With an appendix on the phonology of Cantonese. [A Chinese dictionary in Cantonese and Mandarin pronunciations.]
喬硯農：廣州音國音中文字典

1790 Chung-hua shu-chü (comp.): *P'u-t'ung-hua Yüeh-yin Chung-hua hsin tzu-tien.*—Hong Kong: Chung-hua, 1978, 66, 698 p. [A new Chinese Common Language-Cantonese dictionary.]
中華書局：普通話粵音中華新字典

1791 Cowles, Roy T.: *A pocket dictionary of Cantonese. Cantonese-English with English-Cantonese index.*—Hong Kong: Kelly & Walsh, 1914, xiii, 296, 124 p.; Kowloon: South China Peniel Press, 1949, 2nd ed., 2 vols., xii, 268, 44; iv, 123 p.
〔廣州話袖珍字典〕

1792 Cowles, Roy T.: *The Cantonese speaker's dictionary.*—Hong Kong: Hong Kong U. Press, 1965, xvii, 1318, iv, 232 p./ *RBS* 11, 1965, 440, F.K. Li; *Anthropos* 62, 1967, 972–973, Hermann Köster; *BSOAS* 30, 1967, 435, G.B. Downer; *JAS* 26:3, 1967, 476–477, Parker Po-fei Huang; *ZDMG* 117, 1967, 450, Herbert Franke; *AO* 36, 1968, 702, O. Švarný.
〔粵語辭淵〕

1793 Eitel, Ernest John: *A Chinese-English dictionary in the Cantonese dialect.*—London: Trübner & Co. & Hong Kong: Lane, Crawford & Co., 1877, xxxv, 1018, xviii p.; Hong Kong: Kelly & Walsh, 1910, rev. ed. by Immanuel Gottlieb Genähr, 2 vols., xlvii, 3, xviii, 1417 p.

1794 Feng, Szu-yü: *Kuang-chou-yin tzu-hui.*—Hong Kong: Shih-chieh, 1962, [xiii], 76, [58] p./ Index by radicals. [A Cantonese glossary.]
馮思禹：廣州音字彙（附部首檢字部身檢字表）

1795 Feng, Szu-yü: *Kuang-chou-yin Kuo-yü-yin hsin-pien Chung-wen tzu-tien.*—Hong Kong: Yu-wen shu-wu, 1969, 14, 538 p. [A new Chinese Cantonese-Mandarin dictionary.]
馮思禹：廣州音國語音新編中文字典

1796 Fujitsuka, Shōichi: Kantongo hatsuon jiten.—*AGK* 8, 1955, 153 p. [A Cantonese pronouncing dictionary.]
藤塚將一：廣東語發音字典

1797 Gomes, Luís Gonzaga: *Vocabulário Cantonese-Português.*—Macao: Imprensa Nacional, 1941, xvi, 225 p.
〔高美士：粵葡辭典〕

1798 Gomes, Luís Gonzaga: *Vocabulário Português-Cantonese.*—Macao: Imprensa Nacional, 1942, 235 p.
〔高美士：葡粵辭典〕

1799 Huang, Parker Po-fei: *Cantonese dictionary: Cantonese-English, English-Cantonese.*—New Haven & London: Yale U. Press, 1970, xxi, 487 p./ *JAS* 30, 1970–1971, 892–893, Wang Fang-yu; *JAOS* 92, 1972, 564–566, Charles N. Li; *JCLTA* 8:1, 1973, 31–37, James Dew; *Linguistics* 162, 1975, 84–90, Diana L. Kao; *OLZ* 70:3, 1975, 299–300, Klaus Kaden.

1800 Huo, Pao-ts'ai: *Kuo-Yüeh chu-yin Han-Ying ho-chieh yin hsing chieh chien tzu-tien.*—Hong Kong: Huo-shih ch'u-pan kung-szu, 1977, 2, 2, 1, 376, 79 p./ English title: Fok Bo-choi: *Chinese-English dictionary with simple key to pronunciation and finding (Phonetic lists of Cantonese and Mandarin are provided).*

霍寶材：國粵注音漢英合解音形捷檢字典

1801 Karlgren, B.: *Analytic dictionary of Chinese and Sino-Japanese.*—Paris: Geuthner, 1923, 436 p.; Taipei: Ch'engwen, 1966, repr./ Mandarin-Cantonese-Ancient Chinese; *BSOS* 3, 1923–1925, 362–365, Arthur Waley.

1802 Lau, Sidney: *A practical Cantonese-English dictionary.*—Hong Kong: Government Printer, 1977, xxiii, 1001 p.

〔劉錫祥：實用粵英詞典〕

1803 Li, Cho-min: *Hsing-sheng pu-shou Kuo-yin Yüeh-yin Li-shih Chung-wen tzu-tien.*—Hong Kong: The Chinese U. Press, 1980, 2, 22, 6, 62, 86, 370, 138 p. [Li's Mandarin-Cantonese dictionary arranged according to phonetic compounds.]

李卓敏：形聲部首國音粵音李氏中文字典

1804 Lobscheid, W.: *English and Chinese dictionary with the Punti and Mandarin pronunciation.*—Hong Kong: Daily Press Office, in 4 parts, 4 vols., 1866–1869, 38, 2013 p./ Including Table of sounds in Cantonese, Hakka, Hoklo, Amoy, and Mandarin dialects.

〔英華字典〕

1805 Lobscheid, W.: *A Chinese and English dictionary.*—Hong Kong: Noronha & Sons, 1869, ix, 592 p.

1806 Mello, A. H. de, et al.: *Dicionário Chinês-Português.*—Macao: Imprensa Nacional, 1962, xi, 921 p./ Cantonese-Portuguese.

〔中葡字典〕

1807 Meyer, Bernard Fr. & Wempe, Theodore F.: *The student's Cantonese-English dictionary.*—Hong Kong: St. Louis Industrial School Printing Press, 1935, iv, 843, Radical index, 136 p.; New York: Field Afar Press, 1947, 3rd ed. *English-Cantonese index.*—Hong Kong: Salesian Printing Press, 1941, 187 p.

1808 Morrison, Robert: *A vocabulary of the Canton dialect.*—Macao: East India Company's Press, 1828, 3 pts.; Pt. I. English and Chinese; Pt. II. Chinese and English; Pt. III. Chinese and English, Chinese words and phrases.

〔廣東省土話字彙〕

1809 Robinson, Jack [Casey, G. Hugh]: *The 4000 commonest characters Cantonese-English.*—Hong Kong: Kelly & Walsh, 1976, 2nd ed., [85] p.

1810 Robinson, Jack [Casey, G. Hugh]: *Ten thousand characters Cantonese-Mandarin-English: An analytic dictionary.*—Hong Kong: Kelly & Walsh, 1980, 420 p.

〔祁祖堯：粵語・國語・英語一萬字分析字典〕

1811 Savina, François-Marie: *Dictionnaire étymologique Français-Nùng-Chinois.*—Hong Kong: Nazareth, 1924, xvi, 528 p./ Chinois=Cantonese; based on Aubazac's dictionary (1781).

1812 Servus, M.E.P.: *Locutions modernes dialecte cantonnais.*—Hong Kong: Imprimerie de la Société des Missions Étrangères, 1934, ii, 6, 826, 20 p./ *CCS* 7:5–6, 1934, 526–567, Anonymous (in Latin).

〔粵法新詞句〕

1813 Tipson, Ernest: *A Cantonese syllabary index to Soothill's pocket dictionary.*—London: Routledge & K. Paul, 1951, 79 p.

1814 U.S. Army Language School: *Chinese-Cantonese military terminology.*—Presidio of Monterey: U.S. Army Language School, 1956, 55 p.

1815 U.S. Defense Language Institute: *Dictionary of common Chinese-Cantonese characters.*—Washington, D.C.: U.S. Defense Language Institute, 1959, ii, 250 p.

1816 Wells, Herbert Richmond: *Cantonese for everyone* and *An English-Cantonese dictionary* (1765).

1817 Wells, Herbert Richmond: *An English-Cantonese dictionary.*—Kelly & Walsh, 1931, 227 p.

1818 Williams, Samuel Wells: *A tonic dictionary of the Chinese language in the Canton dialect.*—Canton: Office of the Chinese Repository, 1856, xxxvi, 40, 41, 571 p.
〔英華分韻撮要〕

14.2. Kwangtung (1819–1849)

14.2.1. Hong Kong (1819–1821)

1819 Chang, Hung-nien: *Hsiang-kang Yüeh-yü yü-fa te yen-chiu.*—Hong Kong: Hsiang-kang Chung-wen ta-hsüeh, 1972, ii, 2, 235 p./ 233–235: Bibliography./ *JCL* 2, 1974, 237–246, John McCoy. [Studies on Cantonese grammar as spoken in Hong Kong.]
張洪年：香港粵語語法的研究

1820 Chang, Jih-sheng: Hsiang-kang Yüeh-yü yin-p'ing-tiao chi pien-tiao wen-t'i.—*HKCW* 2:1, 1969, 81–107; 106–107: E.S. [A study on the upper even tone and tone sandhi in the Cantonese dialect as spoken in Hong Kong.]
張日昇：香港粵語陰平調及變調問題

1821 Nakajima, Motoki: Honkon Etsugo no on'in taikei—shu boin o chūshin toshite.—*AAGB* 5, 1972, 145–162. [The phonological structure of Cantonese as spoken in Hong Kong—Focusing on the main vowels.]
中嶋幹起：香港粵語の音韻體系——主母音を中心として

14.2.2. Tungkuan (1822–1825)

1822 Ball, James Dyer: The Tung-Kwún dialect.—*CR* 18, 1890, 284–299./ Subtitle: A comparative syllabary of the Tung-Kwún and Cantonese pronunciations, with observations on the variations in the use of the classifiers, finals, and other words, and a description of the tones, etc., etc.
〔東莞〕

1823 Ch'en, Po-t'ao, et al.: Tung-kuan fang-yen.—*Tung-kuan hsien-chih* (Tungkuan: Yang-ho shu-chü, 1911), Chüan 10 and 11; *Chung-kuo fang-chih so-lu fang-yen hui-pien* (0454), 1: 62–104. [The Tung-kuan dialect.]
陳伯陶等：東莞方言——『東莞縣志』

1824 Saunders, C.J.: The Tungkwun dialect of Cantonese.—*CR* 22, 1897, 465–476.

1825 Wang, Li & Ch'ien, Sung-sheng: Tung-kuan fang-yin.—*LNHP* 10:1, 1949, 119–150; E.S. [Phonetics of the Tungkuan (Tungkwun) dialect.]
王力，錢淞生：東莞方音

14.2.3. Szeyap (1826–1840)

14.2.3.1. General (1826–1828)

1826 McCoy, William J.: *Szeyap data for a first approximation of Proto-Cantonese* (1527).

1827 Wang, Li & Ch'ien, Sung-sheng: Chu-chiang san-chiao-chou fang-yin tsung lun.—*LNHP* 10:2, 1950, 57–66; 213–214: E.S. [General introduction to the study of the Cantonese dialect in the Pearl River Delta.]
王力，錢淞生：珠江三角洲方音總論

1828 Yee, Shu-nam [Yü, Shao-nan]: *Tsui-hsin Hua-Ying hui-hua ch'üan pi.*—Boston: Chinese Co-operative Society, 1930, 587 p. [An Anglo-Chinese general conversation and classified phrases.]/ English transliterated into Szeyap dialect pronunciation.
余召南：最新華英會話全璧（四邑土談翻譯英語）

14.2.3.2. Hsinhui (1829–1831)

1829 Ball, James Dyer: The San Wúi dialect.—*CR* 18, 1890, 178–195./ Subtitle: A comparative syllabary of the San Wúi and Cantonese pronunciations, with observations on the variations in the use of the classifiers, finals, and other words, and a description of the tones, etc., etc.

〔 新會 〕

1830 Chao, Chung-i: Hsin-hui fang-yen k'ao lüeh.—*Hsin-sheng pao Yü-yen yü wen-hsüeh* 15, 1947, Jan. 27; 16, 1947, Feb. 3. [A short study on the Hsinhui dialect.]

趙仲邑：新會方言考略

1831 Kühnert, Franz: *The San-Wúi dialect.*—Hong Kong: (?), 1890, 18 p.

14.2.3.3. T'aishan (1832–1840)

1832 Chao, Yüan-jen: T'ai-shan yü-liao hsü-lun.—*FSNC* 1951, 61–66. [Preface to the T'aishan linguistic materials (1833).]

趙元任：台山語料序論

1833 Chao, Yüan-jen: T'ai-shan yü-liao.—*BIHP* 23, 1951, 25–76./ *Orbis* 2, 1953, 172–173, W.A. Grootaers. [T'aishan linguistic materials.]

趙元任：台山語料

1834 Ch'en, Hsi-wu: T'ai-shan fang-yen t'e-shu pien-tiao ch'u t'an.—*CKYW* 1966:1, 34–36. [A preliminary study on the special tone sandhi in the T'aishan dialect.]

陳錫梧：台山方言特殊變調初探

1835 Cheng, Teresa M.: The phonology of Taishan.—*JCL* 1:2, 1973, 256–322.

1836 Don, A.: The Llin-nen variation of Cantonese.—*CR* 11, 1883, 236–247; 12, 1884, 474–481./ T'aishan dialect.

〔 新寧 〕

1837 Hashimoto, Anne Yue: *A guide to the T'ai-shan dialect.* — Washington, D.C.: Center for Applied Linguistics, n.d., iv,

360 p.; map./ ERIC Microfilm Series, #061855.

1838 McCoy, John: The phonology of Toi-shan City: A Chinese dialect of Kwang-tung Province.—*Orbis* 18, 1969, 108–122.

1839 Wang, Li & Ch'ien, Sung-sheng: T'ai-shan fan-yin.—*LNHP* 10:2, 1950, 67–104. [The T'aishan dialect.]

王力，錢淞生：台山方音

1840 Yiu, Tung: *The T'ai-shan dialect.*—Princeton: Princeton U., 1952, vi, 133 p./ Unpubl. doc. diss.; *DA* 12–295; UM 3073.

〔 尤桐 〕

14.2.4. Yangchiang (1841–1844)

1841 Huang, Po-jung: [T'an-t'an] Yang-chiang-hua yü-fa te liang-ko t'e-tien.—*YWCS* 1955:8, 37–38; *FPC* 1, 1958, 60–61. [Discussion on two special grammatical features in the grammar of the Yang-chiang dialect.]

黃伯榮：〔談談〕陽江話語法的兩個特點

1842 Huang, Po-jung: Kuang-tung Yang-chiang-hua wu-liang-tz'u te yü-fa t'e-tien.—*CKYW* 1959:3, 128–129. [Grammatical features of noun classifiers in the Yangchiang dialect, Kwangtung.]

黃伯榮：廣東陽江話物量詞的語法特點

1843 Huang, Po-jung: Yang-chiang-hua ju-sheng fei sheng shih-yen pao-kao.—*Kan-su shih-fan ta-hsüeh hsüeh-pao* 1960:1, 123–128. [A report on an experimental study of the non-tonal status of the *ju* tone in the Yangchiang dialect.]

黃伯榮：陽江話『入聲非聲』實驗報告

1844 Huang, Po-jung: Yang-chiang-hua te chi-chung chü-shih.—*CKYW* 1966:3, 218, 222. [Several types of sentence patterns in the Yangchiang dialect.]

黃伯榮：陽江話的幾種句式

14.2.5. Other Localities in Kwangtung (1845–1849)

1845 Ball, James Dyer: The Hŏng Shan or Macao dialect.—*CR* 22, 1897, 501–531./ Subtitle: A comparative syllabary of the Hŏng Shan and Cantonese pronunciations, with observations on the variations in the use of the classifiers, finals, and other words, and a description of the tones, etc.
〔香山〕

1846 Ball, James Dyer: The Shun Tak dialect.—*CR* 25, 1901, 57–69, 121–140./ Subtitle: A comparative syllabary of the Shun Tak and Cantonese pronunciations, with observations on the variations in the use of the classifiers, finals, and other words, and a description of the tones, etc.
〔順德〕

1847 Chao, Yüan-jen: Chung-shan fang-yen. —*BIHP* 20, 1948, 49–73. [The Chung-shan dialect.]
趙元任：中山方言

1848 Li, Ch'üan-chia: Wu-ch'uan fang-yen. —*Wen feng hsüeh-pao* 2–3, 1948, 49–58. [The Wuch'uan dialect.]
李全佳：吳川方言

1849 Liang, Yu-kang: Hua-chou-hua te d. —*CKYW* 1979:5, 354–355. [The voiced d initial in the Huachou dialect, Kwangtung.]
梁猷剛：化州話的 d

14.3. Kwangsi (1850–1860)

1850 Ch'en, Chu: Yüeh hsi Pei Yü Jung fang-yen.—*CSTY* 2:19, 1928, 195–196. [The dialects of Peiliu, Yülin and Junghsien of western Kwangsi.]
陳柱：粵西北鬱容方言

1851 Ch'en, Chu: Pei Jung Yü san-i fang-yen.—*T'ung-sheng yüeh-k'an* 3:5, 1943, 13–16. [The dialect of Peiliu, Junghsien and Yülin, Kwangsi.]
陳柱：北容鬱三邑方言

1852 Hashimoto, Anne Y.: *The Teng-xian dialect of Chinese: Its phonology, lexicon and texts with grammatical notes.*— Tokyo: Project on Lexicological Analysis, 1979, iv, 357 p., map./*CAAAL* Monogr. Series, #3.

1853 Liu, Ts'e-ch'i: Kuang-hsi yü-yen kai-lun.—*KYAO* 81, 1925, 1–2. [An outline of the languages of Kwangsi.]
劉策奇：廣西語言概論

1854 Ou, Yang-i, et al.: Fang-yen.—*Kuei-hsien chih* (1934 ed.); *Chung-kuo fang-chih so-lu fang-yen hui-pien* (0454), 1:197–201. [Dialects.]
歐仰義等：方言——『貴縣志』

1855 Pi, K'o-ch'ao: Heng-hsien fang-yen tan-yin hsing-jung-tz'u te AxA ch'ung-tieh shih.—*CKYW* 1979:5, 348–353, 327. [The reduplication pattern AxA of monosyllabic adjectives in the Henghsien dialect.]
閉克朝：橫縣方言單音形容詞的 AxA
重疊式

1856 Tsuji, Nobuhisa: *Comparative phonology of Guangxi Yue dialects.*—Tokyo: Kazama Shobō, 1980, xii, 273 p., 3 maps./ 261–273: Bibliography.
〔辻新久：廣西粵語比較音韻論〕

1857 Wang, Fu-shih: Kuang-hsi Lung-sheng Ling-hua chi-lüeh.—*FY* 1979:2, 137–141; 3, 231–240. [A sketch of the Ling dialect of Lungsheng, Kwangsi.]
王輔世：廣西龍勝伶話記略

1858 Wang, Li: Liang Yüeh yin shuo (1540)./ Including Popai and Yülin.
王力：兩粵音說

1859 Wang, Li: *Une prononciation chinoise de Po-pei* (Province de Kouang-si).— Paris: Librairie Ernest Leroux, 1932, xii, 158 p., 1 map, illus.

1860 Wu, Shou-sung, et al.: Chao-p'ing fang-yen.—*Chao-p'ing hsien-chih* (Canton, 1934); *Chung-kuo fang-chih so-lu fang-yen hui-pien* (0454), 1:195–196. [The Chaop'ing dialect.]
吳壽崧等：昭平方言——『昭平縣志』

15. SOUTH MIN DIALECTS (1861–2220)

15.1. South Min Dialects in General (1861–1981)

15.1.1. Historical Studies (1861–1904)

15.1.1.1. General (1861–1864)

1861 Ch'en, Che-san: Min Yüeh fang-yen chih lai-yüan chi ch'i so pao-ts'un te ku-yin ku-yü (1522). [The origin of the Min and Yüeh dialects and the old pronunciations and words they preserved.]
陳哲三：閩粵方言之來源及其所保存的古音古語

1862 Forrest, R.A.D.: T'ang Min.—*The Chinese language* (0508), 249–251.

1863 Lin, Yü-t'ang: Min Yüeh fang-yen chih lai-yüan (0490). [The origin of the Min and Yüeh dialects.]
林語堂：閩粵方言之來源

1864 Loon, Piet van der: The Manila incunabula and early Hokkien studies.—*AM* 12, 1966, 1–43; 13, 1967, 95–186.

15.1.1.2. Phonetics and Phonology (1865–1882)

1865 Anonymous: Liao Lun-chi *P'ai chang chih yin* ying-yin pen.—*FY* 1979:2, 141–154. [A facsimile reprint of Liao Lun-chi's *P'ai chang chih yin*, a rhyme table of the South Min dialect.]/ See (1871).
無名氏：廖綸璣『拍掌知音』影印本

1866 Hirayama, Hisao: Chūgokugo Binnan Binhoku sohōgen no seichō chōchi.—*Tokyō daigaku bungakubu kenkyūshitsu hōkoku*, 5. *Bungaku tetsugaku* (Tokyo: U. of Tokyo, 1974), 193–248. [The tonemes of the Proto South/North Min dialects of China.]
平山久雄：中國語閩南閩北祖方言の聲調調值――『東京大學文學部研究室報告，5.文學哲學』

1867 Hsü, Yü: *Shih-wu yin* yen-chiu.—*NYHP* 1:1, 1940, 61–74. [A study on *Shih-wu yin.*]

許鈺：『十五音』研究

1868 Hsü, Yün-ch'iao: *Shih-wu yin yen-chiu.*—Singapore: Shih-chieh, 1961, 114 p. [A study on *Shih-wu yin.*]
許雲樵：十五音研究

1869 Hsüeh, Teng-ch'ing: *Shih-wu yin* yü Chang Ch'üan tu-shu yin.—*CSTY* 8:85–87, 1929, 30–39. [*Shih-yu yin* and Chang-chou and Ch'üanchou literary readings.]
薛澄清：『十五音』與漳泉讀書音

1870 Huang, Ching-an: *Min-nan fang-yin cheng ching chü-li.*—Taipei: Taiwan Normal University, 1973, 240 p./ M.A. thesis. [South Min dialect words traced to the Chinese classics.]
黃敬安：閩南方音證經舉例

1871 Huang, Tien-ch'eng: *P'ai chang chih yin* shuo-ming.—*FY* 1979:2, 155–156. [Explanations on *P'ai chang chih yin* (1865).]
黃典誠：『拍掌知音』說明

1872 Li, San-jung: *Min-nan Shih-wu yin chih yen-chiu.*—Taipei: Cheng-chih ta-hsüeh Chung-wen yen-chiu so, 1969, 2, 315 p. [A study on the *Shih-wu yin* of the South Min dialect.]
李三榮：閩南十五音之研究

1873 Norman, Jerry: Tonal development in Min.—*Chi-Lin* 7, 1971, 1–32; *JCL* 1:2, 1973, 222–238.

1874 Norman, Jerry: The initials of Proto-Min.—*JCL* 2:1, 1974, 27–36.

1875 Shen, Fu-chin: *Tseng pu Hui-yin pao-chien.*—Meishanhsiang: Wen-i hsüeh-she, 1970, 674 p., 1 portr. [A revised edition of *Hui-yin pao-chien* (South Min phonetic tables).]
沈富進：增補彙音寶鑑

1876 Wang, Yü-te: *Jūgoon* ni tsuite.—*TICOJ* 13, 1968, 57–69; E.S. [On *Shih-wu yin.*]
王育德：『十五音』について

1877 Wu, Huai: Min-nan-yü ku yin k'ao.—
TWFW 24:4, 1974, 25–63. [A study of
old pronunciations preserved in the South
Min dialects.]

吳槐： 閩南語古音考

1878 Wu, Shou-li: *Pa-yin ting-chüeh* yü
*Shou-ch'ao Shih-wu yin.—Wen-shih hui-
k'an* 2, 1960, 1–21. [*Pa-yin ting-chüeh*
and *Shou-ch'ao Shih-wu yin.*]

吳守禮：『 八音定訣 』與『 手抄十五音 』

1879 Wu, Shou-li: *Li-ching-chi hsi-wen yen-
chiu—Yün tzu p'ien.*—Taipei: The Au-
thor, 1962, 104 p.; mimeogr. [A study on
the drama *Li-ching-chi*—rhyming characters.]/ With commentary and critical
notes.

吳守禮： 荔鏡記戲文研究──韻字篇

1880 Wu, Shou-li: *Shih-yin ch'üan-shu chung
te Min-nan-yü tzu-liao yen-chiu.*—Taipei:
The Author, 1977, 45 p. [A study on
South Min dialect materials found in *Shih-
yin ch'üan-shu.*]

吳守禮：『 什音全書 』中的閩南語資料
研究

1881 Yeh, Kuo-ch'ing: Min-nan fang-yin yü
Shih-wu yin.—CSTY 8:85–87, 1929, 24–
29. [The sounds of the South Min dialect
and *Shih-wu yin.*]

葉國慶： 閩南方音與『 十五音 』

1882 Yen, Sian-lin [Yen, Hsiang-lin]: *Studies
in the phonological history of Amoy
Chinese.*—Urbana: U. of Illinois, 1965,
iv, 234 p./ Unpubl. doc. diss.; 227–233:
Bibliography; *DA* 26:2741; UM 65–11,
898.

〔 顏祥霖 〕

15.1.1.3. Vocabulary and Grammar (1883–1904)

1883 Chiang, Wen-chung: Min-nan-yü hsiao
k'ao.—*DBDK* 13, 1975, 133–146. [A
short etymological study on the South Min
dialect.]

江文種： 閩南語小考

1884 Ch'iu, Li: Min-nan fang-yen k'ao.—
TFHP 1:2, 1958, 51–68; 2:1, 1959, 1–
39. [An etymological study on the South
Min dialect.]

邱立： 閩南方言考

1885 Chou, Fa-kao: Ts'ung ta-po tsa-bo
shuo-tao t'an-chiu yü-yüan te fang-fa.—
TLTC 23:7, 1961, 1–3; *Chung-kuo yü-
wen lun-ts'ung* (Taipei: Cheng-chung,
1962), 161–168. [A method of probing
etymology from explanations of the words
ta-po and *tsa-bo.*]/ A critical review of
(1891).

周法高： 從『 查哺 』『 查某 』說到探究
語源的方法──『 中國語文論叢 』

1886 Hsü, Tu-jen: Min-yü cheng-ku.—*Chih-
chiang hsüeh-pao* 4, 1934, 1–26. [Etymo-
logical verification and explanation of Min
dialect words.]

許篤仁： 閩語證詁

1887 Huang, Ching-an: *Min-nan-hua k'ao-
cheng.*—Taipei: Wen shih che, 1977, ii,
257 p. [Etymological research on the
South Min dialects.]

黃敬安： 閩南話考證

1888 Kuo, I-chou: Fu-chien-yü te ku-yü yen-
chiu.—*NYWH* 1953:9, 1–2. [A study on
archaisms in the Fukien dialect.]

郭一舟： 福建語的古語研究

1889 Norman, Jerry: The verb *chi*—A note
on Min etymology.—*FY* 3, 1979, 179–
181; C.S.

〔 羅杰瑞： 閩語的『 治 』字 〕

1890 Norman, Jerry: Chronological strata in
the Min dialects.—*FY* 4, 1979, 268–274;
C.S.

〔 羅杰瑞： 閩語詞滙的時代層次 〕

1891 Wu, Shou-li: Ta-po tsa-bo yü-yüan te
shih t'an.—*Li-ching-chi hsi-wen yen-chiu*
(1902), 192–202. [A preliminary study
on the etymology of *ta-po* ('a male') and
tsa-bo ('a female').]

吳守禮：『 查哺 』『 查某 』語源的試探

1892 Wu, Shou-li: Tāi-chì pen-tzu k'ao.—*TPWW* 6:4, 1958, 1–10. [A study on the original characters for the word *tāi-chì* ('a matter, affair').]

吳守禮： 『事情』本字考

1893 Wu, Shou-li: Shih taⁿ.—*TLTC* 16:4, 1958, 2–4. [An etymological study of *taⁿ*.]/ A note on a study of the South Min dialects.

吳守禮： 釋『搭』

1894 Wu, Shou-li: Shih ang, ang, bó.—*TLTC* 18:1, 1959, 17–23. [An etymological study of *ang*, *ang*, and *bó*.]/ A note on a study of the South Min dialects.

吳守禮： 釋『翁』、『公』、『厶』

1895 Wu, Shou-li: Min-nan-yü te tàn tzu chi ch'i chou-pien.—*TLTC* 18:7, 1959, 4–10. [The character *tàn* and its cognates in the South Min dialects.]

吳守禮： 閩南語的『呾』字及其周邊

1896 Wu, Shou-li: Shih thit-thô/thiek-thô.—*TLTC* 19:10, 1959, 12–16; 19:11, 1959, 20–26. [A study of *thit-thô/thiek-thô*.]/A note on the South Min dialect etymology.

吳守禮： 釋『彳亍』──『得桃』

1897 Wu, Shou-li: Shih niû kán.—*TLTC* 21:3, 1960, 21–24. [An etymological study of *niû* and *kán*.]/ A note on a study of the South Min dialects.

吳守禮： 釋『娘簡』

1898 Wu, Shou-li: (*Ming k'an*) Li-ching-chi hsi-wen yen-chiu—Chiao k'an p'ien.—Taipei: The Author, 1961, 222 p.; mimeogr. [A study on the South Min drama *Li-ching-chi*, published during the Ming dynasty—Textual criticisms.]

吳守禮： （明刊）荔鏡記戲文研究──校勘篇

1899 Wu, Shou-li: Shih chhōa, i-chi chhōa, chhóa, chhú, chhōa, jiá.—*TLTC* 23:3, 1961, 13–16. [An etymological study of the word *chhōa* and its cognates *chhōa, chhóa, chhú, chhōa, jiá*.]/ Notes on the text of *Li-ching-chi*.

吳守禮： 釋『𨑨』以及『迌』、『擦』、『娶』、『引』、『惹』

1900 Wu, Shou-li: Shih bā.—*TLTC* 25:3, 1962, 5–6. [Etymological study of the word *bā*.]/ Notes on a study of the drama *Li-ching-chi*.

吳守禮： 釋『覓』

1901 Wu, Shou-li: *Shun-chih k'an pen Li-chih-chi yen-chiu—Chiao k'an p'ien.*—Taipei: The Author, 1968, 138 p.; mimeogr. [A study on the South Min drama *Li-chih-chi*, published during the Shun-chih period (1644–1661)—Textual criticisms.]

吳守禮： 順治刊本荔枝記研究──校勘篇

1902 Wu, Shou-li: *Li-ching-chi hsi-wen yen-chiu.*—Taipei: Tung-fang wen-hua kung-ying-she, 1970, 272 p. [Studies on *Li-ching-chi*: A folk play.]/ Including studies on dialect vocabulary (reprinted articles).

吳守禮： 荔鏡記戲文研究

1903 Wu, Shou-li: *Ch'ing Ch'ien-lung chien k'an T'ung-ch'uang ch'in-shu-chi chiao li.*—Taipei: The Author, 1975, 236 p.; 11–56: photo copy of *T'ung-ch'uang ch'in-shu-chi* text. [Commentary and critical notes on *T'ung-ch'uang ch'in-shu-chi* of the Ch'ien-lung period (1736–1795), Ch'ing dynasty.]/ With rhyme tables and classified vocabulary.

吳守禮： 清乾隆間刊同窗琴書記校理

1904 Wu, Shou-li: *Ch'ing Kuang-hsü chien k'an Li-chih-chi chiao li.*—Taipei: The Author, 1978, 588 p.; 17–100: photo copy of *Li-chih-chi* text. [Commentary and critical notes on the *Li-chih-chi* of the Kuang-hsü period (1875–1908), Ch'ing dynasty.]/ With classified dialect vocabulary, and curriculum vitae of the author.

吳守禮： 清光緒間刊荔枝記校理

15.1.2. General Studies (1905–1923)

1905 Chao, Chen-chi: Fu-chien yü-yen chih ch'eng-fen.—*Hua-nien chou-k'an* 3:41, 1934, 805–807. [The components of the dialects of Fukien.]

趙振紀： 福建語言之成分

1906 Ch'ih, P'ing: Fu-tsa te Fu-chien fang-yen.—*YWCS* 1955:7, 32–33. [The complexity of the Fukien dialects.]
持平： 複雜的福建方言

1907 Chou, Fa-kao: Min-yü.—*Chung-kuo yü-wen yen-chiu* (0099), 14. [Min dialects.]
周法高： 閩語

1908 Forrest, R.A.D.: Min.—*The Chinese language* (0508), 242–249.

1909 Fu-chien-sheng Han-yü fang-yen tiao-ch'a chih-tao tsu, et al. (ed.): *Fu-chien-sheng Han-yü fang-yen kai-k'uang.*— Amoy, 1962–1963, 2 vols., 4, 425; 228, 148 p., 51 maps. [General survey of the dialects of Fukien province.]/ A preliminary draft for discussion and evaluation.
福建省漢語方言調查指導組，福建省漢語方言概況編寫組： 福建省漢語方言概況（ 討論稿 ）

1910 Gotō, Asatarō: Fukken hōgen.—*Teikoku hyakka zensho* (Tokyo: Hakubunkan, 1908), 17:7, 146–183. [Fukien dialects.]
後藤朝太郎： 福建方言——『 帝國百科全書 』

1911 Huang, Tien-ch'eng: Min-nan-hua.— *YWCS* 1954:10, 9–11; 11, 12–14. [The South Min dialect.]
黃典誠： 閩南話

1912 Huang, Tien-ch'eng: Min-nan fang-yen ho Han min-tsu yü te pi-chiao.—*HMTH* (wen shih pan) 1954:5, 10–17; 1955:2, 133–159. [A comparison between the Min dialects and the languages of the Han race.]
黃典誠： 閩南方言和漢民族語的比較

1913 Kuo, Ming-k'un: Fu-lao-hua fang-yen te yen-chiu.—*Chūgoku no kazokusei oyobi gengo no kenkyū* (1926), 449–500. [Studies on the Hoklo dialect.]
郭明昆： 福佬話方言的研究

1914 Liu, Ming-shu: Ch'ü-wei te Ch'in Shu Min san ti fang-yin fang-yen (0535). [Interesting dialect sounds and dialect voca-

bulary of the Ch'in (Shensi), Shu (Szechwan) and Min (Fukien) areas.]
劉銘恕： 趣味的秦蜀閩三地方音方言

1915 Nakajima, Motoki: Fukienese.—*Ajia-Afurika bunpō pinran* No. 12b (Tokyo: Ajia-Afurika Gengo Bunka Kenkyūjo, 1976), 37 p.
中嶋幹起： Fukienese. —— 『 アジア・アフリカ文法便覽 』

1916 Norman, Jerry: A characterization of the Min dialects.—*Chi-Lin* 6, 1970, 19–34.

1917 P'an, Mao-ting, et al.: Fu-chien Han-yü fang-yen fen-ch'ü lüeh-shuo (1166). [A short discussion on the divisions of the Chinese dialects of Fukien.]
潘茂鼎等： 福建漢語方言分區略說

1918 Ting, Nan-ch'uan: Hsia-men fang-yen tiao-ch'a.—*P'ing-nü hsüeh-pao* 1, 1975, 21–38. [A survey of the Amoy dialect.]
丁南川： 廈門方言調查

1919 Tōdō, Akiyasu: Binhōgen to Amoigo. —*Chūgokugo on'inron* (0634), 130–132. [The Min dialects and the Amoy dialect.]/ Historico-descriptive.
藤堂明保： 閩方言と廈門語

1920 Wang, Yü-te: Fukken no kaihatsu to Fukkengo no seiritsu.—*NCGH* 21, 1969, 123–142; 1 map; E.S. [The development of Fukien and establishment of the Fukien dialect.]
王育德： 福建の開發と福建語の成立

1921 Wu, Huai: Ho-lo-hua ts'ung t'an.— *TPWW* 7:4, 1958, 1–19; 8:1, 1959, 8:2, 99–105; 8:3, 127–139; 8:4, 1960, 132–139; 9:1, 120–128; 9:2–3, 131–136; 9:4, 73–80; 10:1, 1961, 122–125; 10:2, 68–75. [Discussions on the Hoklo dialect.]
吳槐： 河洛話叢談

1922 Wu, Shou-li: Fu-chien-yü yen-chiu tao-lun.—*Jen-wen k'o-hsüeh lun-ts'ung* 1, 1948, 125–194./ *Orbis* 1, 1952, 213–214, W.A. Grootaers. [An introduction to the study of the Fukien dialects.]/ Fukien people and language.
吳守禮： 福建語研究導論

1923   Yüan, Chia-hua: Min-nan fang-yen.—*Han-yü fang-yen kai-yao* (0146), Chap. X. [The South Min dialects.]
袁家驊：閩南方言

15.1.3.   Sociocultural Aspects (1924–1930)

1924   Ch'un, Hsüeh: Fu-chien nung-chia yen.—*Fu-chien wen-hua* 3:23, 1936, 21–30. [Farmer's proverbs at Fukien.]
春雪：福建農家諺

1925   Egerod, Søren: Swatow loan words in Siamese.—*AcOr* 23:3–4, 1959, 137–156.

1926   Kuo, Ming-k'un: *Chūgoku no kazoku-sei oyobi gengo no kenkyū*.—Tokyo: Tōhō Gakkai, 1962, 16, 564 p./ *RBS* 8, 1962, Lü Chiung-chen. [Studies on the family system and languages of China.]/ Including South Min dialects.
郭明昆：中國の家族制及び言語の研究

1927   Kuo, Ming-k'un: Fukurowa hōgen ni okeru shinzoku shōi no ni-san ni tsuite.—*Chūgoku no kazokusei oyobi gengo no kenkyū* (1926), 295–316. [Notes on kinship terms in the Hoklo dialect.]
郭明昆：福老話方言に於ける親族稱謂の二三について

1928   Manuel, E. Arsenio: *Chinese elements in the Tagalog language.*—Manila: Filipiniana Publications, 1948, 139 p./ Subtitle: With some indications of Chinese influence on other Philippine languages and culture, and an excursion into Austronesian linguistics./ Including South Min dialect loan-words; *Anthropos* 47, 1952, 675–676, Anonymous.

1929   Matsumoto, Kazuo: Binnango ni okeru jinmei to shinzoku no yobikake kata ni tsuite.—*CGGG* 1960:6, 8–12. [Personal names and kinship terms in the South Min dialects.]
松本一男：閩南語における人名と親族の呼びかけ方について

1930   Yap, Gloria Chan: Sound changes in Tagalog words of Chinese origin.—*PJL* 4–5:1–2, 1973–1974, 48–54./ Hokkien dialect and Tagalog.

15.1.4.   Phonetics and Phonology (1931–1946)

1931   Chan, Fong-lam Rosie: *A study of Hokkien vowel sounds: a spectrographic analysis of their properties in phonetic contexts and when modified by speakers' locutions.*—Hong Kong: Hong Kong University, 1972, v. p.; illus./ M. Phil. thesis.
〔陳芳琳〕

1932   Dyer, S.: Remarks on the Hokkien dialect.—*Chinese Repository* 4, 1835, 172–176.

1933   Egerod, Søren: Tonal splits in Min.—*JCL* 4:1, 1976, 108–111.

1934   Hsü, Ch'eng-chang: Min-nan-yü te yin yü tzu wen-t'i.—*TWFW* 19:1–2, 1969, 10–16. [The problems of sounds and characters in the South Min dialects.]
許成章：閩南語的音與字問題

1935   Li, Hsien-chang: Fukurōwa no on'in henka.—*Kakyō Seikatsu* 2:1–2, 1963, 21–30. [Phonological changes in the Hoklo dialect.]
李獻璋：福老話の音韻變化

1936   Lin, Chin-ch'ao: *Min-nan-yü yen-chiu.*—Hsinchu: Chu-i ch'u-pan-she, 1975, 191 p. [A study on the South Min dialects.]/ Phonetic system compared with *Kuang-yün.*
林金鈔：閩南語研究

1937   Matsumoto, Kazuo: Seibo no men kara mita Kantongo to Fukkengo.—*CGGG* 1959:1, 3–7, 17. [The Cantonese and Fukien dialects as seen from their initials.]
松本一男：聲母の面から見た廣東語と福建語

1938   Matsumoto, Kazuo & Wang, Yü-te: Fukkengo no onkei.—*Chūgoku gogaku jiten* (0093), 168–172. [The phonetic system of the Fukien dialect.]
松本一男，王育德：福建語の音系

1939 Nakajima, Motoki: Fukkengo ni okeru ikutsuka no onseiteki tokuchō.—*AAGB* 4, 1971, 143–151. [Some special phonetic features of the Fukien dialect.]
中嶋幹起：福建語におけるいくつかの音聲的特徴

1940 Nakajima, Motoki: Fukkengo no seichō kōtai ni tsuite.—*AAGB* 5, 1972, 43–59. [On tone sandhi in the Fukien dialect.]
中嶋幹起：福建語の聲調交替について

1941 Nakajima, Motoki: Fukkengo no tōshion ni tsuite.—*AAGB* 6, 1973, 75–104. [The initials of the Fukien dialect.]
中嶋幹起：福建語の頭子音について

1942 Tay, Mary Wan Joo: *A phonological study of Hokkien.*—Edinburgh: U. of Edinburgh, 1968./ Unpubl. doc. diss.

1943 Tay, Mary W.J.: Hokkien phonological structure.—*JL* 6:1, 1970, 81–88.

1944 Tung, Chao-hui: Min-nan-yü te liang t'iao tz'u-yao pien-tiao kuei-lü.—*STHP* 18, 1973, 259–271. [Two rules for secondary tone sandhi in the South Min dialects.]
董昭輝：閩南語的兩條次要變調規律

1945 Wu, Huai: Min-nan-yü yü-yin chih yen-chiu.—*TWWH* 26–27, 1976, 126–147. [A study on the phonetics of the South Min dialect.]
吳槐：閩南語語音之研究

1946 Yeh, Ch'ang-ch'ing: Lun Min-yin.—*Kuo-hsüeh chuan-k'an* 1:2, 1926, 1–10. [A discussion on the Min dialects.]
葉長青：論閩音

15.1.5. Vocabulary (1947–1952)

1947 Anonymous: *A vocabulary of the Hok-këen dialect as spoken in the country of Tshëang-tshew. To which is prefixed a treatise on the Hok-këen tones.*—Foochow: Anglo-Chinese College Press, 1838, 6, 96, 20 p.

1948 Anonymous: *Triglot vocabulary: English, Malay, Chinese (Hok-kien, Hak-ka).*

—Singapore: (?), 1904, 4th ed., vii, 144 p.

1949 Cheng, I: Min-nan-hua ho pei-fang-hua tsai tz'u-hui shang te ch'a-pieh.—*YWCS* 1955:5, 38–40. [The lexical differences between the South Min and the Northern dialects.]
鄭溢：閩南話和北方話在詞彙上的差別

1950 Li, Hsien-chang: Fu-lao-hua fang-yen chih mei-yu sheng-mu te tz'u.—*NYWH* 3:3–4, 1956, 1–14; 4:1, 1956, 97–116. [Words without initials in the Hoklo dialect.]
李獻璋：福佬話方言之沒有聲母的詞

1951 Li, Hsien-chang: Fu-lao-hua tz'u-hui.—*TWFW* 6:2, 1956, 11–14; 6:3–4, 1956, 1–10; 6:5–6, 1956, 1–25; 6:7–8, 1956, 1–24. [Hoklo vocabulary.]
李獻璋：福佬話詞彙

1952 Nakajima, Motoki: *Fukken Kango hōgen kiso goi shū.*—Tokyo: Ajia-Afurika Gengo Bunka Kenkyūjo, 1979, 16, 353 p.; map. [A comparative lexicon of the Fukien dialects.]/ Foochow, P'ut'ien, Tungshantao, Ch'aoyang, Yungan.
中嶋幹起：福建漢語方言基礎語彙集

15.1.6. Grammar (1953–1968)

1953 Higuchi, Yasushi: Fukkengo no hiteishi bo to m ni tsuite.—*CGGG* 224, 1977, 70–77. [On the negatives *bo* and *m* in Fukienese.]
樋口靖：福建語の否定詞boとmについて

1954 Huang, Ting-hua: Min-nan fang-yen hsü-tzu-yen te a- ho -a.—*CKYW* 1958:1, 21–24. [The particles *a-* and *-a* in the South Min dialects.]
黃丁華：閩南方言虛字眼的『阿』和『仔』

1955 Huang, Ting-hua: Min-nan fang-yen te hsü-tzu-yen tsai, cho, li.—*CKYW* 1958:2, 81–83. [The particles *tsai (ai, ti, te), cho (to?, tiau, tio?)* and *li (di, de)* in the South Min dialect.]
黃丁華：閩南方言的虛字眼『在』、『着』、『里』

1956 Huang, Ting-hua: Min-nan fang-yen li te ch'ang-yung fou-ting-tz'u.—*CKYW* 1958:4, 189–196. [The commonly used negatives in the South Min dialects.]
黃丁華： 閩南方言裏的常用否定詞

1957 Huang, Ting-hua: Min-nan fang-yen li te jen-ch'eng tai-tz'u.—*CKYW* 1959:12, 571–574. [Personal pronouns in the South Min dialects.]
黃丁華： 閩南方言裏的人稱代詞

1958 Huang, Ting-hua: Min-nan fang-yen li te chih-shih tai-tz'u.—*CKYW* 1961:12, 23–29. [Demonstrative pronouns in the South Min dialects.]
黃丁華： 閩南方言裏的指示代詞

1959 Huang, Ting-hua: Min-nan fang-yen li te i-wen tai-tz'u.—*CKYW* 1963:4, 299–308, 298./ *RBS* 9, 1963, 520, M. Désirat. [Interrogative pronouns in the South Min dialects.]
黃丁華： 閩南方言裏的疑問代詞

1960 Kōsaka, Jun'ichi: Ka-nan hōgen no tokushoku.—*Kakyō Seikatsu* 2:5–6, 1963, 23–29. [Special features of the South China (Min) dialects.]/ A review article of Li's *Fukken gohō josetsu* (1961).]
香坂順一： 華南方言の特性

1961 Li, Hsien-chang: *Fukken gohō josetsu.*—Tokyo: Nan-feng shu-chü, 1950, xvii, 423 p./ *Orbis* 1, 1952, 213, W.A. Grootaers. [An introduction to the grammar of the Fukien dialect.]
李獻璋： 福建語法序說

1962 Murakami, Yoshihide: Binnan hōgen no ninshō daishi ni tsuite.—*TRGH* 96, 1975, 75–86. [Personal pronouns in the South Min dialects.]
村上嘉英： 閩南方言の人稱代詞について

1963 Nakajima, Motoki: Fukkengo ni okeru u⁷, bə⁵ no gohō hanchū.—*AAGB* 4, 1971, 75–85. [On the grammatical category of u^7 and $bə^5$ in the Fukien dialect.]
中嶋幹起： 福建語における『有』、『無』の語法範疇について

1964 Tzu, Shih: Min-nan-hua chung te a tzu.—*YWCS* 1956:6, 48; *FPC* 1, 1958, 103–104./ *YWCS* 1956:8, 37–42, Chang Chao-chi, et al.; *FPC* 1, 1958, 104–107, Chang Chao-chi, et al. [The suffix -*a* in the South Min dialects.]
子實： 閩南話中的『仔』字 / 張兆基等評

1965 Wang, Yü-te: Fukkengo ni okeru tioʔ no gohō ni tsuite.—*CGGG* 1969:7, 1–5. [On the grammatical function of *tioʔ* or *ti* in the Fukien dialect.]
王育德： 福建語における『著』の語法について

1966 Wen, Tuan-cheng: Che-nan Min-yü li hsing-jung-tz'u ch'eng-tu te piao-shih fang-fa.—*CKYW* 1957:12, 36. [The method of expressing degree with adjectives in the Min dialects of southern Chekiang.]
溫端政： 浙南閩語裏形容詞程度的表示方法

1967 Wen, Tuan-cheng: Che-nan Min-yü li te a, tçi ho nīū.—*CKYW* 1958:5, 222–224. [The *a*, *tçi*, and *nīū* in the Min dialect of southern Chekiang.]
溫端政： 浙南閩語裏的『仔』、『子』和『孥』

1968 Wu, Huai: Ho-lo (Min-nan) yü chih shu-tz'u.—*TWFW* 19:3–4, 1969, 68–75. [Numerals in the South Min dialect.]
吳槐： 河洛（閩南）語之數詞

15.1.7. Contrastive Studies (1969–1974)

1969 Ch'en, Ch'ui-min: Min-nan-hua ho P'u-t'ung-hua ch'ang-yung liang-tz'u te pi-chiao.—*CKYW* 1958:12, 591–593. [A comparison of the commonly used classifiers in the South Min dialects and the Common Language.]
陳垂民： 閩南話和普通話常用量詞的比較

1970 Cheng, I: Min-nan-hua ho pei-fang-hua tsai tz'u-hui shang te ch'a-pieh.—*YWCS* 1955:5, 38–40. [Lexical differences between the South Min dialects and the northern dialects.]
鄭溢： 閩南話和北方話在詞滙上的差別

1971 Ho, Tzu-ch'ien: Min-nan-jen hsüeh
Pei-ching-yin.—*YWCS* 1956:2, 41–44;
4, 41–46; 7, 37–40; 10, 42–48; 12, 31–
38. [South Min dialect speakers learning
Peking pronunciation.]
何子乾： 閩南人學北京音

1972 Hsia-men ta-hsüeh Chung-wen-hsi Yü-
yen chiao-yen shih (comp.): *Fu-chien-jen
tsen-yang hsüeh-hsi P'u-t'ung-hua.*—Foochow: Fu-chien jen-min, 1979, 2, 96 p.
[How a Fukien dialect speaker should
learn the Common Language.]
廈門大學中文系語言教研室： 福建人怎
樣學習普通話

1973 Kuo, Hou-chüeh: *Min Yüeh yü ho
Kuo-yü tui-chao chi.*—Shanghai: Erh-
t'ung, 1938, 161 p. [Min and Yüeh dialects and Mandarin compared.]
郭後覺： 閩粵語和國語對照集

1974 Lin, Shuang-fu: Min-nan yü-yin chieh-
kou tui-yü hsüeh-hsi Kuo-yü te ying-
hsiang.—*YSYK* 43, 1976, 35–37; *Chung-
kuo yü-yen-hsüeh lun-chi* (0113), 166–
174. [The influence of South Min dialect
structure on learning Mandarin.]
林雙福： 閩南語音結構對於學習國語的
影響

15.1.8. Textbooks (1975–1977)

1975 Hare, G.T.: *The Hokkien vernacular.*—
Singapore: Government Printing Office,
1897–1904, 2 vols. [not seen].

1976 Jou, Bien-ming [Chou, Pien-ming]:
*English-Mandarin-Hokkien everyday sen-
tences in spoken English* by Harold E.
Palmer and F.G. Blandford, re-edited
with parallel Quoyu-Halgur-character
texts for instruction in English and
Chinese conversation.—Singapore: Nan-
yang Book Co., publ. for the Shu-tung-
wen Institute, 1951, 207 p.

1977 Kao, L.: *The comprehensive book on
Hokkien dialect.*—Singapore: Marican,
1957, 78 p.

15.1.9. Dictionaries (1978–1981)

1978 Chiang, Ker-chiu: *A practical English-
Hokkien dictionary.*—Singapore: Chin
Fen Book Store, 1956 (?), 100 p.
〔 蔣克秋： 英廈註音新辭典 〕

1979 Embree, Bernard L.M.: *A dictionary of
Southern Min.*—Hong Kong: Language
Institute, 1973, xlv, 305 p.; 302–305:
Bibliography.

1980 Legge, James: *A lexilogus of the English, Malay and Chinese language, com-
prehending the vernacular idioms of the
last in the Hok-keen and Canton dialects.*
—Malacca: Anglo-Chinese College Press,
1841, 111 p.

1981 Medhurst, Walter Henry: *Dictionary of
the Hok-këën dialect of the Chinese language, according to the reading and colloquial idioms.*—Macao: East India Company's Press, 1832, lxiv, 860 p.

15.2. Amoy (1982–2023)

15.2.1. Phonetics and Phonology (1982–1999)

1982 Chiang, Helen T.: *Phonology of an
Amoy dialect.*—Bloomington: Indiana
U., 1966, iv, 183 p./ Unpubl. doc. diss.;
DA 28, 1967: 212–A; UM 67–3658.

1983 Chiang, Helen T.: Amoy-Chinese tones.
—*Phonetica* 17, 1967, 100–115.

1984 Chiu, Bien-ming [Chou, Pien-ming]:
The phonetic structure and tone behavior
in Hagu (commonly known as the Amoy
dialect) and their relation to certain questions in Chinese linguistics.—*TP* 28,
1931, 245–342./ *TP* 28, 1931, 343–345,
Paul Pelliot.

1985 Chu, Chao-hsiang: Hsia-yü sheng-tiao
li-lun te pien-cheng.—*Yü-wen i-k'an* 60–
70, 1950. [A theoretical discussion
on the tones of the Amoy dialect.]
朱兆祥： 廈語聲調理論的辯正

1986 Chu, Chao-hsiang: Hsia-men yin-yün te chien-t'ao.—*NYTH* 2, 1963, 63–77. [An examination of the phonology of the Amoy dialect.]

朱兆祥：廈門音韻的檢討

1987 Chu, Chao-hsiang: Chang Ch'üan Hsia-yü yü-yin te ting-hsing miao shu.—*NYTH* 7, 1973, 127–142. [A qualitative description of the Changchou and Ch'üan-chou varieties of the Amoy dialect.]

朱兆祥：漳泉廈語語音的定性描述

1988 Hirayama, Hisao: Hsia-men-hua ku tiao-chih te nei-pu kou-ni.—*JCL* 3:1, 1975, 3–15. [Internal reconstruction of the ancient tonemes in the Amoy dialect.]

平山久雄：廈門話古調值的內部構擬

1989 Ko, Te-ch'un: Hsia-men sheng-tiao yü chü-tzu chieh-kou chi Ying-yü chiao-hsüeh te kuan-hsi.—*HMTH* 1957:2, 167–193. [Tones and sentence structure of the Amoy dialect and the relationship in the teaching of English.]

葛德純：廈門聲調與句子結構及英語教學的關係

1990 Li, Ju-lung: Hsia-men-hua te pien-tiao ho ch'ing-sheng.—*HMTH* 1962:3, 78–114. [Tone sandhi and the neutral tone in the Amoy dialect.]

李如龍：廈門話的變調和輕聲

1991 Li, Ju-lung: Hsia-men-hua te wen pai i-tu.—*HMTH* 1963:2, 57–100. [The differences between literary and colloquial reading in the Amoy dialect.]

李如龍：廈門話的文白異讀

1992 Lo, Ch'ang-p'ei: *Hsia-men yin-hsi.*— Peiping: Academia Sinica, 1930, xiv, 278 p; Peking: K'o-hsüeh, 1956, ix, 286 p.; tab. [The phonetic system of the Amoy dialect.]

羅常培：廈門音系

1993 Mo, Chien-ch'ing: A contrastive study of the initial, final and tone of the Amoy

and Foochow dialects.—*CTHP* 37–38, 1978, 45–58.

〔莫建清〕

1994 Peng, Fred C. C.: Amoy phonology: Phonemization of the three nasal consonants [m, n, ŋ].—*AO* 34, 1966, 411–416.

1995 Sung, Margaret M. Y.: A study of literary and colloquial Amoy Chinese.—*JCL* 1:3, 1973, 414–436.

〔宋嚴棉〕

1996 Sung, Margaret M. Y.: *A study of literary and colloquial Amoy Chinese.*— Stanford: Stanford U., 1974, 127 p./ Unpubl. doc. diss.; *DAI* 34: 7735-A; UM 74–13,693.

1997 Tung, T'ung-ho: Hsia-men fang-yen te yin-yün.—*BIHP* 29, 1957, 231–253; *Tung T'ung-ho . . . . hsüan chi* (0110), 275–297./ *RBS* 4, 1958, 556, Chang Kun. [The phonology of the Amoy dialect.]

董同龢：廈門方言的音韻

1998 Tung, T'ung-ho: Szu-ko Min-nan fang-yen.—*BIHP* 30, 1959, 729–1042./ *RBS* 5, 1959, 493, Ta Trong Hiep. [Four South Min dialects.]/ Amoy, Chinchiang, Lunghsi, Chiehyang.

董同龢：四個閩南方言

1999 Wang, Yü-te: An investigation about literary reading and colloquial reading in the Amoy dialect.—*TICOJ* 3, 1958, 67–70.

15.2.2. Grammar (2000–2005)

2000 Brosnahan, Irene Teoh: *Interrogative structures in Amoy Chinese: A transformational approach.*—Washington, D. C.: Georgetown U., 1972, iii, 188 p./ Unpubl. doc. diss.; *DA* 33, 1973: 6335-A; UM 73–11,804.

2001 Dy, Carmen J.: The syntactic structures of Amoy as used in the Philippines.— *PJL* 3, 1972, ii, 75–94.

2002 Piñol, Francisco: *Gramática China del dialecto de Amoy.*—Hong Kong: Nazareth, 1928, vi, 357, v. p.

2003 Piñol, Francisco: *Grammar of the Amoy dialect.* Transl. by students of the Major Seminary at Maryknoll, New York. —Hong Kong: Maryknoll Fathers, 1952, iv, 219 p./ *Orbis* 9:1, 1960, 180–181, Paul Yang Fu-mien.

2004 Teoh, Irene: Auxiliary verbs and the A-not-A question in Amoy.—*MS* 26, 1967, 295–304.

2005 Wu, Chung-p'ing: Hsia-men-hua te yü-fa t'e-tien.—*FPC* 1, 1958, 84–103. [Special grammatical features of the Amoy dialect.]
吳仲平：廈門話的語法特點

15.2.3. Textbooks (2006–2012)

2006 Bodman, Nicholas C.: *Spoken Amoy Hokkien.*—Kuala Lumpur: Government Federation of Malaya, 1955 & 1958, 2 vols., iv, 367; v, 261 p./ *RBS* 4, 1958, 557, P. Kratochvíl.

2007 Bunkyōkyoku Gakumuka: *Nichi-Ka kaiwa.*—Taipei: Taiwan Sōtokufu Bunkyōkyoku, 1938, 8, 306 p. [Japanese-Amoy conversations.]
文教局學務課：日廈會話

2008 Chiang, Ker-chiu: *Amoy vernacular lessons for beginners with a vocabulary.* Book I.—Singapore: The Author, 1940, 45 p.
〔蔣克秋：廈語易解（卷一）〕

2009 Chiang, Ker-chiu: *Hokkien vernacular lessons for beginners.*—Singapore: Chin Fen Book Store, 1952, 2 vols., 62; 62 p.
〔蔣克秋：廈語易解〕

2010 Doty, E.: *Anglo-Chinese manual with romanized colloquial in the Amoy dialect.*—Canton: S. Wells Williams, 1853, xii, iii, 214 p.

2011 MacGowan, John: *A manual of the Amoy colloquial.*—Hong Kong: De

Sousa, 1869, iii, 200 p.; Amoy: Man Shing, 1880, iii, 206 p.; Amoy: Chui Keng Tong, 1892, 3rd ed., iii, 222 p.; 1898, 4th ed., iii, 216 p.
〔馬約翰：英華口才集〕

2012 Warnshuis, A.L. & De Pree, Henry P.: *Lessons in the Amoy vernacular.*—Amoy: Amoy U. Press, 1930, rev. & enl. by H. P. De Pree & K. G. Chiu, ix, 266 p.; Manila: Shangkuan Press & School Supply, 1955, 3rd ed., rev. & enl. by H. P. De Pree & Peter Hsieh, ix, 269 p.

15.2.4. Dictionaries (2013–2023)

2013 Campbell, William: *A dictionary of the Amoy vernacular spoken throughout the prefectures of Chinchiu, Chiang-chiu and Formosa.*—Yokohama: The Fukuin Printing Co., 1913, 1067 p.; Tainan: T'ai-wan chiao-hui kung pao she, 1952, 5th ed., ii, 1134 p.
〔甘爲霖：廈門音新字典〕

2014 Douglas, Castairs: *Chinese-English dictionary of the vernacular or spoken language of Amoy, with the principal variations of the Chang-chew and Chin-chew dialects.*—London: The Presbyterian Church of England, 1899, xix, 612 p. *Supplement* by Thomas Barclay. Shanghai: Commercial Press, 1923, iv, 276 p.; Taipei: Ku T'ing, 1970, repr.

2015 Francken, J.J.C. & De Grijs, C.F.M.: *Chineesch-Hollandsch voordenboek van het Emoi dialekt.*—Batavia: Landsdrukkerij, 1882, viii, 774 p./ Chinese-Dutch dictionary of the Amoy dialect.

2016 MacGowan, John: *English and Chinese dictionary of the Amoy dialect.*—Amoy: A.A. Marcal, 1885, vii, 611 p.; London: Kegan Paul, Trübner & Co., 1905, vii, 601 p.

2017 Piñol, Francisco y Andreu: *Diccionario Chino-Español del dialecto de Amoy, Chiang-chiu, Choan-chiu, Formosa.*—Hong Kong: Nazareth, 1937, xii, 790 p.
〔華班辭典〕

2018 Prat, Pedro: *Diccionario Español-Chino del dialecto de Amoy y Formosa.*—Amoy: Imprenta de la Misión Católica, 1925, x, 767 p.

2019 Schlegel, Gustaaf: *Nederlandsch-Chineesch woordenboek met de transcriptie der Chineesche karakters in het Tsiang-tsiu dialekt. Hoofdzakelijk ten behoeve der tolken voor de Chineesche taal in Nederlandsch-Indie bewerkt.*—Leiden: E.J. Brill, 1886–1890, 8 vols., 4 parts, Pt. I, viii, 1470 p.; Pt. II, iv, 1134 p.; Pt. III, iv, 1212 p.; Pt. IV, iv, 1403 p.; *Supplement,* 61 p. Chinese title: *Hó Hoâ bûn gí lūi ts'am* [荷華文語類參].

2020 Táⁿ, Má-jī: *Ê-mn̂g īm ê jī-tián.*—Amoy: Kó-lōng-sū Chūi-keng-tông, 1902, 449 p. [A dictionary of the Amoy dialect.]

2021 Tipson, Ernest: *Pocket dictionary of the Amoy vernacular. English-Chinese.*—Singapore: Lithographers, 1934, 215 p.; Shanghai: Commercial Press, 1940, 2nd ed., 446 p.; Mimeogr. repr. by Maryknoll Fathers, 1954, ii, 205 p.

2022 Tipson, Ernest: *Pocket dictionary of the Amoy vernacular. Chinese-English.*—Singapore: Printers, 1935, 476 p.; Taichung: Maryknoll Language School, 1953, iv, 366 p.; Mimeogr.

2023 Winn, J.A.: *A vocabulary of the Hokien dialect as spoken at Amoy and Singapore.*—Singapore: (?), 1866. [not seen].

15.3.   Ch'aochou and Swatow (2024–2064)
15.3.1.   Ch'aochou (2024–2051)
15.3.1.1.   General Studies (2024–2028)

2024 Akagi, Osamu: Chōshūgo gaisetsu.—*OGDG* 23, 1972, 1–34. [A general introduction to the Ch'aochou dialect.]
赤木攻：潮州語概說

2025 Chan, Po-hui: Ch'ao-chou fang-yen.—*FPT* 2, 1959, 39–120. [The Ch'aochou dialect.]
詹伯慧：潮州方言

2026 Li, Yung-ming: *Ch'ao-chou fang-yen.*—Peking: Chung-hua, 1959, v, 385 p.; Hong Kong: Sun Chau Book Co., [1978], repr./ *RBS* 5, 1959, 492, Li Fang-kuei; *Orbis* 15, 1966, 143–144, Paul Yang.
李永明：潮州方言

2027 Wang, Yung-ta: *Ch'ao-chou-hua ch'ien chieh.*—Singapore: Yüan-yang wen-hua kung-szu, 1972, [ii], 239 p. [An easy explanation of the Ch'aochou dialect.]
王永大：潮州話淺解

2028 Weng, Hui-tung: *Ch'ao-Shan fang-yen.*—Shanghai: Han-hui lou, 1943, 16 chüan; Nagoya: Tenzan shuppansha, 1976, repr., 160 p.; The author's name was erroneously changed to Tung Tzu-kuang (東子光). [The Ch'aochou and Swatow dialects.]
翁輝東：潮汕方言

15.3.1.2.   Phonetics and Phonology (2029–2038)

2029 Chang, Sheng-yü: Ch'ao-yang fang-yen te lien-tu pien-tiao.—*FY* 1979:2, 93–121. [Tone sandhi in the Ch'aoyang dialect.]
張盛裕：潮陽方言的連讀變調

2030 Chang, Sheng-yü: Ch'ao-yang fang-yen te wen pai i-tu.—*FY* 1979:4, 241–267. [Colloquial and literary readings in the Ch'aoyang dialect.]
張盛裕：潮陽方言的文白異讀

2031 Cheng, Chin-chuan & Wang, William Shih-yüan: Tone change in Chaozhou Chinese: A study of lexical diffusion.—*Papers in linguistics in honor of Henry and Kenee Kahane* (Ed. by B. Kachru, et al., 1972), 99–113.

2032 Chiang, Ju-lin: *Ch'ao-yü shih-wu yin.*—Swatow: Wen-ming shang-wu shu-chü, 1921, 4 chüan; Hong Kong: Wu-kuei-t'ang shu-chü, n.d., repr., 5, 50, 45, 41, 38 p. [Fifteen initial sounds of the Ch'aochou dialect..]
蔣儒林：潮語十五音

2033 Chiang, Ju-lin: *Ch'ao-yü t'ung-yin tzu-hui.*—Shanghai: Ching-chang shu-chü, 1931; 1938, 11th print., 4 chüan./ Same book as (2032) with changed title. [Homophonous vocabulary of the Ch'aochou dialect.]

蔣儒林： 潮語同音字彙

2034 Hsieh, I-hsien: *Tseng san Ch'ao sheng shih-wu yin.*—Kowloon: The Author, 1965, 14, 36, 125 p. [Three additional initials to the fifteen initial sounds of the Ch'aochou dialect.]

謝益顯： 增三潮聲十五音

2035 Huang, Chi-yü: Ch'ao-chou pa-sheng wu-tu piao shuo.—*Shan-tung ta-hsüeh wen shih ts'ung-k'an* 1, 1934, 19–21. [A table showing eight erroneous readings of the Ch'aochou dialect.]

黃際遇： 潮州八聲誤讀表說

2036 Huang, Chia-chiao: Ch'ao-chou fang-yin kai-shuo.—*Lan-chou ta-hsüeh hsüeh-pao* 1958:1, 103–126. [A general introduction to the Ch'aochou dialect sounds.]

黃家教： 潮州方音概說

2037 Lin, Lien-hsien: *Ch'ao-tu fan-ch'ieh yin-piao liang-yung cheng-yin piao.*—Hong Kong: Chung-wen ta-hsüeh Chung-kuo yü-yen wen-hsüeh-hsi, 1977, [vii], 367 p. [A standard table of phonetics for the Ch'aochou dialect.]

林蓮仙： 潮讀反切音標兩用正音表

2038 Liu, Sheng-i: Ch'ao-chou fang-yin chih yen-chiu.—*Ch'ao-chou liu ching hsüeh-hui nien-k'an* 2, 1926, 1–21. [A study on the phonetics of the Ch'aochou dialect.]

劉聲繹： 潮州方音之研究

15.3.1.3. Grammar (2039–2042)

2039 Chan, Po-hui: Ch'ao-chou-hua te i-hsieh yü-fa t'e-tien.—*CKYW* 1958:5, 218–220. [Some special grammatical features of the Ch'aochou dialect.]

詹伯慧： 潮州話的一些語法特點

2040 Chang, Sheng-yü: Ch'ao-yang fang-yen te ch'ung-tieh shih.—*CKYW* 1979:2, 106–114. [Reduplication in the Ch'aoyang dialect.]

張盛裕： 潮陽方言的重疊式

2041 Li, Hsin-k'uei: Ch'ao-chou fang-yen te shu-liang-tz'u.—*CKYW* 1958:5, 221. [Quantitatives in the Ch'aochou dialect.]

李新魁： 潮州方言的數量詞

2042 Pai, Hsing, et al.: Ch'ao-chou fang-yen i-hsieh yü-fa t'e-tien te t'ao-lun.—*CKYW* 1959:1, 36–38. [A discussion of certain special grammatical features of the Ch'aochou dialect.]

白星等： 潮州方言一些語法特點的討論

15.3.1.4. Contrastive Studies (2043–2045)

2043 Chou, Yao-wen: Ch'ao-chou-hua yü P'u-t'ung-hua yu shen-ma ch'a-pieh.—*FPC* 1, 1958, 140–142. [What the differences are between the Ch'aochou dialect and the Common Language.]

周耀文： 潮州話與普通話有甚麼差別

2044 Kuang-tung sheng fang-yen tiao-ch'a chih-tao tsu: *Ch'ao-chou-jen hsüeh-hsi P'u-t'ung-hua shou-ts'e.*—Canton: Kuang-tung jen-min, 1959, iv, 108 p. [A handbook for Ch'aochou dialect speakers in learning the Common Language.]

廣東省方言調查指導組： 潮州人學習普通話手冊

2045 Li, Hsin-k'uei: Ch'ao-chou-jen hsüeh-hsi Pei-ching-yin.—*FPC* 1, 1958, 62–67. [How a Ch'aochou dialect speaker should learn Peking pronunciation.]

李新魁： 潮州人學習北京音

15.3.1.5. Textbooks and Dictionaries (2046–2051)

2046 Dean, William: *First lessons in the Tie-chiw dialect.*—Bangkok: (?), 1841, 48 p.

2047 Goddard, Josiah: *A Chinese and English vocabulary in the Tie-chiu dialect.*—Bangkok: Mission Press, 1847, ix, 248 p.

2048 Hua-nan shih-fan hsüeh-yüan Chung-wen hsi (ed.): *P'u-t'ung-hua Ch'ao-Shan fang-yen ch'ang-yung tzu-tien.*—Canton: Hua-nan shih-fan hsüeh-yüan, 1971, 286 p. [A common usage Common Language-Ch'aochou-Swatow dictionary.]

華南師範學院中文系編：普通話潮汕方言常用字典

2049 Kuang-t'ai shu-chü (ed.): *Ch'ao Shan tzu-tien.*—Hong Kong: Kuang-t'ai shu-chü, 1969, 666 p. [A Ch'aochou-Swatow dialect dictionary.]

廣泰書局編：潮汕字典

2050 Ts'ai, Chün-ming: *Ch'ao-yü tz'u-tien.*—Taipei: San-min shu-chü, 1976, 26, 482, iv, 38 p. [A Ch'aochou dialect dictionary.]

蔡俊明：潮語詞典

2051 Ts'ai, Chün-ming: *Ch'ao-yü tz'u-tien pu-pien. Kuo-Ch'ao yü-hui.*—Taipei: T'ai-wan hsüeh-sheng, 1979, 370 p. [Supplement to *Ch'ao-yü tz'u-tien* (2050). Mandarin-Ch'aochou vocabulary.]

蔡俊明：潮語詞典補編　國潮語彙

15.3.2. Swatow (2052–2064)

15.3.2.1. Phonetics and Phonology (2052–2053)

2052 Lin, Lien-hsien: Lüeh lun Shan-tou-hua te sheng-mu.—*CCHP* 1:2, 1962, 171–186. [A short discussion on the initials of the Swatow dialect.]

林蓮仙：略論汕頭話的聲母

2053 Steele, John: *The Swatow syllabary, with Mandarin pronunciations.*—Shanghai: The Presbyterian Mission Press, 1924, 2nd ed., iv, 384 p.

〔潮正兩音字集，粵省潮音類列，北方正韻編行〕

15.3.2.2. Vocabulary and Grammar (2054–2056)

2054 Ashmore, William: *Primary lessons in Swatow grammar.*—Swatow: English Presbyterian Mission Press, 1884, x, 155 p./ Pages 125–155 contain a list of syllables representing the sounds used in pronouncing the Tie Chiu dialect, prepared by S.B. Partridge.

2055 Childe, Chi-shun Nellie: *A transformation-generative outline of Swatow grammar.*—Hong Kong: Hong Kong U., 1971, ii, [8], 249 p.; illus., maps./ Unpubl. M.A. thesis.

〔蔡志純〕

2056 Giles, Herbert Allen: *Handbook of the Swatow dialect with a vocabulary.*—Shanghai: (?), 1877, 57 p.

15.3.2.3. Textbooks (2057–2061)

2057 Anshige, Kamesaburō: *Jitsuyō Nichi-San-go shōkei.*—Swatow: Tōei gakkō, 1920. [not seen]. [A practical Japanese-Swatow snap course.]

安重龜三郎：實用日汕語捷徑

2058 Bunkyōkyoku Gakumuka (comp.): *Nichi-San kaiwa.*—Taipei: Taiwan Sōtokufu Bunkyōkyoku, 1939, 8, 325 p. [Japanese-Swatow conversations.]

文教局學務課編：日汕會話

2059 Fielde, Adele Marion: *First lessons in the Swatow dialect.*—Swatow: Swatow Printing Office Co., 1878, 427 p.

2060 Gibson, John Campbell: *Manual of Swatow vernacular.*—Swatow: English Presbyterian Mission Press, 1923, 2nd ed., 184 p.

2061 Lim, Hiong-seng: *A handbook of the Swatow vernacular.*—Singapore: Kohn Yen Hean Press, 1886, iv, 169 p., with a dictionary of some of the more important words in the Swatow dialect, 110 p.

15.3.2.4. Dictionaries (2062–2064)

2062 Fielde, A.M.: *A pronouncing and defining dictionary of the Swatow dialect.*—Shanghai: American Presbyterian Mission Press, 1883, xv, 617 p.

2063 Gibson, John Campbell: *A Swatow index to the Syllabic dictionary of Chinese by S. Wells Williams and to the Dictionary of the vernacular of Amoy by Castairs Douglas.*—Swatow: English Presbyterian Mission Press, 1886, 18, viii, 171 p./ See (0525) & (2014).

2064 Lechler, R. Ed. by Ruffus, William: *English-Chinese vocabulary of the vernacular or spoken language of Swatow.*—Swatow: English Presbyterian Mission Press, 1883, 302 p./ Romanized.

15.4. Other Localities in Fukien and Kwangtung (2065–2075)

2065 Chang, Shuang-ch'ing: Tung T'ung-ho *Szu-ko Min-nan fang-yen* Chin-chiang pu-fen ting pu.—*Lien-ho shu-yüan hsüeh-pao* 10, 1972, 167–185. [Corrigenda and addenda to the section on the Chinchiang dialect in Tung T'ung-ho's *Four South Min dialects* (1998).]

張雙慶 ： 董同龢『四個閩南方言』晉江部分訂補

2066 Chang, Yü-hung: *The Hinghwa dialects of Fukien: A descriptive linguistic study.*—Ithaca: Cornell U., 1972, vi, 225 p.; 218–226: Bibliography./ Unpubl. doc. diss.; *DAI* 33:1154–A; UM 72–23,649.

〔張裕宏；興化〕

2067 Chang, Yü-hung: Tone system in Shangfeng dialect: A Southern Min dialect.—*Chi-Lin* 9, 1972, 41–54.

〔張裕宏；上楓〕

2068 Ch'en, Han-kuang: Chin-men-yü yen-chiu.—*FCWH* 3, 1968, 58–66. [A study of the Chinmen (Quemoy) dialect.]

陳漢光 ： 金門語研究

2069 Ch'iu, Julie M.H.: A phonological description of the Yung-ch'un dialect.—*The Linguistic Approach to English Teaching Series* (Publ. of the U. of Texas, print. in Taipei), vol. 9, 1965, 1–78.

〔邱墨荷 ： 永春話音〕

2070 Chung, Lu-sheng: *Fu-chien Hui-an fang-yen.*—Taipei: The Author, 1964, 279 p./ Mimeogr. [The Huian dialect of Fukien.]

鍾露昇 ： 福建惠安方言

2071 Egerod, Søren: *The Lungtu dialect: A descriptive and historical study of a south Chinese idiom.*—Cophenhagen: Ejnar Munksgaard, 1956, xviii, 284 p.; map./ A South Min dialect variety spoken in Kwangtung; *RBS* 2, 1956, 401, N.C. Bodman.

2072 Nakajima, Motoki: *Bingo Tōsantō hōgen kiso goishū.*—Tokyo: Ajia-Afurika Gengo Bunka Kenkyūjo, 1977, 45, 276 p.; map.; 43–45: Bibliography. [A study of the basic vocabulary of the Min dialect in the Tungshan Island.]

中嶋幹起 ： 閩語東山島方言基礎語彙集

2073 Nakajima, Motoki: *Bingo Tōsantō hōgen kiso goishū Nihongo sakuin.*—Tokyo: Ajia-Afurika Gengo Bunka Kenkyūjo, 1977, 52 p. [Japanese index to the Study of the basic vocabulary of the Min dialect in the Tungshan Island (2072).]

中嶋幹起 ： 閩語東山島方言基礎語彙集日本語索引

2074 Wang, Yü-te: Zenshū hōgen no on'in taikei.—*Meiji daigaku Jinbun kagaku kenkyūjo kiyo*, 8–9, 1970, 1–31; 30–31: E.S. [The phonological system of the Ch'üanchou dialect.]

王育德 ： 泉州方言の音韻體系

2075 Yü, Chih-fu: *Feng-hsin yin-hsi.*—Taipei: I-wen, 1975, 165 p.; 164–165: E.S. [The phonetic system of the Fenghsin dialect.]

余直夫 ： 奉新音系

15.5. Taiwan (2076–2196)

15.5.1. Historical Studies (2076–2083)

2076 Chu, Feng: T'ai-wan fang-yen chih yü-fa yü yü-yüan.—*TPWW* 7:3, 1958, 1–24. [The grammar and etymology of the Taiwanese dialect.]

朱鋒 ： 臺灣方言之語法與語源

2077   Ebara, Fumitane: Chūgoku no hōgen ni tsuite—Taiwan gengo no rekishiteki hensen.—*Chūgoku sōgō kenkyū* 2, 1977, 40–47. [On the dialects of China—The historical development of the languages of Taiwan.]
江原文種：中國の方言について──臺灣言語の歴史的變遷

2078   Lin, Pen-yüan: Kuang-fu nien-to-nien lai te T'ai-wan-hua ta yen-pien.—*TPWH* 13–14, 1970, 84–96. [The great changes in Taiwanese during the past twenty years.]
林本元：光復念多年來的臺灣話大演變

2079   Liu, Chien-jen: T'ai-yü k'ao shih.—*TWFW* 18:2, 1968, 97–99; 20:1, 1970, 63–64; 22:3, 1972, 14–16; 23:3, 1973, 16–17. [Etymological study on Taiwanese.]
劉建仁：臺語考釋

2080   Noguchi, Masayuki: Taiwango no keitō to sono rekishi.—*Tōyō Kenkyū* 29, 1972, 114–137. [The lineage and history of Taiwanese.]
野口正之：臺灣語の系統たその歴史

2081   Sun, Hsün-hou: *T'ai-wan-hua k'ao cheng.*—Taipei: Shang-wu, 1964, 2, ix, 70 p. [Etymological study on Taiwanese.]
孫洵侯：臺灣話考證

2082   Ting, Pang-hsin: *T'ai-wan yü-yen yüan-liu.*—Taichung: T'ai-wan sheng-cheng-fu hsin-wen-ch'u, 1970, ii, ii, 127 p.; 3 maps. [The origin and development of the languages of Taiwan.]
丁邦新：臺灣語言源流

2083   Wang, Yü-te: Taiwango no keitō.—*TWSN* 1, 1960, 27–31. [The lineage of Taiwanese.]
王育德：臺灣語の系統

15.5.2.   General Studies (2084–2097)

2084   Chao, Li-ming: T'ai-wan te yü-yen.—*Hsin Ya-hsi-ya yüeh-k'an* 4:3, 1932, 133–134. [Languages of Taiwan.]
趙立明：臺灣的語言

2085   Ch'en, Wen-pin: T'ai-wan te Han-yü fang-yen.—*CKYW* 1954:10, 43–44. [The Chinese dialects of Taiwan.]
陳文彬：臺灣的漢語方言

2086   Chung, Lu-sheng: *Min-nan-yü tsai T'ai-wan te fen-pu.*—Taipei: The Author, 1967, 650 p.; maps; mimeogr. [The distribution of the South Min dialects in Taiwan.]
鍾露昇：閩南語在臺灣的分佈

2087   Ferguson, D.: Formosan Chinese.—*ChinRec* 40, 1909, 494–502.

2088   Hsü, Ch'eng-chang: T'ai-wan Min-nan-yü te yen-chiu.—*NYWH* 10, 1965, 97–112; 12, 1967, 1–30. [A study on the South Min dialect of Taiwan.]
許成章：臺灣閩南語的研究

2089   Hsü, Ch'eng-chang: Yen-chiu T'ai-wan Min-nan-yü te hsin lu li-ch'eng.—*TWFW* 28:1, 1978, (reprint) 25 p. [Psychological processes in the study of the South Min dialects of Taiwan.]
許成章：研究臺灣閩南語的心路歷程

2090   Ku, Pai-li [Cornelius C. Kubler]: *P'eng-hu ch'ün-tao fang-yen tiao-ch'a.*—Taipei: T'ai-wan ta-hsüeh Chung-wen yen-chiu-so, 1978, vi, 118 p.; 12 maps; E.S./ M.A. thesis. [A dialect survey of the Pescadores Islands.]
顧百里：澎湖羣島方言調查

2091   Lin, Pen-yüan: T'ai-wan te yü-hsüeh. —*T'ai-wan wen-hua lun-chi* (Taipei: Chung-hua wen-hua, 1954), Vol. 3, 353–370. [Linguistics of Taiwan.]/ A general description of Taiwanese.
林本元：臺灣的語學──『臺灣文化論集（三）』

2092   Lin, Pen-yüan: T'ai-wan fang-yen lun. —*TPWW* 7:1, 1958, 89–96. [On the dialects of Taiwan.]
林本元：臺灣方言論

2093 Liu, Chi-yüan: T'an T'ai-wan chih yü-yen.—*TPWW* 5:2–3, 1957, 63–65. [On the languages of Taiwan.]

劉寄園：談臺灣之語言

2094 Ogawa, Naoyoshi: Taiwan no gengo.—*Nippon chiri daikei* (Tokyo: Kaizōsha, 1930), 11, 333–336. [Languages of Taiwan.]

小川尚義：臺灣の言語——『日本地理大系』

2095 Ts'ai, Mao-t'ang: Kuan-yü T'ai-yü yen-chiu te chi-ko wen-t'i.—*TWFW* 13:5, 1963, 3–10. [Some problems concerning the study of Taiwanese.]

蔡懋棠：關於臺語研究的幾個問題

2096 Tung, T'ung-ho; Chao, Jung-lang & Lan, Ya-hsiu: *Chi T'ai-wan te i-chung Min-nan-hua.*—Taipei: Academia Sinica, 1967, 158 p. [A South Min dialect of Taiwan.]/ Spoken in the city of Taipei.

董同龢，趙榮琅，藍亞秀：記臺灣的一種閩南話

2097 Wu, Shou-li: *T'ai-wan t'ung-chih kao*, Chüan 2: *Jen-min chih yü-yen p'ien.*—Taipei: T'ai-wan wen-hsien, 1954, iii, 252 p.; 1 map. [Provincial gazetteer of Taiwan, Chüan 2: Taiwanese people and languages.]

吳守禮：臺灣通志稿　卷二：人民志語言篇

15.5.3. Sociocultural Aspects (2098–2105)

2098 Fang, Hao: T'ai-wan yü-yen yü wen-hua ch'uan-t'ung.—*T'ai-wan shih nien* (Taipei: T'ai-wan hsin-sheng-pao she, 1955), 28–33; *Fang Hao liu-shih tzu ting kao* (Taipei: The Author, 1969), Vol. I, 763–776 (rev. version).

方豪：臺灣語言與文化傳統——『臺灣十年』；『方豪六十自定稿』上冊

2099 Li, Hsien-chang: Fukurōwa no kenkyū to Taiwan wabun undō to.—*Kakyō Seikatsu* 2:7, 1963, 15–28. [The study of the Fukien dialect and the Taiwanese literary movement.]

李獻章：福老話の研究と臺灣話文運動と

2100 Liao, Han-ch'en: T'ai-wan yen-yü te hsing-shih ho nei-jung.—*TWWH* 6:3, 1955, 37–42. [The form and import of Taiwanese proverbs.]

廖漢臣：臺灣諺語的形式和內容

2101 Murakami, Yoshihide: Binnango ni okeru Nihongo goi no juyō yōtai.—*TRGH* 119, 1979, 27–43. [The condition of receptiveness of Japanese vocabulary in the South Min dialect.]

村上嘉英：閩南語における日本語語彙の受容樣態

2102 Taiwan Sōtokufu Gakumubu: *Taiwan rigan shūran.*—Taipei: Taiwan Sōtokufu, 1914, 4, 6, 620, (Index) 213, 5 p. [Collection of Taiwanese idioms and proverbs.]/ Classified.

臺灣總督府學務部：臺灣俚諺集覽

2103 Tong, John S.: Taiwanese sociolinguistic profile and bilingual status.—*JCLTA* 5:3, 1970, 119–126.

〔董守綱〕

2104 Wu, Ying-t'ao: *T'ai-wan yen-yü.*—Taipei: T'ai-wan ying-wen, 1975, 12, 747 p. [Taiwanese proverbs.]/ Proverbs, popular sayings, folk songs, puns, etc.

吳瀛濤：臺灣諺語

2105 Yao, Han-ch'iu: Min-nan-yü yü T'ai-wan te li yen.—*TWWH* 28, 1977, 133–143. [The South Min dialect and the idioms and proverbs of Taiwan.]

姚漢秋：閩南語與臺灣的俚諺

15.5.4. Phonetics and Phonology (2106–2126)

2106 Carroll, Thomas: *Some practical notes on the pronunciation of Taiwanese.*—Taichung: Maryknoll Amoy Language School, 1956 (?), 64 p.

2107 Cheng, Liang-wei & Cheng, Hsieh Shu-chüan: *T'ai-wan Fu-chien-hua te yü-yin chieh-kou chi piao-yin fa.*—Taipei: T'ai-wan hsüeh-sheng, 1977, xvii, 220 p. [Phonological structure and Romanization of Taiwanese Hokkien.]

鄭良偉，鄭謝淑娟：臺灣福建話的語音結構及標音法

2108 Cheng, Robert L.: Tone sandhi in Taiwanese.—*Linguistics* 41, 1968, 19–42.

2109 Cheng, Robert L.: Some notes on tone sandhi in Taiwanese.—*Linguistics* 100, 1973, 5–25, 9 tab.

2110 Hsieh, Hsin-i: The psychological reality of tone sandhi rules in Taiwanese.—*Papers from the Ninth Regional Meeting, Chicago Linguistic Society, April 13–15, 1973* (Ed. by Claudia Corum, et al., Chicago, 1973), 489–503, 4 tab.

2111 Huang, Yu-shih: *T'ai-wan shih-wu-yin tz'u-tien.*—Taipei: Nan-shan t'ang, 1972, 572 p. [A Taiwanese dictionary arranged according to the 15 initials of the South Min dialect.]

黃有實：臺灣十五音辭典

2112 Kappart, Gilbertus: Woordboek der Favorlangsche taal.—*Bataviaasch Genootschap van Kunsten en Wetenschappen, Verhandelingen* 18, 1842, 31–488./ Probably the oldest recording of Taiwanese pronunciation.

2113 Li, Paul Jen-kuei: Tones of Taiwanese.—*Concentric* 4, 1966, 55–59.

〔李壬癸〕

2114 Liao, Ch'iu-chung: *The syntactic environments of tone sandhi in Taiwanese.*—Taipei: National Taiwan U., 1971, 62 p./ Unpubl. M.A. thesis.

〔廖秋忠〕

2115 Lin, Shuang-fu: On some aspects of the semantics and tonal behavior of Taiwanese *lai*.—*JCL* 3:2–3, 1975, 108–128.

2116 Lu, Shu-mei: *T'ai-wan Min-nan-yü yin-yün yen-chiu.*—Taipei: Wen-shih-che, 1977, 122 p. [A study of the phonology of the South Min dialect of Taiwan.]

盧淑美：臺灣閩南語音韻研究

2117 Roberts, Thomas H. & Li, Ying-che: Problems in the phonology of the South Min dialect of Taiwan.—*THHP* 5:1, 1963, 95–108; C.S.

〔羅道明，李英哲：臺灣閩南語的音系問題〕

2118 Taiwan Sōtokufu Gakumubu (ed.): *Taiwan jūgoon oyobi jibo shōkai.*—Taipei: Taiwan Sōtokufu Gakumubu, 1896, 38 p.; 1901, rev. ed., 101 p. [A detailed explanation of the fifteen initial sounds and an alphabetization of the Taiwanese dialect.]

臺灣總督府學務部：臺灣十五音及字母詳解

2119 Tung, Chao-hui: The phonology of Taiwanese as spoken in the Kaohsiung area (a sketch).—*STHP* 9, 1964, 195–204, tab.

〔董昭輝：高雄地區臺語語音系統綱要〕

2120 Tung, Chao-hui: The phonological system of Gaoxiong, a Min dialect of Chinese.—*POLA* 2:5, 1968./ Kaohsiung dialect of Taiwan.

2121 Tung, Jeffrey C.H.: Taiwanese tones and Taiwanized Japanese.—*Papers in linguistics in honor of A.A. Hill* (Ed. by Charles T.C. Tang, et al. Taipei: Rainbow Bridge Co., 1972), 179–213.

2122 Wang, Yü-te: Taiwango no seichō.—*CGGG* 1955:8, 3–11. [Tones in Taiwanese.]

王育德：臺灣語の聲調

2123 Wang, Yü-te: Taiwango no on'in taikei.—*TWSN* 2, 1960, 34–38; 3, 37–42, 22; 4, 35–39. [The Taiwanese phonological system.]

王育德：臺灣語の音韻體系

2124 Wang, Yü-te: Bungen'on to hakuwaon to kundoku to.—*TWSN* 16, 1962, 51–54, 63; 18, 50–54; 19, 49–53. [Literary and colloquial readings, and *kun* readings.]
王育德： 文言音と白話音と訓讀と

2125 Weingartner, Fredric F.: *Tones in Taiwanese: An instrumental investigation.*—Taipei: National Taiwan U., 1970, 98 p./ *Phonetica* 24:1, 1971, 58–63, Helen T. Chiang.
〔 温知新： 使用儀器研究臺語的聲調系統〕

2126 Wu, Huai: T'an T'ai-wan chih yü-yin yü tzu-yin.—*HKHP* 5, 1969, 79–116. [Discussion on colloquial and literary pronunciations in Taiwanese.]
吳槐： 談臺灣之語音與字音

15.5.5. Vocabulary (2127–2130)

2127 Lien, Heng: *T'ai-wan-yü tien.*—Taipei: Chung-hua ts'ung-shu, 1957, ii, iv, 152 p.; 1973, repr./ A phonetic index compiled by Liu Chien-jen, appeared in *TPWH* 10:12, 1965, 315–347. [A handbook of Taiwanese vocabulary.]
連橫： 臺灣語典 / 劉建仁：音讀索引

2128 Wang, Yü-te: *Taiwango jōyō goi.*—Tokyo: Eiwa Gogaku shuppan, 1957, xxviii, 475 p./ *RBS* 5, 1959, 536, Li Fang-kuei; *Orbis* 15, 1966, 146, Paul Yang. [Basic vocabulary of Taiwanese.]
王育德： 臺灣語常用語彙

2129 Wang, Yü-te: Taiwango no goi.—*TWSN* 8, 1961, 37–40; 9, 53–56; 11, 32–36. [Vocabulary of Taiwanese.]
王育德： 臺灣語の語彙

15.5.6. Grammar (2130–2141)

2130 Chen, Betty Hsiu-ying: The uses of *ho* in Taiwanese.—*Papers in linguistics in honor of A.A. Hill* (Taipei: Rainbow Bridge Co., 1972), 5–31.

2131 Ch'en, Hui-lung: *Taiwan gohō.*—Taipei: Taiwan Gogakusha, 1934, 6, 4, 9, 14, 402, 2 p. [A grammar of Taiwanese.]
陳輝龍： 臺灣語法

2132 Cheng, Robert L.: Causative constructions in Taiwanese.—*JCL* 2:3, 1974, 279–324.

2133 Cheng, Robert L.: Taiwanese question particles.—*JCL* 5:2, 1977, 153–185.

2134 Cheng, Robert L.: Tense interpretation of four Taiwanese modal verbs.—*Proceedings of Symposium on Chinese Linguistics,* 1977 Linguistic Institute of the Linguistics Society of America (Ed. by Robert L. Cheng, et al.; Taipei: Student Book Co., 1978), 245–266.

2135 Cheng, Robert L.: Taiwanese morphemes in search of Chinese characters. --*JCL* 6:2, 1978, 306–314; C.S.
〔 鄭良偉 ： 用漢字代表臺灣話特殊詞素〕

2136 Huang, Ching-hsing: *Double object construction in Taiwanese.*—Hsinchuang: Fu Jen Catholic U., 1977, iii, 104 p./ Unpubl. M.A. thesis.
〔黃景星：閩南語的雙賓結構〕

2137 Lai, S.H.: *Tagmemics in Taiwanese.*—Hsinchuang: Fu Jen Catholic U., 1971, 58 p./ Unpubl. M.A. thesis.
〔賴信夫〕

2138 Li, Paul Jen-kuei: Two negative markers in Taiwanese.—*BIHP* 43, 1971, 201–220.

2139 Lin, Shuang-fu: *The grammar of disjunctive questions in Taiwanese.*—Chapel Hill: U. of North Carolina, 1974, iii, 243 p./ Unpubl. doc. diss.; *DAI* 35:3713–A; UM 74–26,903; Taipei: Taiwan Students Book Co., 1975, iii, 243 p.
〔 林雙福〕

2140 Lin, Shuang-fu: Reduction of Taiwanese A-not-A questions.—*JCL* 2:1, 1974, 37–78.

2141 Wang, Yü-te: Taiwango no bunpō.—
TWSN 35, 1963, 44–49; 36, 50–63; 37,
39–45. [Taiwanese grammar.]
王育德：臺灣語の文法

15.5.7. Contrastive Studies (2142–2147)

2142 Cheng, Liang-wei: *T'ai-yü yü Kuo-yü
tzu-yin tui-ying kuei-lü te yen-chiu.*—
Taipei: T'ai-wan hsüeh-sheng, 1979, iv,
157 p. [A study of rules for phonetic correspondences between Taiwanese and
Mandarin.]
鄭良偉：臺語與國語字音對應規律的研
究

2143 Hsü, Hui-hao: *Kuo-T'ai yü-hui.*—
Taichung: The Author, 1952, viii, 186 p.
[Mandarin-Taiwanese vocabulary.]/ With
dialogues.
徐輝浩：國臺語彙

2144 Sun, Shu-hui: The phonological systems
of Mandarin and Taiwanese.—*Kao-hsiung
Shih-yüan hsüeh-pao* 4, 1976, 506–567.
〔孫淑惠〕

2145 T'ai-wan sheng Kuo-yü t'ui-hsing wei-
yüan-hui (ed.): *Kuo-T'ai tzu-yin tui-chao
lu.*—Taipei: T'ai-wan sheng Kuo-yü t'ui-
hsing wei-yüan-hui, n. d., 3, 90 p. [A list
of Chinese characters with Mandarin and
Taiwanese pronunciations compared.]
臺灣省國語推行委員會：國臺字音對照
錄

2146 Ts'ai, P'ei-huo: *Kuo-yü Min-yü tui-
chao ch'u-pu hui-hua.*—Taipei: Cheng-
chung, 1976, 158 p. [Beginning Man-
darin-Min dialect conversations.]
蔡培火：國語閩語對照初步會話

2147 Wang, Yü-te: Taiwango to Pekingo no
aida.—*TWSN* 22, 1962, 43–47; 25, 50–
54; 26, 1963, 49–54. [Phonetic correspondences between Taiwanese and Pekinese.]
王育德：臺灣語と北京語の間

15.5.8. Textbooks (2148–2181)

2148 Chang, Yao-t'ang: *Shinsen Taiwango
kyōkasho.*—Taipei: Shinkōdō, 1935, 2
vols., 5, 8, 208; 6, 216 p. [New textbook
for the Taiwanese dialect.]
張耀堂：新撰臺灣語教科書

2149 Ch'en, Hui-hao: *Shih-yung T'ai-yü hui-
hua.*—Panch'iao: Hua-hsing, 1975, 8, 186
p. [Practical Taiwanese conversations.]/
Character text with Chu-yin fu-hao
phonetic symbols.
陳輝浩：實用臺語會話

2150 Ch'en, Lien-huan: *T'ai-yü hui-hua.*—
Taipei: Kuo-yü jih-pao-she, 1941, 5, 78
p. [Taiwanese conversations.]
陳璉環：臺語會話

2151 Hayashi, Kyūzō: *Keisatsu kaiwa hen.*—
Taipei: Taiwan Nichinichi shinpōsha,
1903, 169 p. [Police conversations.]/ Taiwanese-Japanese.
林久三：警察會話篇

2152 Hayashi, Kyūzō: *Nichi-Tai kaiwa shoho.*—Tainan: Hoseidō, 1908, 233 p. [Be-
ginning Japanese-Taiwanese conversations.]
林久三：日臺會話初步

2153 Hayashi, Kyūzō: *Nichi-Tai kaiwan
shinan.*—Takao (Kaohsiung): Yūhōsan,
1909, 552 p. [A guide to Japanese-Taiwanese conversations.]
林久三：日臺會話指南

2154 Hayashi, Kyūzō: *Nichi-Tai kaiwa
nyūmon.*—Tainan: Hayashi Shashinkan,
1911, 6th ed., 2, 2, 282 p. [Elementary
Japanese-Taiwanese conversations.]
林久三：日臺會話入門

2155 Imada, Shukuzō: *Keimujo yō Taiwango
shū.*—Taipei: Shinkōdō shoten, 1929;
1933, rev. ed., 11, 6, 466 p. [Colletced
prison official's Taiwanese.]
今田祝藏：刑務所用臺灣語集

2156 Iwasaki, Keitarō: *Shinsen Nichi-Tai gengoshū.*—Taipei: Shinsen Nichi-Tai gengoshū hakkōjo, 1913, 3, 2, 14, 686 p. [A new Japanese-Taiwanese collection.]/ Pronunciation, conversation with grammatical notes.

岩崎敬太郎：新撰日臺語言集

2157 Iwasaki, Keitarō: *Taiwango ten.*— Taipei: Taiwango ten, 1922, 2nd ed., 5, 9, 140 p. [A handbook of Taiwanese.]

岩崎敬太郎：臺灣語典

2158 Kawai, Sanenaga: *Shinsen jitsuyō Nichi-Tai kaiwa jizai.*—Taipei: Sugita shoten, 1913, 5, 3, 5, 9, 420 p.; 1938, repr. [New practical Japanese-Taiwanese conversations.]/ Grammar, conversation.

川合眞永：新撰實用日臺會話自在

2159 Kawai, Sanenaga: *Shinsen chūkai Nichi-Tai kaiwa dokushū.*—Taipei: Taiwango Tsūshin Kenkyūkai, 1916, 406 p. [New annotated Japanese-Taiwanese conversations self-taught.]

川合眞永：新撰註解日臺會話獨修

2160 Ko, Chek-hoan [Kao, Chi-huan] & Tan, Pang-tin [Ch'en, Pang-chen]: *An introduction to Taiwanese colloquial.*—Taichung: Maryknoll Amoy Language School, 1955, 3 vols., 365 p.; 1960, rev. ed., 2 vols., 732 p./ *Orbis* 9:1, 1960, 181, Paul Yang.

高積煥，陳邦鎮：初步臺語會話及文法

2161 Kumagai, Yoshimasa: *Taiwango no kenkyū.*—Taipei: Taiwan Nihinichi Shinpōsha, 1931, 3, 28, 1187, 9 p. [A study of the Taiwanese dialect.]/ Pronunciation, vocabulary, methods of conversation with grammatical notes.

熊谷良正：臺灣語之研究

2162 Kumagai, Yoshimasa: *Shinsen jitsuyō Nichi-Taigo nyūmon.*—Taipei: Sugita shoten, 1942, 7, 6, 153 p. [New practical introduction to Japanese-Taiwanese conversations.]

熊谷良正：新撰實用日臺語入門

2163 Lin, Shao-hsien: *Shih-yung T'ai-yü hui-hua.*—Taipei: The Author, 1950, 8, 74 p. [Practical Taiwanese conversations.]/ Chinese character text with romanization.

林紹賢：實用臺語會話

2164 Liu, K'o-ming: *Kokugo taiyaku Taigo daisei.*—Taipei: Kokugo taiyaku Taigo daisei hakkōjo, 1916, 5, 3, 12, 399 p. [A comprehensive collection of Taiwanese with Japanese translations.]/ Phonetics, grammar, grammatical exercises, conversations.

劉克明：國語對譯臺語大成

2165 Maryknoll Language School: *Taiwanese colloquial* Vol. I.—Taichung: Maryknoll Language School, n.d., 134, 30 p.

2166 Maryknoll Language School: *Campus talk, a Yale University textbook, in Taiwanese romanization.*—Taichung: Maryknoll Language School, 1963, 39 p.

2167 Maryknoll Language School: *Chinese dialogues, in Taiwanese romanization.*—Taichung: Maryknoll Language School, 1964, v.p.

〔華語對話〕

2168 Maryknoll Language School: *Talks on Chinese culture, a Yale University textbook, in Taiwanese romanization.*—Taichung: Maryknoll Language School, 1964, 256 p.

〔中國文化叢譚〕

2169 Maryknoll Language School: *Chinese dialogues in the Amoy vernacular.*—[Taichung], 1969, xix, 437, 66 p.; illus./ Based on the Yale U. text: *Chinese dialogues.*

〔中國閩南語對話〕

2170 Mizukami, Umehiko: *Nichi-Tai kaiwa daizen.*—Tokyo: Minyūsha, 1896, 348 p. [Comprehensive Japanese-Taiwanese conversations.]

水上梅彦：日臺會話大全

2171 Saso, Michael: *Taiwanese talks on Hsinchu.*—Hsinchu: Chabanel Language Institute, n.d., 36 p.

2172 Sugi, Fusanosuke: *Nichi-Tai kaiwa shinpen.*—Taipei: Hakubundō, 1888; 1900, 5th ed., 2, 24, 6, 281, 33 p. [New Japanese-Taiwanese conversations.]

杉房之助：日臺會話新編

2173 Sugi, Fusanosuke: *Nichi-Tai kaiwa daizen.*—Taipei: Hakubundō, 1902, 3rd ed., 8, 13, 444 p.; Taipei: Shinkōdō, 1937, 23rd ed. [Comprehensive Japanese-Taiwanese conversations.]

杉房之助：日臺會話大全

2174 Taipei Language Institute: *Speak Taiwanese Hokkien.*—Taipei: Taipei Language Institute, Book I, 1965, vii, 326 p., Book II, 1969, 343 p.; Book III, 1969, 150 p.

〔臺北語文學院：臺語會話〕

2175 Taiwan Sōtokufu: *Taiwango kyōkasho.*—Taipei: Mumeikai, 1940, 11, 452 p., tab.; 1944, 11th rev. ed., 6, 213 p., tab. [A Taiwanese dialect textbook.]

臺灣總督府：臺灣語教科書

2176 Taiwan Sōtokufu Senbaikyoku: *Senbaikyoku Taiwango ten.*—Taipei: Taiwan Sōtokufu Senbaikyoku, 1922, 3, 5, 9, 140 p. [Monopoly Bureau's handbook of Taiwanese.]/ Taiwanese-Japanese, with romanization.

臺灣總督府專賣局：專賣局臺灣語典

2177 Tokuyasu, Teruo: *Kokugo taiyaku Taiwango kaiwa.*—Taipei: Taiwan gogaku kenkyūkai, 1942, 4, 4, 2, 2, 6, 8, 303, 3 p. [Japanese-Taiwanese conversations.]

德安輝龍：國語對譯臺灣語會話

2178 Wang, Ts'ai-wei: *Chung-kuo kuang-po kung-szu Min-nan-yü chiao-hsüeh k'open.*—Tainan: T'ai-wan chiao-hui kungpao-she, n.d., 4 vols., 32, 30, 31, 31 p. [China Broadcasting Co. South Min dialect textbook.]

王采薇：中國廣播公司閩南語教學課本

2179 Wang, Yü-te: *Taiwango nyūmon.*—Tokyo: The Author, 1972, 158 p. [Elementary Taiwanese.]/ Conversations and classified vocabulary.

王育德：臺灣語入門

2180 Wu, Su-chu (adapted from Bodman, Nicholas C.): *Spoken Taiwanese.*—Taipei: Inter-University Program for Chinese Language Studies, n.d., 206 p.

2181 Wu, Su-chu: *An introduction to Taiwanese.*—Yung Ziang Press, 1967, 46 p., fold charts.

15.5.9. Dictionaries (2182–2196)

2182 Ch'en, Chia-te: *Hsin i Han-Ying tz'utien.*—Taipei: Liu Pi-kuei, 1970, 1173, (Index) 38 p. [A new Chinese-English dictionary.]/ Taiwanese-English.

陳嘉得：新譯漢英辭典（ 發行者：劉必貴 ）

2183 Embree, L. M.: *A dictionary of Southern Min.*—Hong Kong: Hong Kong Language Institute, 1973, xlvi, 305 p./ *JCL* 7:1, 1979, 120–124, Cornelius C. Kubler.

2184 Higashikata, Takashi: *Tai-Nichi shin jisho.*—Taipei: Taiwan Keisatsu Kyōkai, 1931, 39, 1320, 13 p. [A new Taiwanese-Japanese dictionary.]

東方孝義：臺日新辭書

2185 Hsü, Ch'eng-chang: T'ai-wan Min-nanyü tz'u-tien.—*TWFW* 20:2, 1970, 27–67; 20:4, 69–108; 21:1, 1971, 108–129; 21:2, 128–150; 21:3, 151. [A Taiwan South Min dialect dictionary.]

許成章：臺灣閩南語辭典

2186 Hsü, Ch'eng-chang: Kuan-yü T'ai-wan Min-nan-yü tz'u-tien hui-pien chih pienchi.—*TWFW* 26, 1976, 127–149. [On the compilation of a collection of dictionaries of the Taiwan South Min dialect.]

許成章： 關於臺灣閩南語辭典滙編之編輯

2187 Ko, Chek-hoan & Tan, Pang-tin: *A basic vocabulary for colloquial Taiwanese.*—Taichung: Maryknoll Amoy Language School, 1956, 751 p.

〔 高積煥， 陳邦鎮： 臺灣白話基礎語句 〕

2188 Mackay, George Leslie: *Chinese-Romanized dictionary of the Formosan vernacular.*—Shanghai: Mei-hua shu-kuan, 1891, [not seen].

〔 馬偕：中西字典 〕

2189 Maryknoll Language School: *A basic vocabulary for beginners in Taiwanese.*—Taichung: Maryknoll Language School, 1956, 334 p.

2190 Maryknoll Language School: *Amoy-English dictionary.*—Taichung: Maryknoll Language Service Center, 1976, 946 p./ *JCL* 7:1, 1979, 120–124, Cornelius C. Kubler.

〔 中國閩南語英語字典 〕

2191 Sugi, Fusanosuke: *Nichi-Tai shin jiten.*—Taipei: Nihon Bussan Gōshi Kaisha, 1903, 616 p. [A new Japanese-Taiwanese dictionary.]

杉房之助：日臺新辭典

2192 Taiwan Sōtokufu: *Nichi-Tai dai jiten.*—Taipei: Taiwan Sōtokufu, 1907, 4, 212, 18, 7, 1184, 66, 10, 8, 4 p.; map. [A comprehensive Japanese-Taiwanese dictionary.]

臺灣總督府：日臺大辭典

2193 Taiwan Sōtokufu: *Nichi-Tai shō jiten.*—Tokyo: Dai Nippon Tosho, 1908, 5, 9, 1010 p. [A small Japanese-Taiwanese dictionary.]

臺灣總督府：日臺大辭典

2194 Taiwan Sōtokufu: *Tai-Nichi dai jiten.*—Taipei: Taiwan Sōtokufu, 1932, 2 vols., 10, 677; 2, 1043 p. [A comprehensive Taiwanese-Japanese dictionary.]

臺灣總督府：臺日大辭典

2195 Taiwan Sōtokufu: *Tai-Nichi shō jiten.*—Taipei: Taiwan Sōtokufu, 1932, 1238 p. [A small Taiwanese-Japanese dictionary.]

臺灣總督府：臺日小辭典

2196 Taiwan Sōtokufu: *Shintei Nichi-Tai dai jiten.*—Taipei: Taiwan Sōtokufu, Vol. I, 1938, 10, 1132 p. [A new comprehensive Japanese-Taiwanese dictionary.]

臺灣總督府： 新訂日臺大辭典（上卷）

15.6. Hainan Island (2197–2220)

15.6.1. General Studies (2197–2200)

2197 Feng, Mao-sung: Hai-nan-hua p'in-yin tzu-mu.—*CSTY* 8:85–87, 1929, 57–63. [A phonetic alphabet for the Hainan dialect.]

馮茂松：海南話拼音字母

2198 Gilman, Frank P.: Notes on the Hainanese dialect.—*CR* 19, 1891, 194.

2199 Han, S. Y.: "hainani:z".—*Maître Phonétique* 107, 1957, 13–14. [Hainanese.]

2200 Shibayama, Takenori: *Kainantō.*—Tokyo: Nihon Takushoku Kyōkai, 1942, 5, 180 p./ 37–39: Chinese dialects. [Hainan Island.]

柴山武德：海南島

15.6.2. Haik'ou and Wanning (2201–2203)

2201 Chan, Po-hui: Wan-ning fang-yin kai-shu.—*WHTH* 1958:1, 89–108. [An outline of the phonetics of the Wanning dialect.]

詹伯慧：萬寧方音概述

2202 Chang, Hsien-pao: *Hai-k'ou fang-yen.*—Taipei: National Taiwan U., 1976, 2 vols., 215 p./ Unpubl. M.A. thesis; Phonology, conversation, vocabulary. [The Haik'ou dialect.]

張賢豹：海口方言

2203 Liang, Yu-kang: Hai-nan-tao Hai-k'ou fang-yen chung te hsi-ch'i-yin.—*CKYW* 1958:1, 27–28, 34. [Clicks in the Haik'ou dialect of Hainan Island.]

梁猷剛： 海南島海口方言中的吸氣音

15.6.3. Wench'ang (2204–2220)

15.6.3.1. Phonetics and Phonology (2204–2214)

2204 Chan, Po-hui: Hai-nan fang-yen chung t'ung-i tzu te hsün-tu hsien-hsiang.—*CKYW* 1957:6, back cover. [The phenomena of *'kun* readings' of synonymous characters in the Hainan dialect.]

詹伯慧： 海南方言中同義字的『訓讀』現象

2205   Hashimoto, Mantarō J.: A contribution to the study of Chinese phonology.—*TICOJ* 5, 1960, 25–32./ On Hainanese and Sino-Annamese.

2206   Hashimoto, Mantarō J.: The Bonshio (文昌) dialect of Hainan.—*GK* 38, 1960, 106–135./ *RBS* 6, 1960, 387, Li Fang-kuei.

2207   Hashimoto, Mantarō J.: The phonemic structure of the Bonshio dialect of Hainan. —*GK* 38, 1960, 154–157.

2208   Hashimoto, Mantarō J.: Bilabial and alveolar implosives in a south Chinese dialect.—*ONK* 9, 1961, 255–263.

2209   Hashimoto, Mantarō J.: Kainango no seichō taikei.—*TSGH* 7, 1961, 35–52./ *RBS* 7, 1961, 446, Li Fang-kuei. [The tonemic system of the Hainan dialect.]
橋本萬太郎：海南島の聲調體系

2210   Hashimoto, Mantarō J.: Kainango Bunshō hōgen.—*AAGB* 11, 1976, 65–86. [The Wench'ang dialect of the Hainan language.]
橋本萬太郎：海南語文昌方言

2211   Hashimoto, Mantarō J. & Norman, Jerry L.: *A guide to the Wen-ch'ang and Ting-an dialects.*—Washington, D.C.: Center for Applied Linguistics, n.d., iv, 345 p./ ERIC Microfilm Series, #061854.

2212   Liang, Yu-kang: Hai-nan fang-yen yü-yin chung sheng-mu te t'e-tien.—*Hua-nan shih-yüan hsüeh-pao* 1960:2, 109–144. [Special phonetic features of initials in the Hainan dialect.]
梁猷剛：海南方言語音中聲母的特點

2213   Liang, Yu-kang: Hai-nan fang-yen chung te hou-sai-yin.—*CKYW* 1964:6, 463–465. [Glottal stops in the Hainan dialect.] *RBS* 10, 1964, 471, A. Rygaloff.
梁猷剛：海南方言中的喉塞音

2214   Woon, Wee-lee: A synchronic phonology of Hainan dialect.—*JCL* 7:1, 1979, 65–100; 7:2, 268–302.

15.6.3.2.   Grammar and Textbooks (2215–2220)

2215   Dell, François: Structure du syntagme nominal dans le dialecte Chinois de Hainan.—*CLAO* 2, 1977, 5–29./ Wench'ang dialect.

2216   Katsumata, Yoshihisa: *Nichi-Kaigo shūsei.*—Taipei: Takekoshi Shōten, 1939, 6, 69, 35, 147 p. [A collection of Japanese-Hainanese words and sentences.]/ Conversation, vocabulary, grammar.
勝間田義久：日海語集成

2217   Murakami, Katsudai: *Kainango shoho.* —Taipei: Taiwan Sōtokufu Kanpō Chō-saka, 1922, 2, 2, 310, 10 p. [Introductory Hainanese.]/ Haik'ou dialect.
村上勝太：海南島語初步

2218   Sousa, S.C. de: *A manual of the Hailam colloquial* (Būn-sio dialect).—Singapore: The Government Printing Office, 1903, iii, 84 p.
〔文昌方言〕

2219   Taiwan Nanpō Kyōkai: *Kainantōgo kaiwa.*—Tokyo: Sanseidō, 1941, 2, 2, 3, 6, 4, 237 p., 2 maps. [Japanese-Hainanese conversations.]/ Wench'ang dialect.
臺灣南方協會：海南島語會話

2220   Wang, Chin-hsiu & Ch'en, Shao-tsung: *Jitsuyō sokusei Kainango tokuhon.*—Taipei: Nikkōdō shōkai, 1941, 5, 16, 283 p. [A practical intensive Hainanese dialect reader.]/ Japanese-Hainanese phonetics, vocabulary, conversation.
王錦繡，陳紹宗：實用速成海南語讀本

16. NORTH MIN DIALECTS (2221–2275)

16.1. North Min Dialects in General (2221–2226)

2221 Lin, T'ung-shu: Fu-chou-ch'eng yü-yen chih ch'i-yüan chi ch'i ti-pien.—*Fu-chien wen-hua* 2:11, 1933, 16–22. [The origin and development of the language of the city of Foochow.]

林同鈵：福州城語言之起源及其遞變

2222 Mei, Tsu-lin & Lo, Chieh-jui [Jerry Norman]: Shih lun chi-ko Min-pei fang-yen chung te lai-mu S- sheng-tzu.—*CHHP* 9:1–2, 1971, 96–105. [*CL-* > *S-* in some Northern Min dialects.]

梅祖麟，羅杰瑞：試論幾個閩北方言中的來母S-聲字

2223 Norman, Jerry: A preliminary report on the dialects of Mintung.—*Chi-Lin* 10, 1972, 20–35./ Compares dialects of Futing, Cheyang, Fuan, Ningteh and Foochow.

2224 P'an, Mao-ting & Liang, Yü-chang: T'an-t'an *Han-yü fang-yen kai-yao* Min-pei fang-yen pu-fen te i-hsieh wen-t'i.—*Fu-chien shih-fan hsüeh-yüan hsüeh-pao* 1962:1, 187–193. [A discussion of the section on the North Min dialects in the *Han-yü fang-yen kai-yao* (0146).]

潘茂鼎，梁玉璋：談談『漢語方言概要』閩北方言部分的一些問題

2225 Weng, Kuo-liang: Min-pei fang-yen shu.—*CSTY* 10:110, 1929, 40–44. [Notes on the North Min dialects.]

翁國樑：閩北方言述

2226 Yüan, Chia-hua: Min-pei fang-yen.—*Han-yü fang-yen kai-yao* (0146), Chap. XI. [The North Min dialects.]

袁家驊：閩北方言

16.2. Foochow (2227–2259)

16.2.1. Phonetics and Phonology (2227–2238)

2227 Anonymous: Tonic and vocal modification in the Foochow dialect.—*CR* 8, 1879–1880, 182–187.

2228 Hsü, Yü: *Ch'i-lin pa-yin* te yen-chiu.—*NYHP* 6:2, 1950, 26–36. [A study on *Ch'i-li pa-yin*.]/ Foochow rhyme book.

許鈺：『戚林八音』的研究

2229 Kao, Ming-k'ai: Fu-chou-yü chih yü-ts'ung sheng-mu t'ung-hua.—*YCHP* 33, 1947, 129–144. [The assimilation of initials in polysyllabic words in the Foochow dialect.]

高名凱：福州語之語叢聲母同化

2230 Kao, Yü-chen: Fu-ch'ing fang-yen te sheng-mu lien-tu yin-pien.—*CKYW* 1978: 4, 258–259. [The assimilation of initials in the Fuch'ing dialect.]

高玉振：福清方言的聲母連讀音變

2231 Lan, Ya-hsiu: Fu-chou yin-hsi.—*WSCH* 6, 1953, 241–331, 2 tab. [Phonetic system of the Foochow dialect.]

藍亞秀：福州音系

2232 Li, Ju-lung; Liang, Yü-chang & Ch'en, T'ien-ch'üan: Fu-chou-hua yü-yin yen-pien kai-shuo.—*CKYW* 1979:4, 287–293. [General remarks on the phonetic evolution of the Foochow dialect.]

李如龍，梁玉璋，陳天泉：福州話語音演變概說

2233 Norman, Jerry L.: *A guide to the Foochow dialect.*—Washington, D.C.: Center for Applied Linguistics, n.d., 2 vols., iii, 333 p.

2234 Parker, Edward Harper: Foochow syllabary.—*CR* 9, 1881, 63–82.

2235 T'ao, Yü-min: Min-yin yen-chiu.—*CSTY* 1:4, 1930, 455–470; Peking: K'o-hsüeh, 1956, repr., 26 p., tab. [A study on Foochow phonetics.]

陶燠民：閩音研究

2236 Wang, T'ien-ch'ang: Fu-chou-yü tzu-yin hua-yin te fen-hsi.—*THHP* 7:1, 1965, 101–121; 121: E.S. [An analysis of the spoken and literary pronunciations in the Foochow dialect.]

王天昌：福州語字音話音的分析

2237 Wang, T'ien-ch'ang: Fu-chou-yü li chieh-yin te hun-yao hsien-hsiang.— *THHP* 9:1, 1968, 45–51; 51: E.S. [The phenomenon of confusion of medial vowels in the Foochow dialect.]

王天昌：福州語裏介音的混淆現象

2238 Wang, T'ien-ch'ang: *Fu-chou yü-yin yen-chiu.*—Taipei: Shih-chieh, 1969, 162 p. [A study on Foochow phonetics.]

王天昌：福州語音研究

16.2.2. Vocabulary (2239–2243)

2239 Cheng, Li-i: Fu-chou-hua chung pao-liu hsia-lai te ku-tai yü-tz'u.—*FPC* 4, 1958, 1–9. [Ancient words preserved and passed down in the Foochow dialect.]

鄭立儀：福州話中保留下來的古代語詞

2240 Hsü, Chih-ch'ing: Fu-chou fang-yen tz'u-hui tien-ti.—*FPC* 1, 1958, 130–131. [Notes on the vocabulary of the Foochow dialect.]

徐志清：福州方言詞彙點滴

2241 Kuo, Yü-lin: Fu-chou fang-yen hsiao shih.—*Fu-chien wen-hua* 1:6, 1932, 16–18. [A small collection from the Foochow dialect.]

郭毓麟：福州方言小拾

2242 Parker, Edward Harper: New Foochow colloquial words.—*CR* 7, 1879, 415–418.

2243 Yeh, Ch'ang-ch'ing: Min-hou fang-yen k'ao-cheng.—*Kuo-hsüeh chuan-k'an* 1:1, 1926, 55–58. [Etymological research on the Minhou dialect.]

葉長青：閩侯方言考證

16.2.3. Grammar (2244–2245)

2244 Chen, Leo: Foochow reduplication.— *CHHP* 6:1–2, 1967, 200–214; 214: C.S.

〔陳曉六：福州話裏的疊詞〕

2245 Cheng, Li-i: Fu-chou fang-yen kou-tz'u-fa te t'e-tien.—*FPC* 1, 1958, 132–134. [Special morphological features of the Foochow dialect.]

鄭立儀：福州方言構詞法的特點

16.2.4. Contrastive Studies (2246–2248)

2246 Cheng, Li-i: Fu-chou-yin ho Pei-ching-yin te pi-chiao.—*FPC* 1, 1958, 110–122. [A comparison of Foochow and Peking pronunciations.]

鄭立儀：福州音和北京音的比較

2247 Cheng, Li-i: Fu-chou fang-yen ho P'u-t'ung-hua te tz'u-hui pi-chiao.—*FPC* 1, 1958, 122–130. [A lexical comparison of the Foochow dialect and the Common Language.]

鄭立儀：福州方言和普通話的詞彙比較

2248 Kao, Ming-k'ai & Lin, T'ao: *Fu-chou-jen tsen-yang hsüeh-hsi P'u-t'ung-hua.*—Peking: Wen-hua chiao-yü, 1956, 112 p./ *YWHH* 1956:9, 39–40, Meng Hsiang. [How a Foochow dialect speaker should learn the Common Language.]

高名凱，林燾：福州人怎樣學習普通話 / 夢湘評

16.2.5. Textbooks (2249–2255)

2249 Baldwin, C.C.: *A manual of the Foochow dialect.*—Foochow: Methodist Episcopal Press, 1871, viii, 256 p.; Foochow: Foochow College Press, 1909, rev. & enl. ed., iii, 264 p.

〔摩嘉立：榕腔初學撮要〕

2250 Bunkyōkyoku Gakumuka: *Nichi-Bin kaiwa.*—Taipei: Taiwan Sōtokufu Bunkyōkyoku, 1938, 8, 319 p. [Japanese-Foochow conversations.]

文教局學務課：日閩會話

2251 Champness, C.S. & Champness, A.E.: *A manual of the Foochow dialect in twenty lessons.*—Foochow: (?), 1904, 147 p.

2252 Chen, Leo & Norman, Jerry L.: *An introduction to the Foochow dialect.*—San Francisco: San Francisco State College, 1965, iv, v.p./ 15 lessons with Foochow narrative texts.

〔陳立鷗，羅杰瑞：閩語入門（中文本）〕

2253 Corbató, Hermenegildo: *Manual of the Foochow dialect.*—Los Angeles: U. of California, L.A., 1945, rev. by Paul P. Wiant, xviii, 206 p.

2254 Kitahara, Kishio, et al.: *Nikka taiyaku Fukushūgo.*—Taipei: Takekoshi Shōten, 1940, 2, 4, 326 p. [A Japanese-Chinese Foochow dialect lessons.]/ Pronunciation, vocabulary, conversation.
北原癸巳男等：日華對譯福州話

2255 White, Moses Clark: *The Chinese language spoken at Fuh Chau.*—Concord, N.H.: Missionary Society of the Methodist General Biblical Institute, 1856, 44 p.

16.2.6. Dictionaries (2256–2259)

2256 Chen, Leo & Norman, Jerry L.: *Foochow-English glossary.*—San Francisco: San Francisco State College, 1965, n.p.
陳立鷗，羅杰瑞合編：閩英辭典

2257 Chen, Leo: *Foochow-English, English-Foochow glossary.*—San Francisco: Asian Language Publication, 1969, iv, 260; 365 p.
陳立鷗：英語—福州語，福州語—英語辭典

2258 Maclay, Robert Samuel & Baldwin, C.C.: *An alphabetic dictionary of the Chinese language in the Foochow dialect.*—Foochow: Methodist Episcopal Mission Press, 1870, xxiv, 1107 p.; 1898, rev. ed., xx, 754 p./ *ChinRec* 3, 1870, 132–134, Justus Doolittle.

2259 Maclay, R.S. & Baldwin, C.C.: *Dictionary of the Foochow dialect.*—Shanghai: The Presbyterian Mission Press, 1929, rev. & enl. by Leger, Samuel H., xxvii, 1874 p.

16.3. Kienow, Kienyang, and Shaowu (2260–2266)

16.3.1. Kienow (2260–2261)

2260 Huang, Tien-ch'eng: Chien-ou fang-yen ch'u-t'an.—*HMTH* 1957:1, 255–299. [A

preliminary investigation of the Kienow dialect.]
黃典誠：建甌方言初探

2261 Norman, Jerry L.: Phonology of the Kienow dialect.—*AAGB* 12, 1976, 171–190.

16.3.2. Kienyang (2262–2263)

2262 Norman, Jerry L.: *The Kienyang dialect of Fukien.*—Berkeley: U. of California, 1969, v, 349 p.; 345–349: Bibliography./ Unpubl. doc. diss.; *DA* 30: 4439–A; UM 70–6181.

2263 Norman, Jerry L.: *A guide to the Chien-yang dialect.*—Washington, D.C.: Center for Applied Linguistics, n.d., 3 vols., iv, 390 p./ ERIC Microfilm Series, #061853.

16.3.3. Shaowu (2264–2266)

2264 Chang, Ching-ch'i, et al.: Shao-wu fang-yen.—*Ch'ung tsuan Shao-wu fu-chih* (1877 ed.), 3 p.; *Chung-kuo fang-chih so-lu fang-yen hui-pien* (0454), 9:61–63. [The Shaowu dialect.]
張景祁等：邵武方言——『重纂邵武府志』

2265 Hsiung, Cheng-hui: Kuang-tse, Shao-wu-hua li te ku ju-sheng tzu.—*CKYW* 1960:10, 310. [Ancient *ju* tone words in the Kuangtse and Shaowu dialects.]
熊正輝：光澤、邵武話裏的古入聲字

2266 Norman, Jerry L.: The Shaowu dialect.—*Orbis* 23:2, 1974, 328–334.

16.4. P'ut'ien and Hsienyu (2267–2275)

16.4.1. P'ut'ien (2267–2271)

2267 Huang, Ching-hu: P'u-t'ien-hua te liang-tzu lien-hsü yin-pien.—*CKYW* 1962:11, 510–516./ *RBS* 8, 1962, 470, A. Rygaloff. [Consonantal sandhi in di-syllabic words of the P'ut'ien dialect.]
黃景湖：莆田話的兩字連續音變

2268   Huang, Chün-t'an: Min-chung fang-yen ho-yü ku-yin k'ao.—*KHTK* 15, 1945, 22–27. [A study of the agreement of the Central Min dialects with ancient phonology.]
黃君坦：閩中方言合于古音考

2269   Lin, Wen-chin: P'u-t'ien-hua te ming-tz'u tz'u-wei gia.—*CKYW* 1957:12, 35. [The noun suffix *gia,* etc. in the P'ut'ien dialect.]
林文金：莆田話的名詞詞尾『子』

2270   Lin, Wen-chin: P'u-t'ien-hua te shih-tz'u ch'ung-tieh hsing-shih.—*FPC* 1, 1958, 136–139. [The plerematic reduplicative forms in the P'ut'ien dialect.]
林文金：莆田話的實詞重叠形式

2271   Lin, Wen-chin: P'u-t'ien-hua te wu-liang tz'u.—*CKYW* 1979:6, 445–450. [Object classifiers in the P'ut'ien dialect.]
林文金：莆田話的物量詞

16.4.2.   Hsienyu (2272–2275)

2272   Tai, Ch'ing-hsia: Min-yü Hsien-yu-hua te pien-tiao kuei-lü.—*CKYW* 1958:10,

485, 487. [The rules for tone sandhi in the Hsienyu dialect of Min.]
戴慶厦：閩語仙游話的變調規律

2273   Tai, Ch'ing-hsia & Wu, Ch'i-lu: Hsien-yu-hua te yü-yin.—*FPC* 1, 1958, 134–136. [The phonology of the Hsienyu dialect.]
戴慶厦，吳啓祿：仙游話的語音

2274   Tai, Ch'ing-hsia & Wu, Ch'i-lu: Min-yü Hsien-yu-hua te wen-pai i-tu.—*CKYW* 1962:8–9, 393–398./ *RBS* 8, 1962, 469, K. Kaden. [Literary and colloquial pronunciations in the Hsienyu dialect of Min.]
戴慶厦，吳啓祿：閩語仙游話的文白異讀

2275   Wu, Ch'i-lu & Tai, Ch'ing-hsia: Min-yü Hsien-yu-hua te yin-pien kuei-lü.—*CKYW* 1961:1, 25–27. [The rules for sound changes in the Hsienyu dialect of Min.]
吳啓祿，戴慶厦：閩語仙游話的音變規律

LIST OF CHINESE AND JAPANESE PUBLISHERS

Ajia-Afurika gengo bunka kenkyūjo.　Tokyo.
アジア・アフリカ言語文化研究所　東京

An-hui jen-min—ch'u-pan-she.　Hofei.
安徽人民出版社　合肥

Bunkyūdō.　Tokyo.
文求堂　東京

Ch'an-shan shu-chü.　Canton (?).
禪山書局　廣州（？）

Cheng-chih ta-hsüeh Chung-wen yen-chiu-so.
Taipei.
政治大學中文研究所　臺北

Cheng-chung — shu-chü.　Shanghai,　Chungking, Taipei.
正中書局　上海，重慶，臺北

Cheng-yu—ch'u-pan-she.　Taipei.
正友出版社　臺北

Chi-lin jen-min—ch'u-pan-she.　Ch'angch'un.
吉林人民出版社　長春

Ch'i-lu ta-hsüeh Kuo-hsüeh yen-chiu-so.　Chinan.
齊魯大學國學研究所　濟南

Chiang-su jen-min—ch'u-pan-she.　Nanking.
江蘇人民出版社　南京

Chin-hsüeh shu-chü.　Taipei.
進學書局　臺北

Ch'ing-hua hsüeh-hsiao yen-chiu-yüan.　Peking.
清華學校研究院　北京

Ch'ing-hua hsüeh-pao-she.　Taipei.
清華學報社　臺北

Ch'iu-chin shu-wu.　Shanghai.
求進書屋　上海

Chu-i ch'u-pan-she.　Hsinchu.
竹一出版社　新竹

Chūgoku gogaku kenkyūkai.　Tokyo.
中國語學研究會　東京

Chün-te-ch'ang nan-chih yin-shua-chü.　Tsingtao.
俊德昌南紙印刷局　青島

Ch'un-ming—ch'u-pan-she.　Shanghai.
春明出版社　上海

Chung-hua—shu-chü.　Shanghai, Peking, Hong
Kong, Taipei.
中華書局　上海，北京，香港，臺北

Chung-hua ts'ung-shu—pien shen wei-yüan-hui.
Taipei.
中華叢書編審委員會　臺北

Chung-hua t'u-shu-kuan hsieh-hui.　Peking.
中華圖書館協會　北京

Chung-hua wen-hua—ch'u-pan shih-yeh wei-
yüan-hui.　Shanghai, Taipei.
中華文化出版事業委員會　上海，臺北

Chung-kuo ta tz'u-tien pien-tsuan-ch'u. Peking.
中國大辭典編纂處　北京

Chung-kuo yü-wen yüeh-k'an-she.　Taipei.
中國語文月刊社　臺北

Chung-ting wen-hua.　Taipei.

鐘鼎文化　臺北

Chung-wen ta-hsüeh Chung-kuo yü-yen wen-
hsüeh-hsi.　Hong Kong.
中文大學中國語言文學系　香港

Ch'ung-cheng tsung-hui.　Hong Kong.
崇正總會　香港

Ch'ung-ch'ing jen-min—ch'u-pan-she.　Chungking.
重慶人民出版社　重慶

Ch'ung-wen—shu-tien.　Hong Kong.
崇文書店　香港

Dai Nippon tosho—kabushiki kaisha. Tokyo.
大日本圖書株式會社　東京

Daitō shuppansha. Tokyo.
大東出版社　東京

Dōshisha daigaku. Kyoto.
同志社大學　京都

Eiwa gogaku shuppan. Tokyo.
永和語學出版　東京

Erh-t'ung—shu-chü. Shanghai.
兒童書局　上海

Fu-chien jen-min—ch'u-pan-she. Foochow.
福建人民出版社　福州

Fu-hsing shu-chü. Canton (?).
復興書局　廣州（？）

Fu-lun-she. Canton.
扶輪社　廣州

Fukudai kōshi. Taipei.
福大公司　臺北

Gaigo gakuin shuppansha. Tokyo.
外語學院出版社　東京

Gaimushō Jōhōbu. Tokyo.
外務省情報部　東京

Hakubundō. Taipei.
博文堂　臺北

Han-hui lou. Shanghai.
涵暉樓　上海

Han-lin shu-chü. Nant'ung.
翰林書局　南通

Harada Shanhai shiten. Shanghai.
原田上海支店　上海

Harima shobō. Tokyo.
播磨書房　東京

Hayashi shashinkan. Tainan.
林寫眞館　臺南

Heibonsha. Tokyo.
平凡社　東京

Ho-pei jen-min—ch'u-pan-she. Paoting, Tientsin.
河北人民出版社　保定，天津

Hōseidō. Taipei.
補生堂　臺北

Hsi-shan shu-ts'ang. Hsingning.
希山書藏　興寧

Hsiang-kang chiao-yü—ch'u-pan-she. Hong Kong.
香港教育出版社　香港

Hsiang-kang Chung-wen ta-hsüeh. Shatin, N.T., Hong Kong.
香港中文大學　香港新界沙田

Hsiang-kang P'u-t'ung-hua yen-hsi-she. Hong Kong.
香港普通話研習社　香港

Hsin chih-shih—ch'u-pan-she. Shanghai.
新知識出版社　上海

Hsin min-chu—ch'u-pan-she. Hong Kong.
新民主出版社　香港

Hu-nan jen-min—ch'u-pan-she. Ch'angsha.
湖南人民出版社　長沙

Hu-pei jen-min—ch'u-pan-she. Wuhan.
湖北人民出版社　武漢

Hua-ch'iao yü-wen—ch'u-pan-she. Hong Kong.
華僑語文出版社　香港

Hua-hsing—ch'u-pan-she. Panch'iao.
華星出版社　板橋

Hua-nan jen-min—ch'u-pan-she. Canton.
華南人民出版社　廣州

Hua-nan shih-fan hsüeh-yüan. Canton.
華南師範學院　廣州

Hui-t'ung shu-tien. Hong Kong.
滙通書店　香港

Hui-wen t'ang—shu-chü. Shanghai.
會文堂書局　上海

Hung-yeh shu-chü.　Hong Kong.
宏業書局　香港

Huo-shih ch'u-pan kung-szu.　Hong Kong.
霍氏出版公司　香港

I-wen—yin-shu-kuan.　Taipei.
藝文印書館　臺北

Iwanami shoten.　Tokyo.
岩波書店　東京

Jen-min—ch'u-pan-she.　Peking.
人民出版社　北京

K'ai-ming—shu-tien.　Shanghai, Peking,
　Taipei.
開明書店　上海，北京，臺北

Kazama Shobō.　Tokyo.
風間書房　東京

Kenkyūsha.　Tokyo.
研究社　東京

K'o-hsüeh—ch'u-pan-she.　Peking.
科學出版社　北京

Kōbe Gaikokugo daigaku.　Kobe.
神戸外國語大學　神戸

Kōbeshi Gaikokugo daigaku Chūgokugaku
　kenkyūshitsu.　Kobe.
神戸市外國語大學中國學研究室　神戸

Kokugo taiyaku Taigo daisei hakkōjo.　Taipei.
國語對譯臺語大成發行所　臺北

Kōnan shoin.　Tokyo.
江南書院　東京

Kōseikan.　Tokyo.
光生館　東京

Kuang-ch'i—ch'u-pan-she.　Taichung.
光啓出版社　臺中

Kuang-t'ai shu-chü.　Hong Kong.
廣泰書局　香港

Kuang-tung jen-min—ch'u-pan-she.　Canton.
廣東人民出版社　廣州

Kuang-wen—shu-chü.　Taipei.
廣文書局　臺北

Kuang-wen t'u-shu kung-szu.　Hong Kong.
廣文圖書公司　香港

Kuei-chou jen-min—ch'u-pan-she.　Kweiyang.
貴州人民出版社　貴陽

Kuo-li Chung-yang t'u-shu-kuan.　Taipei.
國立中央圖書館　臺北

Kuo-yü jih-pao-she.　Taipei.
國語日報社　臺北

Kuo-yü t'ui-hsing wei-yüan-hui.　Peiping.
國語推行委員會　北平

Kyōjinsha.　Osaka.
巧人社　大阪

Kyōto daigaku Chūgoku gobungaku
　kenkyūshitsu.　Kyoto.
京都大學中國語文學研究室　京都

Kyōto daigaku Jinbunkagaku kenkyūjo.　Kyoto.
京都大學人文科學研究所　京都

Lai-hsün-ko shu-tien.　Peking.
來薰閣書店　北京

Li-hsing—ch'u-pan-she.　Soochow.
力行出版社　蘇州

Lung-men shu-tien.　Hong Kong.
龍門書店　香港

Mei-hua shu-kuan.　Shanghai.
美華書館　上海

Mei-shu kung-i chih-pan-she.　Shanghai.
美術工藝製版社　上海

Miao-yu Chung-yüan tsa-chih-she.　Miaoli.
苗友中原雜誌社　苗栗

Min'yūsha.　Tokyo.
民友社　東京

Mumeikai.　Taipei.
無名會　臺北

Nan-feng shu-chü.　Tokyo.
南風書局　東京

Nan-k'ai ta-hsüeh. Tientsin.
南開大學　天津

Nan-shan-t'ang—ch'u-pan-she. Taipei.
南山堂出版社　臺北

Nihon bussan gōshi kaisha. Taipei.
日本物產合資會社　臺北

Nihon gakujutsu kaigi. Tokyo.
日本學術會議　東京

Nihon gakujutsu shinkōkai. Tokyo.
日本學術振興會　東京

Nihon takushoku Kyōkai. Tokyo.
日本拓殖協會　東京

Nihondō. Shanghai.
日本堂　上海

Nikkōdō—shōkai. Taipei.
日光堂商會　臺北

Okamura shobō. Tokyo.
岡村書房　東京

Ōsakaya shoten. Tokyo.
大阪屋書店　東京

Ōsakayago shoten. Tokyo.
大阪屋號書店　東京

Oyasato kenkyūjo. Tenri.
おやさと研究所　天理

Saika shorin. Nagoya.
栞華書林　名古屋

San-jen hsing—ch'u-pan-she. Taipei.
三人行出版社　臺北

San-min—shu-chü. Taipei.
三民書局　臺北

San-t'ung shu-chü. Shanghai.
三通書局　上海

Sanseidō. Tokyo.
三省堂　東京

Shan-hsi jen-min—ch'u-pan-she. Sian.
陝西人民出版社　西安

Shan-tung jen-min—ch'u-pan-she. Chinan.
山東人民出版社　濟南

Shan-tung yin-shua-chü. Chinan.
山東印刷局　濟南

Shang-hai chiao-yü—ch'u-pan-she. Shanghai.
上海教育出版社　上海

Shang-hai shu-chü. Hong Kong.
上海書局　香港

Shang-wu—yin-shu-kuan. Shanghai, Peking,
  Hong Kong, Taipei.
商務印書館　上海，北京，香港，臺北

She-hui—ch'u-pan-she. Shanghai.
社會出版社　上海

Shih-chieh—shu-chü. Shanghai, Hong Kong,
  Taipei, Singapore.
世界書局　上海，香港，臺北，新加坡

Shih-fan ta-hsüeh. Peking.
師範大學　北京

Shih-huo—ch'u-pan-she. Taipei.
食貨出版社　臺北

Shih-tai—ch'u-pan-she. Shanghai, Peking.
時代出版社　上海，北京

Shinchikushū keisatsu bunko. Hsinchu.
新竹州警察文庫　新竹

Shinkōdō—shoten. Taipei.
新高堂書店　臺北

Shinsen Nichi-Tai gengoshū hakkōjo. Taipei.
新撰日臺言語集發行所　臺北

Shiseidō shoten. Shanghai.
至誠堂書店　上海

Shōsuidō shoten. Shanghai.
松翠堂書店　上海

Shōzankaku. Osaka.
象山閣　大阪

Shubigunmin seifubu. Tsingtao.
守備軍民政府部　青島

Shun'yōdō. Tokyo.
春陽堂　東京

Sōbunsha. Tokyo.
創文社　東京

Su-chou chu-yin fu-hao t'ui-hsing-hui. Soochow.
蘇州注音符號推行會　蘇州

Sugita shoten. Taipei.
杉田書店　臺北

Szu-ming-t'ang. Hankow.
思明堂　漢口

Ta Chung-kuo—t'u-shu kung-szu. Taipei.
大中國圖書公司　臺北

Ta-t'ung yin-shua-she. Chiaohsien.
大同印刷社　膠縣

T'ai-hsing—shu-chü. Hong Kong.
泰興書局　香港

T'ai-lien kuo-feng ch'u-pan-she. Taipei.
臺聯國風出版社　臺北

T'ai-pei wen-hsien wei-yüan-hui. Taipei.
臺北文獻委員會　臺北

T'ai-wan chiao-hui kung-pao-she. Tainan.
臺灣教會公報社　臺南

T'ai-wan hsin-sheng-pao-she. Taipei.
臺灣新生報社　臺北

T'ai-wan hsüeh-sheng—shu-chü. Taipei.
臺灣學生書局　臺北

T'ai-wan sheng-cheng-fu hsin-wen-ch'u. Taichung.
臺灣省政府新聞處　臺中

T'ai-wan-sheng Kuo-yü t'ui-hsing wei-yüan-hui.
Taipei.
臺灣省國語推行委員會　臺北

T'ai-wan ta-hsüeh Chung-wen yen-chiu-so.
Taipei.
臺灣大學中文研究所　臺北

T'ai-wan ta-hsüeh wen-hsüeh-yüan. Taipei.
臺灣大學文學院　臺北

T'ai-wan wen-hsien—wei-yüan-hui. Taipei.
臺灣文獻委員會　臺北

T'ai-wan ying-wen—ch'u-pan-she. Taipei.
臺灣英文出版社　臺北

Taishūkan. Tokyo.
大修館　東京

Taiwan gogaku kenkyūkai. Taipei.
臺灣語學研究會　臺北

Taiwan gogakusha. Taipei.
臺灣語學社　臺北

Taiwan hōsō kyōkai. Taipei.
臺灣放送協會　臺北

Taiwan keisatsu kyōkai. Taipei.
臺灣警察協會　臺北

Taiwan Nichinichi shinpōsha. Taipei.
臺灣日日新報社　臺北

Taiwan sōtokufu. Taipei.
臺灣總督府　臺北

Taiwan sōtokufu bunkyōkyoku. Taipei.
臺灣總督府文教局　臺北

Taiwan sōtokufu gakumubu. Taipei.
臺灣總督府學務部　臺北

Taiwan sōtokufu kanpō chōsaka. Taipei.
臺灣總督府官房調查課　臺北

Taiwan sōtokufu senbaikyoku. Taipei.
臺灣總督府專賣局　臺北

Taiwangoten hakkōjo. Taipei.
臺灣語典發行所　臺北

Taiwango tsūshin kenkyūkai. Taipei.
臺灣語通信研究會　臺北

Takei shobō. Taipei.
竹井書房　臺北

Takekoshi shōten. Taipei.
竹腰商店　臺北

Teikoku shoin. Tokyo.
帝國書院　東京

Tenzan shoten. Nagoya.
天山書店　名古屋

Tenzan shuppansha. Nagoya.
天山出版社　名古屋

T'ien-ch'eng-ch'ien-chi nan-chih tien. Chinan.
天成謙記南紙店　濟南

T'ien-chin jen-min—ch'u-pan-she. Tientsin.
天津人民出版社　天津

T'ien-i—ch'u-pan-she. Taipei.
天一出版社　臺北

Tōei gakkō. Swatow.
東瀛學校　汕頭

Tōhō gakkai. Tokyo.
東方學會　東京

Tōkaidō. Tokyo.
東海堂　東京

Tōkyō gaigokugo daigaku. Tokyo.
東京外國語大學　東京

Torii Hisayasu kyōju kakō kinenkai. Tenri.
鳥居久靖教授華甲紀念會　天理

Tōto shoseki—kabushiki kaisha. Taipei.
東都書籍株式會社　臺北

Tso-hsin-t'ang. Shanghai.
作新堂　上海

Tung-fang jih-pao-she. Canton.
東方日報社　廣州

Tung-fang—shu-tien. Shanghai.
東方書店　上海

Tung-fang wen-hua kung-ying-she. Taipei.
東方文化供應社　臺北

Tung-Ya t'ung-wen shu-yüan. Shanghai.
東亞同文書院　上海

T'ung-su tu-wu—ch'u-pan-she. Shanghai.
通俗讀物出版社　上海

Wan-li—shu-tien. Hong Kong.
萬里書店　香港

Wang Shou-ching (Mrs. Tung T'ung-ho).
    Taipei.
王守京　臺北

Waseda daigaku gogaku kyōiku kenkyūjo.
    Tokyo.
早稻田大學語學教育研究所　東京

Wen-fang ch'u-pan-she. Hong Kong.
文放出版社　香港

Wen-hsing—shu-chü. Taipei.
文星書局　臺北

Wen-hua chiao-yü—ch'u-pan-she. Shanghai,
    Peking.
文化教育出版社　上海，北京

Wen-i hsüeh-she. Meishanhsiang.
文藝學社　梅山鄉

Wen-ming shang-wu shu-chü. Swatow.
文明商務書局　汕頭

Wen-shih-che—ch'u-pan-she. Taipei.
文史哲出版社　臺北

Wen-tzu kai-ko—ch'u-pan-she. Peking.
文字改革出版社　北京

Wu-kuei-t'ang. Canton.
五桂堂　廣州

Wu-kuei-t'ang shu-chü. Hong Kong.
五桂堂書局　香港

Yang-ho shu-chü. Tungkuan.
養和書局　東莞

Yokohama shiritsu daigaku. Yokohama.
橫濱市立大學　橫濱

Yoshimura shōkai. Taipei.
吉村商會　臺北

Yu-shih wen-hua shih-yeh kung-szu. Taipei.
幼獅文化事業公司　臺北

Yu-wen shu-wu. Hong Kong.
右文書屋　香港

Yüan-yang wen-hua kung-szu. Singapore.
遠洋文化公司　新加坡

Yuhōsan. Kaohsiung (Takao).
又鳳山　高雄

Yün-hsüan ch'u-pan-she. Shanghai.
雲軒出版社　上海

Yün-nan jen-min—ch'u-pan-she. Kunming.
雲南人民出版社　昆明

ROMANIZED INDEX OF AUTHORS

A. P.   1057

Abe, Tadashi   安倍貞   0795

Ai, Ch'iang   艾羌   0440

Akagi, Osamu   赤木攻   2024

Akimoto, Ichirō   秋元一郎   1374

Alekséev, V.M.   0605

Alleton, V.   0545

Amundsen, Edward   1036

An, Ju-p'an   安汝盤   0745

An-hui-sheng fang-yen tiao-ch'a chih-tao tsu   安徽省方言調查指導組   1008, 1009

Anderson, Olov Bertril   0281, 0302

Anshige, Kamesaburō   安重龜三郎   2057

Ara, Motoi   荒基   1016

Arendt, Carl   0544

Arimoto, Takeshi   有元剛   1410

Arisaka, Hideyo   有坂秀世   0097, 0413, 0803

Arlotto, Anthony   0414

Ashmore, William   2054

Aubazac, Louis   何類思   1543, 1780, 1781, 1782, 1783, 1784

Azuma, Torazō   東寅三   0788, 0845

Bailey, Charles-James N.   0625

Baker, Hugh D.R.   0289, 1568

Baldwin, C.C.   摩嘉立   0551, 2249, 2258, 2259

Ball, James Dyer   1489, 1490, 1675, 1676, 1677, 1822, 1829, 1845, 1846

Ballard, William L.   0173, 0636, 1169, 1170, 1171

Barclay, Thomas   2014

Barnett, K.M.A.   0303

Baron, Stephen P.   0228

Baronsfeather, C.G.S.   1612, 1678

Barrau, Jacques   1591

Bauer, Robert S.   1613

Belt, Walter   皮泰德   1717

Bentley, Charles William   1104

Bernard, Henri   0763

Berval, René de   1753

Bielenstein, Hans   0062

Blandford, F.G.   1976

Blatchford, Charles H.   1560

Bodman, Nicholas C.   包擬古   0384, 2006, 2071, 2180

Bollini, Robert J.   1441

Boltz, William G.   1521, 1544

Bonney, Samuel W.   1679, 1680

Boucher, Henri   0733

Bourgeois, Albert   1225, 1226, 1227, 1231, 1263

Bousack, Christian   0841

Boyle, Elisabeth L.   1681

Bradley, Cornelius Beach   0712, 1593

Bridgman, Elijah Coleman   神治文   1682

Bridie, William   0304

Brosnahan, Irene Teoh   2000

Browning, Larry K.   1645

Bröring, Theodor   卞志一   0804, 0805, 0842

Bruce, R.   1683, 1684

Bugazov, Kh.   1145, 1147

Buhot, Ed.   1085

Bunkyōkyoku Gakumuka   文教局學務課   1685, 2007, 2058, 2250

Campbell, William   甘爲霖   2013

Carroll, Thomas   賀子緘   2106

Cartier, M.   0454

Cartier, S.N. 0341, 0431, 0859, 0983, 1023, 1075, 1166, 1331, 1459

Casey, G. Hugh 祁祖堯 See Robinso, Jack

Castañeda, Benjamin 1623

Caysac, Georges-Philippe 1686

Chabanel Language Institute 1491, 1492

Ch'ai, Jan-chih 柴然之 1048

Chalmers, John 湛約翰 1646, 1785, 1786

Champness, A.E. 2251

Champness, C.S. 2251

Chan, Fong-lam Rosie 陳芳琳 1931

Chan, Jachin Yin-man 1561

Chan, Po-hui 詹伯慧 0258, 0259, 0273, 0483, 1023, 1028, 1030, 1031, 1167, 1624, 1670, 2025, 2039, 2201, 2204

Chan, Yeung-kwong 陳陽光 1687, 1688

Chan, Yuen-yuen Angela 陳婉媛 See Fok, Chan Yuen-yuen 1594

Ch'an, Chan-sin 1595

Chang, Chao 張照 0282

Chang, Chao-chi 張兆基 1964

Chang, Chao-yü 張兆鈺 0846

Chang, Che-sheng 張喆生 0232, 0260, 0856

Chang, Ch'eng-ts'ai 張成材 0935, 0936, 0937, 0944, 0945

Chang, Ch'i-hua 張其華 0374

Chang, Ch'i-huan 張啓煥 0875

Chang, Chia-mao 張家茂 1277

Chang, Ching 張靜 0606

Chang, Ching 張敬 1029

Chang, Ching-ch'i 張景祁 2264

Chang, Ching-su 張景蘇 0575

Chang, Ch'ing-ch'ang 張清常 0955

Chang, Ch'ün 覃羣 0001

Chang, Ch'ün-yen 張羣鷹 0818

Chang, Fen-ch'ien 張奮前 1401

Chang, Hsi-chen 張席珍 0099

Chang, Hsiang-chen 張相臣 0789

Chang, Hsien-pao 張賢豹 2202

Chang, Hsün-ju 張洵如 0642, 0646, 0669, 0686, 0761

Chang, Hui-chih 張撝之 1214

Chang, Hui-ying 張惠英 1299

Chang, Hung-nien 張洪年 1625, 1819

Chang, Jih-sheng 張日昇 1820

Chang, Kun 張琨 0338, 0487, 0526, 1327, 1997

Chang, Kung-kuei 張拱貴 0152, 0249, 0250, 1185, 1304, 1305

Chang, Lien-ch'iang 張鍊強 1626

Chang, Lu 覃輅 0415

Chang, Nien-chuang Ting 1066, 1067

Chang, P'ei-chung 張培中 0949, 0956

Chang, Ping-lin 覃炳麟 0457, 1428

Chang, Sheng-yü 張盛裕 1166, 2029, 2030, 2040

Chang, Shih-lu 張世祿 0114

Chang, Shuang-ch'ing 張雙慶 2065

Chang, Tzu-p'ing 張資平 1647

Chang, Wei-ching 張衛經 0441

Chang, Wei-kang 張爲綱 0332, 0647, 1387, 1391, 1531

Chang, Wei-szu 張維思 1049

Chang, Yao-t'ang 張耀堂 2148

Chang, Yü-hung 張裕宏 2066, 2067

Chang, Yüan-hsiang 張源祥 1689

Chang, Yung-mien 張永綿 0433

Ch'ang-li-hsien hsien-chih pien-tsuan wei-yüan hui, Chung-kuo k'o-hsüeh-yüan yü-yen yen-chiu-so fang-yen tsu 昌黎縣縣志編纂委員會，中國科學院語言研究所方言組 0767

Chao, Chen-chi 趙振紀 0594, 1905

Chao, Chen-to 趙振鐸 0176

Chao, Ch'i 趙琪　0819

Chao, Ch'ien 趙前　0570

Chao, Chün 趙浚　0926, 0932

Chao, Chung-i 趙仲邑　1830

Chao, Hui-hsien 趙輝賢　1300

Chao, Jung-kuang 趙榮光　1690

Chao, Jung-lang 趙榮琅　2096

Chao, Li-ming 趙立明　2084

Chao, Lin-sen 趙林森　0946

Chao, Ping 趙秉　0221

Chao, Ping-hsüan 趙秉璇　0905, 0914

Chao, Po-yü 趙伯愚　1114

Chao, Yüan-jen　See Chao, Yuen Ren

Chao, Yüeh-p'eng 趙月朋　0871, 0872, 0873

Chao, Yuen Ren 趙元任　0063, 0064, 0098,
　0115, 0153, 0174, 0175, 0214, 0223,
　0251, 0297, 0463, 0488, 0494, 0495,
　0519, 0527, 0528, 0529, 0607, 0637,
　0687, 0697, 0698, 0699, 0700, 0770,
　0962, 1003, 1004, 1010, 1029, 1176,
　1273, 1274, 1292, 1297, 1366, 1691,
　1692, 1832, 1833, 1847

Chapman, Tim　1693

Char, Tin-yuke 謝廷玉　See Hsieh, T'ing-yü
　1415

Chavannes, Ed. 沙畹　1268

Chen, Betty Hsiu-ying 陳秀英　2130

Chen, Janey 陳周家齊　0735

Chen, Leo 陳曉六　2244, 2252, 2256, 2257

Chen, Mathew Y. 陳淵泉　0252, 0530

Chen, Shang-ling 甄尚靈　1068

Ch'en, Chang-t'ai 陳章太　1166

Ch'en, Che-san 陳哲三　1522, 1861

Ch'en, Chen-ai 陳眞愛　1429

Ch'en, Ch'eng-yung 陳承融　1344

Ch'en, Chi-wu 陳激悟　1032

Ch'en, Ch'i-sheng 陳祺生　1298

Ch'en, Ch'i-t'ung 陳啓彤　0458

Ch'en, Chia-te 陳嘉得　2182

Ch'en, Chih-liang 陳志良　1215

Ch'en, Chih-wen 陳治文　0688

Ch'en, Chu 陳柱　1850, 1851

Ch'en, Ch'ui-min 陳垂民　1969

Ch'en, Han-ch'ing 陳漢淸　0224

Ch'en, Han-kuang 陳漢光　2068

Ch'en, Hsi-wu 陳錫梧　1834

Ch'en, Hui-hao 陳輝浩　2149

Ch'en, Hui-lung 陳輝龍　2131

Ch'en, Hui-ying 陳慧英　1614, 1627, 1648

Ch'en, Kang 陳剛　0701

Ch'en, K'uei-miao 陳癸森　1089

Ch'en, Li 陳澧　1562

Ch'en, Lien-huan 陳璉環　2150

Ch'en, Pang-chen 陳邦鎭　See Tan, Pang-tin

Ch'en, P'ei-lan 陳培蘭　0820

Ch'en, Po-t'ao 陳伯陶　1823

Ch'en, San-su 陳三蘇　1596, 1628

Ch'en, Shao-ling 陳紹齡　1077

Ch'en, Shao-tsung 陳紹宗　2220

Ch'en, Shih-min 陳世民　0483

Ch'en, Shun-cheng 陳舜政　0825

Ch'en, Sung-mao 陳松茂　1275

Ch'en, Sung-yüan 陳嵩元　1486

Ch'en, T'ieh-pi 陳鐵筆　1694

Ch'en, T'ien-ch'üan 陳天泉　2232

Ch'en, T'ien-fu 陳天福　0875

Ch'en, Tun 陳鈍　0002, 0003, 1545

Ch'en, Tzu-shih 陳子實　0595

Ch'en, Wang-tao 陳望道　0225

Ch'en, Wen-pin 陳文彬　0584, 2085

Ch'en, Yang-kuang 陳陽光　See Chan, Yeung-
　kwong

Ch'en, Yin-k'o 陳寅恪　0402

Ch'en, Yüan-t'an 陳原譚　0496

Ch'en, Yün-tung 陳運棟　1402

Cheng, Chang Shang-fang 鄭張尚芳　1328, 1329, 1330

Cheng, Chao-lin 鄭兆麟　1583, 1587, 1597, 1615, 1629

Cheng, Chien-pai 鄭堅白　0154

Cheng, Chin-chuan 鄭錦全　0561, 1372, 2031

Cheng, Chin-ch'üan　See Cheng, Chin-chuan

Cheng, Hsieh Shu-chüan 鄭謝淑娟　2107

Cheng, I 鄭溢　0875, 1949, 1970

Cheng, Li-i 鄭立儀　2239, 2245, 2246, 2247

Cheng, Liang-wei 鄭艮偉　See Cheng, Robert L.　2107, 2142

Cheng, Robert L.　0226, 0449, 2108, 2109, 2132, 2133, 2134, 2135

Cheng, Susie S.　0497

Cheng, Teresa M.　1563, 1835

Cheng, Yung-pang 鄭永邦　0732, 0733, 0734

Ch'eng, K'ang 程亢　0261, 0670

Cherovenetskii, Tikhon D.　0702

Cheung, Oakman 蔣愛民　1787

Chi-lin ta-hsüeh Chung-wen-hsi fang-yen tiao-ch'a hsiao-tsu 吉林大學中文系方言調查小組 0783

Ch'i, Chih 憩之　0860

Ch'i, T'ieh-hen 齊鐵恨　0596, 0597

Chiang, Ch'eng 江成　0570, 1306

Chiang, Ching-fu 江矜夫　1017

Chiang, Ching-fu 蔣鏡夫　0283

Chiang, Helen T. 蔣田雲　1982, 1983, 2125

Chiang, Hsi-wen 蔣希文　0857, 0858, 0859

Chiang, Ju-lin 蔣儒林　2032, 2033

Chiang, Ker-chiu 蔣克秋　1695, 1788, 1978, 2008, 2009

Chiang, Ming 蔣明　0963

Chiang-su-sheng (ho) Shang-hai-shih fang-yen tiao-ch'a chih-tao tsu 江蘇省（和）上海市方言調查指導組　0991, 0992, 1177, 1307, 1308, 1309, 1310, 1311

Chiang, Wen-chung 江文種　1883

Chiang, Yün 蔣韞　1232

Ch'iao, Yen-nung 喬硯農　1616, 1649, 1789

Chien, Hsiang-jung 菅向榮　1493

Ch'ien, Hsiao-pai 錢小柏　1178

Ch'ien, Sung-sheng 錢淞生　1825, 1827, 1839

Ch'ien, Tseng-i 錢曾怡　0821, 0826

Ch'ien, Wen-chin 錢文晉　0986

Chih, Ko 止戈　0771

Ch'ih, P'ing 持平　1906

Childe, Chi-shun Nellie 蔡志純　2055

Chin, K'ai 金凱　1416

Chin, Kuei-shih 金貴士　0777

Chin, P'eng 金鵬　0274

Chin, Shou-shen 金受申　0671

Chin, Yu-ching 金有景　0216, 1293, 1294, 1345, 1392

Ch'in, Chiung-ling 秦炯靈　1025

China Inland Mission　1510

Chinese Language School　1696, 1697

Chinese Linguistics Project　0215

Ching, Yün-ching 荊允敬　0880

Ch'ing, Ch'ing 青青　1073

Chiu, Bien-ming 周辨明　See Jou, Bien-ming 1984

Chiu, I 九一　1115

Chiu, K.G.　2012

Chiu, Rosaline Kwan-wai　0004

Ch'iu, Julie M.H. 邱墨荷　2069

Ch'iu, Li 邱立　1884

Chmielewski, Janusz　0373, 0552, 1476

Chong, Peter　1494

Chou, Ch'ang-chi 周長輯 0262

Chou, Ching-shao 周景紹 0996

Chou, Fa-kao 周法高 0099, 0116, 0117, 0118, 0119, 0416, 0464, 0514, 1885, 1907

Chou, Hsiao-jo 周孝若 0778

Chou, Kan-t'ing 周幹庭 0796, 0797, 0815

Chou, K'ang-hsieh 周康燮 1564

Chou, Ling-wu 周另吾 1376

Chou, Meng-che 周孟哲 0869

Chou, Pien-ming 周辨明 See Chiu, Bien-ming

Chou, T'ing-feng 周廷峯 1698

Chou, Tso-jen 周作人 0192

Chou, Tsu-mo 周祖謨 0100, 0101, 0243, 0359, 0374, 0403, 0410, 0417, 0418, 0434, 0435

Chou, Wen-yü 周文煜 1116

Chou, Wu-chi 周無忌 0265

Chou, Yao-wen 周耀文 2043

Chou, Yin-meng 周因夢 0065, 0066, 0087

Chou, Yu-kuang 周有光 0333, 0465

Chow, Chung-yu Chen 周陳重瑜 1165

Chow, Tse-tsung 周策縱 0411

Chu, Chao-hsiang 朱兆祥 1985, 1986, 1987

Chu, Chauncey C. 屈承熹 0098

Chu, Chien-sung 朱建頌 0224

Chu, Chin-chiang 朱錦江 0964

Chu, Chü-i 朱居易 0442

Chu, Chün 朱濬 0965

Chu, Fang-p'u 朱芳圃 0404

Chu, Feng 朱鋒 2076

Chu, Hsi-tsu 朱希祖 1430

Chu, Hsing 朱星 0176, 0284

Ch'ü, Wan-li 屈萬里 0798

Ch'uan, Fu 船夫 0193

Ch'uan, Wen 川文 0571

Chūgoku Gogaku Kenkyūkai 中國語學研究會 0005, 0006, 0093, 0094

Ch'ui 鎚 0950

Chün, Ch'in 君勤 1316

Ch'un, Hsüeh 春雪 1924

Chung, Ching-wen 鍾敬文 0482

Chung, Lu-sheng 鍾露昇 2070, 2086

Chung-hua shu-chü 中華書局 1790

Chung-kuo k'o-hsüeh-yüan Ho-pei-sheng fen-yüan Yü-yen wen-hsüeh yen-chiu-so 中國科學院河北省分院語言文學研究所 0746, 0748

Chung-kuo k'o-hsüeh-yüan Li-shih yen-chiu-so Ti-i erh so, Pei-ching ta-hsüeh Li-shih-hsi 中國科學院歷史研究所第一二所，北京大學歷史系 0007

Chung-kuo k'o-hsüeh-yüan Yü-yen yen-chiu-so 中國科學院語言研究所 0008, 0009, 0217, 0218, 0531

Chung-kuo wen-tzu kai-ko yen-chiu wei-yüan-hui mi-shu ch'u p'in-yin fang-an kung-tso tsu 中國文字改革研究委員會秘書處拼音方案工作組 0515

Chung-kuo yü-wen pien-chi-pu 中國語文編輯部 0120

Chung-kuo yü-wen tsa-chih she 中國語文雜誌社 0194

Chung-yang yen-chiu yüan 中央研究院 0147

Chwang, Wang Schu-yün 1276

Clarke, Samuel R. 1108

Cohen, Alvin P. 0098

Cohen, Myron L. 1417

Cole, W.B. 0309

Condax, Iovanna Delano 1393

Cooper, F.C. 1233

Corbató, Hermenegildo 2253

Cordier, Georges 1095

Cordier, Henri 0010, 0067, 0068, 0069, 1780, 1781

Corum, Claudia   2110

Couvreur, Séraphin 顧賽芬   0762

Cowles, Roy T.   1701, 1791, 1792

Crawford, T.P.   0285

Crofoot, Jay William   1234

Csongor, B.   0384, 0419, 0508, 0703

Cubbitt, Beryl   1728

Daly, Charles   1702

Darroch, John   0286

Davidson, Jeremy   0075

Davis, D.H.   1235, 1264, 1265

DeGrijs, C.F.M.   2015

De Nino, Generoso   1011

De Pree, Henry P.   2012

Dealy, Kirkman T.   1786

Dean, William   2046

Dell, François   2215

Deloustal, Raymond   1703

Demiéville, Paul 戴密微   0020, 0211, 0339, 0562, 0906

Deniker, Géorge   0608

Désirat, Michel   1186, 1328, 1329, 1959

Devan, Thomas T.   1704, 1705

Dew, James   1681, 1799

Dietz, F.C.   0754

Dil, Anwar S.   0088, 0098

Doherty, W.   1267

Doleželova-Velingerová, M.   0033

Don, A.   1836

Doolittle, Justus   2258

Doty, E.   2010

Douglas, Castairs   2014

Dow, Francis D.M. 竇道明   0887

Down, J.   1495

Downer, G.B.   0384, 0508, 1510, 1792

Dragunov, A.A. 龍果夫   0074, 0703, 0704, 1121, 1122, 1148, 1377

Dragunova, E.N. 龍果娃   1122, 1377

Dragunova, K.   1121

Draye, H.   0070

Drought, James M.   1496

Ducat, Charles M.   0722

Dunn, Robert 伍相國   0011

Duverger, A.   1067

Dy, Carmen J.   2001

Dyer, S.   1932

Ebara, Fumitane 江原文種   2077

Edkins, Joseph 艾約瑟   0705, 0723, 1216, 1228

Egawa, Kingo 江川金五   1706

Egerod, Søren   0102, 0121, 0305, 0507, 1476, 1766, 1925, 1933, 2071

Eitel, Ernest John 歐德理   0734, 1793

Elizarenkova, T. Ia.   0655

Embree, Bernard L.M.   1979, 2183

Enríquez, Colin Metcalfe Dallas   1096

Essen, O. von   0563

Eun, Boo-ki 殷富基   0555

Fabre, Alfred   1546

Fan, Chi-yen 范繼淹   1074, 1075, 1076

Fan, Kung-yüan 樊恭垣   1346

Fang, Chin 方進   0998

Fang, Ch'ing 方青   0146, 0498, 0499

Fang, Hao 方豪   2098

Fang, Mao 方矛   0780

Fang, Pin-kuan 方賓觀   0300

Fang, Shu-chen 方淑珍   1650

Fang, Tsu-kao 方祖高   0155

Fang, Yung 方勇   0459

Feng, Kuo-jui 馮國瑞   0899

Feng, Liang 馮亮   1630

Feng, Lü 馮履 1050

Feng, Mao-sung 馮茂松 0310, 2197

Feng, Szu-yü 馮思禹 1794, 1795

Ferguson, D. 2087

Fielde, Adele Marion 2059, 2062

Firth, J.R. 1367

Foe, George 1236

Fok, Bo-choi 霍寶材 See Huo, Pao-ts'ai

Fok, Chan Yuen-yuen 霍陳婉媛 1598

Forke, Alfred 福克 0556

Forkes, Eduard 0360

Forrest, R.A.D. 富勵士 0508, 0648, 1862, 1908

Francken, J.J.C. 2015

Franke, Herbert 0122, 1792

Frauchiger, F. 1691

Frei, Henri 0609, 0713, 0915

Fu, Ch'ao-yang 傅朝陽 0451, 0452

Fu, Kuo-t'ung 傅國通 1347

Fu, Mao-chi 傅懋勣 0071, 0233, 0610, 0611

Fu, Tso-chih 傅佐之 1331

Fu, Tung-hua 傅東華 0672, 0673

Fu, Wei 傅爲 0779

Fu-chien-sheng Han-yü fang-yen tiao-ch'a chih-tao tsu 福建省漢語方言調查指導組 1909

Fujitsuka, Shōichi 藤塚將一 1565, 1566, 1707, 1708, 1796

Fujiwara, Teruzō 藤原輝三 0747

Fukuchi, Shigeko 福地滋子 0598

Fukuda, Jōnosuke 福田襄之助 0375

Fukunaga, Seiya 福永靜哉 0420

Fukuya, Masao 福屋正男 1709

Fulton, A.A. 1710

Fung, Iu-ting 馮畱亭 1763

García, Otilio 吉愛慈 1515

Gardner, C.S. 0287

Gaspardone, E. 1691

Gaultier, A. 0320

Gaztelu, J. 1086, 1087

Germain, Robert 0612

Gibson, John Campbell 2060, 2063

Gibson, O. 1711

Giet, Franz 齊德芳 0562, 0563, 0806, 0807

Giles, Herbert Allen 翟理斯 0516, 0731, 0736, 2056

Gilman, Frank P. 2198

Glahn, Else 0089, 0102

Goddard, Josiah 2047

Gomes, Luís Gonzaga 高美士 1712, 1797, 1798

Goodrich, C.S. 0020

Gordon, Leonard H.D. 0012

Gotō, Asatarō 後藤朝太郎 0466, 0532, 1910

Gotō, Kimpei 後藤近平 0013

Gottlieb, Immanuel 1793

Gourdin, Édouard-François 1037

Grainer, Adam 1038

Grootaers, L. 0563

Grootaers, Willem A. 賀登崧 0072, 0123, 0124, 0125, 0148, 0209, 0210, 0211, 0212, 0213, 0321, 0467, 0508, 0563, 0573, 0681, 0892, 0893, 0906, 0916, 0917, 1010, 1833, 1922, 1961

Grosvenor, M. Donald 1018

Guernier, R.C. 0613

Haenisch, Erich 1019

Halliday, M.A.K. 0103, 0442, 0444, 1052, 1369

Han, S.Y. 2199

Han, T'ao 寒濤 1356

Hani, Shin'ichi 羽仁新一 0674

Hang-chou ta-hsüeh Chung-wen-hsi fang-yen tiao-ch'a tsu 杭州大學中文系方言調查組 1335

Hao, Chih 郝志 1532

Hao, Hsi-chiung 郝錫炯 1077

Hao, Ning 郝凝 0999

Harada, Matsuzaburō 原田松三郎 1220

Hare, G.T. 1975

Harkin, George F. 1497

Hartman, Lawton M. 哈忒門 0614

Hashimoto, Anne Yue See Hashimoto, Oi-kan Yue 1533, 1588, 1837, 1852

Hashimoto, Mantarō J. 橋本萬太郎 0048, 0163, 0164, 0165, 0166, 0427, 0509, 0533, 0557, 0894, 0900, 0907, 1123, 1124, 1129, 1130, 1179, 1196, 1431, 1442, 1443, 1444, 1453, 1454, 1466, 1584, 1588, 2205, 2206, 2207, 2208, 2209, 2210, 2211

Hashimoto, Oi-kan Yue 橋本余霭芹 1523, 1567, 1568

Hatano, Tarō 波多野太郎 0126, 0453, 0454, 0675, 1020

Hattori, Shirō 服部四郎 0443, 0615, 0649

Haudricourt, André G. 0031, 1477

Hayashi, Kyūzō 林久三 2151, 2152, 2153, 2154

Hayashi, Morimichi 林盛道 1418, 1419, 1445, 1455

Hei-lung-chiang-sheng chiao-yü-t'ing P'u-t'ung-hua t'ui-kuang k'o 黑龍江省教育廳普通話推廣科 0790

Heibonsha 平凡社 0095, 0096

Hemeling, Karl Ernst Georg 0966

Henne, Henry 1469, 1470, 1471

Hernisz, Stanislas 1713

Herrmann, F. 1420

Hess, Emil 1714

Higashikata, Takashi 東方孝義 2184

Higuchi, Yasushi 樋口靖 1953

Hillier, Walter Caine 0731, 0737

Hirai, Katsutoshi 平井勝利 0650, 0689

Hirayama, Hisao 平山久雄 0616, 0638, 0651, 0652, 0676, 0677, 0777, 1176, 1425, 1866, 1988

Ho, Ai-jen 何靄人 0791

Ho, Ch'an-shan 何禪山 1715

Ho, Charles 1236

Ho, Chiung 何炯 1483

Ho, Chung-ying 何仲英 0127, 0177, 0510, 0511

Ho, Keng-feng 何耿豐 1456

Ho, Keng-yung 何耿鏞 1464

Ho, Ko-en 何格恩 0398

Ho, Shu-yung 何叔永 0227

Ho, Teng-sung 賀登崧 See Grootaers, Willem A.

Ho, Tzu-ch'ien 何子乾 1971

Ho, Wei 賀巍 0263, 0865, 0866, 0867, 0868

Ho, Yü 何育 0204

Ho-fei shih-fan hsüeh-yüan fang-yen tiao-ch'a kung-tso tsu 合肥師範學院方言調查工作組 1005

Ho-nan t'ung-chih kuan 河南通志館 0861

Ho-pei Pei-ching shih-fan hsüeh-yüan 河北北京師範學院 0748

Hobson, Benjamin 1716

Hockett, Charles F. 霍凱特 0617, 0690, 0697

Hoh, Fuk-sz 何福嗣 1717

Holzman, D. 0075

Hopkins, L.C. 金璋 0734, 1763

Hoppōgo Kenkyūkai 北方語研究會 0572, 0888

Hou, Chih-chung 侯直忠 0038

Hou, Ching-i 侯精一 0772

Hsia, Hsi-chün 夏錫駿 0275

Hsia, T'ing-yü 夏廷棫 0014

Hsia-men ta-hsüeh Chung-wen-hsi Yü-yen chiao-yen shih 廈門大學中文系語言教研室 1972

Hsiang, Hsi 向熹 1371

Hsiang, Hsia 向夏 0361, 0362

Hsiang, Shih-yüan 項士元 1348

Hsiang-kang Ch'ung-cheng tsung-hui 香港崇正總會 1404

Hsiao, Hui 小蕙 0749

Hsieh, Hsin-i 謝信一 0228, 0585, 2110

Hsieh, Hsiu-wen 謝秀文 0808

Hsieh, Hsüan 謝璿 0334

Hsieh, I-hsien 謝益顯 2034

Hsieh, Kuo-p'ing 謝國平 See Tse, John Kwock-ping 1651

Hsieh, Peter 2012

Hsieh, Shou-mei 謝壽眉 See Tse, Sou-mei

Hsieh, Shu-hsin 謝樹新 1405

Hsieh, Te-hsien 謝德銑 1349

Hsieh, T'ing-yü 謝廷玉 See Char, Tin-yuke 1406

Hsien, Chou 先舟 0576

Hsien-tai Han-yü kuei-fan wen-t'i hsüeh-shu hui-i mi-shu-ch'u 現代漢語規範問題學術會議秘書處 0103

Hsing, Ju-nan 邢儒南 0993

Hsiung, Cheng-hui 熊正輝 1388, 1389, 2265

Hsü, Ch'eng-chang 許成章 1934, 2088, 2089, 2185, 2186

Hsü, Ch'eng-chün 徐承俊 0881, 1097, 1098

Hsü, Chia-jui 徐嘉瑞 0444

Hsü, Chih-ch'ing 徐志清 2240

Hsü, Fu 徐復 1039, 1394

Hsü, Hsü-ch'ang 徐緒昌 0038

Hsü, Hsüeh-hang 許雪航 1718

Hsü, Hua-fang 1674

Hsü, Hui-hao 徐輝浩 2143

Hsü, Jen-fu 徐仁甫 0350

Hsü, Kao-juan 徐高阮 0073

Hsü, Ling-fang 許令芳 1484

Hsü, Pao-hua 許寶華 0523, 0545, 1199, 1200

Hsü, Mei-chen 徐美貞 1314

Hsü, Shih-jung 徐世榮 0234, 0618, 0619, 0653, 0654, 0679

Hsü, Shu-sheng 許樹聲 0938

Hsü, Te-an 徐德庵 1040, 1041

Hsü, T'ieh-sheng 徐鐵生 0979, 1305

Hsü, Tu-jen 許篤仁 1886

Hsü, Wei-han 許威漢 0235

Hsü, Wei-yü 許維遹 0876

Hsü, Yü 許鈺 1867, 2228

Hsü, Yün-ch'iao 許雲樵 0517, 1868

Hsüeh, Feng-sheng 薛鳳生 0827, 0877

Hsüeh, Ju-hua 薛儒華 0828

Hsüeh, Po-an 薛博盦 0941

Hsüeh, Sheng-min 薛生民 0947

Hsüeh, Teng-ch'ing 薛澄清 1869

Hu, Cheng-hua 胡正華 1012

Hu, Chih-fan 胡芷藩 0374

Hu, Ching-fu 胡景福 1446

Hu, Ching-hsiu 胡經修 1399

Hu, Chiung-t'ang 胡炯堂 See Woo, Kwing-tong

Hu, Hsin 胡新 0957

Hu, Ming-yang 胡明陽 1172, 1350, 1351

Hu, Pei-sheng 湖北生 1237

Hu, P'u-an 胡樸安 0128, 1000

Hu, Shuang-pao 胡雙寶 0922

Hu, Wei-hsin 胡維新 1033

Hu, Ying 胡英 0288

Hu, Yün-yü 胡韞玉　See Hu, P'u-an

Hua-nan shih-fan hsüeh-yüan Chung-wen hsi 華南師範學院中文系　2048

Huang, Chao-p'ing 黃肇平　0229

Huang, Chi-yü 黃際遇　2035

Huang, Ch'i 黃綺　0773, 1002

Huang, Chia-chiao 黃家教　0259, 0260, 0483, 1168, 2036

Huang, Chia-chung 黃家忠　1001

Huang, Ching-an 黃敬安　1870, 1887

Huang, Ching-hsing 黃景星　2136

Huang, Ching-hu 黃景湖　2267

Huang, Chün-t'an 黃君坦　2268

Huang, Hsi-ling 黃錫凌　See Wong, Sik-ling 1569

Huang, Li-chen 黃麗貞　0445

Huang, Parker Po-fei 黃伯飛　1599, 1719, 1720, 1792, 1799

Huang, P'ei-hsü 黃培需　0882

Huang, Po-jung 黃伯榮　0932, 1631, 1632, 1652, 1653, 1841, 1842, 1843, 1844

Huang, Tien-ch'eng 黃典誠　0311, 0678, 1534, 1871, 1911, 1912, 2260

Huang, Ting-hua 黃丁華　1954, 1955, 1956, 1957, 1958, 1959

Huang, Tsai-chiang 黃在江　1238

Huang, Yen-p'ei 黃炎培　1301

Huang, Yu-shih 黃有實　2111

Huber, E.　1780, 1781

Hui 灰　0452

Hulsewé, A.F.P.　0384

Hung, Hui-ch'ou 洪惠疇　0436

Huo, Pao-ts'ai 霍寶材　1800

I, Hsi-wu 易熙吾　1112

I, Jen 異人　1360

I, Ting 一丁　0452

I, Tso-lin 易作霖　0980

Iakhontov, S.E.　0074, 0468, 0484

Ianshansin, Iu　1125, 1131, 1132, 1133, 1137, 1146, 1149, 1150, 1154

Ikeuchi, Hiroshi 池內宏　1174

Imada, Shukuzō 今田祝藏　2155

Imault-Huart, Camille　0724

Imazov, M.X.　1138, 1139

Inaba, Teiichirō 稻葉鼎一郎　1239

Ingle, James Addison　1021

Iriya, Yoshitaka 入矢義高　0446

Ishida, Takeo 石田武夫　0049, 1432, 1447, 1448

Itō, Ryōkichi 伊東良吉　1201

Iusurov, Kh.　1147

Iwaki, Hideo 岩城秀夫　1180

Iwasaki, Keitarō 岩崎敬太郎　2156, 2157

Jabłoński, Witold 夏伯龍　0599

Jao, Ping-ts'ai 饒秉才　0264, 0265, 1484

Jao, Ying-ch'i 饒潁奇　1407

Jasmin, Ernest　0322, 0323, 0324, 0325, 0327, 0328, 0329

Jen, Chün-tse 任均澤　0811, 0862

Jen, I-ch'i 任以奇　1617

Jen, Ming 任明　0573

Jen, Tan 任丹　0768

Jo, Ping 若氷　0809

Jones, Daniel　1570, 1571

Joos, Martin　0104

Jörgens, Otto　0843

Jou, Bien-ming 周辨明　See Chiu, Bien-ming 1976

Juhl, Robert A.　0405, 0406, 0407, 0408, 0409

Jung, Chao-tsu 容肇祖　0230

Kachru, B.　2031

Kaden, Klaus　0435, 0688, 1074, 1799, 2274

Kageyama, Takashi 影山巍　1197, 1240, 1241, 1721

Kalimov, A.A.　1126, 1127, 1146, 1151, 1152, 1153

Kallgren, Gerty　0437, 0822

Kam, Tak Him 甘德謙　1633

Kanagae, Nobumitsu 鐘ヶ江信光　0574, 0889

Kanamaru, Kunizō 金丸邦三　1449

Kanō, Mitsunori 狩野充德　0639

Kao, Chi-huan 高積煥　See Ko, Chek-hoan

Kao, Chih-teng 高志澄　1654

Kao, Chih-yung 高志用　1305

Kao, Ching-ch'eng 高景成　0460

Kao, Diana L. 高勵華　1572, 1799

Kao, Kuang-yü 高光宇　1117

Kao, L.　1977

Kao, Ming-k'ai 高名凱　0178, 0179, 0180, 2229, 2248

Kao, Pen-han 高本漢　See Karlgren, Bernhard

Kao, Wen-ta 高文達　0846, 0847, 0848, 0849

Kao, Yü-chen 高玉振　2230

Kappart, Gilbertus　2112

Karapet'iants, A.M.　0655

Karlgren, Bernhard 高本漢　0516, 0518, 0519, 0725, 0752, 0952, 1801

Katō, Toyotaka 加藤豊隆　0784

Katsumata, Yoshihisa 勝間田義久　2216

Kawai, Sanenaga 川合眞永　2158, 2159

Kawauchi, Katsuaki 川內且昭　0015

Kehl, Frank　1547

Keiya, Toshinobu 慶谷壽信　0566, 1013

Kennedy, George A. 金守拙　0489, 1324, 1325, 1326

Kerr, John G.　1722

Killingley, Siew Yue　1634

Kim, Young-kee 金永基　0546

Kindaichi, Kyōsuke 金田一京助　0097

Kita, Seiji 喜多青滋　1242

Kitahara, Kishio 北原癸巳男　2254

Knectges, David R.　0012

Ko, Chek-hoan 高積煥　2160, 2187

Ko, I-ch'ing 葛毅卿　1190

Ko, Te-ch'un 葛德純　1989

Ko, Yu-p'u 葛幼圃　1302

K'o, Ch'iao 柯喬　1357

Koji, Shinpei 小路眞平　0726

Kok, Gerard P.　1719, 1720

Kollecker, C.A.　1450, 1655

Kong, Jae-sŏk 孔在錫　0376

Kōno, Rokurō 河野六郎　0384, 0421, 1187

Kōno, Tōkisu 河野登喜壽　1498

Kōsaka, Jun'ichi 香坂順一　0111, 0422, 0547, 0548, 0960, 1015, 1058, 1173, 1361, 1535, 1600, 1635, 1636, 1637, 1656, 1657, 1723, 1724, 1960

Köster, Hermann　1792

Kratochvíl, Paul　0469, 0620, 0656, 0657, 0658, 0669, 0700, 0706, 0707, 1003, 1071, 2006

Kratochvíl, Pavel　See Kratochvíl, Paul

Kriukov, M.V.　0340

Ku, Chih 古直　1433

Ku, Pai-li 顧百里　See Kubler, Cornelius C.

Ku, Pen-cheng 古本正　0883

Kuang-chou-shih jen-min cheng-fu wen-chiao-chü 廣州市人民政府文教局　1725

Kuang-t'ai shu-chü 廣泰書局　2049

Kuang-tung-sheng fang-yen tiao-ch'a chih-tao tsu 廣東省方言調查指導組　1485, 1658, 2044

K'uang, Ch'ao 匡超　0823

Kubler, Cornelius C. 顧百里　2090, 2183, 2190

Kubota, Kyūsaku 久保田久作　0812

Kühnert, Franz　0967, 0968, 0969, 1202, 1831

Kumagai, Yoshimasa 熊谷良正　2161, 2162

Künstler, M.J.　0383, 0384

K'ung, Chung-nan 孔仲南　1524

Kuo, Ch'ang-ch'eng See Kwok, C.H.

Kuo, Hou-chüeh 郭後覺　1973

Kuo, I-chou 郭一舟　1888

Kuo, Ming-k'un 郭明昆　1913, 1926, 1927

Kuo, P'u 郭璞　0395

Kuo, Shou-hua 郭壽華　1408

Kuo, Yü-lin 郭毓麟　2241

Kuo, Yü-ts'ai 郭豫才　0399

Kuo-li Chung-yang t'u-shu-kuan 國立中央圖書館　0016

Kuo-li T'ai-wan ta-hsüeh t'u-shu-kuan 國立臺灣大學圖書館　0017

Kuraishi, Takeshirō 倉石武四郎　0901, 1278

Kurata, Junnosuke 倉田淳之助　0045

Kusaka, Tsuneo 日下恒夫　0586, 0587, 0691, 0970

Kwok, C.H.　1415

Kwok, Helen 郭張凱倫　1638

Kyōto Daigaku Jinbun Kagaku Kenkyūjo 京都大學人文科學研究所　0018

Lagarrue, Julien　1726

Lai, S.H. 賴信夫　2137

Lamasse, Henri　0326, 0327, 0328, 0329, 0520

Lan, Ya-hsiu 藍亞秀　2096, 2231

Lan-chou ta-hsüeh 蘭州大學　0933

Lanctot, Benoni　1727

Landi, F.　1014

Lanning, G.　1217

Lao, Chün-fang 勞君方　0552

Lapparent, Joseph de 孔道明　1266, 1267

Lau, Sidney 劉錫祥　1728, 1729, 1730, 1731, 1732, 1733, 1734, 1802

Leblanc, Joseph Alexis Marie　1735

Lechler, R. 黎力基　2064

Lee, K.P. 李桂攀　1747

Lee, S.K. 李錫鈞　1736

Lee, Toong-hin　1499

Leger, Samuel H.　2259

Legeza, Irenus László　0289

Legge, James 理雅各　1980

Lehmann, Winfred　0129

Leont'ev, A.A.　1155, 1156

Leslie, Ronald　0075

Léva, René 杜維禮　0895, 0896

Li, Charles N. 李諾　0500, 1799

Li, Ch'en-tung 李辰冬　0501

Li, Chin-hsi 黎錦熙　0195, 0942

Li, Ch'ing-fu 李慶富　0997

Li, Cho-min 李卓敏　1803

Li, Ch'üan-chia 李全佳　1848

Li, F.K.　See Li, Fang-kuei

Li, Fang-kuei 李方桂　0130, 0146, 0265, 0305, 0307, 0346, 0384, 0470, 0471, 0491, 0519, 0563, 0767, 0907, 1004, 1055, 1064, 1070, 1084, 1099, 1102, 1204, 1443, 1474, 1691, 1792, 2026, 2128, 2206, 2209

Li, Fu-ts'ai 李富才　1478

Li, Hsiao-t'ung 厲嘯桐　0105

Li, Hsien-chang 李獻璋　1935, 1950, 1951, 1961, 2099

Li, Hsin-k'uei 李新魁　0264, 2041, 2045

Li, Hsing-chien 李行健　0750

Li, Hsing-chih 李行之　0351

Li, Jen-chien 李人鑑　0982, 0983

Li, Ju-han 李孺韓　1105

Li, Ju-lung 李如龍　1166, 1990, 1991, 2232

Li, Jung 李榮　0196, 0201, 0219, 0220, 0221, 0222, 0236, 0237, 0238, 0253, 0276, 0341, 0621, 0698, 1336, 1337, 1338

Li, Lin-nei Yeung　0714

Li, Ling 李齡　1080

Li, Liu-shun 李流順　0768

Li, Mao-hsiang 李茂詳　0312

Li, Paul Jen-kuei 李壬癸　2113, 2138

Li, P'ei-chi 李培基　1221

Li, San-jung 李三榮　1872

Li, Sen 李森　0197

Li, Shan 力山　0692, 1541

Li, Shih-yü 李世瑜　0758, 0774

Li, Shou-chih 李瘦芝　1659

Li, Tao-chung 李道中　0400

Li, Tien-yi 李田意　0489, 1324, 1325

Li, T'ien-i　See Li, Tien-yi

Li, Tso-nan 李作南　1458, 1459, 1486, 1487

Li, Tsu-pai 李祖白　0577

Li, Ts'un-chü 李存聚　0884

Li, Ts'ung-yün 李叢雲　0335

Li, Wei 李未　1541

Li, Yih-yuan 李亦園　1421

Li, Ying-che 李英哲　0700, 2117

Li, Ying-ch'uan 李映川　1457

Li, Yü-en 李遇恩　1381

Li, Yüan-shou 李元授　1028

Li, Yün-i 李運益　1090, 1091

Li, Yung-ming 李永明　2026

Liang, Chen-shih 梁振仕　0423

Liang, Yu-kang 梁猷剛　1849, 2203, 2212, 2213

Liang, Yü-chang 梁玉璋　1166, 2224, 2232

Liao, Chiu-chung　See Liao, Ch'iu-chung

Liao, Ch'iu-chung 廖秋忠　0129, 0534, 2114

Liao, Han-ch'en 廖漢臣　2100

Liao, Hsü-tung 廖序東　1279, 1312

Liao, Hsün-ying 廖珣英　0087

Liao-ning ta-hsüeh Chung-kuo yü-yen wen-hsüeh-hsi yü-yen chiao-yen shih　遼寧大學中國語言文學系語言教研室　0785

Lien, Heng 連橫　2127

Light, Timothy　0043, 1589

Lim, Hiong-seng　2061

Lim, Yaw-tjiang　0738

Lin, Chen 林震　1243

Lin, Chin-ch'ao 林金鈔　1936

Lin, Lien-hsien 林蓮仙　0363, 0364, 1525, 1548, 1573, 1574, 1601, 1639, 2037, 2052

Lin, Pen-yüan 林本元　0313, 0314, 2078, 2091, 2092

Lin, Shao-hsien 林紹賢　2163

Lin, Shuang-fu 林雙福　1974, 2115, 2139, 2140

Lin, T'ao 林燾　2248

Lin, T'ung-shu 林同鏻　2221

Lin, Wen-chin 林文金　2269, 2270, 2271

Lin, William C.　0514

Lin, Yü-hsin 林雨新　1462, 1463

Lin, Yü-t'ang 林語堂　0019, 0105, 0181, 0239, 0240, 0352, 0353, 0354, 0355, 0370, 0371, 0372, 0490, 1526, 1863

Lin, Yün-lai 林運來　0198, 1460

Lindauer, Bennett M. 林德本　1468

Ling, James　1230

Ling, Tz'u-fang 凌慈房　1479

Lippert, W.　0704

Liu, Chi-yüan 劉寄園　2093

Liu, Chien-jen 劉健仁　0053, 2079

Liu, Chin 劉進　1618

Liu, Ching-hsüan 劉溚選　1375

Liu, Chung-sheng 劉衆生　0951

Liu, Feng 柳鳳　1059

Liu, Fu 劉復　0622

Liu, Hsing-ts'e 劉興策　1034

Liu, Hsiu-yeh 劉修業　0038

Liu, Hsüeh-chün 劉學濬　1570

Liu, Jen-ch'ien 劉忉千　0829

Liu, K'ai-ming 劉凱鳴　0680

Liu, K'o-ming 劉克明　1500, 2164

Liu, Kuang-hua 劉光華　0775

Liu, Lin 劉琳　0973

Liu, Ming-shu 劉銘恕　0535, 1914

Liu, P'ei-lun 劉培倫　0974, 0975

Liu, Sheng-i 劉聲繹　2038

Liu, T'e-ju 劉特如　0994

Liu, Tse 劉賾　0365, 1024, 1026, 1027

Liu, Tse-hsien 劉澤先　0623

Liu, Ts'e-ch'i 劉策奇　1853

Liu, Wan-chang 劉萬章　1549

Liu, Wen-chin 劉文錦　0902, 0927, 0943

Liu, Wen-ping 劉文炳　0908

Liu, William W. 劉維漢　0879

Liu, Yao-li 劉耀藜　0909

Liu, Yu-hsin 劉又辛　0199

Lo, Ch'ang-p'ei 羅常培　0076, 0106, 0131, 0132, 0133, 0134, 0290, 0291, 0342, 0377, 0410, 0424, 0425, 0519, 0643, 1006, 1118, 1395, 1602, 1992

Lo, Chao-chin 羅肇錦　1480

Lo, Cheng-p'ing 羅正平　1619

Lo, Chi-kuang 羅季光　0241, 0644

Lo, Chieh-jui 羅杰瑞　See Norman, Jerry

Lo, Hsiang-lin 羅香林　1409, 1410

Lo, Hsin-t'ien 羅莘田　See Lo, Ch'ang-p'ei

Lo, Hui-yün 羅翽雲　1434

Lo, Hung-k'ai 駱鴻凱　0366

Lo, Tso-han 羅祚韓　1382

Lobscheid, William　1640, 1705, 1737, 1804, 1805

Lockhart, J.H. Stewart　1575

Loon, Piet van der 龍彼得　0020, 1864

Lou, Po-p'ing 婁伯平　1378

Lu, Chi 陸基　0299, 0300

Lu, Chih-wei 陸志韋　0519, 0624, 0681, 0693

Lu, Shu-mei 盧淑美　2116

Lu, Tan-an 陸澹安　0455

Lü, Hsiang 呂湘　0984

Lü, Shu-hsiang 呂叔湘　0700

Luc, Khynh 盧謹　0325, 0330, 0331

Lucas, A.　0867, 1025, 1421, 1464

Lum, Mun-chak　1742

Lung, Kuo-fu 龍果夫　See Dragunov, A.A.

Lust, John　0021

Lyon, D.　1244

Lyovin, Anatole　0040, 0266, 0522, 0564, 1572

Ma, Hsüeh-liang 馬學良　0267

Ma, Kuang-yü 馬光宇　0378

Ma, P'ei-chih 馬培芝　0885

Ma, Tsung-huo 馬宗霍　0401

Ma, Ying-po 馬鑾伯　0254

MacGillivray, Donald　0685, 0739, 0742

MacGowan, John 馬約翰　1245, 2011, 2016

MacIver, Donald　1511, 1512, 1513, 1514

MacKay, George Leslie 馬偕　2188

MacKenzie, M.C.　1514

Maclay, Robert Samuel　2258, 2259

MacWeigh, Jean　0740

Malmqvist, Göran 1064, 1069, 1070, 1071, 1078, 1079

Malmqvist, N.G.D.　0077, 0410, 0893, 1107, 1469

Man, Szu-ch'ien 滿思謙　See Marsecano, Guerrino

Manuel, E. Arsenio　1928

Mao, Ch'iu-pai 毛秋白　0182

Mao, Hsi-p'ang 毛西旁　0452, 1060

Mao, I-po 毛一波　1081

Mao, K'ai 茅開　0635

Mao, K'un 毛坤　0482

Marsecano, Guerrino 滿思謙　1515

Martinet, A.　0135

Maryknoll Language School　2165, 2166, 2167, 2168, 2169, 2189, 2190

Maspero, Henri 馬伯樂　0426, 0427, 0438

Matake, Naoshi 眞武直　0367

Mateer, Ada Haven　1270

Mateer, Calvin Wilson　0727

Mather, Richard B.　0411, 0874, 0971

Mathews, William R.　0715

Matisoff, James A.　0470

Matsumoto, Akira 松本昭　0111, 0425, 0659, 0660

Matsumoto, Kazuo 松本一男　0536, 0549, 0578, 1576, 1585, 1620, 1929, 1937, 1938

McCoy, John　See McCoy, William John Jr.

McCoy, William John, Jr.　1527, 1819, 1826, 1838

McIntosh, Gilbert　1246, 1247

Medhurst, Walter Henry 麥都思　1981

Mei, Ch'i-hsi 梅啓熙　0830

Mei, Shou 梅瘦　1550

Mei, Tsu-lin 梅祖麟　1191, 2222

Mello, A.H. de　1806

Meng, Ch'ing-hui 孟慶惠　0995

Meng, Hsiang 夢湘　2248

Mercer, Bernard　1501

Meyer, Bernard Fr.　1807

Miao, Chin-an 繆錦安　1568

Miller, Roy A.　0799, 1280

Ming, Yüan 鳴遠　1368

Misawa, Reiji 三澤玲爾　0090

Mittler, Theodor　0813

Miyamori, Tsuneko 宮森常子　1227

Miyata, Ichirō 宮田一郎　1192, 1193, 1218

Mizukami, Umehiko 水上梅彦　2170

Mo, Chao-hsiung 莫朝雄　1738

Mo, Chien-ch'ing 莫建青　1993

Mogi, Ichirō 茂木一郎　0726

Möllendorff, O.F. von　0022

Möllendorff, Paul Georg von　0022, 0485, 1317, 1318

Montgomery, P.H.S.　1332

Morrison, Robert　1808

Morrison, William T.　1319

Moskalev, A.A.　1568

Moule, George Evans　1342, 1343

Moule, Henry W.　1341

Mu, An 木安　1194

Mu, Kung 牧公　1203

Mulder, J.W.F.　0625

Mullie, Joseph L.M. 閔宣化　0292, 0343, 0751, 0752, 0753, 0754, 0755, 0952

Murakami, Katsudai 村上勝太　2217

Murakami, Yoshihide 村上嘉英　0054, 0167, 0168, 0169, 0315, 1962, 2101

N.L.　0785

Nagamochi, Tokuichi 永持德一　0550

Nagano, Seirai 長野政來　1739

Nagao, Mitsuyuki 長尾光之　0537, 0694, 0814

Nagashima, Eiichirō 永島榮一郎　0626

Nakagawa, Manabu　1411

Nakajima, Motoki 中嶋幹起　1568, 1821, 1915, 1939, 1940, 1941, 1952, 1963, 2072, 2073

Nakamura, Kyūshirō 中村久四郎 1174

Nakano, Miyoko 中野美代子 1352

Nakata, Yoshikatsu 中田喜勝 1101

Nan, T'ai 南台 1461

Nan-ching ta-hsüeh Chung-wen-hsi fang-yen tiao-ch'a tsu 南京大學中文系方言調查組 0972

Nan-k'ai ta-hsüeh 南開大學 0759

Nasu, Kiyoshi 那須清 0627, 0628, 0661, 0695

Nei Meng-ku chiao-yü-t'ing fang-yen tiao-ch'a kung-tso tsu 內蒙古教育廳方言調查工作組 0953

Nhật, La-quang 1740

Ni, Chi-yü 倪寄予 0669

Ni, Hai-shu 倪海曙 0107, 0301, 0521, 0565

Nihon Gakujutsu Kaigi 日本學術會議 0023

Nishida, Taiichirō 西田太一郎 0395

Noguchi, Masayuki 野口正之 0344, 1536, 2080

Nolasco da Silva, Pedro 1741

Nomura, Masayoshi 野村正良 0890, 0897, 0898, 0910, 1395

Norman, Jerry L. 羅杰瑞 0043, 1873, 1874, 1889, 1890, 1916, 2211, 2222, 2223, 2233, 2252, 2257, 2261, 2262, 2263, 2266

Novgorodskii, Iu. V. 0891

Oakley, R.H. 1742

Obata, Gabun 御幡雅文 1248, 1249

Obręska-Jabłońska, Antonina 0640, 0641

O'Connor, Kevin A. 1426

Ogaeri, Yoshio 魚返善雄 0472, 0473, 1571

Ogawa, Naoyoshi 小川尚義 2094

Ogawa, Tamaki 小川環樹 0045, 0108, 0157, 0384, 0467, 0471

Ōhara, Nobukazu 大原信一 0579

Okamoto, Kazuo 岡本一雄 1743

Ōkawa, Yosaku 大川與朔 1250

Ōkōchi, Yasunori 大河內康憲 0625

O'Melia, Thomas A. 李重光 1744, 1745

Osada, Natsuki 長田夏樹 0045, 0474, 0588, 1280, 1286

Ōshima, Shōji 大島正二 0428, 1175

Ōta, Tatsuo 太田辰夫 0024, 0045, 0447, 0589

Ou, Ching-huan 區靜寰 1528

Ou, Yang-i 歐仰義 1854

Ou-yang, Chüeh-ya 歐陽覺亞 0265

Ōuchida, Saburō 大內田三郎 0502

Ozaki, Minoru 尾崎實 0682

Pa, Sang 巴桑 0772

Pai, Hsing 白星 2042

Pai, Ti-chou 白滌洲 0293, 0566, 0831, 0928, 0929, 0930, 0931

Pai, Wan-ju 白婉如 1648

Palmer, Harold E. 1976

P'an, Hung-wen 潘鴻文 0716

P'an, Keng 潘庚 0444

P'an, Mao-ting 潘茂鼎 1166, 2224

P'ang, An-fu 龐安福 0776

P'ang, Hung-ch'i 龐鴻祺 1486

Pao, Ming-wei 鮑明煒 0850, 0987

Parker, Edward Harper 0336, 0516, 0551, 0976, 1022, 1042, 1320, 1333, 1451, 1551, 1577, 1621, 2234, 2242

Parker, P. 1270

Parker, R.A. 1251

Partridge, S.B. 2054

Pashkov, B.K. 0590

Paton, Bernard W. 1501

Pei-ching ta-hsüeh Chung-kuo yü-yen wen-hsüeh-hsi Yü-yen hsüeh chiao-yen shih 北京大學中國語言文學系語言學教研室 0522

Pei-ching ta-hsüeh yü-yen-hsüeh chiao-yen shih Han-yü fang-yen-hsüeh chi fang-yen tiao-ch'a hsiao-tsu 北京大學語言學教研室漢語方言學及方言調查小組 0200

Pei-ching yü-yin Ch'ao-chou fang-yin chu-yin hsin tzu-tien pien-chi wei-yüan-hui 北京語音潮州方音注音新字典編輯委員會 0717

Pelliot, Paul 伯希和 0966, 1984

Peng, Fred C.C. 彭哲卿 1994

P'eng, A-mu 彭阿木 1412, 1422

P'eng, Ch'u-nan 彭楚南 1152

P'eng, Kuo-chün 彭國鈞 1106

P'eng, P'ai 彭湃 1082

Permanent International Committee of Linguists 0025

Pétillon, Corentin 貝迪榮 1268

Phillips, Hugh Stowell 0316

Phoon, Mun-kwong 潘文光 1660

Pi, K'o-ch'ao 閉克朝 1855

P'ing, Tzu 平子 1061

Piñol, Francisco y Andreu 2002, 2003, 2017

Pitcher, P.W. 0317

Piton, Ch. 畢安 1451

Playfair, G.M.H. 1552

Po, Han 伯韓 0183

Polivanov, E.D. 1133, 1140, 1154, 1155, 1156

Pop, Sever 0078, 0135

Pott, Francis Lister Hawks 卜舫濟 1252, 1253, 1254

Prat, Pedro 2018

Prjadochin, M. 0452

Pulleyblank, E.G. 0429

P'u, Chih-chen 濮之珍 0379

Quinn, Raymond P. 1502

Rabouin, Paul 1229, 1269

Rai, Tsutomu 賴惟勤 0026, 0027, 0430, 0538, 0634, 0985, 1578, 1590

Ratau, J.R. 0728

Rawlinson, F. 1234

Rey, Charles 1503, 1516, 1517

Rimsky-Korsakoff, Svetlana 1128

Roberts, Thomas H. 羅道明 2117

Robinson, Jack See Casey, G. Hugh 1809, 1810

Rogers, B.B. 1367

Rokkaku, Tsunehiro 六角恒廣 0028, 0029

Rose, Philip John 費國華 1321

Roy, Gilbert W. 0043

Rudlang, W.D. 1353

Rudolph, R.C. 0903

Ruffus, William 2064

Rutten, J. See Luc, Khynh

Rygaloff, Alexis 0222, 0538, 0629, 0656, 0915, 1204, 1591, 1606, 1610, 2267

Sagart, Laurent 1431, 1481

Sakai, Ken'ichi 坂井健一 0439, 0448

Sakamoto, Ichirō 坂本一郎 0045, 0580, 0832, 0939, 1109, 1181, 1188, 1198, 1205, 1255, 1281, 1287

Sallé, Robert 陸若伯 1518

Sampson, Geoffrey 1431

Saso, Michael 蘇海涵 2171

Satō, Akira 佐藤昭 0961

Saunders, C.J. 1824

Savina, François-Marie 撒得 0524, 1811

Schaank, Simon H. 商克 1467, 1468

Scharfenberg, W.A. 1256

Schlegel, Gustaaf 希勒格 0544, 2019

Scott, N.C. 1043, 1051, 1052

Sebeok, Thomas A. 0109

Sedláček, Kamil 1572

Seers, O. 1579

Seidel, A. 0741

Serdiuchenko, G.P. 謝爾久琴珂 0486

Serruys, Paul L.-M. 司禮儀 0345, 0346, 0380, 0381, 0382, 0383, 0384, 0385, 0386, 0387, 0410, 0903

Servus, M.E.P. 1812

Setoguchi, Ritsuko 瀨戶口律子 0662

Shafer, Robert 0031

Shan, Chou-yao 單周堯 1586

Shan, Jung 山榕 1062

Shan-tung ta-hsüeh Chung-wen-hsi she-hui shih-chien fang-yen tiao-ch'a hsiao-tsu 山東大學中文系社會實踐方言調查小組 0833

Shang, Ching 尙靜 0688

Shang, Yün-ch'uan 尙允川 0156, 0792

Shang-hai Wai-kuo-yü hsüeh-yüan, Ha-erh-pin Wai-kuo-yü hsüeh-yüan 上海外國語學院, 哈爾濱外國語學院 0184

Shanghai Christian Vernacular Society 1206, 1270

Shao, Jung-fen 邵榮芬 0431

Shen, Chien-shih 沈兼士 0185

Shen, Ch'un 沈純 0337

Shen, Fu-chin 沈富進 1875

Shen, Shih-ying 沈士英 0769

Shen, Tzu-p'ing 沈子平 1053, 1177

Sherard, Michael Lewis 司馬侃 0046, 0170, 1207, 1208

Shiba, Yoshitarō 吉波吉太郎 1504

Shibayama, Takenori 柴山武德 2200

Shiga, Masatoshi 志賀正年 0032

Shih, Jerome Jen-chung 史仁仲 1661

Shih, Nan-yü 史南育 1662

Shih, Ts'un-chih 史存直 0558, 0630

Shih, Tsung-chou 史宗周 0863

Shih, Wen-t'ao 施文濤 0232, 0255, 0456, 0522, 1322

Shimamura, Shūji 島村修治 0889

Shimizu, Shigeru 清水茂 1568, 1592, 1641

Shimomizu, Kenji 下水憲次 0601

Shinlo, L. 1146, 1157

Shivaza, Ia. 1158, 1159

Shu, Feng 舒鳳 1219

Shulman, Frank Joseph 0012, 0030

Silsby, John Alfred 1209, 1257, 1264, 1265, 1271

Simon, H.F. 0822

Simon, Walter 西門華 0294, 0385, 0437, 1691, 1766

Siulin 0911

Skachkov, P.E. 0033

Slovodchikova, L.A. 1254

Smith, J.F. 1746

Société des Missionnaires 1088

Sogō, Teiji 十河悌次 0916

Sokolov, M.V. 1210, 1211

Solntseva, N.V. 0136

Sousa, S.C. de 2218

Soymié, M. 0629

Sprenger, Arnold Heinrich 孫志文 0718

Stadt, P.A. van de 1519

Stangier, Joseph 商格理 0843

Stedman, T. Lathrop 1747

Steele, John 2053

Stent, George Carter 0685, 0742

Stimson, Hugh M. 司徒修 0102, 0385, 0449, 0559, 0591, 0592, 0600, 0663

Stravanovich, G. 1134

Streenevassa, P. 1323

Streeter, Mary 0268

Su, Ch'ih 蘇遲 1195

Su, Hsi-hung 蘇錫鴻 1748

Su, Jen 蘇人 1288

Su, Wen-cho 蘇文擢 1529

Su, Yün-chung 蘇運中 1091

Suenobu, Yasuo 末延保雄 0090, 1220, 1282, 1289

Sugi, Fusanosuke 杉房之助 2172, 2173, 2191

Sugie, Bōzō 杉江房造 1258

Sui, Shu-hua 隋樹華 0958

Sun, Chin-piao 孫錦標 0981

Sun, Fu-ch'üan 孫福全 0940

Sun, Fu-yüan 孫伏園 1044, 1045

Sun, Hsün-hou 孫洵侯 2081

Sun, Shu-hui 孫淑惠 2144

Sung, Chen-hua 宋振華 0186

Sung, Hok-p'ang 宋學鵬 1749

Sung, Hsüeh 宋學 0793

Sung, Hsüeh-p'eng 宋學鵬 See Sung, Hok-p'ang

Sung, Margaret M.Y. 宋嚴棉 0503, 1995, 1996

Sung, Yüan-chia 宋元嘉 0631

Sushanlo, M. 1157

Suzue, Mantarō 鈴江萬太郎 0601

Suzuki, Naoji 鈴木直治 0111

Švarný, Oldřich 0664, 1792

Szu-ch'uan ta-hsüeh 四川大學 1053

Tagawa, Kazumi 田川一己 0388

Ta, Trong Hiep 1998

Tai, Chen 戴震 0395

Tai, Ch'ing-hsia 戴慶厦 2272, 2273, 2274, 2275

Tai, Chung-chieh 戴仲傑 1663

Tai, Henry H. 戴浩一 0041

Tai, Lei 戴磊 0851

T'ai-wan sheng Kuo-yü t'ui-hsing wei-yüan-hui 臺灣省國語推行委員會 2145

Taipei Language Institute 1505, 1506, 2174

Taiwan Nanpō Kyōkai 臺灣南方協會 2219

Taiwan Sōtokufu 臺灣總督府 1520, 2175, 2192, 2193, 2194, 2195, 2196

Taiwan Sōtokufu Gakumubu 臺灣總督府學務部 2102, 2118

Taiwan Sōtokufu Senbaikyoku 臺灣總督府專賣局 2176

Takada, Hisahiko 高田久彦 1278

Takakura, Shōzō 高倉正三 1290

Takayama, Kizen 高山喜全 1507

Takeji, Sadao 竹治貞夫 0368

Takeuchi, Minoru 竹內實 1221

Tallandier, I. 1750

Tam, Wing-kwong 譚榮光 0306

Tán, Má-jī 2020

Tan, Pang-tin 陳邦鎮 2160, 2187

T'an, Chi-ch'iang 譚季強 1751

Tanaka, Yoshitarō 田中與四太郎 1694

Tang, Charles T.C. 湯廷池 2121

T'ang, Chen-chu 湯珍珠 1200

T'ang, Hung 唐宏 0581

T'ang, Ping-cheng 湯炳正 0800

T'ang, Tso-fan 唐作藩 1379

T'ao, Yü-min 陶燠民 2235

Tateishi, Hiroo 竹石廣男 0389, 0390

Tay, Mary Wan Joo 1942, 1943

Teboul, M. 0602

Teng, Chih-hsien 鄧志賢 1752

Teng, Shou-hsin 鄧守信 0043, 0129, 0719

Teng, Ssu-yü 鄧嗣禹 0432

Tenri Daigaku Chūgokugo Gakka Kenkyūshitsu 天理大學中國語學科研究室 0051

Teoh, Irene 2004

Thom, Robert 0729

Thompson, Robert Wallace 1622

Thompson, Sandra A. 0469, 0500

Thonkum, Theraphan L. 1643

Ti, Chou 荻舟 0710, 0912

Tien, Fu 殿福 0772

Tien, Lu 奠陸 0834

T'ien, Chung-chi 田仲濟 0504

T'ien, Hsi-ch'eng 田希誠 0918, 0922

T'ien, Ju-k'ang 0475

T'ien, Shui 天水 0269, 0270

T'ien, Yüan 田元 1092

Ting, Chieh-min 丁介民 0034

Ting, Chih-k'un 丁志坤 0852

Ting, Cho 丁卓 1259

Ting, Fang-hao 丁方豪 0567

Ting, Hsing-wang 丁興瀆 0356

Ting, Nan-ch'uan 丁南川 1918

Ting, Pang-hsin 丁邦新 0055, 0079, 0080, 0091, 0110, 0137, 0412, 0450, 0988, 2082

Ting, Pei 定北 1303

Ting, Sheng-shu 丁聲樹 0201, 0202, 0220, 0221, 0222, 1010

Ting, Stella 0035

Ting, Ti-hao 丁迪豪 1413

Ting, Wei-fen 丁惟汾 0391, 0801

Tipson, Ernest 1813, 2021, 2022

Tipton, Gary Prior 0720, 1664, 1665

Tjen, Fo-sang 1508

To, Thien-tru 1753

Tōdō, Akiyasu 藤堂明保 0111, 0138, 0357, 0395, 0523, 0582, 0593, 0632, 0633, 0634, 0696, 0708, 0709, 0870, 1182, 1283, 1435, 1436, 1537, 1919

Tokuyasu, Teruo 德安輝龍 2177

Tong, John S. 董守綱 2103

Torii, Hisayasu 鳥居久靖 0036

Trubetskoy, N.S. 1141

Ts'ai, Chün-ming 蔡俊明 2050, 2051

Ts'ai, Feng-ch'i 蔡鳳圻 0392

Ts'ai, Mao-t'ang 蔡懋棠 2095

Ts'ai, P'ei-huo 蔡培火 2146

Ts'ao, Cheng-i 曹正一 0816, 0817, 0853

Ts'ao, Kuang-ch'ü 曹廣衢 0911, 1339, 1340

Ts'ao, Te-ming 曹德明 1063

Tse, John Kwock-ping 謝國平 See Hsieh, Kuo-p'ing 1553, 1603, 1604

Tse, Sou-mei 謝壽眉 1666

Ts'en, Ch'i-hsiang 岑麒祥 0139, 0203, 0204, 0242, 1538, 1554, 1580, 1581, 1605

Tseng, Hsing-li 曾星笠 1437

Tseng, Tzu-fan 曾子凡 1667, 1668

Tseng, Yün-ch'ien 曾運乾 1430

Tso, Ch'i 左企 1222

Tsou, Chia-yen 鄒嘉彥 See T'sou, Benjamin K.

Tsou, Lu 鄒魯 1539

T'sou, Benjamin K. 鄒嘉彥 1555, 1556, 1557, 1642, 1643

Tsu-mo 祖謨 See Chou, Tsu-mo

Ts'ui, Chi 崔驥 0037

Ts'ui, Ying-k'o 崔盈科 0904

Tsuji, Nobuhisa 辻伸久 1362, 1530, 1856

Tsung, Fu-pang 宗福邦 1606

Tsunvazo, Iu. 1142, 1160, 1161, 1162, 1163, 1164

Tu, Nai-keng 杜乃庚 1110

Tu, Shu-t'ien 杜書田 0787

Tu, Sung-shou 杜松壽 1135, 1136

Tu, Tzu-chin 杜子勁 0864

Tu, Yeh-p'ing 杜也平 0948

T'u, Feng 涂鳳 1083

Tung, Chao-hui 董昭輝 See Tung, Jeffrey C.H. 1944, 2119, 2120

Tung, Chün-yen 董俊彥 0393

Tung, Jeffrey C.H. 董昭輝 2121

Tung, Shao-wen 董少文 0244

Tung, Tso-pin 董作賓 0081, 0603

Tung, Tsun-chang 董遵章 0835

Tung, T'ung-ho 董同龢 0110, 0140, 0141, 0149, 0157, 0187, 0369, 0476, 0477, 0539, 0583, 1010, 1093, 1482, 1997, 1998, 2096

Tung, Tzu-kuang 東子光 See Weng, Hui-tung

T'ung, Chen-hua 童振華 0461

T'ung, Wei 童瑋 1119

Tzu, Shih 子實 1964

U.S. Army Language School 1754, 1755, 1756, 1757, 1758, 1814

U.S. Defense Language Institute 1815

U.S. Department of Army 1759

U.S. Office of Strategic Services 0478

U.S. War Department 1760, 1761

Ueda, Kinjirō 上田金次郎 0665

Ulring, Tor 0307

Umehara, Keiun 梅原慧運 0802

Ushijima, Tokuji 牛島德次 0111, 0711

Vaillant, L. 1414

Vance, Timothy J. 1607, 1608

Ven, Canisius van de 1509

Vissière, Arnold Jacques Antoine 0666, 0730

Vitale, Guido 0604

Voegelin, C.F. 0479

Voeglin, F.M. 0479

Vömel, Johann Heinrich 1452

Wade, Thomas Francis 威妥瑪 0731, 0743

Waley, Arthur 威利 1801

Walton, A. Ronald 1212

Wan, Yü-hsiang 萬玉祥 1383

Wang, Chia-chün 王家俊 0760

Wang, Chin-cheng 王今錚 0186

Wang, Chin-hsiu 王錦繡 2220

Wang, Ch'in 王勤 0635

Wang, Ching-ch'uan 王鏡川 0869

Wang, Ching-liu 王敬騮 1354

Wang, Chün 王鋆 1669

Wang, Chung-hsien 汪仲賢 1260

Wang, Chung-min 王重民 0038

Wang, Fang-yü 王方宇 0700, 1799

Wang, Fu-shih 王輔世 0245, 0645, 1857

Wang, Fu-t'ang 王福堂 0767, 1355

Wang, Hsüan 王弦 1223

Wang, Hsün 王迅 0919

Wang, John C. 0877

Wang, Kuang-lü 王光閭 1400

Wang, Li 王力 0142, 0480, 0505, 0540, 0878, 1313, 1540, 1541, 1669, 1670, 1825, 1827, 1839, 1858, 1859

Wang, Li-ko 王立革 1097

Wang, Li-ta 王立達 0143, 0913, 0920, 0923, 0924, 0925

Wang, Liao-i 王了一 See Wang, Li

Wang, Lien 王練 1396

Wang, Lien-tseng 王聯曾 0667

Wang, Lun 王綸 0462

Wang, Meng-hsü 王孟戍 0836

Wang, Nien-fang 王年芳 0977

Wang, P'ei-hsü 王丕煦 0837

Wang, Peter Chin-tang 0506

Wang, Pu-chou 王步洲 0394

Wang, Shih-hua 王世華 0978

Wang, Sung-mao 王松茂 0886

Wang, T'ien-ch'ang 王天昌 2236, 2237, 2238

Wang, T'ing-chüeh 王廷珏 1261

Wang, Ts'ai-wei 王朵薇 2178

Wang, Tsung-yao 王宗瑤 0256

Wang, Tung 汪東 1183

Wang, Tzu-ming 王子明 1762

Wang, William S-Y. 王士元 0039, 0040, 0271, 0633, 0668, 1372, 2031

Wang, Yü 王煜 1046

Wang, Yü-te 王育德   0318, 0319, 0481, 0491, 0536, 0578, 1427, 1876, 1920, 1938, 1965, 1999, 2074, 2122, 2123, 2124, 2128, 2129, 2141, 2147, 2179

Wang, Yung-ta 王永大   2027

Ware, James R. 0209

Warnshuis, A.L. 2012

Wei, Chien-kung 魏建功   0082, 0205, 1007, 1189

Wei, Chü-hsien 衛聚賢   0354, 1224

Wei, Li 魏立   0775

Wei, Tseng-shan 魏曾山   1582

Weingartner, Fredric F. 溫知新   2125

Wells, Herbert Richmond 威禮士   1763, 1764, 1765, 1816, 1817

Welzel, A. 0844

Wemp, Theodore F. 1807

Wen, Chung-ho 溫仲和   1438

Wen, Jui-hua 文瑞華   0959

Wen, Tai-k'uei 溫戴奎   1431

Wen, T'ing-ching 溫廷敬   1465

Wen, Tuan-cheng 溫端政   0204, 1966, 1967

Wen-tzu kai-ko ch'u-pan-she 文字改革出版社   0112, 0308

Weng, Hui-tung 翁輝東   2028

Weng, Kuo-liang 翁國樑   2225

Weys, G. 0281

Whitaker, Katherine Po Kan   1558, 1609, 1610, 1691, 1766, 1767, 1768

White, Moses Clark 2255

Whymant, A. Neville John 1671

Wiant, Paul P. 2253

Wieger, Léon 戴遂艮   0763, 0764, 0765

Williams, Samuel Wells 衛三畏（廉士）   0525, 0744, 1769, 1818

Wils, J. 0755

Winn, J.A. 2023

Wisner, O.F. 1770, 1771

Wong, Le-hing 黃履卿   1772

Wong, Sik-ling 黃錫凌   See Huang, Hsi-ling 1773, 1774

Woo, Kwing-tong 胡炯堂   1570, 1571

Woon, Wee-lee 雲惟利   2214

Wu, C.Y. 0099

Wu, Chao-wan 吳昭婉   0056, 0092

Wu, Ch'i-lu 吳啓祿   2273, 2274, 2275

Wu, Ch'i-t'ai 吳啓太   0732, 0733, 0734

Wu, Chung-p'ing 吳仲平   2005

Wu, Hsiao-ju 吳小如   1370

Wu, Hsiao-ling 吳曉鈴   0374

Wu, Huai 吳槐   1877, 1921, 1945, 1968, 2126

Wu, Hung-hsü 吳宏緒   0869

Wu, Lang 吳朗   0854

Wu, Shou-li 吳守禮   0057, 0058, 0059, 0060, 0171, 0172, 1878, 1879, 1880, 1891, 1892, 1893, 1894, 1895, 1896, 1897, 1898, 1899, 1900, 1901, 1902, 1903, 1904, 1922, 2097

Wu, Shou-sung 吳壽崧   1860

Wu, Su-chu 吳素珠   2180, 2181

Wu, T.C. 1775

Wu, T'ien-shih 吳天石   0158

Wu, Tsung-chi 吳宗濟   0159, 1010

Wu, Ying-t'ao 吳瀛濤   2104

Wurm, S. 0563

Ya, Hsüan 瘂弦   0113

Ya, Yüan 亞元   0231

Yamashita, Noboru 山下昇   1776

Yang, Ch'ang-li 楊長禮   0160, 0257

Yang, Ch'eng-chih 楊成志   1559

Yang, Chia-wen 楊嘉文   1094

Yang, Ch'ien-ming 楊乾明   1334

Yang, Feng 楊峯   0810, 0855

Yang, Fu-mien See Yang, Paul Fu-mien

Yang, Hsi-ling 楊喜齡　0492, 0541

Yang, Hsiao-min 楊筱敏　0206

Yang, Hsiao-min 楊曉敏　0954

Yang, Hsin-an 楊欣安　1054, 1065

Yang, Hsiung 揚雄　0395

Yang, Huan-tien 楊煥典　1113

Yang, Kuo-chu 楊國柱　0934

Yang, Liang 楊戾　1777

Yang, Nai-szu 楊耐思　0246, 0568, 0769, 1380

Yang, Paul　See Yang, Paul Fu-mien

Yang, Paul Fu-mien 楊福綿　0041, 0042, 0047, 0050, 0052, 0061, 0083, 0084, 0093, 0119, 0144, 0145, 0146, 0150, 0161, 0204, 0218, 0219, 0220, 0221, 0222, 0347, 0348, 0349, 0374, 0384, 0442, 0454, 0522, 0523, 0669, 0748, 0756, 0757, 0767, 1177, 1230, 1231, 1263, 1423, 1424, 1431, 1439, 1472, 1473, 1503, 1515, 1517, 1543, 1546, 1686, 1780, 2003, 2026, 2128, 2160

Yang, Shih-feng 楊時逢　0162, 0880, 1004, 1010, 1055, 1056, 1072, 1084, 1099, 1100, 1102, 1103, 1107, 1363, 1364, 1369, 1385, 1390, 1397, 1474, 1475

Yang, Shu-ta 楊樹達　0396, 1370

Yang, Tao-ching 楊道經　1384

Yang, Teresa S.　0041

Yang, Winston L.Y.　0004, 0043

Yao, Han-ch'iu 姚漢秋　2105

Yap, Gloria Chan　1930

Yates, M.T.　1262

Yau, Shun-chiu 游順釗　1644

Yee, Shu-nam 余召南　1828

Yeh, Ch'ang-ch'ing 葉長青　1946, 2243

Yeh, Hsiang-ling 葉祥苓　0232, 1284, 1285, 1295, 1296

Yeh, Kuo-ch'ing 葉國慶　1881

Yeh, Te-chün 葉德均　0989

Yeh, Tzu-hsiung 葉子雄　1314

Yen, Chih-t'ui 顏之推　0432

Yen, Fu-sun 嚴芙孫　1272

Yen, Hsiang-lin 顏祥霖　See Yen, Sian-lin

Yen, Hsüeh-chün 嚴學窘　1398

Yen, Keng-wang 嚴耕望　0397

Yen, P'in-jen 顏品仁　1358

Yen, Sian-lin 顏祥霖　1882

Yin, Huan-hsien 殷煥先　0207, 0208

Yin, Meng 因夢　0194

Yiu, Tung 尤桐　1840

Yoshida, Megumu 吉田惠　0358, 1291

Young, Elizabeth Jen　1213

Yu, Tun-ming 尤敦明　1315

Yu, T'ung　1691

Yü, Ch'e 于車　1047

Yü, Chih-fu 余直夫　2075

Yü, Ch'ing-p'an 于清泮　0838

Yü, Min 俞敏　0508, 0681, 1488

Yü, Shao-nan 余召南　See Yee, Shiu-nam

Yü, Shih-ch'ang 喻世長　0247, 0277, 0931

Yü, Yang 俞揚　0990

Yü-yen yen-chiu-so 語言研究所　0542, 0569

Yuan, Tung-li 袁同禮　0044

Yüan, Chia-hua 袁家驊　0146, 0188, 0189, 0190, 0248, 0272, 0278, 0493, 0512, 0513, 0543, 0553, 0554, 0560, 1184, 1365, 1373, 1386, 1440, 1542, 1923, 2226

Yüan, Shao-ang 袁紹昂　0839

Yüan, Ting 元丁　1035

Yüan, Ying-ts'ai 袁英才　See Yuen, Y.C.

Yüeh, Chai 約齋　1395

Yuen, Irene　1729

Yuen, Y.C. 袁英才　1778

Yün-nan-sheng Chiao-yü-chü 雲南省教育局　1120

Zavjalova, Olga I.　1143, 1144

Zhou, Ning　0794